# Digital Ecologies

Manchester University Press

# Digital Ecologies

## Mediating more-than-human worlds

*Edited by*

Jonathon Turnbull, Adam Searle,
Henry Anderson-Elliott, and Eva Haifa Giraud

MANCHESTER UNIVERSITY PRESS

Copyright © Manchester University Press 2024

While copyright in the volume as a whole is vested in Manchester University Press, copyright in individual chapters belongs to their respective authors, and no chapter may be reproduced wholly or in part without the express permission in writing of both author and publisher.

An electronic version of this book has been made freely available under a Creative Commons (CC BY) licence, thanks to the support of The University of Sheffield Open Access Fund and the European Research Council Horizon 2020 Starting Grant 'The Body Societal' (Grant No. 949577), which permits distribution and reproduction provided the author(s) and Manchester University Press are fully cited. Details of the licence can be viewed at https://creativecommons.org/licenses/by/4.0/

Published by Manchester University Press
Oxford Road, Manchester, M13 9PL

www.manchesteruniversitypress.co.uk

British Library Cataloguing-in-Publication Data
A catalogue record for this book is available from the British Library

ISBN 978 1 5261 8860 1 paperback
ISBN 978 1 5261 7034 7 hardback

First published 2024

The publisher has no responsibility for the persistence or accuracy of URLs for any external or third-party internet websites referred to in this book, and does not guarantee that any content on such websites is, or will remain, accurate or appropriate.

Typeset by Newgen Publishing UK

# Contents

*List of figures* vii
*List of tables* viii
*List of contributors* ix
*Acknowledgements* xv

Introduction: what is Digital Ecologies?    1
    Adam Searle, Eva Haifa Giraud, Jonathon Turnbull, and
    Henry Anderson-Elliott

### Part I Digital encounters

1 Running wild: encountering digital animals through exercise apps    31
    William M. Adams, Chris Sandbrook, and Emma Tait

2 Digital sonic ecologies: encountering the non-human through
   digital sound recordings    50
    Hannah Hunter, Sandra Jasper, and Jonathan Prior

3 Trap-cam of care: conservation and the digital ecology of
   online lobster entrapment    70
    Jon Henrik Ziegler Remme

4 *Our Chicken Life*: byproductive labour in the digital flock    87
    Catherine Oliver

### Part II Digital governance

5 On-bird surveillance: albatrosses, sensors, and the lively
   governance of marine ecologies    105
    Oscar Hartman Davies and Jamie Lorimer

6 #AmazonFires and the online composition of ecological politics    123
    Jonathan W.Y. Gray, Liliana Bounegru, and Gabriele Colombo

7 Children and young people's digital climate action in Australia: co-belonging with place, ecology, and Country  145
   *Jess McLean and Lara Newman*

8 'Saving the knowledge helps to save the seed': generating a collaborative seed data project in London  164
   *Sophia Doyle and Katharine Dow*

### Part III  Digital assemblages

9 Programming nature as infrastructure in the Smart Forest City  185
   *Jennifer Gabrys*

10 Ecological computationality: cognition, recursivity, and a more-than-human political actor  197
   *Andrew C. Dwyer*

11 Mediated natures: towards an integrated framework of analogue and digital ecologies  215
   *Mari Arold*

### Part IV  Digital ecological directions

Afterword: digital ecologies and digital geographies  239
   *Gillian Rose*

Afterword: making digital ecologies visible  248
   *Dolly Jørgensen and Finn Arne Jørgensen*

Afterword: finding the media in digital ecologies  256
   *Eva Haifa Giraud*

Index  267

# Figures

| | | |
|---|---|---|
| 2.1 | Inside the WES archive at the British Library, Euston Road, London | 54 |
| 5.1 | The digitisation of fisheries monitoring | 107 |
| 5.2 | Tracking and vessel location data collected by CEBC | 109 |
| 5.3 | On-bird surveillance | 110 |
| 6.1 | Tweet from *Mother Jones* on 'fake' viral photos | 124 |
| 6.2 | Total number of posts per day associated with several hashtags | 128 |
| 6.3 | Top 40 most shared links per day, 24 August to 2 September 2019 | 131 |
| 6.4 | Co-hashtag network showing hashtags associated with posts containing prominent Amazon fires related hashtags on Twitter | 133 |
| 6.5 | Tracing variations and different visual articulations of pre-2003 burning forest image shared by Macron and others in association with 2019 Amazon fires | 137 |
| 8.1 | The four main tables in the LFSBase | 170 |
| 8.2 | Figure created by Anna Clow to illustrate the linked record fields in the LFSBase | 171 |
| 8.3 | Linked Seed Batches records in the LFSBase Variety record for Bloody Marvel lettuce | 173 |
| 11.1 | Harvester cabin | 224 |
| 11.2 | Frames from SFMC's video clip 'Harvester Operator Kaupo' | 229 |
| 11.3 | Gathering energy and photographs from a holy oak on a sacred groves tour | 231 |

# Tables

6.1 Selection of hashtags identified with EFI to explore issue composition 134
11.1 Forests understood through different conceptual lenses 218
11.2 Co-mediating channels and filters shaping Sepo's forest experience 225

# Contributors

**William M. Adams** is a geographer based in Geneva and Cambridge. He is currently Claudio Segré Professor of Conservation and Development in the Centre for International Environmental Studies at the Geneva Graduate Institute. His research ranges across environmental history and political ecology. He is particularly interested in the way novel technologies shape ideas and practices in nature conservation. His book *Strange Natures: Conservation in the Era of Genome Editing* (co-authored with Kent Redford) was published by Yale University Press in 2021.

**Henry Anderson-Elliott** is an independent scholar. He studied for his PhD and MPhil at the University of Cambridge in the Scott Polar Research Institute and the Department of Geography where he co-founded the Digital Ecologies research group. He has also held an ESRC Grand Union DTP research fellowship at the University of Oxford, and a visiting fellowship at The Arctic Institute, Washington DC. His research focus is on polar bears and the varied human relationships with the species. This has also led to an interest in the role of technologies in mediating human–wildlife relations, encounters, and modes of governance. He has also worked in documentary film on a natural history production for *National Geographic*.

**Liliana Bounegru** is Senior Lecturer in Digital Methods at King's College London. Her research interests include data journalism, digital journalism, digital methods for social and cultural studies, and controversy mapping.

**Gabriele Colombo** is a researcher in the Department of Design at Politecnico di Milano. His research interests include visual methods, communication design, and information visualisation.

**Oscar Hartman Davies** is an environmental and cultural geographer focusing on digital transformations in environmental governance, particularly in marine ecosystems. Oscar's PhD research explored the histories and contemporary uses of seabirds as sentinels of marine environmental change in scientific and marine governance practices. His ongoing research with the Digital Ecologies research group focuses on approaches to tracking and modelling animal movement and creative approaches to visualising environmental change. Oscar is also a co-founder of a youth-led nature recovery organisation and acts as an advisor to initiatives in the UK and Finland focusing on broadening youth participation in nature recovery.

**Katharine Dow** is an independent researcher working on the intersections between reproductive and environmental concerns and activism. She was previously senior research associate and deputy director of the Reproductive Sociology Research Group (ReproSoc) at the University of Cambridge and visiting fellow at the University of Copenhagen. She is the author of several peer-reviewed articles and the monograph *Making a Good Life: An Ethnography of Nature, Ethics, and Reproduction* (Princeton University Press, 2016) and has given keynote lectures at Tampere University, London School of Economics, and the University of Granada. She received her PhD in social anthropology from the LSE.

**Sophia Doyle** is a PhD fellow in the Minor Cosmopolitanisms research training group at Potsdam University. Combining her degree in postcolonial cultural studies at Goldsmiths College, University of London, and practical training in regenerative agriculture, her work explores the imperial histories and political ecology of food and farming and agro-industry's role in consolidating white supremacist capital, state, and military power. Her PhD project interrogates the historical development of the logics and logistics of industrial agriculture through colonial processes of dispossession, genocide, and enslavement to understand how racial-colonial violence structures modern food systems today. She is involved in various grassroots collectives and self-organised learning spaces in Berlin. Sophia is passionate about connecting across movements, geographies and disciplines to support landworkers' struggles as part of a broader anti-capitalist, anti-colonial, and anti-imperialist politics of liberation.

**Eva Haifa Giraud** is Senior Lecturer in Digital Media & Society at Sheffield University, whose research focuses on the (sometimes fraught) relationship between theoretical work focused on relationality and entanglement, and activist practice. Her publications include *What Comes After Entanglement? Activism, Anthropocentrism and an Ethics of Exclusion* (Duke University Press, 2019), *Veganism: Politics, Practice, and Theory* (Bloomsbury Academic, 2021), and articles in journals such as *Theory, Culture & Society*, *New Media & Society*, and *Social Studies of Science*.

*List of contributors* xi

**Jonathan W.Y. Gray** is Director of the Centre for Digital Culture and Reader in Critical Infrastructure Studies at the Department of Digital Humanities, King's College London; co-founder of the Public Data Lab; and a research associate at the Digital Methods Initiative (University of Amsterdam) and the médialab (Sciences Po, Paris). His research explores the role of digital data, methods, and infrastructures in the composition of collective life. More about his work can be found at jonathangray.org and at @jwyg.

**Hannah Hunter** is a PhD candidate and Vanier Scholar in the Department of Geography and Planning at Queen's University in Canada. Her research interests include sonic geographies, historical geographies of nature, and social studies of science. Her doctoral project and recent publications explore sonic geographies of extinction and the history of bird sound recording.

**Sandra Jasper** is Assistant Professor of Geography of Gender in Human-Environment-Systems at Humboldt-Universität zu Berlin. Her research interests are urban nature, soundscapes, and feminist theory. She has published on urban wastelands, the botanical city, acoustic architecture, and the sonic dimensions of landscape design. She is co-author and producer of the documentary film *Natura Urbana: The Brachen of Berlin* (UK/GER, 2017).

**Dolly Jørgensen** is Professor of History, University of Stavanger, Norway, specialising in histories of environment and technology. Her current research agenda focuses on cultural histories of animal extinction. She published *Recovering Lost Species in the Modern Age: Histories of Longing and Belonging* with MIT Press in 2019. She is co-editor-in-chief of the journal *Environmental Humanities* and co-directs The Greenhouse Center for Environmental Humanities at UiS.

**Finn Arne Jørgensen** is Professor of Environmental History and co-director of The Greenhouse Center for Environmental Humanities at the University of Stavanger. His research is placed at the intersection of technology and environment, drawing on history, media studies, and science and technology studies. He has published two books on recycling: *Making a Green Machine* (Rutgers University Press, 2011) and *Recycling* (MIT Press, 2019).

**Jamie Lorimer** is Professor of Environmental Geography at the University of Oxford. His research explores public understandings of nature and how these come to shape environmental governance. Past projects have explored the histories, politics, and cultures of wildlife conservation ranging across scales from elephants to the microbiome. Jamie is the author of *Wildlife* *in the Anthropocene: Conservation after Nature* (University of Minnesota Press, 2015), *The Probiotic Planet: Using Life to Manage Life* (University of Minnesota Press, 2020), and *More-than-Human* (Routledge, 2024). His current research explores transitions in agriculture and conservation in the context of growing concerns about the relationships between farming, biodiversity loss, and global heating.

**Jess McLean** does research on how humans, more-than-humans, environments, and technologies interact to produce geographies of change. Her research focuses on digital technologies, water politics, climate action, and activism. As an associate professor in the School of Social Sciences (Macquarie University), she teaches smart urbanism, Anthropocene politics, and environmental justice. Her book *Changing Digital Geographies: Technologies, Environments and People* (Springer, 2020) has contributed to the emerging subdiscipline of digital geographies. Jess is an associate editor of *Transactions of the Institute of British Geographers*; she enjoys writing for and speaking with multiple audiences, within and beyond academia, and builds collaborations across disciplines and in applied settings.

**Lara Newman** engages in interdisciplinary research in the areas of activism, social justice, Indigenous methodologies, ocean geographies, film studies, and GIS. Her current research focuses on Black and Indigenous women with disabilities' connections to the Pacific Ocean. Lara's previous research includes work on Indigenous healing programmes and audience relationships with animal rights films. Lara currently works as an academic in human geography at the University of Newcastle, where her work focuses on mapping and Indigenous presence on and connections with urban Country. She also works as part of a research team in the School of Health and Society at the University of Wollongong researching Indigenous women and gender-based violence.

**Catherine Oliver** is a geographer and lecturer in the Sociology of Climate Change at Lancaster University. Her research interests include animals (specifically birds), more-than-human theory, and urban studies. Between 2020 and 2022, Catherine was researching the history and contemporary resurgence of backyard hens and their keepers in gardens and allotments in London. She is currently writing a book about this research, *The Chicken City*, to be published with Manchester University Press. Previously, she researched veganism in Britain; her first book *Veganism, Archives and Animals* was published with Routledge in 2021 and her second book, *What Is Veganism For?* will be published in 2024 with Bristol University Press. Currently, Catherine is researching the birds of Morecambe Bay and, when not teaching or writing, can be found walking and watching the seabirds and the sands, or on the 2p machines at the arcades. She can also be found online at @katiecmoliver, and on her website, https://catherinecmoliver.com/.

**Jonathan Prior** is Senior Lecturer in Human Geography at Cardiff University. His research spans cultural geography, environmental philosophy, sound studies, and landscape research. He has published on the use of sonic methods in human geography; the relationship between landscape design and sonic perception; environmental aesthetics; and ecological restoration and rewilding strategies.

**Jon Henrik Ziegler Remme** is an Associate Professor in the Department of Social Anthropology, University of Bergen. His previous research dealt with the relations between humans, animals, and spirits among the Ifugao, the Philippines. Recently his research interests have turned towards the multispecies biopolitics of human–marine relations. He investigates this through looking at the affective relationalities of recreational lobster fishery in Norway and through studying the temporal dimensions of human–lobster relations in the commercial lobster fisheries in Maine, US.

**Gillian Rose** is Professor of Human Geography at the University of Oxford and a Fellow of the British Academy and of the Academy of Social Sciences. She is the author of *Feminism and Geography* (Polity, 1993) and *Doing Family Photography* (Ashgate, 2010); the fifth edition of *Visual Methodologies* (Sage) was published in 2023. The year 2022 saw the publication of a collection of essays on *Seeing the City Digitally*, available open access from Amsterdam University Press, as well as *The New Urban Aesthetic: Digital Experiences of Urban Change*, co-authored with Monica Degen (Bloomsbury). She has written many papers on images, visualising technologies, and ways of seeing in urban, domestic, and archival spaces.

**Chris Sandbrook** is Professor of Conservation and Society in the Department of Geography, University of Cambridge. He is Director of the MPhil in Conservation Leadership at Cambridge, and a Fellow of Darwin College. He is a conservation social scientist with a range of research interests around the central theme of biodiversity conservation and its relationship with society. His current research addresses the relationship between conservation and development in theory and practice, the values and viewpoints of conservationists and how these influence conservation practice, as well as the social and political implications of new technologies for conservation.

**Adam Searle** is a cultural, historical, and environmental geographer at the University of Nottingham broadly researching the relations between humans, other species, and technologies. He is particularly interested in how developments in science and technology implicate the lives of animals and environmental governance within the overlapping crises of climate breakdown and mass extinction. He has a PhD in geography from the University of Cambridge, an MSc in Nature, Society, and Environmental Governance from the University of Oxford, and a BSc (Hons) in Ecological and Environmental Sciences from the University of Edinburgh. In 2020, he co-founded the international, interdisciplinary Digital Ecologies research group with other early-career researchers.

**Emma Tait** is a data scientist and visualisation engineer with an extensive background in geographic information systems, cartography, web and database development, creative design, and visual art. Her academic interest is centred on feminist digital natures, particularly the interplay between lived human experience, fantasy worlds, and the power of play within digital games. She worked for the Forest Ecosystem Monitoring Cooperative at the University of Vermont, and has a Master's degree from the Department of Geography at the University of Cambridge. She is currently a product engineer for Esri.

**Jonathon Turnbull** is a cultural, environmental, and urban geographer at the University of Oxford. His research examines how understandings of nature are produced and contested across geographical contexts and why this matters for more-than-human social, political, and economic life. Jonny received his PhD from the University of Cambridge, funded by the ESRC. This research examined the cultural and ecological fallout from the Chornobyl nuclear catastrophe in Ukraine. In 2020, Jonny co-founded the Digital Ecologies research group. He has conducted research into the digitisation of more-than-human worlds in diverse contexts, from urban peregrine falcons to free-roaming dogs in the Chornobyl Exclusion Zone. In 2021, he co-founded the Ukrainian Environmental Humanities Network.

# Acknowledgements

The Digital Ecologies research group emerged at the height of the COVID-19 pandemic when, for many people, many aspects of everyday life went online. It started as a series of informal conversations about the digitisation of human–nature relationships between Jonny, Adam, and Henry who were in Kyiv, Barcelona, and Cambridge at the time. These conversations quickly grew into research interests and, driven by the desire to connect with scholars during lockdown, the trio organised an online conference exploring the digital mediation of more-than-human worlds. The conference received widespread interest and took place over two days in March 2021 with Etienne Benson and Jennifer Gabrys delivering keynote presentations. Many of the contributions in this collection are reworkings of initial presentations which took place at the 2021 conference: thank you to all of the contributing authors to this collection who have each been a pleasure to work with over the past three years. Eva has been involved with the Digital Ecologies group since this time, initially as a discussant at the conference, and later as an active collaborator within the book project and broader intellectual project of Digital Ecologies.

In 2022, the group grew to include Oscar Hartman Davies, Pauline Chasseray-Peraldi, Jennifer Dodsworth, and Julia Poerting, each of whom have played an enormous role in shaping the contributions of this book. Without them, Digital Ecologies – as a research group and community, as well as a field of practical and intellectual inquiry – wouldn't exist. We are very grateful also to other members of our advisory board – Jennifer Gabrys, William M. Adams, Jamie Lorimer, and Erica Von Essen – who have each offered feedback and guidance on various aspects of our group's work and organisation. We are also grateful to the Digital Ecologies blog contributors who have shaped the ideas throughout this book in various ways, who are, by the time of full draft submission, in order of blog publication: Will Bindley, Ben Platt, Catherine Oliver, Erica von Essen, Alexandra Palmer, Adam Fish, Mónica Amador, Ben Newport, Juan Felipe Riaño, Georgios Tzoumas,

Siddharth Unnithan Kumar, Samuel Cushman, Timothy Hodgetts, Theo Stanley, Noemi Duroux, Daniël de Zeeuw, Tommaso Campagna, Eleni Maragkou, Jesper Lust, Carlo de Gaetano, Michelle Lai, John Carillo, and Matthew Halpenny.

Our second conference – Digital Ecologies in Practice – took place in Bonn, Germany, in July 2022. This event involved engaging with practitioners and artists, expanding the scope of the research group and starting new and interdisciplinary conversations. The event included keynote lectures from Ron Wakkary and Mari Bastashevski, with the latter also exhibiting a multimedia installation in a local gallery space. Our team once again expanded to include Noemi Duroux and Kira Bautz as research assistants, and Karolina Uskakovych and Matthew Halpenny as artists-in-residence. The Digital Ecologies project has taken on new lines of flight through these collaborations, for which we are very grateful. Many of the interventions from this conference seeking to foster dialogue between the intellectual foundations of Digital Ecologies and artistic, creative, or activist practice have been published in a special issue of *cultural geographies*.

We have held further Digital Ecologies events, workshops, and conferences at Wageningen University in The Netherlands and the Oslo School of Environmental Humanities in Norway, with the support of Clemens Driessen and Hugo Reinert, Malene Bøyum, and Rachel Douglas-Jones. Thank you to all the speakers and panellists at or around these events, with a special mention to the artists who welcomed us into their studios: Polymorf, Ingrid Bjørnaali, Carolina Vásquez, Isak Wisløff, and Siri Austeen.

We are grateful to Karolina Uskakovych for producing the cover image for this book. Thanks also go to Will Bindley who designed our website and conference materials in 2021. Working with Karolina and Will involved conscious and deliberate attempts to translate key ideas and concepts from digital ecologies into visual form, informed by several discussions. We are lucky to have such wonderful interlocutors.

At the University of Sheffield, we are grateful to animal studies, STS, and digital media colleagues, particularly ShARC (Sheffield Animal Studies Research Centre), STeMiS (Science, Technology and Medicine in Society), iHuman, and the Digital Media & Society team. We are grateful for the wider support and mentorship of the Vital Geographies Research Group, the Winged Geographies group, and the Urban Ecologies project at the University of Cambridge, in addition to everyone at King's College who helped us get this project off the ground. Thank you to the More-than-human Geography cluster at the University of Oxford, who cultivated a thriving and supportive research community throughout pandemic lockdowns and beyond, and who have generously given feedback at multiple occasions on the

Digital Ecologies research agenda. In Liège, we are grateful for the support of everyone involved in the Centre Spiral STS group, and especially those working on the Body Societal ERC project. Our thanks also to colleagues at the Institute for Science and Society, Cultural and Historical Geography, and Environment and Society groups at the University of Nottingham.

As this book was developed between periods of industrial action in UK higher education, thanks also to colleagues on our various picket lines; a special shout out to everyone on the Elmfield picket in Sheffield, South Entrance picket in Nottingham, Downing Street picket in Cambridge, and South Parks Road picket in Oxford!

Thanks to our original editor Tom Dark for getting this project off the ground and to our new editors Shannon Kneis and Laura Swift who, along with colleagues at MUP such as Deborah Smith, have been hugely supportive in helping us deal with unexpected challenges during the process of developing the book.

This project has been supported by European Research Council Horizon 2020 Starting Grant 'The Body Societal' (Grant No. 949577) and the University of Sheffield Institutional Open Access Fund. We would like to issue huge thanks to these funders for enabling us to make this book open access.

Additionally, the Digital Ecologies research group has received funding from King's College, University of Cambridge (2021); the Vital Geographies research group, Department of Geography, University of Cambridge (2021); the Institute of Geography, University of Bonn (2022); the Cultural Geography group, Wageningen University (2022); the German Research Foundation, Deutsche Forschungsgemeinschaft project number 446600467 (2022); the Oslo School of Environmental Humanities (2023); the Technological Life research cluster, School of Geography and the Environment, University of Oxford (2021; 2023); and the Economic and Social Research Council (ESRC) project number: ES/W006952/1 (2022). The financial support of these funders allowed us to host conferences, workshops, art installations, and exhibitions, all of which have importantly shaped the intellectual contribution of Digital Ecologies.

Special personal thanks for the love and support of Anne and Nigel Turnbull and Clive and Wendy Searle whose encouragement spurred on certain editors of this book for many, many years. We are grateful to our partners, families, and friends for all you have done and continue to do for us.

# Introduction: what is Digital Ecologies?

*Adam Searle, Eva Haifa Giraud, Jonathon Turnbull,
and Henry Anderson-Elliott*

In an era of mass extinction, climate emergency, and biodiversity collapse, what role might digital media play in securing liveable futures across species lines? To what extent are digital media ameliorating or exacerbating environmental crises? And what theoretical, empirical, and methodological frameworks are needed to make sense of digitally mediated ecologies? In order to confront these questions, this collection draws together scholars from across more-than-human and digital geographies, the digital and environmental humanities, social anthropology, and media theory, among other fields. Collectively, these authors trace relationships between digital media and environmental politics that are often fraught, sometimes hopeful, and always complex.

Interrogating the mediation of more-than-human worlds is increasingly urgent. As rare and endangered species find digital prominence online, many of them are fading out of corporeal existence. Yet online afterlives of extinct animals continue to circulate in digitised form.[1] In 2021, for instance, the National Film and Sound Archive of Australia released a colourised YouTube video of a thylacine, an extinct marsupial, to commemorate National Threatened Species Day. Numerous contemporary 'thylacine sighting' videos continue to circulate on the same platform.[2] Virtual reality technologies now facilitate encounters with extinct species, such as Jakob Kudsk Steensen's video installation *RE-ANIMATED* (2018–19), which brings the Hawaiian Kauaʻi ʻōʻō bird back from the dead for the public to consume. Environmental activism, moreover, is frequently organised and coordinated via social media. Widespread protests by Just Stop Oil and Extinction Rebellion in the UK and beyond are obvious examples of activism that is tailored to being liked, shared, and debated online. Within academia, researchers now deploy digital technologies to study, manage, and conserve species, landscapes, and ecologies: from the everyday logging of birding lists via smartphone apps to advanced satellite tags being used to track turtle dove flightpaths,[3] and artificial intelligence being utilised in identifying plant species.

At the same time, digital media open up new regimes of environmental governance and surveillance. CCTV and camera traps are increasingly deployed to police wildlife in ways that risk reconfiguring colonial violence.[4] Meanwhile, the manufacture, maintenance, and disposal of digital technologies have vast material footprints, contributing towards and intensifying ecological crises.[5] Digital technologies are thus evermore entangled with more-than-human life, often with ambivalent results. Rather than detached, neutral, and objective intermediaries between bodies, digital technologies are situated, political, and affective mediators with manifold implications for the ecologies in which they are intentionally or unintentionally embedded.

Ideas for this collection of interdisciplinary interventions – each with their own objectives, perspectives, and contributions – emerged during the COVID-19 lockdowns in the early 2020s. As a group of scholars working across the social sciences and humanities who were interested in the complex nexus of human social relations with other species and technologies, but were unable to venture far from our homes, we began to search for alternative insights into, and encounters with, the more-than-human worlds we simultaneously study and co-constitute.[6] Many substituted the gaze of binoculars for that of the webcam to observe the daily lives of non-human animals.[7] Conversations about nature took place in alternative spaces and reached new publics online, meaning the very nature of nature itself seemed to change.[8] Organisations and scientists utilised an emergent arsenal of digital devices to mobilise publics (themselves with more spare time) to monitor the natural world at an unprecedented scale through a plethora of citizen science initiatives.[9] Although the global pandemic was heterogeneously experienced and characterised across cultural, historical, and geographical contexts, it resulted in the widespread intensification and normalisation of both digital media and digital mediation in everyday life.

Yet digitisation, and its varied social and political implications for more-than-human worlds, is a socio-technological process far pre-dating contemporary (post-) pandemic scholarship and practice. Technologies necessarily mediate countless human understandings of and engagements with ecology,[10] for example the vast assemblages of devices and implements which facilitate travel, understanding, or communication. The ontological foundations of what different people or cultures might call 'nature' or 'natural' are inseparable from the epistemological implications of the contrasting – and often contradicting – practices and processes used to understand it. Natural histories are technologically mediated, and contemporary ecological situations are known or made knowable by technological histories, to the extent where 'natural' or 'technological' do not make sense without each other, and the narration of ecology is fundamentally shaped by 'technonatural histories'.[11]

However, to emphasise the enmeshment of nature and culture is a non-innocent critical gesture. In empirical terms, as Ryan Bishop and AbdouMaliq Simone foreground in relation to Bernard Stiegler's late scholarship, the large-scale technical systems that are necessary for detecting, visualising, and mobilising around climate change simultaneously contribute to it.[12] This framing of digital media as pharmakon, concurrently culprit and cure for socio-ecological crises, could equally be applicable to the framework of technonatural histories itself. As we discuss in more depth shortly, the act of replacing a nature/technics distinction with an emphasis on the co-constitutive relations between these realms, or recognition of hybridity, has been embraced by hopeful posthumanist and new materialist theories in order to highlight interdependencies and resist anthropocentrism.[13] Yet some of the most prominent technological and conceptual lineages that this body of theory draws upon (notably cybernetics) are grounded in cold war legacies of militarisation and control.[14] As N. Katherine Hayles points out in *How We Became Posthuman*, early cybernetic theory – emerging from conferences sponsored by the Josiah Macy foundation – was intended to 'extend liberal humanism, not subvert it'.[15] In practical terms, moreover, Adam Wickberg highlights that these developments had particular significance for environmental politics, because:

> Early computers like ENIAC – the Electronic Numerical Integrator and Computer – were first developed to calculate complex wartime ballistics tables between 1943 and 1945 and were then received by civil society as a revolutionary means to increase efficiency in engineering, modelling and predicting weather, and would also be part of revolutionizing the understanding of the environment.[16]

Against this backdrop, the prospect of dissolving meaningful separations between mediating technologies and more-than-human worlds is an ambivalent prospect. It is thus important, we suggest, to find ways of understanding processes of mediation without uncritically celebrating them, and to resist treating the description of these relations as an ethico-political end in itself. Instead, this book functions as an ethical entry point, generative of critical lines of inquiry into the futures of ecological politics.

It is among these frictions and tensions we position *Digital Ecologies*. We take the mediation of more-than-human worlds as a starting point, looking to provoke more questions than answers. As such, the intervention we make with this book is not diagnostic or deterministic; it cannot and should not claim any authority over this shifting technological and ecological landscape. Our goal, instead, is to foster dialogue in the emergent space of mediated more-than-human relations and create opportunity for further epistemic multiplicity while at the same time insisting on the need to centralise ethico-political questions about what these developments mean for more-than-human worlds.

This introductory chapter offers readers a roadmap to *Digital Ecologies* as an intervention. First, we chart the contemporary situations within which these interventions are made, asking what digital ecologies can provide both intellectually and politically in the technonatural present. We position digital ecologies, within the nexus of society–environment–technology, as an epistemological approach to question how and where the mediation of more-than-human worlds occurs, for whom, and with what political consequences?[17] Second, we detail the conceptual framing of this work by establishing a common vernacular through attending to and defining some key concepts such as 'digitisation', 'mediation', 'ecologies', and 'more-than-human'. Third, we explore the empirical articulations of this book, across three interrelated sections of 'digital encounters', 'digital governance', and 'digital assemblages', in addition to introducing the theoretical reflections offered by leading scholars in the social sciences, environmental humanities, and media theory. Lastly, in dialogue with our final trio of chapters, we suggest future directions for critical scholarship in the field.

## Situations: the technonatural present

Complex global ecological issues such as climate dysfunction, biodiversity breakdown, and mass extinction now affect all aspects of life. Even activities, practices, and scholarship that were perhaps once thought of as separate from this overarching environment – for example, identity, creativity, or politics – are all dynamically related to the contemporary ecological catastrophe.[18] Notoriously difficult to grasp or imagine across spatio-temporal scales of great magnitude, these ecological frictions are known, communicated, and acted upon through scientific and technological practices associated with the proliferating use of digital media.[19] Agnieszka Leszczynski calls the ongoing intensification of socio-spatial digital mediation the 'technological present': characterised by significant changes in everyday life through the use of media – technical objects such as hardware or software – and forms of mediation.[20] But the complex nexus of technology, society, and environment is further complicated and reimagined in what we call the 'technonatural present'. We understand the technonatural present as rife with digital expressions of 'entanglement', a term deployed by scholars across the environmental humanities and cognate disciplines to decentre human exceptionalism and emphasise the agencies of other-than-human bodies, affects, and practices.[21]

*Introduction* 5

Media theorist Sy Taffel, for instance, has made strides in thinking through digital mediation and the environment through the concept of digital entanglement.[22] In particular, Taffel's work is adept at thinking materialities and encounters – or infrastructure and experience – simultaneously. Drawing from Félix Guattari's influential work that conceptualises the inseparable ecologies of mind, society, and environment, Taffel deploys a relational approach to demonstrate how Guattari's 'three ecologies' are entangled through the mediation of more-than-human worlds. As Taffel underlines, moreover, digital entanglements should not just neutrally be described; instead, they are deeply political – while digital technologies are rooted in systems of exploitative and extractive capitalism through their very materiality, they are not necessarily bound to them. Following this observation, while much scholarship attending to more-than-human agencies tends to celebrate entanglement as something inherently good or progressive, our question here is to ask what comes after digital entanglement?[23] What futures are rendered imaginable or impossible in the technological present, as some technonatural entanglements are materialised while others are foreclosed?

To examine the technonatural present, a relational approach is therefore favourable. On the one hand, this involves acknowledgement that digital mediation has become ubiquitous across diverse societal practices. On the other hand, it involves recognition that digital mediation is itself ecological, underpinned by vast material infrastructures. The technonatural present can thus be characterised as an assemblage of relations that includes human and non-human bodies, environments, and technologies.[24] Digital ecologies, we propose, is one approach to examining the implications of this entanglement across species, spaces, and practices. As an epistemological approach, it asks how situated and politicised accounts of the technonatural present may stimulate alternative future constellations. In the media and public imaginary, speculative futures concerning the digital mediation of more-than-human worlds are commonly situated within a binary narrative of either techno-utopian futures or techno-apocalyptic despair. The former finds unwarranted hope in speculations of 'digital solutionism',[25] hoping for technofixes to the ecological catastrophe that often accommodate some form of 'business as usual'. The latter has long-standing prominence in environmentalist literatures articulated through popular ideas like 'nature deficit disorder',[26] arguing that screens and technologies inherently sever human connections with more-than-human worlds. As such, 'reconnection with nature' 'has become the mantra for addressing humanity's severance from the natural world',[27] which, as Robert Fletcher aptly highlights, is a gross simplification.[28]

Breaking down this narrative binary of techno-utopian hope versus techno-dystopian despair is a key task for digital ecologies scholarship. Such a progressive environmental politics, we argue, can be found in the *glitches* of the technonatural present.[29] Such glitches involve grounded and empirical stories that elucidate digital entanglement otherwise. In software studies, glitches in computation have long been conceived as moments of disruption that enable 'insight beyond the customary, omnipresent and alien computer aesthetics', a moment that 'reminds us of our cultural experience at the same time as developing it by suggesting new aesthetic forms'.[30] Work in digital geographies, likewise, contends that glitches function as 'generative fissures within the spaces and practices' of digital mediation.[31] Building on Legacy Russell's *Glitch Feminism*,[32] this epistemological approach to glitches 'acknowledges the simultaneous ability for error and erratum in digitally mediated formations' whereby 'each rupture offers an opportunity to correct for a different and better outcome'.[33] Glitches provide opportunities to look beyond necessary, but insufficient, criticism of digitisation in the technonatural present and to speculate on digitisation otherwise through affirmative scholarship.

Taffel's work hints at this glitchiness, whereby technologies can be repurposed and experimented with towards more just socio-environmental ends. One example of such glitch-hacking is artist-researcher Matthew Halpenny's work, which attends to the extractive qualities and materialities of digital mediation through attention to temporality. Halpenny's creation *Slow Serif* makes digital materiality palpable by provoking viewers to consider alternative temporalities of digitality.[34] Harnessing electricity from fuel cells powered by moss photosynthesis, Halpenny's research-creation powers artificial intelligence to write a novella on slowness. The electricity generated through the fuel cells can manage to generate one word per day, which makes palpable the relatively enormous amount of energy required for instantaneous and rapid transmission of text, images, and sound that have become customary for fossil fuel powered societies.

Within this framing, then, *Digital Ecologies* employs both critical and affirmative approaches to the mediation of more-than-human worlds, and searches for progressive means of questioning technologies otherwise. In the interstices of sweeping speculation about technologies and their polarised implications for ecologies, *Digital Ecologies* follows minor stories rooted in the everyday. Such work, following Leszczynski,[35] counters the majoritarian view of digitisation as a 'techno-apocalyptic phenomenon' to move towards 'more open – and ultimately more hopeful' futures in scholarship, thought, and praxis. *Digital Ecologies* is situated within the cracks of these narratives, looking for generative openings in thought and practice that awkwardly dwell with friction and modestly provoke inquiry.

## Provocations: conceptual framing

To facilitate critically urgent scholarship on the mediation of more-than-human worlds, we need a shared conceptual vocabulary capable of working across disciplinary and practical perspectives. Many terms used throughout this book draw from important theoretical advances made by the 'more-than-human' and 'digital' turns that recently swept across the social sciences and humanities. These 'turns' are heterogeneous and complex, and multiple books could be dedicated to understanding the intricacies of each. In the interests of brevity, though, we will focus here on the contributions central to our conceptual framing of *Digital Ecologies*, defining some of the key concepts that inform the book, such as 'digitisation', 'mediation', 'ecologies', and 'more-than-human'. Strands of media theory have long defined, debated, and nuanced some of the key terms operationalised in this collection.[36] But rather than delving into their specific intellectual histories, here we are concerned with outlining working definitions intended for interdisciplinary audiences. As such, our understandings of these key terms are informed by digital geographies; media theory; science and technology studies (and how insights of this work have been reshaped by the environmental humanities); and transdisciplinary more-than-human theory.

Digital worlds are proliferating and are evermore the subject of academic inquiry, so much so that James Ash, Rob Kitchin, and Agnieszka Leszczynski have traced the emergence of a 'digital turn' in scholarship around the late 2010s, particularly in the context of geography.[37] Despite the digital receiving heightened attention as a matter of concern, the continued definitional ambiguity of 'the digital' is well documented. Daniel Miller and Heather Horst define the digital as 'all that which can be ultimately reduced to binary code, but which produces a further proliferation of particularity and difference'.[38] Digitisation converts the messy worlds of organic information into 'digits': the zeros and ones constituting binary code. Acknowledging digitisation as productive of multiplicity, Ash et al. warn against singular 'monolithic' depictions of 'the digital', instead invoking 'digital' in multiple ways to conceptualise the interconnected things produced through digital modes and mechanisms.[39] In relation to the non-human world, these multiple processes of digitisation work, in turn, to produce a multiplicity of natures.[40] As some of this book's editors and authors have argued elsewhere, 'digitisation thus shapes human–nature relations in multiple ways, enabling and foreclosing connections across more-than-human assemblages, events, and processes'.[41]

This conception of digitisation highlights its political and ethical stakes. Elsewhere, editors and authors in this book have noted that two 'ontological shifts' are inaugurated by the use of digital technologies in mediating more-than-human worlds.[42] First, 'digitisation enables new ways of encountering nonhumans that were (and are) encountered without digital mediation'.[43] Second, 'entirely novel encounters are facilitated by digitisation, involving aspects of nature inaccessible to encounter without the use of digital technologies'.[44] What is at stake in these two modes of mediation, however, are very different. Indeed, two very different kinds of ontological politics – or the enactment of particular worlds – take place in each. The former involves changing understandings of already existing human–nature relations, whereby new affects can be generated that may co-exist with non-digitised encounters. Such encounters can be harnessed for a variety of purposes from entertainment to education, and we might view this mode as a kind of proliferation of the ways one might relate to nature. At stake here is whether these encounters may displace 'actual' human–nature encounters or enhance in-person encounters. As such, they carry the risk of rendering ecologies spectacular.[45] The latter, however, involves bringing previously inaccessible aspects of the non-human world into the realm of encounter and, thus, governance. Encounters with the deep sea or with certain microbial worlds, for example, are (arguably) *only* possible through digital mediation.[46] The type of digital mediation thus matters as there is a risk of singularly representing such worlds or excluding others – intentionally or unintentionally – from view. Both *how* more-than-human worlds are digitised as well as *what* is being digitised invoke very different ontological and ethical questions, which a digital ecologies framework is attentive to. Thinking across these two distinct modes of digital mediation, we come to understand how digital entanglement gives rise to different modalities of biopower, which, in turn, casts digitisation as an opportunity for 'activists, researchers, designers, artists, and others seeking to refashion how environmental governance takes place and [to] subvert technocratic hegemony'.[47]

Our second key term, 'media', is perhaps still more complex than 'digital' or 'digitisation'. Even in fields that take media as their object of inquiry – such as media studies itself – it can be challenging to pin down what the term 'media' actually means. As Nick Couldry points out, the difficulty is that: 'media themselves are always at least doubly articulated, as both transmission technology and representational content'.[48] These challenges are compounded when moving to other academic fields. Different disciplines offer alternative frameworks and approaches for studying media, producing diverse conceptualisations that mutate and evolve in pluralistic ways.[49] Perhaps the most well-known early theory of mediated communication is Claude Shannon and Warren Weaver's 'mathematical theory of communication' from 1948. This model breaks mediation down into discrete elements (information source, transmitter, signal/received signal, receiver, and destination), in order to identify how 'noise' generated by semantic, technical, and efficacy problems could disrupt the smooth communication of messages from A to B. This rendering of mediation as a neutral process of transporting messages – only disrupted by external forces – seems far removed from widespread understandings of mediation in sociology or science and technology studies (STS) as any process that makes a difference in the composition of social life.[50]

Yet between Shannon and Weaver and contemporary, broader, conceptions of mediation, there is a rich tradition of media theory that has expanded what mediation means by thinking across different intellectual traditions. In their pithy overview and definition of digital media activism, for instance, Emiliano Treré and Anne Kaun find cultural theorist Raymond Williams' definition of media especially useful due to its emphasis on transformation.[51] For Williams, media should be analysed in terms of three forms of mediation, or transformation: amplification, duration, and alternative symbolic production. This engagement with Williams is productive, then, in combining a broad sociological conception of mediation as a process that makes a difference with a theorisation of *specific* modes of transformation associated with media technologies. In the context of digital ecologies research, this conception of media – and mediation – is productive in centralising questions about how, and in what specific ways, matter and meaning are being transformed at the interface of digital media technologies and more-than-human worlds.

Take livestreamed animal webcams as an example: to examine the digital mediation of peregrine falcons it is important to ask how the newfound visibility of nesting birds might amplify the plight of vulnerable urban species or what forms of ethical response-ability are generated as species are made accessible to wide audiences. It might also be important to ask about the ethical implications of this imagery in terms of its capacity to generate data: what does the production and storage of these data mean for the human and non-human animals enrolled in these mediated encounters? Finally, it seems vital to ask what new meanings are generated by the novel circulation of affectively charged representations? In sum, what role do these technologies play in transforming material relations and cultural narratives?[52] This approach necessitates careful reflection on the relationship between the content of media and its materiality. What is the ethical relation, for instance, between installing and maintaining a camera in a hard-to-reach, intimate site and the affective livestreamed imagery of vulnerable chicks this camera produces? These concerns speak to wider questions in media theory regarding the production of what Sean Cubitt calls 'ecomedia', or texts that are designed to raise environmental consciousness. For Cubitt, the ethics of ecomedia is only partially located in the content of these texts and it is equally important to understand how this content intersects with the material production of media.[53]

The risk of framing media technologies in terms of the forms of complex socio-material transformation they inaugurate is that this emphasis can give rise to a deterministic understanding of media as forces that shape society – or in the context of this book, transform more-than-human worlds – in accordance with particular technological properties. From this deterministic perspective, for instance, the uptake of sensor technologies in industrialised farming could be interpreted as transforming agriculture in line with productivist logics; or the rise of tracking apps to monitor domesticated animals could be conceived as precipitating new forms of trans-species surveillance. Yet, as lively and valuable scholarship on these topics elucidates,[54] it is important to resist overly neat conclusions about technologies causing or determining social change, as this presumption neglects how media have themselves been shaped by wider socio-cultural assemblages.

To circumvent determinism, Treré and Kaun avoid making neat, linear claims about the types of social transformation that are created by particular forms of mediation. Instead, they reframe mediation in ecological terms, drawing on a tradition of scholarship that conceives of media as 'complex environments' constituted by 'newer and older media formats, physical and digital spaces, internal and external forms of communication, as well as alternative and corporate social media platforms'.[55] In the context of digital ecologies scholarship, therefore, specific media technologies might be entangled with particular forms of technonatural transformation, but should not be understood in isolation and instead conceived as one element of a complex environment. Also central to media ecological thought is the premise that the affordances of media are not static and unchanging, but emerge through practice and their (evolving) relationship with other media.[56] Although media ecological scholarship has a long history, as illustrated by several of the chapters in this book this approach has particularly flourished in the theoretical realm of software studies and ethnographic scholarship on social movement media use. Both these bodies of work have, in turn, drawn inspiration from a range of other disciplines (particularly continental philosophy, critical theory, and STS) to conceptualise media.[57] As Taffel foregrounds, while this approach might carry its risks – not least due to the appropriation of ecological language by corporate forces – an ecological approach retains political and ethical value.[58]

The insights offered by media ecological theory are thus productive for digital ecologies scholarship, in attending to the specific and situated transformations fostered by media environments while resisting deterministic narratives about the nature of these transformations. As Jody Berland underlines in *Virtual Menageries*,[59] developments in media theory mean that three elements need to be interrogated in order to grasp the ethical implications of mediation for more-than-human worlds. It is vital, Berland argues, to understand both the 'ecology of species' and the 'ecology of media', but it is equally essential to grasp the relations between these ecologies and how they entwine and co-constitute one another. As traced across many of the chapters in this book, these arguments are also applicable to other non-human beings in addition to animals: from seeds and forests to ecosystems themselves.

Debates in media theory are complex and risk, at times, generating too many moving parts (especially when summarising decades of debate into such a condensed form, as we have done here). In sum, though, several key aspects of the above conceptions of mediation are especially informative for this book. First, our approach is informed by the broad conceptual understanding of mediation as a process that makes a difference in the composition of social life, as refined through a focus on the more specific ways that media technologies transform material relations and semiotic meanings. Second, as touched on previously, we adopt an ecological understanding of the affordances of media rather than a deterministic conception of how media shape social relations. Rather than possessing static properties, we understand the affordances of media as emerging through co-constitutive relationships with other elements in complex assemblages. This approach to mediation means that entities beyond the apps, television screens, newspapers, platforms, and phones that are conventionally understood as 'media' can become mediators. In other words, through their relationship with other entities, sometimes surprising entities emerge as important material-semiotic actors – such as the animal mediators described by Berland. This approach, third, means that we take an expansive understanding of what constitutes media, resonating with John Durham Peters' conception of 'elemental media',[60] wherein entities – from clouds to water – can, in Stefan Helmreich's terms, be understood 'not just as an ambient surround, but as a medium through which living and knowing happen'.[61] As Melody Jue points out, understanding the specific ways that elements act as mediators is generative for rethinking some of the central tenets of mediation.[62]

While our *conceptions* of digital media(tion) are informed by digital geographies and media theory, our *ethical orientation* in analysing mediation is informed by approaches originating in science and technology studies (STS) that have flourished in the context of the environmental humanities. As hinted at by many of the recurring conceptual touchstones throughout these opening pages – and throughout this book as a whole – theoretical work from STS informs both our own engagements with digital ecologies and arguments made in many of the other chapters. There are several key traditions within STS (though some have historically seen more uptake beyond this field than others),[63] but our reference points are grounded in feminist science studies in light of its influence in the environmental humanities and more-than-human geographies.[64] This branch of STS is useful as it combines the recognition of non-human agency and dissolution of boundaries between humans, technologies and non-human animals with an insistence on centring ethico-political questions about the implications of these relationships. As Susan Leigh Star argues in her influential essay, 'Power, Technology and the Phenomenology of Conventions', this tradition starts with the premise that 'it is more politically just to begin with a question, *cui bono?* [who benefits] than to begin with a celebration of the fact of human/nonhuman mingling'.[65]

For Star, what is missed in celebratory narratives of entanglement is recognition that socio-technical infrastructures organise worlds in ways that are difficult to reverse and become normalised as a fact of social life. It is thus important to ask how these infrastructures come into being and to interrogate the work they do in order to foreground who benefits from them (and crucially who is harmed). Put differently, when analysing digital infrastructures, it is vital to address questions of power and inequality. To do this, Star contends, it is important to ask who does the 'invisible work' of negotiating exclusionary infrastructural arrangements because this focus not only highlights inequity but disrupts infrastructural naturalisation by highlighting that: 'There is nothing necessary or inevitable about science or technology, all constructions are historically contingent, no matter how stabilized'.[66] As Star goes on to emphasise in her landmark book on the politics of classification with Geoffrey Bowker, *Sorting Things Out*: 'Each standard and each category valorizes some point of view and silences another. This is not inherently a bad thing – indeed it is inescapable. But it is an ethical choice, and as such it is dangerous – not bad, but dangerous'.[67] What is underlined by Star and Bowker, then, is the importance of understanding how categories and standards mediated by spreadsheets, filing cabinets, and computer desktops might seem mundane – and, as such, are difficult to even notice – they nonetheless organise worlds in profound ways.

As evoked by the title of *Sorting Things Out*'s first chapter, 'To classify is human', the book's focus is on the implications of information infrastructures for the organisation of *human* lifeworlds.[68] Thus, while *Digital Ecologies* is animated by similar ethical questions and points of emphasis to Bowker and Star, we differ in our focus on the implications of mediation for more-than-human worlds. In other words, we place non-human animals, plants, and ecosystems front and centre in questions about who benefits and who is excluded by assemblages of digital mediation.

As illustrated by the above discussion, the phrase 'more-than-human' is used regularly throughout this book. This term's use has proliferated since the beginning of the twenty-first century, perhaps signifying a political choice to decentre human experience as the focal point of analysis in social research. More-than-human approaches to research broadly seek to conceptualise and examine the agency of non-human beings and materials in what were previously considered the sole domains of human activities: culture, society, politics, and the economy. Digital media (and mediation) are co-constituted with more-than-human environments. The theoretical lens of ecologies allows us to make sense of this in greater detail. 'Ecology' is conventionally defined as the biological study of relations and interactions between living and non-living bodies. However, the term has been adopted and reworked in the social sciences (as exemplified by media theory) because of its focus on relations, connections, assemblages, and entanglements between more-than-human actants.[69] New materialist scholars, for instance, have explored ecological frameworks for elucidating the relations between matter, bodies, environments, and their interactions. Digital geographers have, likewise, deployed an ecological lens to study the agencies of cybernetic matter such as algorithms and malware,[70] and ecological metaphors are commonly evoked in the study of human–computer interactions.[71]

We are drawn to the multiple interdisciplinary, collaborative, and conceptual potentials of 'ecologies', and thus find it preferable to alternative terms like 'digital nature'[72] and 'digital Anthropocene' (even though these frameworks are also critically important).[73] Our use of the term 'ecologies', however, is due to it being multiple from the outset, explicitly focused on interrelations between actants across species and spaces. Moreover, it refers to the critical tradition of political ecology, which combines the theoretical lenses of political economy and ecology to examine the relations between humans, non-humans, and capital.[74] As Taffel argues, in the context of digital mediation: 'A political ecology of media must additionally consider the relations that are embedded in and propagated by the infrastructures that support the production of content – the code, algorithms and programs which exist at the scale of software, and the components, cabling, cell towers and other entities which comprise the scale of hardware'.[75]

In co-authored work elsewhere, with a range of other scholars from across geography, media theory, and political ecology – namely Pauline Chasseray-Peraldi, Jennifer Dodsworth, Oscar Hartman Davies, Julia Poerting, and Erica von Essen – we have presented digital ecologies as an analytical framework to empiricise these overlapping areas of conceptual interest.[76] The structure of this book reflects this framework, although the areas are by no means mutually exclusive. The interrelated sections of the book – digital encounters, digital governance, and digital assemblages – develop the conceptual framing of digital ecologies still further and highlight the importance of multiplicity, reflexivity, and adaptability in this approach.

## Articulations: empirical engagements

*Digital Ecologies* is divided into three thematic parts, followed by three reflections from academics working in different fields related to the contributions of this book. These parts are by no means mutually exclusive, and some chapters certainly could have worked elsewhere within the collection. For us, this highlights the entanglements between theoretical, methodological, and empirical dimensions of the material and political realities of research in digital ecologies.

Starting with 'Digital encounters', Part I of the book highlights the heterogeneity of mediation across cultural, historical, technological, and ecological contexts. Encounters materialise in a given space and time when two or more entities come into contact. In the cases explored in this collection, these encounters are brokered through a variety of digital media.[77] Digitisation enables new ways of encountering non-humans that were (and are) encountered without digital mediation. These are encounters that took place before digitisation but which are now mediated by it. But also, entirely novel encounters are facilitated by digitisation, involving aspects of nature inaccessible to encounter without the use of digital technologies. To start with encounter, then, is to situate digital mediation and digital media, to ask what encounters they inaugurate, and to explore what knowledges are produced through these processes.[78]

In 'Running wild', William M. Adams, Chris Sandbrook, and Emma Tait examine the possibilities of augmented reality and smartphone gaming to foster a form of digital empathy towards far-away species on the brink of extinction. The role of games and gamification here is significant. While games can encourage human users to change their attitudes towards corporeal animals through building affinities towards digital avatars, gamification points to ethico-political tensions that arise through making life playable. Indeed, more broadly in the sociological literature, gamification has been accused of: 'replacing older forms of labour surveillance and oversight with seemingly "playful" forms'.[79] Speaking directly to the potentials and tensions of play, Catherine Oliver's chapter on the Twitch stream *Our Chicken Life* notes the affective atmospheres of gamification for fostering multispecies connection. In this case, direct user control is crucial: unlike many forms of online nature streaming that are unidirectional castings of wildlife (like AfriCam's gaze upon watering holes of Southern Africa),[80] *Our Chicken Life* relies on viewer input to directly shape the daily activities of chickens.

Yet both livestreams and exercise apps ultimately mobilise digital encounters in the pursuit of value generation, whereby non-human animals and their labour are used in the context of platform capitalism.[81] Whether for private wealth accumulation or for the benefit of conservation organisations, these chapters highlight the ways in which digital encounters can produce spectacular versions of nature,[82] as well as critical reflection on the new regimes of 'encounter value' instigated by these assemblages.[83]

While the aforementioned chapters bring well-known, widely documented, or even mundane ecological contexts into widespread public gaze through digitisation, Jon Henrik Ziegler Remme's 'Trap-cam of care' questions the novel ecologies brought into view through digital mediation itself. Prior to the installation of camera networks in traps, the captive behaviour of lobsters was left to the imagination. Remme's chapter shows how digitisation brings publics closer to these encounters – similarly to Oliver's detailing of user engagement, trap-cam viewers can offer suggestions to scientists about which foods to offer captive lobsters. Subaquatic ecologies are often argued to engage humans due to their inaccessibility and the need for them to be imagined.[84] However, through digital mediation, these more-than-human worlds are made knowable, and forms of digital intimacy have the potential to emerge. Again, though, while Remme's chapter underlines that mediation might foster new forms of knowledge and, in turn, care, these modes of care can also be entangled with violence, here due to the complex relations between lobster trap-cams and the fishing industry. In 'Digital sonic ecologies', Hannah Hunter, Sandra Jasper, and Jonathan Prior offer a different set of provocations for multispecies ethics, in turning to digital sound archives and sonic encounters. For instance, one of the chapter's many empirical illustrations discusses how digital traces of the now-extinct Kauaʻi ʻōʻō bird – once native to the Hawaiian archipelago – are found readily online. The spectral listening experience is now haunted by the knowledge of the animal's eventual demise and, the authors argue, provokes affectively charged responses critical of the settler colonial and capitalist processes underpinning its extinction. Ultimately, Hunter, Jasper, and Prior show how digital sonic recordings carry a multitude of material implications for more-than-human life.

Part II of the book, 'Digital governance', explores how digitisation generates opportunities for understanding pasts, governing presents, and forecasting futures across ecological contexts. Digital tools inaugurate many opportunities for the command and control of non-human life, and profoundly implicate the knowledge practices involved in mediating more-than-human worlds. For example, large conservation organisations are increasingly deploying algorithmic forms of governance that make 'smart' or 'real-time' decisions affecting non-human life anywhere in the world, such as from a computer in California, which often comes at the expense of decentring local and embodied knowledge practices.[85] But there are also frictions within this techno-hegemonic narrative, and as work in this collection demonstrates, online spaces have capacities to foster alternative versions of environmental politics – whether progressive or conservative.

'On-bird surveillance' by Oscar Hartman Davies and Jamie Lorimer explores the novel modes of governance used by marine ecologists and inaugurated by a range of digital tracking devices. Animals have been made knowable to humans through their tracks since prehistoric times, but in recent decades the growing arsenal of digital devices on hand to movement ecologists has left wilderness well and truly 'wired'.[86] But Hartman Davies and Lorimer trace the emergence of an important shift for digital ecological governance: from the human tracking *of* animals to humans tracking other human activities *with* animals. Particularly in an oceanic context, this carries fascinating implications for 'smart' governance regimes that demand fluidity, leading certain actors to create more urgency for further technological intervention. The agencies of non-human animals often come to the fore through the deployment of 'lively surveillance', whereby human actors exploit the ecological adaptabilities of non-human life to an environment, in their case the mounting of tracking devices onto albatrosses covering vast oceanic distances to monitor fishing activities.

In a similar vein, '"Saving the knowledge helps save the seed"' by Sophia Doyle and Katherine Dow details where non-human agencies – in this instance, those of technologies themselves – can be used by other human actors for politically just means. The London Freedom Seed Bank uses the same tools and techniques associated with biopolitical governance – in this case databases and database infrastructures – to forge multispecies connections, centre non-human genetic knowledges, and cultivate more liveable futures. Their chapter emphasises the non-neutrality of environmental data,[87] and illustrates technological agency itself, showing how the use of – and socio-ecological relations mediated by – certain technologies differs significantly from their originally intended purpose. These arguments thus resonate with Star's reminder that technologies could always have been 'otherwise', as with *Sorting Things Out*'s observation that everyday datagathering technologies are often dangerous due to becoming so routinely, and mundanely, used that they escape critical attention, thus obscuring the possibility of alternative ways of doing things. In Bowker and Star's words: 'when a seemingly neutral data collection mechanism is substituted for ethical conflict about the contents of the forms, the moral debate is partially erased'.[88] Speaking to these arguments, what is so critical about Doyle and Dow's chapter is that it does not solely work to denaturalise data-gathering software, but offers a concrete sense of how socially and environmentally just alternatives could be realised.

Digital objects, technologies, and techniques are therefore deeply engaged and involved in ecological politics, as the '#AmazonFires' chapter by Jonathan W.Y. Gray, Liliana Bounegru, and Gabriele Colombo attests. They detail how political frictions can develop on social media platforms through digital objects like hashtags and images, and how such digital objects reconfigure knowledge practices concerning environmental events online. Alternative visions of the 2019 #AmazonFires can be understood through digital archiving, which emphasises the methodological potentials and complications digitisation poses to the praxis of historical research – as such the digital archive is an ever-expansive space in the perpetual process of recombination.[89] Yet far from being understood after the fact, digital tools are also used in a prefigurative politics with the objectives of inclusivity and visibility across diverse social groups, as discussed by Jess McLean and Lara Newman regarding 'Children and young people's digital climate action in Australia'. Through digitisation, the School Strike 4 Climate movement has facilitated alternative visions of environmentalism that are not inherently exclusive along lines of race, gender, age, or class, and provide important links between activism across spatial and temporal scales. Importantly, McLean and Newman explore the decolonial potentials of digital mediation through centring on place and co-belonging and discuss its implications for identity and activism online.

These chapters, in conversation, allow for broader reflections concerning how digital ecologies are mobilised in search of progressive ethics and political potential. As ethics are always situated and emergent,[90] these chapters highlight the importance of paying close attention to ecologists, policymakers, and other practitioners experimenting with digital technologies to determine the responsibilities and obligations they inaugurate.[91]

Part III, 'Digital assemblages', questions the broader material foundations and implications of digital mediation. Materiality is a key theme throughout this part of the book, which highlights the diversity of non-human actants implicated in the co-fabrication of social, political, and economic worlds. This diversity is frequently obscured by the seemingly immaterial character of digitised worlds – for example, those characterised by imaginaries of an invisible 'cloud'.[92] Thus, chapters in this section draw attention to the materials, devices, and infrastructures that are fundamental to the digitisation process. These chapters learn from conceptual discussions in media ecology in the 2010s and 2020s that advance the idea that ecologies do not surround or adjoin media, but rather support and enable them.[93] Contributions in this part of the book thus take an expanded view of infrastructure, attentive to the ways in which non-human life is implicated in, and can be enrolled as part of, the biopolitics of infrastructure.[94]

Jennifer Gabrys offers a critical analysis of 'Programming nature as infrastructure in the Smart Forest City', proposed by its supporters as the meeting of technological and ecological urban design. This chapter was initially presented as one of the keynote lectures at the inaugural Digital Ecologies conference in 2021, inciting debate among attendees.[95] In contrast to many other chapters in this collection that examine the subversion of digital technologies by human and non-human actors, Gabrys importantly shows how smart green urbanism and its socio-technical – and ecological – formations potentially exacerbate urban inequalities. In considering the work of Lauren Berlant and the attestation that otherwise infrastructures carry transformative political potential while attending to their interrelations with social life,[96] Gabrys thinks through Smart Forest City infrastructures 'otherwise' to highlight the possibilities for less extractive and exploitative future practices.

Dwyer and Arold continue this expansion of what and how media ecologies are conceived, further strengthening dialogue between media theory and geographical and environmental humanities scholarship. Dwyer's chapter 'Ecological computationality' foregrounds potentials – and further complexity – opened up when conceiving of media in ecological terms, taking seriously the proposition that media have their own form of agency rather than simply mediating human intentions. Drawing on vignettes from the ethnography of malware, Dwyer traces how layers of self-referential relationships among code manifest agency in ways that disrupt the work of software engineers. Thinking across software studies, more-than-human and digital geographies, Dwyer thus poses provocations for digital ecologies research about how to accommodate the ecologies and agencies of digital media themselves. In 'Mediated natures', Arold draws on ethnographic observations from forest activism in Estonia, likewise offering an important provocation for digital ecologies in the rejoinder to remember the analogue. In other words, whereas Dwyer asks what can be gained from understanding software in ecological terms, Arold offers a reminder that the communications ecologies associated with environmental politics are always 'hybrid media' systems:[97] co-constituted, as Arold traces, not only by digital GPS and GIS technologies, but (in the case of forest activism) by discourse, diggers, and the agency of humans and non-humans with a stake in the forest. Arold's chapter, then, offers a framework for understanding how hybrid media systems are entangled with more-than-human worlds, expanding what counts as mediation in this context.

Together, the book's central chapters point to new disciplinary alliances and directions, and the value of thinking across academic fields. It should be emphasised, however, that although we have divided the book into three parts, this is for heuristic purposes rather than a neat dividing line. Echoing Taffel, it is futile to examine the agencies of content, software, and hardware in isolation from one another, but it is not merely enough to describe these digital entanglements.[98] Instead it is vital to foster situated understandings of the political stakes of particular entanglements, in terms of the more-than-human worlds they enact and those they foreclose.

### Directions: beyond the book

Part IV of *Digital Ecologies*, 'Digital ecological directions', consists of three invited reflections from academics working in different disciplinary domains – geography and visual studies, environmental history and humanities, media theory and sociology – about future directions for research in the overlapping remit of digital ecologies. Our hope with this part of the book is to acknowledge the aforementioned importance of interdisciplinarity to current and future digital ecologies scholarship while resisting the problems of hazy disciplinary boundaries – cognisant of critiques made by Cary Wolfe who suggests, in the context of animal studies, 'it is only through our disciplinary specificity that we have something specific and irreplaceable to contribute to this "question of the animal"'.[99] Echoing Wolfe's sentiment, in the context of digital ecologies, our hope in closing with reflections that are grounded in three specific disciplinary traditions that inform this book is threefold. First, these chapters elucidate some of the specific ways these disciplines shape – or could further inform – digital ecologies research. Conversely, and second, this part of the book foregrounds what digital ecologies scholarship might contribute to geographical, media, and environmental humanities research moving forwards. Third, and finally, these closing chapters also made us reflect back on the original conception of *Digital Ecologies*, what has changed over the years the book was being elaborated, and work that still needs to be done.

This book has developed over three years, and the ideas that have shaped it have come from many sources and interdisciplinary engagements, for which we are grateful. We had initially planned to hold a series of paper sessions at an international conference on the theme of digital ecologies. However, this event was due to take place in 2020 and shifted to a virtual format. At the height of the pandemic and its social and economic burden, many lacked the resources to pay high attendance or participation fees for an online event, which led us to withdraw. Instead, we ran a two-day conference online, with an open call for attendees across disciplines. This collection brings together some of the papers from these two days in

March 2021, in addition to other contributions from people working in the field.

The book's history, then, was beset with challenges. We were able to negotiate some of these challenges successfully, such as organising our first – then second – event, and working with an emerging community of scholars and practitioners engaged with digital ecologies. Other challenges were more complex. As with many books that have grown out of existing networks and collaborations, there are shared emphases and shared omissions in this collection. For instance, the geographical background of three of the editors and several authors means that there is rich engagement with care ethics, more-than-human agency, biopolitics, and the spatial dynamics of digitisation. In contrast, debates in media studies concerning datafication or media theory's reconceptualisation of what constitutes media began as more peripheral and have been intentionally integrated through ongoing interdisciplinary conversation.

Similarly, the theoretical background of the editors and many authors is grounded in literature from more-than-human thought, STS, animal studies, and the environmental humanities. This context means that a vocabulary of entanglement and relationality is threaded throughout the book and the lives of non-human animals and ecosystems is centralised. While this is (we hope) an important collective intervention, it also risks broader questions of data sovereignty and the relationship between digital ecologies, human labour, and precarity playing a less significant role in the conversation. Or, as Gillian Rose puts it in her afterword, there is less attention to the 'big social media platforms ... their harvesting of user data and their algorithmic mediation of environmental data, nor their commodification of nonhuman life'. The book's focus on the way more-than-human worlds are mediated, moreover, at times risks rendering mediation itself as something all-pervasive. While contemporary ways of knowing and understanding environments are difficult to detach from media systems, these dynamics should not be taken for granted. Human relations with more-than-human worlds are always political and demand materialist (as well as new materialist) analysis, in order to identify extractive relationships fostered by mediation and carve out space for alternative imaginaries.[100] At times this might entail deciding to purposefully resist or contest the enrolment of non-human beings into media assemblages, to leave certain non-human animals alone, or allow particular ecologies to remain strange.[101] Our aspiration, therefore, in closing the book with reflections about pathways forward is to offer entry points into future conversations about what digital ecologies scholarship might be – not only serving to highlight the work undertaken by chapters in the book, but as an invitation for dialogue about possible future directions.

# Notes

1. Adams, 'Digital animals.'
2. NFSA Films, 'Tasmanian tiger in colour.'
3. eBird, for instance, describes itself as 'among the world's largest biodiversity-related science projects, with more than 100 million bird sightings contributed annually by eBirders around the world and an average participation growth rate of approximately 20% year over year.' See: E-bird, Cornell Lab of Ornithology, https://ebird.org/about. Operation Turtle Dove is an international collaboration between conservation organisations in Western Europe and North Africa to address sharp declines in turtle dove populations due to disruption in their migration routes. See: 'Tracking turtle doves.' Operation Turtle Dove. RSPB, Pensthorpe Conservation Trust, and Natural England, https://operationturtledove.org/turtle-doves/titan/.
4. On camera traps and securitisation, respectively, see Mathur, 'Entrapment'; Duffy, 'Security technologies and biodiversity conservation.'
5. Cubitt, *Finite Media*.
6. We were not alone in doing so, either. See Turnbull et al., 'Quarantine encounters with digital animals'; Turnbull et al., 'Quarantine urban ecologies.'
7. For example, Schultz-Figueroa, 'Abandoned aquariums.'
8. Turnbull et al., 'Anthropause environmentalisms.'
9. See Basile et al., 'Birds seen and not seen during the COVID-19 pandemic'; Saraswat and Saraswat, 'Research opportunities in pandemic lockdown.'
10. Jørgensen, 'The armchair traveller's guide to digital environmental humanities.'
11. Searle et al., 'The digital peregrine.'
12. Bishop and Simone, 'Volumes of transindividuation.'
13. For a genealogy and critique of these theoretical moves, see Hörl (ed.), *General Ecology*.
14. Beck and Bishop, *Technocrats of the Imagination*.
15. Hayles, *How We Became Posthuman*, p. 7.
16. Wickberg, 'Environing media and cultural techniques.'
17. This line of questioning is informed by the book's engagement with insights from feminist science studies, which we elaborate upon subsequently. In particular, our perspective resonates with Donna Haraway's argument that, to unearth the ethical and political stakes of any socio-political context, it is vital to ask: 'what counts as nature, for whom, and at what cost?' Haraway, *Modest_Witness@Second_Millennium*.
18. Braun and Whatmore, *Political Matter*; Davis and Turpin, *Art in the Anthropocene*.
19. Edwards, *A Vast Machine*; Stengers, *In Catastrophic Times*.
20. Leszczynski, 'Spatial media/tion.'
21. Haraway, *When Species Meet*.
22. See in particular Taffel, *Digital Media Ecologies*; 'Data and oil'; 'Technofossils of the Anthropocene.'
23. See Giraud, *What Comes After Entanglement?*

24 Taffel, *Digital Media Ecologies*.
25 Kuntsman and Rattle, 'Towards a paradigmatic shift in sustainability studies.'
26 Louv, *Last Child in the Woods*.
27 Zylstra et al., 'Connectedness as a core conservation concern,' p. 120.
28 Fletcher, 'Connection with nature is an oxymoron.'
29 This argument is made in more detail with colleagues from the Digital Ecologies research group. See Searle et al., 'Glitches in the technonatural present.'
30 Goriunova and Shulgin, 'Glitch,' pp. 114–115.
31 Leszczynski and Elwood, 'Glitch epistemologies for computational cities,' p. 362.
32 Russell, *Glitch Feminism*.
33 Maalsen, 'Algorithmic epistemologies and methodologies,' p. 207.
34 Halpenny, 'Post-extractivist gardening.'
35 Leszczynski, 'Glitchy vignettes of platform urbanism,' p. 196.
36 Wickberg, 'Environing media'; Wickberg and Gärdebo (Eds.), *Environing Media*.
37 Ash et al., *Digital Geographies*.
38 Miller and Horst, 'The digital and the human,' p. 3.
39 Ash et al., *Digital Geographies*.
40 Nelson et al., 'Feminist digital natures.'
41 Turnbull et al., 'Digital ecologies,' p. 6.
42 Ibid., p. 11.
43 Ibid.
44 Ibid.
45 Arts et al., 'Information technology and the optimisation of experience.'
46 Helmreich, *Alien Ocean*; Herrera, 'Microbes and other shamanic beings.'
47 Turnbull et al, 'Digital ecologies', p. 20.
48 Couldry, 'Mediatization or mediation?' p. 375.
49 For a comparison between STS and media studies approaches, see Wajcman and Jones, 'Border communication.'
50 Bruno Latour's definition(s) of mediation is perhaps exemplary here, e.g. Latour, 'On interobjectivity.'
51 Treré and Kaun, 'Digital media activism.'
52 For more sustained reflections in relation to this case study, see Searle et al., 'The digital peregrine.'
53 Cubitt, 'Decolonizing ecomedia.' Here Cubitt makes the broader point that media industries are often bound up with regimes of racial capitalism.
54 E.g. Bellet, 'Reconfiguring the senses'; Langstone, ' "No shit Sherlock"!'
55 Treré and Kaun, 'Digital media activism,' p. 201.
56 For a succinct overview of media ecological thoughts, see Treré and Mattoni, 'Media ecologies and protest movements.'
57 For especially valuable work in this tradition from software studies, see Fuller, *Media Ecologies*; Taffel, *Digital Media Ecologies*; for social movement media studies, see Mattoni, 'A situated understanding of digital technologies in social movements'; Treré, *Hybrid Media Activism*.
58 Taffel, 'Digital media ecologies.'

# Introduction 23

59 Berland, *Virtual Menageries*.
60 Peters, *The Marvelous Clouds*.
61 Helmreich, *Sounding the Limits of Life*, p. 186. For an alternative theorisation of seawater, as a route into 'milieu-specific analysis' that transforms conception of the fundamental elements of media theory 'interface, inscription, database storage', see Jue, *Wild Blue Media*.
62 Jue, *Wild Blue Media*.
63 Outside of the field itself, STS can sometimes be conflated with a comparatively small number of thinkers and frameworks that have had the most prominence in other disciplines, e.g. Bruno Latour and Michel Callon in relation to actor-network theory, or influential and important interventions made by feminist, postcolonial, and queer science studies, such as Donna Haraway's companion species, Sandra Harding's standpoint theory, Karen Barad's agential realism, and Maria Puig de la Bellacasa's theorisations of care. For particularly helpful accounts of the different traditions of STS, some of which are contemporary and others which retain value despite being over twenty years old, see Biagioli, 'Introduction'; Cipolla et al. (eds.), *Queer Feminist Science Studies*; Law and Singleton, 'Performing technology's stories.'
64 This valuable exchange between STS and the environmental humanities is crystallised, for instance, by Thom van Dooren's engagement of conceptions of 'entanglement' from feminist science studies in van Dooren, *Flight Ways*.
65 Star, 'Power, technology and the phenomenology of conventions,' p. 38.
66 Ibid.
67 Bowker and Star, *Sorting Things Out*, p. 6.
68 This is not to say that other non-human beings are omitted; indeed, in the opening pages of the book (p. 7) seed categorisation is referred to as an instance of classification, but the book's emphasis is on IT infrastructures and their implications for work and biomedicine.
69 Latour, *Reassembling the Social*.
70 Dwyer, 'Cybersecurity's grammars.'
71 Helmreich, 'What was life?'
72 Nelson et al., 'Feminist digital natures.'
73 McLean, *Changing Digital Geographies*.
74 For more on digital political ecology, see Tait and Nelson, 'Nonscalability and generating digital outer space natures in no man's sky.'
75 Taffel, 'Digital media ecologies,' p. 16.
76 Turnbull et al., 'Digital ecologies.'
77 For more on the ethics of encounter, see Wilson, 'Contact zones.'
78 Haraway, 'Situated knowledges.'
79 Woodcock and Johnson, 'Gamification,' p. 544.
80 See Kamphof, 'Webcams to save nature.'
81 Barua, 'Nonhuman labour, encounter value, spectacular accumulation.'
82 See Büscher, *The Truth About Nature*; Igoe, *The Nature of Spectacle*.
83 Haraway, *When Species Meet*, pp. 45–68.
84 See Bastian, 'Whale calls, suspended ground, and extinctions never known.'

85 Adams, 'Conservation by algorithm'; Bakker and Ritts, 'Smart Earth'; Duffy, *Security and Conservation*.
86 Benson, *Wired Wilderness*.
87 Nost and Goldstein, 'A political ecology of data.'
88 Bowker and Star, *Sorting Things Out*, p. 24.
89 Hodder and Beckingham, 'Digital archives and recombinant historical geographies.'
90 Haraway, *When Species Meet*.
91 Stengers, *Cosmopolitics I*.
92 For conceptualisations and imaginaries of the cloud, which stress its epistemological and ethical significance, see Amoore, *Cloud Ethics*; Peters, *The Marvelous Clouds*.
93 For example, Kember and Zylinska, *Life After New Media*; Parikka, *The Anthrobscene*.
94 Barua, 'Infrastructure and non-human life.'
95 A recording of this lecture is currently hosted on the *Digital Ecologies* website and YouTube channel, in addition to the other keynote lecture, delivered by Etienne Benson. See: https:/youtube.com/watch?v=IX7pXHfjzKE.
96 Berlant, 'The commons.'
97 See Chadwick, *The Hybrid Media System*.
98 Taffel, *Digital Media Ecologies*
99 *What is Posthumanism?* p. 115.
100 Wadiwel, 'Animals & capital.'
101 Davé, *Indifference*; Neimanis, 'Stygofaunal worlds.'

# Bibliography

Adams, W.M. 2018. Conservation by algorithm. *Oryx*, 52(1): 1–2.
Adams, W.M. 2020. Digital animals. *The Philosopher*, 108: 17–21.
Amoore, L. 2020. *Cloud ethics: Algorithms and the Attributes of Ourselves and Others*. Durham, NC: Duke University Press.
Arts, I., Fischer, A., Duckett, D., and van der Wal, R. 2021. Information technology and the optimisation of experience – the role of mobile devices and social media in human-nature interactions. *Geoforum*, 122: 55–62.
Ash, J., Kitchin, R., and Leszczynski, A. 2019. *Digital Geographies*. London: Sage.
Bakker, K. and Ritts, M. 2018. Smart Earth: A meta-review and implications for environmental governance. *Global Environmental Change*, 52: 201–211.
Bastian, M. 2020. Whale calls, suspended ground, and extinctions never known. *Environmental Humanities*, 12(2): 454–474.
Barua, M. 2017. Nonhuman labour, encounter value, spectacular accumulation: The geographies of a lively commodity. *Transactions of the Institute of British Geographers*, 42(2): 274–288.
Barua, M. 2021. Infrastructure and non-human life: A wider ontology. *Progress in Human Geography*, 45(6): 1467–1489.
Basile, M., Russo, L.F., Russo, V.G., Senese, A., and Bernando, N. 2021. Birds seen and not seen during the COVID-19 pandemic: The impact of lockdown measures on citizen science bird observations. *Biological Conservation*, 256: 109079.

Beck, J. and Bishop, R. 2020. *Technocrats of the Imagination: Art, Technology, and the Military-Industrial Avant-garde*. Durham, NC: Duke University Press.

Bellet, C. 2023. Reconfiguring the senses: Sensor technologies and the production of a new sensorium in cattle farming. In L. Tallberg and L. Hamilton (Eds.) *The Oxford Handbook of Organization Studies* (pp. 101–114). Oxford: Oxford University Press.

Benson, E. 2010. *Wired Wilderness: Technologies of Tracking and the Making of Modern Wildlife*. Washington, DC: Johns Hopkins University Press.

Berland, J. 2019. *Virtual Menageries: Animals As Mediators in Network Cultures*. Cambridge, MA: MIT Press.

Berlant, L. 2016. The commons: Infrastructures for troubling times. *Environment and Planning D: Society and Space*, 34(3): 393–419.

Biagioli, M. 1999. Introduction. *The Science Studies Reader*. New York: Routledge

Bishop, R. and Simone, A. in press. Volumes of transindividuation. *Cultural Politics*, 19(2).

Bowker, G.C. and Star, S.L. 2000. *Sorting Things Out: Classification and Its Consequences*. Cambridge, MA: MIT Press.

Braun, B. and Whatmore, S. (Eds.) 2010. *Political Matter: Technoscience, Democracy, and Public Life*. Minneapolis, MN: University of Minnesota Press.

Büscher, B. 2021. *The Truth About Nature: Environmentalism in the Era of Post-Truth Politics and Platform Capitalism*. Oakland, CA: University of California Press.

Cipolla, C., Gupta, K., Rubin, D.A., and Willey, A. 2017. *Queer Feminist Science Studies: A Reader*. Washington, DC: University of Washington Press.

Chadwick, A. 2017. *The Hybrid Media System: Politics and Power*. 2nd ed. Oxford: Oxford University Press.

Couldry, N. 2008. Mediatization or mediation? Alternative understandings of the emergent space of digital storytelling. *New Media & Society*, 10(3): 373–391.

Cubitt, S. 2014. Decolonizing ecomedia. *Cultural Politics*, 10(3): 275–286.

Cubitt, S. 2016. *Finite Media: Environmental Implications of Digital Technologies*. Durham, NC: Duke University Press.

Davé, N. 2023. *Indifference: On the Praxis of Interspecies Being*. Durham, NC: Duke University Press.

Davis, H. and Turpin, E. (Eds.) 2014. *Art in the Anthropocene: Encounters Among Aesthetics, Politics, Environments and Epistemologies*. London: Open Humanities Press.

Duffy, R. 2022a. *Security and Conservation: The Politics of the Illegal Wildlife Trade*. New Haven, CT: Yale University Press.

Duffy, R. 2022b. Security technologies and biodiversity conservation. In R. Duffy *Security and Conservation: The Politics of the Illegal Wildlife Trade* (pp. 136–164). New Haven, CT: Yale University Press.

Dwyer, A.C. 2023. Cybersecurity's grammars: A more-than-human geopolitics of computation. *Area*, 55(1): 10–17.

Edwards, P.N. 2010. *A Vast Machine: Computer Models, Climate Data, and the Politics of Global Warming*. Cambridge, MA: MIT Press.

Fletcher, R. 2017. Connection with nature is an oxymoron: A political ecology of "nature-deficit disorder". *The Journal of Environmental Education*, 48(4): 226–233.

Fuller, M. 2005. *Media Ecologies: Materialist Energies in Art and Technoculture*. Cambridge, MA: MIT Press.

Giraud, E.H. 2019. *What Comes After Entanglement? Activism, Anthropocentricism, and an Ethics of Exclusion*. Durham, NC: Duke University Press.

Goriunova, O. and Shulgin, A. 2008. Glitch. In M. Fuller (Ed.) *Software Studies: A Lexicon* (pp. 110–119). Cambridge, MA: MIT Press.

Grusin, R. 2015. Radical mediation. *Critical Inquiry*, 42: 124–148.

Halpenny, M. 2023. Post-extractivist gardening: Seeding symbiotic relations between soil, microbial communities, & energy technologies through research-creation. *Digital Ecologies Blog* [online], 15 August. Available from: www.digicologies.com/2023/08/15/matthew-halpenny/.

Haraway, D.J. 1988. Situated knowledges: The science question in feminism and the privilege of partial perspective. *Feminist Studies*, 14(3): 575–599.

Haraway, D.J. 1997. *Modest_Witness@Second_Millennium. FemaleMan©_Meets_OncoMouse™*. London: Routledge.

Haraway, D.J. 2008. *When Species Meet*. Minneapolis, MN: University of Minnesota Press.

Hayles, N.K. 1999. *How We Became Posthuman: Virtual Bodies in Cybernetics, Literature, and Informatics*. Chicago, IL: University of Chicago Press.

Helmreich, S. 2009. *Alien Ocean: Anthropological Voyages in Microbial Seas*. Berkeley, CA: University of California Press.

Helmreich, S. 2011. What was life? Answers from three limit biologies. *Critical Inquiry*, 37(4): 671–696.

Helmreich, S. 2015. *Sounding the Limits of Life: Essays in the Anthropology of Biology and Beyond*. Princeton, NJ: Princeton University Press.

Herrera, C.G. 2018. *Microbes and Other Shamanic Beings*. Basingstoke: Palgrave Macmillan.

Hodder, J. and Beckingham, D. 2022. Digital archives and recombinant historical geographies. *Progress in Human Geography*, 46(6): 1298–1310.

Hörl, E. 2017. *General Ecology: The New Ecological Paradigm*. London: Bloomsbury Academic.

Horst, H. and Miller, D. 2012. *Digital Anthropology*. London, Berg.

Igoe, J. 2017. *The Nature of Spectacle: On Images, Money, and Conserving Capitalism*. Tucson, AZ: The University of Arizona Press.

Jørgensen, F.A. 2014. The armchair traveller's guide to digital environmental humanities. *Environmental Humanities*, 4(1): 95–112.

Jue, M. 2020. *Wild Blue Media: Thinking Through Seawater*. Durham, NC: Duke University Press.

Kamphof, I. 2011. Webcams to save nature: Online space as affective and ethical space. *Foundations of Science*, 16(2): 259–274.

Kember, S. and Zylinska, J. 2012. *Life After New Media: Mediation as a Vital Process*. Cambridge, MA: MIT Press.

Kuntsman, A. and Rattle, I. 2019. Towards a paradigmatic shift in sustainability studies: A systematic review of peer reviewed literature and future agenda setting to consider environmental (un)sustainability of digital communication. *Environmental Communication*, 13(5): 567–581.

Langstone, D. 2021. "No shit Sherlock"! Canine DNA and policing public space. *International Journal of Sociology and Social Policy*, 41(3–4): 455–474.

Latour, B. 1996. On interobjectivity. *Mind, Culture, and Activity*, 3(4): 228–245.

Latour, B. 2004. Why has critique run out of steam? From matters of fact to matters of concern. *Critical Inquiry*, 30(2): 225–248.

Latour, B. 2007. *Reassembling the Social: An Introduction to Actor-Network Theory*. Oxford: Oxford University Press.

Law, J. and Singleton, V. 2000 Performing technology's stories: On social constructivism, performance, and performativity. *Technology and Culture*, 41(4): 765–775.
Leszczynski, A. 2015. Spatial media/tion. *Progress in Human Geography*, 39(6): 729–751.
Leszczynski, A. 2020. Glitchy vignettes of platform urbanism. *Environment and Planning D: Society and Space*, 38(2): 189–208.
Leszczynski, A. and Elwood, S. 2022. Glitch epistemologies for computational cities. *Dialogues in Human Geography*, 12(3): 361–378.
Louv, R. 2005. *Last Child in the Woods: Saving Our Children from Nature-Deficit Disorder*. London: Atlantic.
Maalsen, S. 2023. Algorithmic epistemologies and methodologies: Algorithmic harm, algorithmic care and situated algorithmic knowledges. *Progress in Human Geography*, 47(2): 197–214.
Mathur, N. 2021a. *Crooked Cats: Beastly Encounters in the Anthropocene*. Chicago, IL: University of Chicago Press.
Mathur, N. 2021b. Entrapment. In N. Mathur *Crooked Cats: Beastly Encounters in the Anthropocene* (pp. 127–152). Chicago, IL: University of Chicago Press.
Mattoni, A. 2017. A situated understanding of digital technologies in social movements. Media ecology and media practice approaches. *Social Movement Studies*, 16(4): 494–505.
McLean, J. 2020. *Changing Digital Geographies: Technologies, Environments and People*. London: Springer.
Miller, D. and Horst, H.A. 2012. The digital and the human: A prospectus for digital anthropology. In Horst, H.A. and Miller, D. (Eds.) *Digital Anthropology* (pp. 3–35). London: Berg.
Neimanis, A. 2023. Stygofaunal worlds: Subterranean estrangement and otherwise knowing for multispecies justice. *Cultural Politics*, 19(1): 18–38.
Nelson, I.L., Hawkins, R., and Govia, L. 2023. Feminist digital natures. *Environment and Planning E: Nature and Space*, 6(3): 2096–2109.
NFSA Films. 2021. Tasmanian Tiger in Colour. YouTube video [online], 7 September. Available from: www.youtube.com/watch?v=6gt0X-27GXM.
Nost, E. and Goldstein, J.E. 2022. A political ecology of data. *Environment and Planning E: Nature and Space*, 5(1): 3–17.
Parikka, J. 2015. *The Anthrobscene*. Minneapolis, MN: University of Minnesota Press.
Peters, J.D. 2015. *The Marvelous Clouds*. Chicago, IL: University of Chicago Press.
Russell, L. 2020. *Glitch Feminism*. London: Verso.
Saraswat, R. and Saraswat, D.A. 2020. Research opportunities in pandemic lockdown. *Science*, 368(6491): 594–595.
Schultz-Figueroa, B. 2020. Abandoned aquariums: Online animal attractions during quarantine. *Journal of Environmental Media*, 1: 5.1–5.8.
Searle, A., Turnbull, J., and Adams, W.M. 2023. The digital peregrine: A technonatural history of a cosmopolitan raptor. *Transactions of the Institute of British Geographers*, 48(1): 195–212.
Searle, A., Turnbull, J., Hartman Davies, O., Poerting, J., Chasseray-Peraldi, P., Dodsworth, J., and Anderson-Elliott, H. 2023. Glitches in the technonatural present. *Dialogues in Human Geography*. https://doi.org/10.1177/20438206231174633.
Star, S.L. 1990. Power, technology and the phenomenology of conventions: On being allergic to onions. *The Sociological Review*, 38(1): 26–56.
Stengers, I. 2010. *Cosmopolitics I*. Minneapolis, MN: University of Minnesota Press.

Stengers, I. 2015. *In Catastrophic Times: Resisting the Coming Barbarism*. Ann Arbor, MI: Open Humanities Press.

Taffel, S. 2016. Technofossils of the anthropocene: Media, geology, and plastics. *Cultural Politics*, 12(3): 355–375.

Taffel, S. 2019. *Digital Media Ecologies: Entanglements of Content, Code and Hardware*. London: Bloomsbury.

Taffel, S. 2023. Data and oil: Metaphor, materiality and metabolic rifts. *New Media & Society*, 25(5): 980–998.

Tait, E.R. and Nelson, I.L. 2022. Nonscalability and generating digital outer space natures in no man's sky. *Environment and Planning E: Nature and Space*, 5(2): 694–718.

Treré, E. 2018. *Hybrid Media Activism: Ecologies, Imaginaries, Algorithms*. London: Routledge.

Treré, E. and Kaun, A. 2021. Digital media activism. In G. Balbi, N. Ribeiro, V. Schafer, and C. Schwarzenegger (Eds.) *Digital Roots* (pp. 198–199). Berlin: De Gruyter.

Treré, E. and Mattoni, A. 2016. Media ecologies and protest movements: Main perspectives and key lessons. *Information, Communication & Society*, 19(3): 290–306.

Turnbull, J., Searle, A., and Adams, W.M. 2020. Quarantine encounters with digital animals: More-than-human geographies of lockdown life. *Journal of Environmental Media*, 1: 6.1–6.10.

Turnbull, J., Searle, A., and Adams, W.M. 2020. Quarantine urban ecologies. *Cultural Anthropology* Editor's Forum. https://culanth.org/fieldsights/quarantine-urban-ecologies.

Turnbull, J., Searle, A., and Lorimer, J. 2023. Anthropause environmentalisms: Noticing natures with the Self-Isolating Bird Club. *Transactions of the Institute of British Geographers*, 48(2): 232–248.

Turnbull, J., Searle, A., Hartman Davies, O., Dodsworth, J., Chasseray-Peraldi, P., Von Essen, E., and Anderson-Elliott, H. 2023. Digital ecologies: Materialities, encounters, governance. *Progress in Environmental Geography*, 2(1–2): 3–32.

van Dooren, T. 2014. *Flight Ways: Life and Loss at the Edge of Extinction*. New York: Columbia University Press.

Wadiwel, D.J. 2023. *Animals & Capital*. Edinburgh: Edinburgh University Press.

Wajcman, J. and Jones, P.K. 2012. Border communication: Media sociology and STS. *Media, Culture & Society*, 34(6): 673–690.

Whatmore, S. 2006. Materialist returns: Practising cultural geography in and for a more-than-human world. *cultural geographies*, 13(4): 600–609.

Wickberg, A. 2023. Environing media and cultural techniques: From the history of agriculture to AI-driven smart farming. *International Journal of Cultural Studies*, 26(4): 392–409.

Wickberg, A. and Gärdebo, J. (Eds.) 2022. *Environing Media*. London: Routledge.

Wilson, H.F. 2019. Contact zones: Multispecies scholarship through *Imperial Eyes*. *Environment and Planning E: Nature and Space*, 2(4): 712–731.

Wolfe, C. 2010. *What is Posthumanism?* Minneapolis, MN: University of Minnesota Press.

Woodcock, J. and Johnson, M.R. 2018. Gamification: What it is, and how to fight it. *The Sociological Review*, 66(3): 542–558.

Zylstra, M.J., Knight, A.T., Esler, K.J., and Le Grange, L. 2014. Connectedness as a core conservation concern: An interdisciplinary review of theory and a call for practice. *Springer Science Reviews*, 2(1): 119–143.

# Part I

Digital encounters

# 1

# Running wild: encountering digital animals through exercise apps

*William M. Adams, Chris Sandbrook, and Emma Tait*

## Introduction

In October 2019, the start-up Internet of Elephants launched *Run Wild*, a collaboration with the sports company Adidas, the Snow Leopard Trust, and UNEP.[1] Over ten days in the autumn of 2019, users of the Adidas running app Runtastic signed up for a 'challenge',[2] competing against a snow leopard (*Panthera uncia*) from the high mountain ranges of Central Asia. The human athlete was told: 'Check Uuliin's daily running stats and push yourself to outrun him. Connect with your wild side and enjoy a little friendly competition'.[3]

The snow leopard is a rare animal, with an estimated wild population of only 4,000–6,000 individuals across 2 million km² of remote terrain. In 2017, it was reclassified from 'endangered' to 'vulnerable' on the IUCN Red List of threatened species.[4] The data that powered the Runtastic challenge were provided by the US-based conservation charity the Snow Leopard Trust and its partner, the Snow Leopard Conservation Foundation, and came from an animal that had been fitted with a radio collar as part of a long-running research programme in southern Mongolia.[5]

The snow leopard whose movement powered the *Run Wild* game was given the name Uuliin Ezen by the winners of an auction. Uuliin Ezen is Mongolian for 'ghost of the mountain', and the name replaced the technical identifier previously used for the animal ('M12').[6] In and through the *Run Wild* game, the snow leopard not only acquired a human name but an online personality. His invitation to runners was disseminated via Twitter: 'Hi, my name is Uuliin Ezen, I'm a real wild snow leopard from Mongolia'.[7]

Users received daily updates of Uuliin's movements in the newsfeed of the Runtastic app. The posts were presented as micro-stories about his daily activities (hunting or foraging, social encounters) and challenges (including poaching). These posts were written as a first-person narrative and were accompanied by photographs taken from the animal's point of view. *Run Wild* sought to offer 'a fun and positive way for people to dive deeper into the world of endangered species'. It was, the organisers suggested, 'as close to wildlife as most of us will ever get'.[8]

Apart from posting about his 'athletic performance' and the challenges of finding food and staying safe, Uuliin also promoted snow leopard conservation. The *Run Wild* campaign sought 'to create a positive and powerful connection between runners and an endangered species, to grow their understanding of the complexity of conservation, and to harness support for the hard work it takes to keep Uuliin and others of his species safe'.[9] Dr Charu Mishra, Executive Director of the Snow Leopard Trust and an avid endurance runner, said, 'To be able to connect running with nature conservation – a most worthy social cause – is just wonderful'.[10] It was hoped that Uuliin's digital life would 'encourage people to get outdoors, and through physical activity, help them create a meaningful connection with nature'.[11]

*Run Wild* attracted considerable attention. Over 12 days, 499,000 people joined the competition, running 5.3 million kilometres (on average 19.5 km each). Twenty-one thousand people 'outran' Uuliin, who covered 50.1 km (and 5,800 m of climbing and descending), hunted and caught prey twice, and met a real human once.[12]

The snow leopard in the *Run Wild* challenge is a digital animal, not a sentient being.[13] Etienne Benson would describe it as a 'minimal animal', a mere trace of the fleshly beast.[14] Yet the digital leopard is an entity with a distinct set of affects moored to the fleshy leopard, even though separate from it. It is both active and mobile in the digital realm. This digital liveliness is based on the movements of a real animal, but its digital presence lies within the silicon and flickering bytes of the mobile phone. The digital leopard's trajectory parallels the movements of the fleshy leopard in Mongolia. Yet it is also distinct and separate, with a measure of independence: the real snow leopard never runs the streets of New York or London, let alone sniffs around the database of leopard scientists or the server farms that process 'his' data; the digital leopard has never roamed in the Mongolian hills; it has never left the labyrinthine virtual ecosystems of the digital world. The connection between the actual and the digital leopard is the tracking device attached to a collar around the living leopard's neck: a physical device that converts fleshy movement into digital data.

Digital animals, represented, enrolled, and created within digital networks, are proliferating. Scholars argue that we live in the 'digital Anthropocene', an era in which our understanding of nature and interactions with wild and domestic animals, and the wider environment, is increasingly mediated via screens and digital devices.[15] Digital entanglement is becoming ever more ubiquitous, producing novel encounters between humans and non-human animals.[16] In and through a bewildering variety of digital devices (e.g. computers, mobile phones, camera traps, tracking devices, and webcams) and apps, digital natures simulate, mediate, or augment actual nature.[17] Digitisation, and the increasing familiarity of digital environments, undermines binary distinctions such as 'virtual' and 'real'.[18] Meaningful encounters happen in both digital and non-digital spaces that are interlaced in increasingly subtle, complex, and profound ways.[19]

Digital games in particular have begun to attract attention for their capacity to represent nature and shape human thinking about animals.[20] Games offer unique opportunities for virtual encounters between humans and animals. These may mimic those of real life (on Twitter/X, the runner is invited to 'meet' the snow leopard through the data on the app as if they were passing on a mountain trail) but are mediated digitally.[21] Digital game environments offer immersive approaches to animal lives that avoid some of the physical and logistical challenges of attempts to enter the world of animals directly.[22] Moreover, the activity of play suggests the possibility of particular kinds of sharing of animal experience by the human.

In this chapter, we explore digital games as places of human–animal encounter and the role of games and gamification in mediating those encounters. We focus in particular on games based on the movement of wild animal bodies, using data captured by digital tracking technologies. To stay with Uuliin the snow leopard, we ask what it means for him to be enrolled in digital form in a mobile phone game and what significance (if any) we should attach to the digital encounter between hunting leopard and phone-toting human runner.

## Digital games

The world of digital gaming, especially on handheld devices, has grown rapidly since the beginning of the twenty-first century.[23] Digital games are played in a wide range of ways, from casual viewing through occasional playing to intensive daily engagement. Online games allow social interaction through shared experiences, collaboration, and competition, as well as in-game messaging.[24]

Games can be thought of as 'structured activities carried out for pleasure, according to certain written or unwritten rules'.[25] They are often dismissed as leisure activities that serve only to entertain. However, digital games are important in the daily lives of more than 2 billion people globally, with mobile games comprising the majority of the $137.9 billion worldwide games market.[26] The gaming industry provides an infrastructure that enables novel commodification under digital capitalism, interlocks play and labour ('playbour' or 'playbor'), and contributes to significant material consumption (such as energy demands, mineral extraction, and e-waste).[27]

Game studies researchers draw attention to the power of games to serve positive purposes beyond mere human entertainment.[28] There has been considerable interest in 'serious games' which speak to (and potentially help address) problems in the real world such as poverty, health, environment, or science.[29] Many games explore contexts like crime, violence, war, and apocalypse. But others offer experiences related to urban planning, sports, or the state of the environment.[30] 'Serious games' have found a place in education, training, and human behaviour change in a wide range of sectors.

Gameplay dynamics (competition with others within set rules, the winning of points or rewards) have been even more widely applied.[31] This process of 'gamification' is routinely used in fields such as education, shopping, diet, or exercise, in the hope that the sense of play engendered by games will make activities more enjoyable and rewarding and promote continued user engagement.[32]

Digital gaming worlds often draw on detailed representations of nature, be it a dystopian post-apocalypse land or an impassable jungle. These digital natures emerge from the digitally mediated interactions between the concepts of nature that developers employ in games and the assumptions, choices, and experiences of players who encounter them.[33] Digital natures incorporate both accurate and interpreted representations of earth environments and species as well as imagined, interplanetary, science-fictional and fantastical ecosystems, often merging the two.[34] Digital natures are diverse and complex both in the understandings of natures they engage and the digital spaces in and through which they are produced.[35]

Digital animals are a common presence in digital games. As Tom Tyler points out in *Game*, video games offer a wide range of ways in which a player may encounter, understand, and engage with non-human animals.[36] They range from comprising an element of the backdrop of ecosystems or landscapes to resources or non-player characters, to hunter or prey, to the player's in-game character, as in *Never Alone*, where the player's character is alternately an Iñupiaq girl and her companion, an arctic fox.[37]

While some worry that digital games might reduce direct encounters with actual nature, especially in young people,[38] others argue that digital games might contribute to better human understanding of actual nature, and that this might perhaps promote more benign relations with the natural world.[39] In *Games of Empire* in 2009, Nick Dyer-Witheford and Greg de Peuter suggested that 'games of multitude' that engaged with the climate emergency might open up alternatives to global capitalism and unsustainable consumption.[40]

There has been growing interest in the possibility that 'games for nature' might contribute to biodiversity conservation goals.[41] This notion seeks to take advantage of the expansion of the games industry and the growing significance of 'technological nature' in people's daily lives.[42] Animals (particularly large and charismatic species) have a prominent place in debates about 'conservation games', reflecting their importance in conservation.[43]

Digital games offer novel opportunities for humans to engage with non-human animals through digital mediation. As Tom Tyler argues, games can generate novel affects between humans and non-humans.[44] Games can potentially inspire curiosity about and empathy with other species, although how games shape human–non-human relations depends on complex factors, including personal circumstances and previous experience of nature.[45] They provide a means of seeing and engaging with animals that avoids the physical and logistical difficulties of direct physical encounter. This expands the number and diversity of people who can observe wild animals from the relatively narrow circle of skilled naturalists or wealthy ecotourists to gamers in their millions. Moreover, through their detailed digital worlds and the close engagement engendered by gameplay, games can potentially provide approaches to animal lives that are not only immersive but also intimate.

## Digital animals

Digital animals can be created from the raw material of actual nature in various ways. They can be imagined fictional characters whose entire existence is digital, even if loosely built on nature, either as a cute cartoon character (as in *Sonic the Hedgehog*, or *Donkey Kong*) or as the denizen of a complete fantasy world (*Avatar* or *The Mandalorian*).[46] Alternatively, they can be rendered from actual animals, either through photography (e.g. webcams and camera traps) or by the attachment of a digital tracking device.

Recent advances in digital technology such as small lightweight digital devices, the collection of GPS location data, and the automatic and continuous uploading of data to geographic information systems have offered new opportunities for tracking the movement of animals through space and time.[47] Tags range in size and capacity, from those uploading positions daily or even hourly to satellites, to tiny geolocators weighing less than 0.3 grams that calculate position from time and day length.[48] Tags are now routinely fitted to birds, mammals, fish, reptiles, and other taxa. As tags get smaller, the range of species that can be tracked expands, and other data such as body temperature, altitude or depth, blood pressure, or pulse rate can also be collected.[49]

Digital tracking has become an increasingly mainstream dimension of conservation, encouraged by reductions in the size and cost of tags and the increasing availability of computer capacity.[50] Digital tracking technologies extend human abilities to observe the lives of animals beyond the scope of direct observation,[51] allowing the separation of the movement of individuals from population-level patterns,[52] the mapping of territories, the tracing of migration routes, and discovery of key sites for conservation. They also draw attention to the ways in which the mobilities of human and non-human animals shape each other.[53]

The human animal can also be tracked using digital technologies. GPS devices within mobile phones or smartwatches allow continuous location monitoring. This is the basis of both user-initiated apps such as Google Maps, and the commercial market in location data (for example, allowing retail corporations to analyse how long which kind of consumer spends viewing different shop displays).[54] These technologies also underlie a boom in the market for digital self-tracking of location and biological function. Digital devices attached to the human body have become an increasingly common accompaniment to both sporting activities and daily lives, a phenomenon described as the 'Quantified Self' (QS) movement.[55] Exercise and movement tracking apps (such as Strava, Map My Run, Runtastic, and MyFitness Pal)[56] and devices (such as smartwatches and Fitbits) that collect data on metrics such as location, distances travelled, and calories burned are widely used. The experience of self-tracking using such devices can create motivation to exercise and new forms of engagement with particular places where exercise occurs, although the motivational responses of users vary.[57] While literatures on the tracking of human and non-human animals have developed independently, it is important to note that a human runner using a digital watch to collect a stream of location and physiological data is as much a digital animal as a tagged albatross fishing in the southern ocean or a collared snow leopard in Mongolia.

## The search for digital empathy

Human researchers have suggested that after prolonged observation of wild animals they begin to develop a sense of how those animals experience mobility.[58] Vinciane Despret describes this as 'embodied empathy', the exploration of non-human relationships by 'making the body available for the response of another being'.[59] Can encounters with digital animals create an equivalent sense of 'digital empathy'?

Digital technologies have a recognised capacity to create a sense of intimacy between humans and other animals for human observers.[60] Digital video, streamed through devices such as fixed cameras, encourages the curation of affective relations between humans and animals by transforming the movement of animal bodies into media that can be stored, re-run as 'highlights', edited, and shared.[61] 'Nestcams' that livestream the nests of birds of prey on public buildings have become a significant social phenomenon, attracting audiences across the world.[62]

Digital devices focused on actual animals, such as webcams or tracking devices, appear to offer an unmediated view of wild animals, free from human 'intrusion', but they involve a technological and physical separation of watchers and the watched.[63] In his chapter in this book, Jon Henrik Ziegler Remme describes how the lobster trap-cam on the floor of a Norwegian bay enables a form of 'digital intimacy', an 'affective trap' as well as a physical one. However active a remotely observed animal portrayed through digital media seems to be, however freely it traverses land or sea, it remains the object of the human viewer's gaze. The observed animal is not, usually, aware of the observer, and certainly does not have the opportunity to watch in the same way as it is watched. The intimacy is therefore one-sided. Indeed, as Maan Barua points out, the power relations of observer and observed are integral to the affective non-human labour of charismatic zoo animals such as giant pandas.[64]

However, some forms of digitally based interaction go some way towards overcoming this one-sidedness. During the COVID-19 pandemic in 2020, the Sumida Aquarium in Tokyo found that burrowing marine garden eels, popular with visitors (and already livestreamed), were becoming shy with aquarium staff. They installed a line of tablets alongside the tank and invited the public to view the eels using FaceTime on their iPad or iPhone – to keep them habituated to human faces.[65] Also during the COVID lockdown, livestreamed video of rescued, sanctuary, and farm animals, and virtual guided walks with feral dogs in the Chornobyl Exclusion Zone provided lockdown distractions for observers and new digital channels for attunement to animal life.[66] In these encounters, digital technology created, for the human observer, a sense of proximity to physically distant animals despite (or because of) the physical separation between watchers and the watched. Technology both linked and distanced human and animal. The experience of intimacy was dependent on a complex array of linked digital technologies (including mobile phones, laptops, multi-person conference software, and the Internet), the mediation of human 'guides' on the ground, and novel complexions of capital in the services provided by multinational corporations, for example, Zoom, Google (Meet), and Microsoft (Teams).[67] However, to some extent at least, interaction was mutual (if profoundly mediated): the garden eels became accustomed once again to the staring human face; the sheep on the Zoom call could see the camera and the people watching the video stream from their desk; the dogs could choose whether to respond to the human guide who curated the virtual tour experience.

Other forms of digital technology also provide the opportunity for digital engagement and the creation of a sense of empathy between observing humans and observed animals. The attachment of digital tracking tags to animals, and the collection of data on their location and their movement, can have powerful affective implications for human observers. Jamie Lorimer describes how constant radio location of corncrakes changes the perceptions of bird researchers in the Hebrides, leading to 'corncrake-mindedness'.[68] Using such research techniques, the human observer could be said to share 'embodied life and movement' with an animal.[69]. Such sharing could potentially be radically extended through the combination of data streams from self-tracking devices worn by humans and tracking devices attached to non-human animals. Such a combination brings into play the possibility of direct comparison between the movements of a human and a non-human animal.

## Animals in digital games

The use of digital devices to track the movements of animals opens up the possibility of incorporating that movement into a digital game, as *Run Wild* did in 2019. In that game, Internet of Elephants created a direct link between actual animal movements and the movements of human athletes playing against them.[70] Their vision was to 'engage massive new audiences with nature' through the gamification of animal movement data, the imparting of knowledge and the creation of empathy.[71] In 2020, Internet of Elephants launched an augmented reality game *Wildeverse* that allowed players to 'find' and protect digital versions of great apes, teaching the player about the challenges of conservation.[72]

Internet of Elephants' approach harnesses the ways in which mixed or augmented reality (AR) games allow elements of the actual and digital worlds to be combined through the sensory components in mobile devices that facilitate integration of computer-generated images or sound with actual-world features.[73] We use the term AR broadly to include senses and modes of augmentation beyond the visual.

AR gaming environments offer a novel context for human–non-human interactions and new insights into the lives of animals through experience of their movements. AR games such as *Pokémon Go* enable gamers to physically move through their environment in order to encounter virtual Pokémon.[74] While this can enhance their fitness and time outdoors, it does not necessarily enhance their connection to the non-digital nature around them. People are glued to screens while out playing the game – potentially disturbing animals or trampling plants and insects.[75] This leads to questions about what kinds of encounters AR spaces produce and how they might facilitate different interactions with actual natures.

To date, digital animals within AR games have tended to be based on detached representations of actually existing animals. For example, apps such as Wildlife AR and Safari Central allow users to insert moving simplistic three-dimensional representations of charismatic animals into the smartphone video feed of their desk or their street.[76] *Run Wild*, launched in 2019, offered a different approach to engagement with animals in an AR environment, blending data collected from tracked wild animals with the gamified human of the 'Quantified Self' movement. The game allows people to see their daily movement and exercise in relation to the movements of geotagged wildlife such as elephants and migrating birds. It has some similarities to a game concept called *Race the Wild*, conceived in 2011, and an idea proposed in 2017 to create an app to combine tracking data from humans and animals.[77] In 2021, *Run Wild* ran again in expanded form. This time, runners could compete with three different animals: Pamoja the pangolin in Kenya, Tendrel Zangmo the tiger in Bhutan, and Adjany the elephant in Angola.[78] Over 1 million runners participated in the 2021 challenge, covering a collective 12,870,639 km.[79]

In order to investigate their experience of running against wild animals, we sent a short survey to participants in the 2021 *Run Wild* challenge who had signed up to receive updates from Runtastic. We received 238 responses.[80] Two thirds had raced against both the tiger and the pangolin, one third against the elephant. Ninety-two per cent said they had learnt about wild animals and their conservation by completing the challenge, 36% learning 'quite a lot' or 'a lot'. The results suggested that participation increased motivation to exercise (70%), and that this motivation was linked to the fact that the animal being raced was real (65%). Most respondents felt more connected to nature after participating (65%) and particularly to the animal they had been racing (72%). This translated into increased concern for conservation in general (68%) and for the species they had raced against (78%). Most also claimed to be more likely to support conservation in the future (68%) and to be interested in future 'races' against wild animals (85%).

In an open response question asking for thoughts on the experience of participating, several users described how they found the challenge motivating. For example, one said: 'It motivated me a lot to exercise and to track it more than usual. I sometimes went walking only with the scope to beat the tiger'. Some participants clearly found the game stimulated empathy – one said 'the distance the animals walk or run is in some ways comparable to my way to work. I need money to buy food, the animals need to walk miles and miles to hunt or to go to the water hole'. Many respondents made suggestions on how to improve the experience: by increasing the period over which the challenge ran, offering more animals or animals with different capabilities, providing comparisons with the performance of other human runners or rewards for those participating, and so on. While most comments were positive, some concerns were expressed, such as: 'I did not like the challenge; I felt it was wrong to disturb wild animals'.

## Playing with animals

*Run Wild* provides some evidence that the gamification of wildlife movement data can contribute to learning and empathy on the part of human participants for the lives of their animal 'running companions'. Several runners reported some form of connection and learning, suggesting it is possible that empathy with animals stimulated by the game might lead players to become interested in the welfare and conservation of the species and the places in which they live, for example through financial contributions or volunteering. There is clearly potential for game design to influence the form and depth of engagement for human players, such as in the way that the lives of animals, or the threats they face in the wild, are portrayed.[81] Participants in the 2021 survey suggested that they would have been interested in the use of video, more frequent updates, or more exact information about where animals were and what they were experiencing. It would, for example, be possible to attach explicit 'conservation stories' to the racing challenge in the form of a larger 'play space' beyond the 'run against a snow leopard' challenge and more extensive links to conservation organisations on the ground.

Games that link animal and human movement could also have a role in animal behaviour research. As discussed above, field researchers already learn to 'see like their subject'. Games that match bodily movement by a researcher to that of their research might help to create the conditions for 'embodied empathy' and could become a tool for conducting multispecies ethnography.[82] It might also enable researchers who have worked directly with study animals in the field to continue some form of relationship with that study animal remotely, with its movements faithfully tracked by the unsleeping digital tag.

So, from the human perspective digital games incorporating the tracking of animals seem to offer the possibility of engagement and the emergence of some level of cross-species understanding and empathy. But what about the animal? Does the snow leopard in any sense 'play' with the human runners who compete with it? Not in the sense of fun: this is not 'play' as in a cat with a ball of wool or a dog chasing a stick. The sense of play is entirely one-sided. Indeed, you could say that the leopard is being 'played', as in tricked or 'made sport of'.

Participation in the 'challenge' of running against thousands of humans in cities across the world might be considered a passive experience for digital animals, who can run as tirelessly, repeatedly, and endlessly as the cloud computing database specifies. But the data come from an actual physical animal that is fitted with a tag. In the case of the snow leopard, this is a collar which requires the animal to be tranquilised, a risky and invasive procedure even when done under humane conditions. The collar must then be carried for an extended period. Other animals are caught and tagged in different ways – methods vary between species, but they are inevitably invasive.

Whether its purpose is scientific data collection or the promotion of empathy, the tagging and surveillance of animals therefore inevitably have the potential to impose harm on the animal. These include the potential trauma of capture, anaesthetisation and fitting of the collar or other device, and any measurement and biological sampling activities carried out as part of the process.[83]

Digital interactions between humans and animals are not symmetrical. Digital capture has been likened to domestication, resulting in a form of human control.[84] The observed animal is not, usually, aware of the observer and certainly does not have the opportunity to watch in the same way as it is watched. Animal celebrities are not aware of their status: intimacy is one-sided, creating an animal *Truman Show*.[85] Animals under surveillance may be presented to human audiences as independent agents living their own lives, but the combination of surveillance technologies and associated digitally mediated storytelling is an obvious exercise of non-human biopower.[86]

The enrolment of animals to provide data for a digital game creates encounters rich in affect linked to non-human charisma. Surplus value is created through the affective labour of the tagged animal.[87] If a game is linked to payments (whether as donations to conservation or payments to a commercial entity), the interaction between human and animal potentially generates capital for those (such as game designers) harnessing animal liveliness. In her chapter in this volume, Katie Oliver argues that the chickens portrayed in the *Our Chicken Life* webstream undertake (involuntarily) 'byproductive labour', involving the disposal and accumulation of affect for the human viewer. The labour of animals whose tags provide digital location data could be thought of in the same way. The data comprise a new form of what Maan Barua calls encounter value, 'the value produced in regimes of capital where the commodity is a living, breathing thing'.[88] The game recasts the target animals as lively commodities – commodities that depend on the creature in question being alive and, in this case, on the move.

Animals are widely made digital and serve in this way, featuring in the photographs of tourists taken from a safari vehicle for example, or on wildlife documentaries. But the animal whose movement is captured and held as digital data has a particular form of endless digital life. The tagged animal's digital avatar can move again and again, racing against joggers in multiple countries around the world. Its digital servitude is potentially endless, limited only by the currency of algorithms, the maintenance of databases, and the fickle spotlight of consumer attention.

Human encounters with digital animals who are representing the liveliness of an actual animal in AR games like *Run Wild* may have the potential to enhance awareness, increase understanding and compassion, or generate meaningful human actions. However, they are limited. They may be able to offer curated and simplified insights into the actual lived experience of the real animal from which the data for the challenge have been obtained. But they are one-sided interfaces. The animal that has been enrolled into the game can have no awareness that the encounter with a human 'competitor' is taking place. They are not active participants in the encounter beyond having to deal with carrying a tracking device. On the basis of AR games like *Run Wild*, digital encounters would seem at present to offer limited prospects of truly 'knowing' the experience of the non-human lives of the animals represented. Nevertheless, their potential to open human minds and hearts to animals remains. Future research should explore the potential of this in more detail.

## Acknowledgements

We would like to thank Gautam Shah and colleagues at Internet of Elephants (www.internetofelephants.com/),with whom we have been sharing ideas on conservation games for the last five years, and colleagues (especially Bruno Monteferri, Peter Damerell, and Anandhi Vivek) for discussions and contributions to work exploring the use of animal movement data in games based on running apps. We would like to thank Runtastic for sharing survey response data on the 2019 and 2020 *Run Wild* projects, and the editors for comments and suggestions.

## Notes

1 *Internet of Elephants*, www.internetofelephants.com/; *Run Wild*, www.internetofelephants.com/adidas-runtastic-runwild; *Adidas*, www.adidas.co.uk/. The other partners were the United Nations Environment Programme (UNEP), www.unep.org/; and the Snow Leopard Trust, https://snowleopard.org/. Adams and Sandbrook were unpaid advisers to Internet of Elephants during the development of this game.

2  Runtastic, www.runtastic.com. Running apps allow users to track and archive their routes and times, as well as to compare times (and so compete) with other runners.
3  Screenshot shown in the video 'Run Wild with Uuliin Ezen the Snow Leopard', www.internetofelephants.com/adidas-runtastic-runwild.
4  Snow Leopard Trust, https://snowleopard.org/snow-leopard-facts/; IUCN Red List of Threatened Species, www.iucnredlist.org/species/22732/50664030.
5  Collaring began in 2006; see the Snow Leopard Trust, https://snowleopard.org/our-work/research/research-tools/#gps.
6  https://snowleopard.org/snow-leopard-named-in-honor-of-late-mongolian-researcher/.
7  Twitter/X, https://twitter.com/unep/status/1185956974288089090.
8  Quotes from *Run Wild*, www.internetofelephants.com/adidas-runtastic-runwild.
9  Snow Leopard Trust, https://snowleopard.org/run-wild-for-snow-leopards/.
10  Ibid.
11  Ibid.
12  www.internetofelephants.com/adidas-runtastic-runwild.
13  On digital animals, see Adams, 'Digital animals'; Adams, 'The digital animal'; Searle et al., 'The digital peregrine.'
14  Benson, 'Minimal animal.'
15  Arts et al., 'Digital technology and the conservation of nature'; Jørgensen, 'The armchair traveler's guide to digital environmental humanities'; Turnbull et al., 'Quarantine encounters with digital animals'; von Essen et al., 'Wildlife in the digital Anthropocene.'
16  Turnbull et al., 'Digital ecologies.'
17  Adams, 'Geographies of conservation II'; Kahn, *Technological Nature*.
18  Ash, *The Interface Envelope*; McLean, *Changing Digital Geographies*; Morrow et al., 'Feminist research in online spaces'; Shaw and Warf, 'Worlds of affect'; Stinson, 'Re-creating wilderness 2.0.'
19  Boellstorff, *Coming of Age in Second Life*; Graham et al., 'Augmented reality in urban places'; Haraway, *The Haraway Reader*; Morrow et al., 'Feminist research in online spaces.'
20  Sandbrook et al., 'Digital games and biodiversity conservation.'
21  Twitter/X, https://twitter.com/unep/status/1185956974288089090.
22  Buller, 'Animal geographies II'; Hodgetts and Lorimer, 'Methodologies for animals' geographies.'
23  Chatfield, *Fun Inc.*
24  Newzoo 'Global games market report.'
25  Chatfield, *Fun Inc*, p. 4.
26  Newzoo, 'Global games market report.'
27  Dyer-Witheford and de Peuter, *Games of Empire*; Dyer-Witheford and de Peuter, 'Postscript'; Scholz, *Digital Labor*.
28  Bos, 'Answering the call of duty'; McGonigal, *Reality Is Broken*.
29  Bavelier and Davidson 'Brain training'; Kato 'Video games in health care'; McGonigal, *Reality Is Broken*; Radchuk et al., '*Homo politicus* meets *Homo ludens*.'

30 Examples include: *Minecraft* (Windows/OSX), Majong Studios, 2011; *Cities: Skylines* (Windows/OSX), Paradox; *FIFA* (Windows/OSX/Console), EA Sports, 1993.
31 Rapp et al., 'Strengthening gamification studies.'
32 Chatfield, *Fun Inc*; Woodcock and Johnson, 'Gamification.'
33 Driessen et al., 'What could playing with pigs do to us?'; Rutherford and Bose 'Biopower and play'; Tait and Nelson, 'Nonscalability and generating digital outer space natures in *No Man's Sky*.'
34 Tait and Nelson, 'Nonscalability and generating digital outer space natures in *No Man's Sky*.'
35 Ibid.; Elliot, 'Contesting Nature 2.0 or "the power of naming".'
36 Tyler, *Game*.
37 *Never Alone* (Windows/OSX), Upper One Games, 2015; Tyler, *Game*.
38 Kahn, *Technological Nature*; Louv, *Last Child in the Woods*.
39 Fletcher, 'Gaming conservation'; Sandbrook et al., 'Digital games and conservation.'
40 Dyer-Witheford and de Peuter, *Games of Empire*; Dyer-Witheford and de Peuter, 'Postscript'; Reyes, 'Nick Dyer-Witheford and Greig de Peuter.'
41 Dorward et al., 'Pokémon Go'; Fisher, 'Could Nintendo's *Animal Crossing* be a tool for conservation messaging?'; Fletcher, 'Gaming conservation'; Sandbrook et al., 'Digital games and conservation.'
42 Fletcher, 'Gaming conservation'; Sandbrook et al., 'Digital games and conservation'; Turnbull et al., 'Digital ecologies.'
43 Lorimer, 'Nonhuman charisma'; Sandbrook et al., 'Digital games and conservation.'
44 Tyler, *Game*.
45 Frey et al., 'Wild animals in daily life.'
46 *Sonic the Hedgehog*, Sega, 1991; *Donkey Kong*, Nintendo, 1981; *Avatar*, directed by James Cameron, 20th Century Studios. 2009; *The Mandalorian*, produced by J. Bartnicki, Lucasfilms, 2019.
47 Adams, 'Geographies of conservation II'; Benson, 'Trackable life'; Benson, *Wired Wilderness*; Lupton, *The Internet of Animals*.
48 Atkinson, BTO: www.bto.org/understanding-birds/articles/bird-tracking-masterclass.
49 Beiser, 'Where the things were wild'; Katzner and Arlettaz, 'Evaluating contributions of recent tracking-based animal movement ecology to conservation management.'
50 Katzner and Arlettaz, 'Evaluating contributions of recent tracking-based animal movement ecology.'
51 Hodgetts and Lorimer, 'Methodologies for animals' geographies.'
52 Lorimer, *Wildlife in the Anthropocene*.
53 Barua 'Bio-geo-graphy'; Buller, 'Animal geographies II'; Hodgetts and Lorimer, 'Animals' mobilities'; Hodgetts and Lorimer, 'Methodologies for animals' geographies.'
54 'Retail dwell time the route to higher spending: retail sensing: people counting and footfall systems,' 11 June 2020, www.retailsensing.com/people-counting/retail-dwell-time-metric/.

55 Wolf, *The Quantified Self*, TED@Cannes, June 2010, www.ted.com/talks/gary_wolf_the_quantified_self; Lupton, *The Quantified Self*.
56 www.strava.com; www.mapmyrun.com; www.runtastic.com; www.myfitnesspal.com
57 Attig and Franke, 'I track, therefore I walk.'
58 Hodgetts and Lorimer, 'Animals' mobilities.'
59 Despret, 'Responding bodies and partial affinities in human–animal worlds,' p. 70.
60 Turnbull et al., 'Quarantine encounters with digital animals'; Verma et al., 'Microscope and spectacle.'
61 Adams, 'Geographies of conservation'; Verma et al., 'Microscope and spectacle.'
62 Searle et al., 'The digital peregrine'; Turnbull et al., 'Quarantine encounters with digital animals.'
63 Chambers, '"Well it's remote, I suppose, innit?"'; Verma et al., 'Microscope and spectacle.'
64 Barua, 'Affective economies, pandas, and the atmospheric politics of lively capital.'
65 Marras Tate, 'Hello, garden eel here'; Meisenzahl, 'Meisenzahl, 'A Tokyo aquarium.'
66 Turnbull et al., 'Quarantine encounters with digital animals.'
67 Ibid.
68 Lorimer, *Wildlife in the Anthropocene*.
69 Buller, 'Animal geographies II,' p. 5.
70 Internet of Elephants, www.internetofelephants.com/. Sandbrook and Adams have both contributed as unpaid advisers to Internet of Elephants on the use of animal tracking data in digital games.
71 Internet of Elephants, www.internetofelephants.com/#consumer-engagement-wildlife.
72 Internet of Elephants, *Wildeverse*, www.wildeversegame.com/.
73 Gotow et al., 'Addressing challenges with augmented reality applications on smartphones.'
74 *Pokémon Go* (iOS, Android), Niantic, 2016; see Dorward et al., 'Pokémon Go.'
75 Carlton, 'Pokémon Go.'
76 Internet of Elephants, www.internetofelephants.com/safari-central/#safari-central-1; Wildlife AR, Playrock Studios, 2020.
77 Frey et al., 'Wild animals in daily life'; Sandbrook et al., 'Race the wild'; *Race the Wild* was first conceived by Chris Sandbrook, William M. Adams, Bruno Monteferri, and Ken Banks as part of a project on conservation games. The practicalities of a link between sports apps and animal movement data were explored by Peter Damerell, who conducted the first experiment interfacing the movement of wild elephants and human athletes, using the Endomondo app and data supplied by the NGO Space for Giants. Anandhi Vivek built an experimental app for interfacing athlete and animal movement data. Emma Tait conducted further trials of the concept. The idea was shared with Internet of Elephants, who in turn worked with Runtastic to create *Run Wild*.
78 *Run Wild*, www.internetofelephants.com/adidas-runtastic-runwild.

79 www.linkedin.com/posts/runtastic-gmbh_remembering-run-wild-on-world-wildlife-day-activity-6772785618482200576-PxUP.
80 NB, this is a tiny sample size relative to the approximately 1 million people who played the game. Apart from information volunteered by respondents to this survey, no other data were collected on participants.
81 See discussion in Sandbrook et al., 'Race the wild.'
82 Buller, 'Animal geographies II'; Despret, 'Responding bodies and partial affinities in human–animal worlds'; Kirksey and Helmreich, 'The emergence of multispecies ethnography.'
83 von Essen et al., 'Wildlife in the digital Anthropocene.'
84 Kamphof, 'Webcams to save nature.'
85 von Essen et al., 'Wildlife in the digital Anthropocene'; *The Truman Show* (film 1998, directed by Peter Weir) concerned a reality television show whose star did not know he was being filmed
86 von Essen et al., 'Wildlife in the digital Anthropocene.'
87 Barua, 'Affective economies, pandas, and the atmospheric politics of lively capital'; Barua, 'Nonhuman labour, encounter value, spectacular accumulation.'
88 Barua, 'Nonhuman labour, encounter value, spectacular accumulation,' pp. 278–279.

## Bibliography

Adams, W.M. 2019a. Digital animals. *The Philosopher*, 108: 17–21.

Adams, W.M. 2019b. Geographies of conservation II: Technology, surveillance and conservation by algorithm. *Progress in Human Geography*, 43: 337–350.

Adams, W.M. (in press) The digital animal: tracking technology and wild nature. In B. Minteer and J. Losos (Eds.) *Heart of the Wild: Essays on Nature, Ecology and the Human Future*. Princeton, NJ: Princeton University Press.

Arts, K., van der Wal, R., and Adams, W.M. 2015. Digital technology and the conservation of nature. *Ambio*, 44(4): 661–673.

Ash, J. 2015. *The Interface Envelope: Gaming, Technology, Power*. New York: Bloomsbury Academic.

Attig, C. and Franke, T. 2019. I track, therefore I walk – exploring the motivational costs of wearing activity trackers in actual users. *International Journal of Human-Computer Studies*, 127: 211–224.

Barua, M. 2014. Bio-geo-graphy: Landscape, dwelling, and the political ecology of human-elephant relations. *Environment and Planning D: Society and Space*, 32: 915–934.

Barua, M. 2017. Nonhuman labour, encounter value, spectacular accumulation: The geographies of a lively commodity. *Transactions of the Institute of British Geographers*, 42: 274–288.

Barua, M. 2020. Affective economies, pandas, and the atmospheric politics of lively capital. *Transactions of the Institute of British Geographers*, 45: 678–692.

Bavelier, D. and Davison, R.J. 2013. Brain training: Games to do you good. *Nature*, 494: 425–426.

Beiser, V. 2021. Where the wild things were wild: What happens when hyper surveillance comes to conservation. *Red Canary Magazine* [online]. Available from: https://redcanarycollective.org/magazine/where-the-things-were-wild/.

Benson, E. 2010. *Wired Wilderness: Technologies of Tracking and the Making of Modern Wildlife*. Baltimore, MD: Johns Hopkins University Press.

Benson, E. 2014. Minimal animal: Surveillance, simulation, and stochasticity in wildlife biology. *Antennae*, 30: 39–53.

Benson, E. 2016. Trackable life: Data, sequence, and organism in movement ecology. *Studies in History and Philosophy of Science Part C: Studies in History and Philosophy of Biological and Biomedical Sciences*, 57: 137–147.

Boellstorff, T. 2008. *Coming of Age in Second Life*. Princeton, NJ: Princeton University Press.

Bos, D. 2018. Answering the Call of Duty: Everyday encounters with the popular geopolitics of military-themed videogames. *Political Geography*, 63: 54–64.

Buller, H. 2015. Animal geographies II: Methods. *Progress in Human Geography*, 39: 374–384.

Carlton, J. 2016. "Pokémon Go" gives boost to national parks. *Wall Street Journal* [online], 13 July. Available from: www.wsj.com/articles/pokemon-go-gives-boost-to-national-parks-1468447301.

Chambers, C. 2007. 'Well it's remote, I suppose, innit?' The relational politics of birdwatching through the CCTV lens. *Scottish Geographical Journal*, 123: 122–134.

Chatfield, T. 2010. *Fun Inc: Why Games are the Twenty-first Century's Most Serious Business*. London: Virgin Books.

Despret, V. 2013. Responding bodies and partial affinities in human–animal worlds. *Theory, Culture & Society*, 30(7–8): 51–76.

Dorward, L.J., Mittermeier, J.C., Sandbrook, C., and Spooner, F. 2017. Pokémon Go: Benefits, costs, and lessons for the conservation movement. *Conservation Letters*, 10(1): 160–165.

Driessen, C., Alfrink, K., Copier, M., Lagerweij, H., and van Peer, I. 2014. What could playing with pigs do to us? Game design as multispecies philosophy. *Antennae*, 30, 79–102.

Dyer-Witheford, N. and de Peuter, G. 2009. *Games of Empire: Global Capitalism and Video Games*. Minneapolis, MN: University of Minnesota Press.

Dyer-Witheford, N. and de Peuter, G. 2021. Postscript: Gaming while empire burns. *Games and Culture*, 16(3): 371–380.

Elliot, G. 2016. Contesting Nature 2.0 or 'the power of naming'. *Geoforum*, 77: 192–195.

Fisher, J.C., Yoh, N., Kubo, T., and Rundle, D. 2021. Could Nintendo's *Animal Crossing* be a tool for conservation messaging? *People and Nature*, 3: 1218–1228.

Fletcher, R. 2017. Gaming conservation: Nature 2.0 confronts nature-deficit disorder. *Geoforum*, 79: 153–162.

Frey, R.M., Miller, G.A., Ilic, A., Fleisch, E., and Pentland, A.S. 2017. Wild animals in daily life. *38th International Conference on Information Systems Proceedings*. Seoul: ICIS.

Gotow, J.B., Zienkiewicz, K., White, J., and Schmidt, D.C. Addressing challenges with augmented reality applications on smartphones. *Mobilware*, 48: 129–143.

Graham, M., Zook, M., and Boulton, A. 2014. Augmented reality in urban places: Contested content and the duplicity of code. *Transactions of the Institute of British Geographers*, 38(3): 464–479.

Haraway, D.J. 2004. *The Haraway Reader*. London: Routledge.

Hodgetts, T. and Lorimer, J. 2015. Methodologies for animals' geographies: Cultures, communication and genomics. *cultural geographies*, 22(2): 285–295.

Hodgetts, T. and Lorimer, J., 2020. Animals' mobilities. *Progress in Human Geography*, 44(1): 4–26.
Jørgensen, F.A. 2014. The armchair traveler's guide to digital environmental humanities. *Environmental Humanities*, 4: 95–11.
Kahn, P. 2009. *Technological Nature: Adaptation and the Future of Human Life*. Cambridge, MA: The MIT Press.
Kamphof, I. 2011. Webcams to save nature: Online space as affective and ethical space. *Foundations of Science*, 16: 259–274.
Kato, P.M. 2010. Video games in health care: Closing the gap. *Review of General Psychology*, 14(2): 113–121.
Katzner, T.E. and Arlettaz, R. 2020. Evaluating contributions of recent tracking-based animal movement ecology to conservation management. *Frontiers in Ecology and Evolution*, 7: Article 519.
Kirksey, E. and Helmreich, S. 2010. The emergence of multispecies ethnography. *Cultural Anthropology*, 25(4): 545–576.
Lorimer, J. 2007. Nonhuman charisma. *Environment and Planning D: Society and Space*, 25: 911–932.
Lorimer, J. 2015. *Wildlife in the Anthropocene: Conservation After Nature*. Minneapolis, MN: University of Minnesota Press.
Louv, R. 2005. *Last Child in the Woods: Saving Our Children from Nature-Deficit Disorder*. Chapel Hill, NC: Algonquin Books.
Lupton, D. 2016. *The Quantified Self*. London: Wiley.
Lupton, D. 2023. *The Internet of Animals: Human–Animal Relationships in the Digital Age*. Cambridge: Polity Press.
Marras Tate, J.C. 2023. "Hello, garden eel here:" Insights from emerging humanature relations at the aquarium during COVID-19. *Environmental Communication*, 17(3): 218–219.
McGonigal, J. 2011. *Reality is Broken: Why Games Make Us Better and How They Can Change the World*. London: Penguin.
McLean, J. 2020. *Changing Digital Geographies: Technologies, Environments and People*. London: Palgrave Macmillan.
Meisenzahl, M. 2020. A Tokyo aquarium needs you to FaceTime their shy eels right now. *Science Alert* [online]. Available from: www.sciencealert.com/tokyo-aquarium-needs-your-help-reminding-their-eels-to-not-fear-humans.
Morrow, O., Hawkins, R., and Kern, L. 2015. Feminist research in online spaces. *Gender, Place and Culture*, 22: 526–543.
Neimanis, A. 2023. Stygofaunal worlds: Subterranean estrangement and otherwise knowing for multispecies justice. *Cultural Politics*, 19(1): 18–38.
Newzoo. 2022. *Global Games Market Report 2023*. Amsterdam: Newzoo.
Radchuk, O., Kerbe, W., and Schmidt, M. 2017. Homo politicus meets Homo ludens: Public participation in serious life science games. *Public Understanding of Science*, 26(5): 531–546.
Rapp, A., Hopfgartner, F., Hamari, J., Linehan, C., and Cena, F. 2019. Strengthening gamification studies: Current trends and future opportunities of gamification research. *International Journal of Human-Computer Studies*, 127: 1–6.
Reyes, I. 2017. Nick Dyer-Witheford and Greig de Peuter, Games of Empire: Global Capitalism and Video Games (2009). *Markets, Globalization, and Development Review*, 2(1): Article 8.
Rutherford, S. and Bose, P.S. 2013. Biopower and play: Bodies, spaces, and nature in digital games. *Aether*, 12: 1–29.

Sandbrook, C., Adams, W.M., and Monteferri, B. 2015. Digital games and biodiversity conservation. *Conservation Letters*, 8: 118–124.

Scholz, T. 2012. *Digital Labor: The Internet as Playground and Factory*. London: Routledge.

Searle, A., Turnbull, J., and Adams, W.M. 2023. The digital peregrine: A technonatural history of a cosmopolitan raptor. *Transactions of the Institute of British Geographers*, 48(1): 195–212.

Shaw, I.G.R. and Warf, B. 2009. Worlds of affect: Virtual geographies of video games. *Environmental Planning A*, 41: 1332–1343.

Stinson, J. 2017. Re-creating wilderness 2.0: Or getting back to work in a virtual nature. *Geoforum*, 79: 174–187.

Tait, E.R. and Nelson, I.L. 2022. Nonscalability and generating digital outer space natures in No Man's Sky. *Environment and Planning E: Nature and Space*, 5(2): 694–718.

Turnbull, J., Searle, A., and Adams, W.M. 2020. Quarantine encounters with digital animals: More-than-human geographies of lockdown life. *Journal of Environmental Media*, 1: 6.1–6.10.

Turnbull, J., Searle, A., Hartman Davies, O., Dodsworth, J., Chasseray-Peraldi, P., Von Essen, E., and Anderson-Elliott, H. 2023. Digital ecologies: Materialities, encounters, governance. *Progress in Environmental Geography*, 2(1–2): 3–32.

Tyler, T. 2022. *Game: Animals, Video Games, and Humanity*. Minneapolis, MN: University of Minnesota Press.

Verma, A., van der Wal, R., and Fischer, A. 2015. Microscope and spectacle: On the complexities of using new visual technologies to communicate about wildlife conservation. *Ambio*, 44(4): 648–660.

von Essen, E., Turnbull, J., Searle, A., Jørgensen, F.A., Hofmeester, T.R., and van der Wal, R. 2023. Wildlife in the digital Anthropocene: Examining human-animal relations through surveillance technologies. *Environment and Planning E: Nature and Space*, 6(1): 679–699.

Woodcock, J. and Johnson, M.R. 2018. Gamification: What it is, and how to fight it. *The Sociological Review*, 66(3): 542–558.

# 2

# Digital sonic ecologies: encountering the non-human through digital sound recordings

*Hannah Hunter, Sandra Jasper, and Jonathan Prior*

## Introduction

In a degraded part of Australia's Great Barrier Reef, where the coral was bleached and the fish had lost interest, scientists suspended a loudspeaker underwater. For six weeks in 2017, this speaker broadcast the recorded digital sounds of a nearby 'healthy' reef in an attempt to restore the ecosystem through acoustic enrichment. It worked: the fish followed the sound and, at least temporarily, reinhabited the site.[1]

On the site AllPredatorCalls.com, one can browse 'one of the largest selections of electronic game calls on the Internet'. A popular choice is the MOJO Triple Threat E-Caller: retailing for 239.99 USD, it includes an SD card holding eighty sounds and a spinning feathered appendage which, together, are 'irresistible' to animals like coyotes and deer.[2] Users also have the option of downloading additional sounds for the device. For instance, for 300 USD, one can purchase '50 ... top killing sounds in an easy to download .ZIP file'.[3]

In a Hawaiian swamp in 1986, Jim Jacobi recorded one of the last known Kauaʻi ʻōʻō birds using a handheld tape recorder. The recording captures a male bird singing half of a duet – calling out to a mate, with no response. Seemingly, there is no one left to call back. When the recording was digitised in 2019, it circulated online rapidly: news articles, podcast episodes, and remixes all lamented the tragic loss of this now-extinct species to destructive colonial capitalism. Listeners widely report that they find the recording heartbreaking, and they can't listen to it without crying.[4]

This chapter examines human encounters with non-human beings and places through digital sound, and the role digital sound plays in interspecies relations. In all of the above vignettes, digital sound recordings seem to, for better or worse, 'enhance' human–non-human encounters, ostensibly resulting in livelier reefs, easier kills, and deeper relationships. However, there are more to these encounters than initially meets the ear: these relations are multiple, partial, and politically charged. What does it mean to listen to an animal that can't listen back? Whose voices are recorded, by whom, and where do they end up? What are the implications of trying to 'trick' non-humans through digital sound? What about the physical infrastructures that make these encounters possible?

Digital sound can reflect, enable, alter, and intensify human–non-human relationships to variegated, complex, and sometimes unexpected ends. In this chapter, we first reflect upon the recent proliferation of digital sound archives and sonic ecological monitoring techniques and technologies, asking what types of human–non-human relationships they represent and afford. Here, we explore the promises of digital archives and ecological monitoring systems, including their contributions to environmental conservation efforts and their ability to forge new kinds of encounters with the non-human world. Along the way, we highlight some concerns that have been raised in relation to these modes of listening, such as the role of Big Tech companies in producing ecological data sets and the asymmetrical power relations that are reproduced through digital listening. Second, we consider how digital sound alters material ecologies in multi-faceted ways, ranging from the luring or deterring of non-human beings to the environmental damage involved in creating and consuming this ostensibly intangible medium.

Throughout the chapter, we draw upon recent case studies and relevant literature from across the natural and social sciences, as a means to highlight the status of what we term 'digital sonic ecologies'. Through this term, we aim to critically theorise the multifarious interrelations between the digital, the sonic, and the non-human. Our chosen case studies throughout this chapter address just some of the ways that digital sonic ecologies manifest as we begin to investigate the promises and tensions of this terrain. We thus end our discussion by identifying new avenues for further critical research in this area. Though cognisant of literature that eschews human–non-human binaries, here we retain the framing of 'human–non-human relationships' to reflect and assess the stated promises of many digital sonic interventions, as well as to foreground the asymmetrical power relations often perpetuated by them.

## Digital bioacoustics and environmental sound archives

The scientific study of animal communication through sound, termed bioacoustics, blossomed during the latter half of the twentieth century, though it has a longer history. This has been facilitated by the introduction of relatively lightweight and mobile recording technologies and, as Rachel Mundy outlines, the advent of the spectrograph recorder, which enabled researchers to visualise the frequency and amplitude of animal sounds.[5] Bioacoustic methods are now used to detect and identify species, trace changes in animal communication across time (often as a result of anthropogenic pressures on aural space), model animal populations, and chart speciation events.

Digital sound recording technologies deepen and extend these long-standing promises of bioacoustics research. The flexibility, durability, and portability of digital recording technologies has enabled bioacoustics researchers to reach near-omnipotent levels of ecological eavesdropping in ways previously unimaginable. Entire ecosystems can be sensed through digital sensors to ascertain their ecological health across long durations of time. Emerging digital technologies and infrastructures combine to make the invariably vast data sets that such systems produce both manageable and comprehensible. Autonomous recording units relinquish the need for constant monitoring by a human operator while recording, and AI systems can detect and log specific sounds either in real time or after recording has ceased.

Concerns have been raised about the role of Big Tech firms in the rapid growth of such sonic data sets, related to the expanding capacity for surveillance and data commodification.[6] Yet there is also a burgeoning number of scientists and activists that are deploying open access digital recording technologies (Raspberry Pi-based recorders are favoured devices) to create decentralised networks of environmental sensors capable of not only monitoring animal calls but also alerting communities to particular environmental threats. Early warning detection systems, such as those that identify the sound of chainsaws as a proxy for illegal deforestation, are emerging tools for conservation efforts. Nonetheless, questions remain about the power relations, privacy, and invasiveness inherent to the production, processing, storage, and dissemination of such big data. Who gets to eavesdrop? On whose behalf? Who has access to the reams of data produced by omnipotent digital sensors, and on what terms?

In addition to species and ecosystem monitoring, omnipotent digital recording techniques are used as a means of engaging broader publics with the non-human world that faces various anthropogenic pressures. Online livestreams of coastal hydrophones continuously recording along cetacean migratory routes are particularly popular in this regard.[7] These enable listeners to encounter species that cannot ordinarily be detected through the human ear or the listening body, the alterity of deep underwater spaces, and the ubiquitous noise pollution that emanates from shipping and other coastal industries, which these species have to contend with. Terrestrial soundscapes streaming online in real time are also becoming a common sound art practice, while long-form digital soundscape recording is now a particular genre of slow radio broadcasting and podcasting.

Digital sound technologies have not only propelled the growth of data collection in the present; they have also reconfigured historical sound archives. Museums, libraries, and research institutions that hold extensive environmental sound archives are being reshaped by digital sound technologies, in terms of the types of recordings being archived, their distribution, the spaces of their audition, and their use. With a few clicks, one can access hundreds of thousands of digital audio recordings through websites such as British Library Sounds, xeno-canto, and the Macaulay Library.[8] The Macaulay Library, part of the Cornell Laboratory of Ornithology (CLO), is a juggernaut of sonic environmental data, with more than 2 million audio recordings representing over 12,000 animal species. The Library's digital collection comprises both born-digital recordings, often uploaded to the site by amateur recordists, and digitised recordings from the CLO's archive of historical tapes. In a matter of minutes, one can sonically travel from an Atlantic puffin's burrow in 1951 New Brunswick to a Sri Lanka frogmouth calling in a forest in Kerala in 2020, to the last known recording of the (now extinct) Kauaʻi ʻōʻō in 1986 Hawaii. For those with internet access, these websites offer sonic ecological encounters far exceeding what would be possible 'in person' in a lifetime. Marketed to scientists, educators, activists, artists, and the public, they aim to encourage and enhance the building of relationships with the natural world.

Single-species recordings of birds and other animals form the backbone of the majority of recordings within environmental sound archives. This is a function of their historic role as repositories of recordings for population-level bioacoustics research, and as reference sites for the identification of species by professionals (mostly scientific taxonomists) and amateurs alike. Nonetheless, there has been a relatively recent and rapid expansion of soundscape-style recordings being archived. For instance, Cheryl Tipp, curator of the British Library's Wildlife & Environmental Sounds (WES) collection, has noticed a shift to atmospheric recordings of rural and urban landscapes, which can be explained by the emergence of digital technologies. First, the accessibility of digital recording devices has democratised sound recording beyond a relatively small cadre of professional and hobbyist wildlife recordists. Notably, increasing numbers of sound artists and experimental musicians are depositing soundscape-style recordings within the archive. Such contributions to the archive, often positioned as creative productions rather than scientific data sets, blur the boundaries between the WES and adjacent musical collections in the Library. Second, the emergence of online repositories of birdsong and calls, notably xeno-canto, and bird identifier apps that can be used in the field has led to a transformation in the ways people access and consume single-species recordings as they are no longer tethered to a physical location. This has meant that the curator is now reluctant to actively seek out such recordings for the WES archive (Figure 2.1).

Figure 2.1 Inside the WES archive at the British Library, Euston Road, London. The boxes in the stores contain single-species recordings that are in the process of being digitised. (Photograph: Jonathan Prior. All rights reserved and permission to use the figure must be obtained from the copyright holder.)

When considering human–non-human relationship building as an outcome of digital sound archives, there are certainly limits to such capacities, especially in relation to single-species recordings. For starters, the 'encounter' of listening to non-humans in this way is almost entirely one-sided: the digital animal cannot listen back. This relationship between the listener and listened-to is thus one of asymmetrical power relations,[9] an asymmetry that begins with the necessarily non-consensual extraction of animals' voices by the recordist. Further, many digital recordings focus not only on single species but individual animals, eliminating background sounds to the deficit of that animal's complex ecological context. Akin to zooming in on a subject with a camera, such recordings use particular microphones, equipment placement, and editing techniques to 'hone in' on individual animal subjects.[10] Soundscape ecologist Bernie Krause criticises such recordings as an exercise in 'fragmentation' that 'distorts a sense of what is wild by giving us an incomplete perspective of the living landscape'.[11] Rather than eschewing all individual animal recordings, however, we would suggest more creative, ecologically attuned techniques, for instance using close mic-ing techniques and non-standard recording technologies (bat detectors, contact microphones) to spatially frame individual animal sounds. This has the potential to amplify and modulate those sounds that are usually imperceptible to humans – for example, the ultrasound of a bat in flight or Orthoptera stridulation – and those individual animal sounds that are otherwise overwhelmed by the complexity or total volume of soundscape-style approaches. We hear ample opportunities here for affective encounters with individual animals – often those that are less acoustically charismatic – in an ecologically meaningful way; that is to say, moments of attunement that may forge positive relations with non-humans, particularly for those species that tend to be misheard or neglected.[12]

Mediation is apparent in many aspects of digital sound archives: which animal is recorded, which segment is uploaded, which recording and editing technologies are used all make a difference to what kinds of relationships are possible with or through digital sonic natures. Given such issues of mediation, we might ask whether we should continue to think of digital sound recordings as representations at least mildly akin to hearing a species 'in the flesh' or if they should be recognised as something else entirely. William M. Adams raises this in regard to 'digital animals' at large, asking if digitalisation 'involve[s] the creation of new digital lives, which have no analogue in nature'.[13] This provocation is particularly interesting in relation to the sonic, as sound studies scholars routinely discuss sound as something (or some relation) that has agential and affective capacities in excess of its source.[14] Also, one never encounters the same sound twice. On playing back a digital recording, the vibrations emitted may be informed by the same stored information each time, but the sounds heard are always new, as they are shaped by the auditory space, technologies, and bodies of the listening event.[15] We might, then, recognise each press of the play button as a discrete sonic event which, though informed by an initial recording encounter and the layers of mediation that followed, has distinct affective and relational capacities. Here, a relationship may be forged *with* the digital sound recording rather than *through* it to the animal represented.

Even after all this is considered, listening to a digital recording of an animal remains a palpable experience. As Rachel Poliquin observes regarding taxidermied animal bodies, despite, and sometimes because of, the layers of abstraction and mediation in animal representation, something of an animal's 'magnetism' remains in taxidermy. She argues that the physical proximity afforded by taxidermy still 'engenders emotional intimacy' between the human and animal-thing.[16] Though sound is not a proximate physical object, the physics of listening can also forge these intimacies. Unlike taxidermy, sound is not an object but an event – an affective, relational, ephemeral force that vibrates through our entire bodies, literally moving us.[17] Listening to a sound recording is therefore intimate and embodied, a potent force for collapsing boundaries between the listener and listened-to.[18] As such, listening *through* digital sound recordings to the species they represent may engender more compassionate relationships with non-humans than, say, viewing a digital image of the same animal. The cultural-political impacts of whale sound recordings have made this clear,[19] and digital sound archives make such affective sonic encounters widely accessible.

It is, nonetheless, difficult to quantify what such relationships might 'do' and to what extent they 'matter' in our time of ecological crisis. A web-based children's game called *BeastBox* created by DJ Ben Mirin with the CLO, for instance, advocates for the importance of encountering digital animal sounds in a more participatory medium. In this game, players act as 'Wildlife DJs', layering digital animal sounds with ecosystem recordings and beatbox beats. Mirin hopes that this game will help you, the player, to open 'a pathway for you to find your own sense of connection and love for nature so that you can be inspired to protect it'.[20] This follows the *raison d'être* of many animal representations: the *hope* that encountering virtual animals will inspire empathy towards, and thus actions to save, 'actual' animals. As demonstrated by Adam Searle, Jonathon Turnbull, and William M. Adams in their study of peregrine falcon nestcams, relations of more-than-human care can indeed emerge from virtual encounters with animals.[21] However, encounters afforded by applications like *BeastBox* – containing many animal voices out of time and context – are less discrete and their impacts are thus trickier to measure. At their most potent, these encounters *could* result in the 'interspecies epiphanies' that Jamie Lorimer describes in his exploration of non-human charisma. Here, childhood encounters with particular non-human beings can be 'the foundations for a lifetime attachment, interest, and concern'.[22] Though Lorimer explores encounters in the flesh, it is interesting to consider if such life-changing epiphanies could also occur through mediated digital encounters such as *BeastBox*, where the curiosity and awe afforded by creating music with non-human sound recordings could provide a spark towards future conservation action.[23]

What of those animals that are beyond saving? While for much of the twentieth century species rarity was treated with excitement and fascination by the custodians of wildlife sound archives, it is now tinged with regret as the biodiversity crisis unfurls. For Cheryl Tipp, the British Library's sound archive is a means of preserving environmental sonic heritage, including the sounds of extinct species: 'in these situations, sound recordings become acoustic relics of something precious that will never return. Sound archives act as the final protectors of expired voices, and have a core role in preserving the memory of our biophonic past'.[24] Similarly, the Director of the Macaulay Library, Mike Webster, asserts that sound archives act as sonic time capsules, preserving how the world used to sound and contemporary sounds for future listeners. Though he believes all the sounds in the archive are important, the sounds of extinct species are absolutely irreplaceable, akin to 'a Rembrandt or Van Gogh'.[25] The archive, then, has an emerging role as a space for ecological memorialisation.[26] At the same time, we need to be acutely aware of the active role that sound recordings play in shaping the future of rare and declining species populations. While we may instinctively celebrate the digitisation of wildlife sound archives because this increases public accessibility and engagement with them, a movement towards unconstrained access raises serious questions for conservation ethics, which we explore in more detail in the following section.

Aside from their assumed ability to promote empathy towards the non-human world, digital sounds are also positioned as a means to create therapeutic spaces for humans.[27] There are abundant apps and long-form audio streams of nature sounds available to aid listeners with meditation, stress relief, and sleep, which draw upon vast online digital archives. Such digital resources are emerging as an important, and profitable, component of the expanding 'wellness' industry, wherein digitised nature is positioned as a surrogate for in situ nature experiences, mental health services, and corporate wellbeing procedures. However, in their investigation of the potential use of digital environmental sound in clinical settings, Victoria Bates and colleagues reject the notion that such sounds should be interpreted as surrogates for the 'real thing', and contend that they produce fundamentally different types of listening experiences to in situ listening.[28] Others have critiqued the social effects of the rapid rise of this use of digitised nature, including sound. In her analysis of digital nature in relation to health and wellbeing, Samantha Walton argues that digital nature apps are cheaper than 'balancing workloads, hiring more staff, or paying struggling workers fairly – providing a perfect sticking plaster for a neoliberal society committed to the project of "unbundling" responsibility for self-care, rather than creating a community dedicated to compassion and quality of life for all'.[29]

## Digital sound and material ecologies

Digital sound recording can impact material ecologies in various ways, ranging from the use of digital voices to lure animals to local habitats, to the extractive terrains of recorded sound that involve more distant places. For a long time, the idea persisted that sound is an intangible medium, and even more so in its virtual form. Recent work on the political ecology of recorded music and media archaeology has challenged the notion that digitalisation involves dematerialisation by tracing the deep time of digital media and the ecological damage caused by sound technologies, including digital forms.[30] Indeed, institutional digital archives have large material footprints, which runs counter to the rhetorical nebulousness of the digital 'cloud'. Data centres that sustain digital library systems are resource intensive in terms of electricity and water use.[31] The British Library's own digital library is replicated across five UK data centres, or 'nodes'. Each centre stores a copy of all digitised recordings, and they are networked with one other; if files on one server become corrupted, then they are restored by the network.[32] Thus, digitised sound archives require constant material reproduction.

If we consider the environmental history of recorded sound, every new format, whether it is shellac, vinyl, tape, or digital data, has come with its distinctive histories and geographies of extraction. The process of extraction that makes digital sound technologies possible involves raw materials, more-than-human labour relations, supply chains, toxic waste, and obsolescent media that are distributed unevenly across the globe. Today, it is possible to stream the first commercial wildlife sound recording in an instant via the British Library History of Recorded Sound collection.[33] This very first recording of a captive nightingale (*Luscinia megarhynchos*) was originally made by the bird collector Carl Reich, who had an aviary in the German city of Bremen, together with the engineer Max Hampe. Released in 1910 by the Gramophone Company, the recording with the title 'Actual Bird Record made by a Captive Nightingale' marks the beginning of commercial wildlife sound recording, a genre that would grow increasingly popular in subsequent decades. Reich released many more records of captive birds, mostly of blackbirds, canaries, thrushes, and other species that were renowned for their versatile song. Copies were distributed widely across Europe, the US, Russia, and Australia.[34] Listening to the digitised song of the nightingale on a computer or mobile phone, we can detect hisses and crackling sounds. The surface noise reveals the historical traces of now obsolete formats. In this case, the audio file we can stream online is a digitised version of a 78 rpm shellac disc from 1910 on which the nightingale was initially recorded. Thus, this audio file appears immaterial only if we fail to hear the acoustic traces of past physical media embedded in digital sound.

Shellac is an interesting material to reflect on encounters with the non-human in digital sound archives. Shellac discs or '78's' reveal the more-than-human agency involved in the production of value in multiple ways. First, shellac, the raw material that was used as a binding agent in the manufacture of records, is created by the labour of the lac bug (*Kerria lacca*), a South Asian scale insect. When we discuss the potential role of sound recording in conservation, we also need to consider those places and more-than-human relations that have been affected dramatically by the extraction of raw materials. The extractive frontiers of shellac include forests in

India, the more-than-human labour of shellac beetles and human harvesters, the local knowledge these highly skilled workers had of distant places and ecosystems, and supply chains and labour relations that – at the time of the first nightingale recording – were deeply exploitative and structured by colonial relations.[35] We can trace such environmental conditions and 'hidden infrastructures' that undergird every recording format, ranging from the petrochemical relations of plastic embedded in vinyl to the networks of fibre optic cables, server farms, routers, consumer electronics, and software involved in the making of digital sound.

Second, the 'Actual Bird Record made by a Captive Nightingale', like the myriad commercial bird recordings to follow, was in fact made by an actual bird whose song was captured for its particular musicality or acoustic charisma. Charismatic species, including those that are valued for their musicality, can be helpful agents in efforts to generate public enthusiasm and funding for conservation efforts.[36] There is also a certain nostalgia that fuels contemporary virtual encounters with the sounds of extinction. Birdsong can recall childhood memories and produce a sense of place. With the disappearance of many farmland birds from the acoustic landscape, a particular sense of loss is invoked, as has been recently expressed with reference to rural England.[37] But what about those birds whose song holds little value to the human ear, that merely squawk, or animals whose voices are not represented in sound archives at all and that don't fall into categories of value such as rarity, charisma, or extinction?

If we are to take seriously the provocation to centre sonic ecologies beyond human sound worlds,[38] it is important to also consider how digital sonic ecologies impact animals' sonic worlds. Intentional interventions into animals' sonic space include the use of digital sound recordings to lure animals to specific locations for scientific surveys and conservation efforts to repopulate habitats. The howlbox, for example, is a device to count and monitor wolves in remote locations without an observer needing to be present. The box repeatedly broadcasts digital recordings of wolf howls and then switches to record the howls made by wolves in response. Researchers at the University of Montana developed this cost-effective device in 2007 with funding from the Nez Perce Tribe, in anticipation of the removal of grey wolves from federal protections under the U.S. Endangered Species Act that would also end federal funding for the monitoring of wolves.[39] Interestingly, in the case of wolves, human-simulated howls have been found to elicit more wolves to respond than recordings of real wolf howls.[40]

This case study is mirrored in the proposed removal of the ivory-billed woodpecker (*Campephilus principalis*) from the Endangered Species Act due to their presumed extinction.[41] The extinction of this species is perhaps the most controversial event in US conservation history, and 'ivorybill searchers' still trawl the Southeastern swamps of the US to capture evidence of the species' survival. Both grassroots and institutional searchers have taken advantage of the public digitisation of an ivory-billed woodpecker recording from 1935, which searchers use to train their ears, as a benchmark against which modern putative ivory-billed woodpecker recordings are measured and as a playback resource to try to locate surviving birds. Some searchers have claimed to hear surviving ivory-billed woodpeckers respond to the playback of the digitised historical recording which, if true, is an intriguing example of digital sonic ecologies in its multispecies, multi-generational, and digital/analogue hybridity. However, as with grey wolves, some searchers have found non-digital methods to be more effective, such as simulating the species' distinctive 'double-knocks' by banging wood against trees or canoes.[42]

A more popularised practice is the use of digital playback in birding, wherein birders broadcast digital sound recordings in bird habitats to increase their chances of seeing a species. Methods include playing mating calls and alarm calls or broadcasting the sounds of predators. Playback has a long history, but the accessibility of digital bird sounds and ease of playing them (often simply from digital sound archives accessed on mobile phones) means this practice has proliferated in recent years. Playback is controversial, as birds' response to digital predators, mates, and alarms is thought to potentially cause unnecessary stress, tricking them into expending energy that could be better utilised for actual threats and survival.[43] Despite these concerns, some studies have found birds habituating to and ignoring digital sounds over time.[44] Here, we can see that the birds are not just passive victims of humans' sonic intrusions, but that non-humans can have their own varying and evolving relationships with and within digital sound.

In the previous section, we saw how digitised recordings held within sound archives may help to forge compassionate relationships with the non-human world. However, digitised recordings are not inherently innocuous in configuring human–non-human relations. Cheryl Tipp notes that she has been approached on a number of occasions by people – mainly located in North America – seeking digitised animal vocalisation recordings to use as hunting aids. Similarly, the pet trade is interested in accessing digitised recordings to help track and capture increasingly rare, and thus lucrative, species. Such requests are turned down on the basis of a commitment to a preservationist ethic that extends beyond species recordings to encompass their non-digitised, living populations. However, Cheryl expressed concern that sound archives internationally are reducing the number of curators while increasing the number of AV specialists employed to digitise and publicise their collections as quickly as possible, which will have ramifications for the ethical custodianship of these recordings.

Beyond these practices to lure animals in the contexts of hunting, conservation, or birding, digital sound recordings are also used as a sonic weapon against birds and other animals in urban, agricultural, or infrastructural spaces where their appearance is considered a threat or nuisance. Around many airports, for example, larger birds whose presence might endanger human air travel are deterred with various technologies including the playback of biosonic alarms and distress calls. Digital sound deterrents are also part of the everyday 'hostile architecture' of cities. There is a flurry of commercial products available, including ultrasonic bird repellers that make use of high frequencies that can't be heard by humans and thus don't interfere in human sound worlds. However, there is no significant empirical evidence that ultrasound has an effect on birds.[45]

One example that has gained media and political attention is the auditory conflict emerging from the presence of Javan mynas (*Acridotheres javanicus*) in Singapore's central tourist areas, including Orchard Road and the residential neighbourhoods of Potong Pasir, where local residents complain about the flocks of birds and their collective squawking causing noise and a lack of sleep.[46] Considering birdsong as noise pollution stands in stark contrast to the charismatic or meditative potential of digital bird recordings discussed earlier. Such real-world sonic relations with birds in cities also call into question the presumption that 'encounters of listening' are always one-directional, fully intentional, and under the control of human listeners. Javan mynas are good urban adaptors, with well over 100,000 birds currently inhabiting Singapore. The Indonesian bird was first introduced to Singapore as a songbird through the caged bird trade in the 1920s. It is native to Java and Bali, where it is now highly endangered. The myna's appropriation of urban space sparks ongoing public debates about whether to battle these birds with various techniques including bioacoustic repellents, hawk patrols, chemicals, and modification of their habitats, or whether to accommodate them and consider Singapore an urban refugium for exotic escapees that might even help save endangered species.[47] These debates also raise wider questions about the colonial and racial legacies underpinning concerns around the presence of non-native birds in cities, including their circulation along trade routes shaped by colonialism.[48] Myna birds have been considered a problem in Singapore since the 1980s, when their numbers started to grow alongside urbanisation processes. Among the numerous methods of wildlife management that have been tested on myna birds is the broadcast of looped digital recordings of myna distress, alarm, and pre-flight calls close to roosting trees. But recent studies show that bioacoustic methods alone are of little effect as the birds quickly habituate to these sonic events.[49] This deviation of non-human bodies from the intended effects of biopolitical management through digital means calls into question the overbearing power asymmetry often ascribed to 'the digital'. It also highlights that, especially in light of the sonic intensity of cities that birds inhabit, digital sound is only one element shaping non-human sensory worlds.

While it is clear that humans and birds alike suffer the damage loud sounds can cause to auditory receptors, we still know very little about how different species of birds hear. The wider effects of digital sound on urban ecologies, the corporeal vulnerability of animals towards excessive sound, and the changing relationships between sound, late capitalism, and urban space that can affect both human and animal health are still largely unclear. In Berlin and other cities, informal outdoor music events and mobile parties in public parks that have sought to compensate for the closure of clubs during the COVID-19 pandemic sparked debates among nature conservationists about the impact of amplified music on urban ecologies.[50] In Tulum, Mexico, a conservationist has recently warned about the negative effects of electronic music raves on birds, monkeys, and other animals.[51] These examples question the idea of the resurgence of nature in cities during the pandemic that proliferated in the media.[52] Rather, they show that in some places we can observe the contrary effect, with increasing pressures on animals through human-induced noise and the intensive use of parks and nature spaces. Preliminary studies on urban and marine ecologies have begun to investigate how animal bodies respond to music events. In Miami, Florida, for example, scientists have measured elevated sound pressure levels caused by the Ultra music festival. Sound pressure in the air and the coastal underwater soundscape caused significant endocrine stress responses in Gulf toadfish (*Opsanus beta*).[53] A study of Daubenton's bats (*Myotis daubentonii*) roosting in the roof of Brinkburn Priory in Northumberland has shown that loud sounds and bright illumination on summer festival nights make bats emerge at a later time of day, so the timing of music festivals can be crucial for bat ecologies.[54] These exploratory studies point to the need for further research that examines how amplified music and digital sound affect the acoustic spaces of non-humans in and beyond cities.

## Conclusion

In this chapter, we have charted some of the ways in which digital sound can shape encounters between humans and non-humans, with a particular focus on digital sound archives and sonic ecological monitoring techniques and technologies, and how digital sound alters material ecologies. Here, we demonstrated how the use of digital sound recordings, from lures to sonic weapons, have repercussions for interspecies relations among multispecies

# Digital sonic ecologies 63

communities. Throughout the chapter, we have discussed some of the limitations and limits to current research. To conclude, we will now describe areas for future research that we envisage would fruitfully build upon and expand digital ecologies scholarship in the sonic sphere.

There are ethico-political tensions between the affective dimensions of experiencing non-human others through digital sound recordings and the environmental damage involved in producing and consuming digital media. These cannot be easily resolved and warrant further investigation. Looking towards the future of digital sound recordings, we need to question 'our expectations of instant access and infinite storage' engendered by digital media.[55] We might want to further explore digital sonic ecologies from a political ecology perspective. Such a perspective involves geographically tracing how digital sound recordings and their 'metabolic vehicles' (minerals, cables, wires, server farms) that are used in conservation efforts in one place produce the destruction of habitats and livelihoods elsewhere. Following feminist epistemologies, future work might also consider, for instance, the implications of sonic surveillance and the data sonification of animal voices.

Second, there are wider ethical questions that need to be addressed when producing and using digital sound recordings in the field. Thus far, there are few ethical protocols asked of researchers working with digital sound recording as an investigative method beyond conventional human procedural ethics, such as using consent forms and participant pseudonyms for human subjects.[56] As the preliminary research on digital sound recording for the tracking and monitoring of animals we have discussed has shown, sound recording devices and digital sound data can be misused for extractive purposes and to detrimental ends. There is also a significant set of questions raised by the often non-consensual nature of field recording, both in the extraction of sounds and their performance. Such questions arise in the use of sonic monitoring and control technologies, but also might be considered in relation to a recent trend of digital sonic transmission in ecological sound art.[57] Further research could help explore in more detail the ethical considerations and protocols that are needed for using digital sonic methods in and beyond the field, and in developing sensitive and caring multispecies methodologies that involve digital sound recording.[58]

A third strand for future directions involves further engagement with the role of curating digital sound archives. As the curator Cheryl Tipp highlights, we currently see a proliferation of digital sound recordings flooding archives and online platforms while, at the same time, the role of curation is significantly underfunded.[59] This situation conflicts with the importance of ethical custodianship and the need to contextualise the various local and global power relations digital sound recordings are embedded in and the types of specific technologies that have been used in the recording process.

There is also still much research to be done on the presence of non-human others in digital and digitised sound archives, and contemporary and future researchers will rely on the expertise of curators and archivists providing context to such sources. Further to this, we think an important component of future digital sonic ecologies research will be to focus on the colonial relations embedded within and reproduced through formal institutional sound archives, as scholars have considered in other contexts.[60]

Lastly, many case studies discussed in this chapter have centred on 'acoustically charismatic' species, neglecting the vast majority of extant species. This is partly a reflection of the field itself, including available archival sources that are overwhelmingly dominated by bird recordings, and the focus of contemporary research within fields such as bioacoustics, but it also reflects our own expertise and interests and thus the limitations of this chapter. We hope that future research will push beyond species deemed to be of positive sonic aesthetic value to also encompass the ugly, the mundane, and those sounds that do not equivocally and directly engender either positive or negative responses due to their alterity.[61]

## Notes

1. Gordon et al., 'Acoustic enrichment can enhance fish community development.'
2. Mojo Outdoors have a range of devices and decoys: https://mojooutdoors.com/products/predator
3. Predator University, 'Tony's top killers.'
4. E.g., the thread beginning u/AwesomeFrito, 2020. See www.reddit.com/r/Naturewasmetal/comments/ew7e0u/song_of_the_last_kauai_oo_singing_to_a_mate_that/.
5. Mundy, 'Birdsong and the image of evolution.'
6. Ritts and Bakker, 'Conservation acoustics.'
7. Hydrophones are waterproofed microphones that can be used in aquatic environments. Many online streaming projects exist, but hear for example the Monterey Bay Aquarium Research Institute's Soundscape Listening Room: www.mbari.org/soundscape-listening-room/.
8. Xeno-canto is an online repository of birdsong and bird call recordings. Users can freely upload and download recordings which are held under a Creative Commons licence. See: www.xeno-canto.org/.
9. Regarding asymmetrical power relations as enacted through digital technologies, see Turnbull et al., 'Quarantine Eencounters with digital animals.'
10. Bruyninckx, *Listening in the Field*.
11. Krause, *The Great Animal Orchestra*.
12. See Bear, 'Being Angelica?' for an examination of the agency and affective capacity of individual animals, in this case an octopus named Angelica viewable in a UK aquarium.

13 Adams, 'Digital animals.'
14 E.g. Born, 'On nonhuman sound'; Gallagher, 'Sound as affect'; Robinson, *Hungry Listening.*
15 Gallagher, 'Field recording and the sounding of spaces.'
16 Poliquin, *The Breathless Zoo*, p. 136.
17 Gallagher, 'Field recording'; Gallagher, 'Sound as affect.'
18 Born, 'On nonhuman sound.'
19 See Ritts, 'Environmentalists abide.'
20 Bascomb, 'Nature and the beat.'
21 Searle et al., 'The digital peregrine.'
22 Lorimer, 'Nonhuman charisma,' p. 921.
23 The participatory nature of *BeastBox* could increase the likelihood of future conservation action by users. However, these encounters are still one-sided, and thus retain the issue of asymmetrical power relations discussed elsewhere in this chapter.
24 Cheryl Tipp, 2018, personal communication.
25 Mike Webster, 2022, personal communication.
26 For a creative sonic response to extinction, listen to the work of Sally Ann McIntyre in Boyle, 'The silence of the Huia.'
27 Berland, *Virtual Menageries.*
28 Bates et al., 'Beyond landscape's visible realm.'
29 Walton, *Everybody Needs Beauty*, p. 251.
30 Devine, *Decomposed*; Parikka, *A Geology of Media.*
31 Siddik et al., 'The environmental footprint of data centers.'
32 See www.bl.uk/legal-deposit/security-for-publications. Interestingly, the location of one of these data centres is unknown – even to Cheryl Tipp – for security reasons.
33 The sound recording can be listened to here: www.bl.uk/collection-items/nightingale-first-commercially-available-wildlife-recording-1910.
34 Tipp, 'The birth of wildlife sound recording.'
35 Melillo, 'Global entomologies.'
36 Lorimer, 'Nonhuman charisma.'
37 Adams, 'Listening and loss.'
38 Gallagher et al., 'Listening geographies.'
39 The Trump administration removed the grey wolf from federal protections under the Endangered Species Act in the lower 48 United States in 2020, a decision that was overturned by a federal judge in February 2022, restoring protection to grey wolves and prohibiting wolf hunting and trapping in states outside of the northern Rocky Mountains. For the discussion around the funding by the Nez Perce Tribe, see Johnson, 'A bid to lure wolves.'
40 Brennan et al., 'Testing automated howling devices.'
41 United States Fish and Wildlife Service, 'Endangered and threatened wildlife and plants.'
42 See Gallagher, *The Grail Bird.*
43 Due to such concerns, many organisations dissuade playback while birding, particularly when it comes to endangered birds (e.g. *Australian Wildlife*

*Conservancy* and *Environment and Climate Change Canada*). However, empirical research on the actual impact of digital playback on birds is limited.
44  Harris and Haskell, 'Simulated birdwatchers' playback.'
45  Beason, 'What can birds hear?'
46  See Choo, '"Cacophony" of mynah birds.'
47  Gibson and Yong, 'Saving two birds with one stone.'
48  Barua, 'Feral ecologies.'
49  Jaimipak et al., 'Effects of distress.'
50  Personal communication with the Berlin-based nature conservationist Rainer Altenkamp.
51  Olufemi, 'Noise pollution is harming wildlife in Tulum.'
52  Searle and Turnbull, 'Resurgent natures?'
53  Cartolano et al., 'Impacts of a local music festival.'
54  Shirley et al., 'Assessing the impact of a music festival.'
55  Devine, *Decomposed*, p. 187.
56  A lack of protocols is the case for much qualitative and especially ethnographically focused research on non-human others that takes place outside the traditional laboratory space. See Oliver, 'Beyond-human ethics.'
57  For instance, the project 'Radio Amnion: Sonic transmissions of care in oceanic space' claims to quietly transmit digital sound art compositions in the Pacific Ocean's Cascadia Basin during each full moon, with the intended listening audience of 'the Ocean itself'; see: https://radioamnion.net/#about.
58  See Wright, 'Listening after nature' for an initial survey of what this might sound like.
59  Cheryl Tipp notes that outside of the WES, The Macaulay Library, and the Animal Sound Archive at the Museum für Naturkunde Berlin, funding streams are not consistent for dedicated wildlife and environmental sound archives.
60  See, for example, Nannyonga-Tamusuza and Weintraub, 'The audible future,' p. 206.
61  An important deviation from the foregrounding of positive aesthetic value in wildlife recording is Michael, 'Toward a dark nature recording.' Michael advocates for a 'Dark Nature Recording,' celebrating practices like Chris Watson's track *Vultures, Nine Birds Feeding on Zebra Carcass, Itong Plains, Kenya* that starkly resists the romantic aesthetics of nature sound recording. For a discussion about the overwhelming focus on positive sonic aesthetics in environmental aesthetics scholarship, see also Prior, 'Sonic environmental aesthetics and landscape research.'

## Bibliography

Adams, W.M. 2019. Listening and loss. *Thinking Like a Human* [online], 28 May. Available from: https://thinkinglikeahuman.com/2019/05/28/listening-and-loss/.
Adams, W.M. 2020. Digital animals. *The Philosopher*, 108(1): 17–21.
Barua, M. 2022. Feral ecologies: The making of postcolonial nature in London. *Journal of the Royal Anthropological Institute*, 28(3): 896–919.

Bascomb, B. 2021. Nature and the beat. *Living on Earth* [online], 5 March. Available from: www.loe.org/shows/segments.html?programID=21-P13-00010&segmentID=5.

Bates, V., Hickman, C., Manchester, H., Prior, J., and Singer, S. 2020. Beyond landscape's visible realm: Recorded sound, nature, and wellbeing. *Health and Place*, 61: 102271.

Bear, C. 2011. Being Angelica? Exploring individual animal geographies. *Area*, 43(3): 297–304. www.jstor.org/stable/41240506.

Beason, R.C. 2004. What can birds hear? *Proceedings of the Vertebrate Pest Conference*, 21(21): 92–96.

Berland, J. 2019. *Virtual Menageries: Animals as Mediators in Network Cultures*. Cambridge, MA: MIT Press.

Born, G. 2019. On nonhuman sound – Sound as relation. In J.A. Steintrager and R. Chow (Eds.) *Sound Objects* (pp. 185–207). Durham, NC: Duke University Press.

Boyle, C. 2019. The silence of the Huia: Bird extinction and the archive. *Journal of New Zealand & Pacific Studies*, 7(2): 219–236.

Brennan, A., Cross, P.C., Ausband, D.E., Barbknecht, A., and Creel, S. 2013. Testing automated howling devices in a wintertime wolf survey. *Wildlife Society Bulletin*, 37(2): 389–393.

Bruyninckx, J. 2018. *Listening in the Field*. Cambridge, MA: MIT Press.

Cartolano, M.C., Berenshtein, I., Heuer, R.H., Pasparakis, C., Rider, M., Hammerschlag, N., Paris, C.B., Grosell, M., and McDonald, D. 2020. Impacts of a local music festival on fish stress hormone levels and the adjacent underwater soundscape. *Environmental Pollution*, 265(Pt A): 114925.

Choo, C. 2018. "Cacophony" of mynah birds a headache for some Potong Pasir residents. *Today* [online], 9 August. Available from: www.todayonline.com/singapore/cacophony-mynah-birds-headache-some-potong-pasir-residents.

Devine, K. 2019. *Decomposed: The Political Ecology of Music*. Cambridge, MA: MIT Press.

Gallagher, M. 2015. Field recording and the sounding of spaces. *Environment and Planning D: Society and Space*, 33(3): 560–576.

Gallagher, M. 2016. Sound as affect: Difference, power and spatiality. *Emotion, Space and Society*, 20: 42–48.

Gallagher, M., Kannigieser, A., and Prior, J. 2017. Listening geographies: Landscape, affect and geotechnologies. *Progress in Human Geography*, 41(5): 618–637.

Gallagher, T. 2005. *The Grail Bird: Hot on the Trail of the Ivory-billed Woodpecker*. Boston, MA: Houghton Mifflin Company.

Gibson, L. and Yong, D.L. 2017. Saving two birds with one stone: Solving the quandary of introduced, threatened species. *Frontiers in Ecology and the Environment*, 15(1): 35–41.

Gordon, T.A.C., Radford, A.N., Davidson, I.K., Barnes, K., McCloskey, K., Nedelec, S.L., Meekan, M.G., McCormick, M.I., and Simpson, S.D. 2019. Acoustic enrichment can enhance fish community development on degraded coral reef habitat. *Nature Communications*, 10: 5414.

Harris, J.B.C. and Haskell, D.G. 2013. Simulated birdwatchers' playback affects the behavior of two tropical birds. *PLoS ONE*, 8(10): e77902.

Jaimipak, T., Kamtaeja, S., Payakkhabutra, S., and Viruhpintu, S. 2019. Effects of distress, alarm, and pre-flight calls on the behavior of Myna birds. *Songklanakarin Journal of Science and Technology*, 41(1): 222–228.

Johnson, K. 2008. A bid to lure wolves with a digital call of the wild. *New York Times* [online], 19 March. Available from: www.nytimes.com/2008/03/19/science/earth/19howl.html.

Krause, B. 2013. *The Great Animal Orchestra*. New York: Little, Brown and Company.

Lorimer, J. 2007. Nonhuman charisma. *Environment and Planning D: Society and Space*, 25(5): 911–932.

Melillo, E.D. 2014. Global entomologies: Insects, empires, and the 'Synthetic Age' in world history. *Past & Present*, 223(1): 233–270.

Michael, D. 2011. Toward a dark nature recording. *Organised Sound*, 16(3): 206–210.

Mundy, R. 2009. Birdsong and the image of evolution. *Society and Animals*, 17: 206–223. https://doi.org/10.1163/156853009X445389.

Nannyonga-Tamusuza, S. and Weintraub, A.N. 2012. The audible future: Reimagining the role of sound archives and sound repatriation in Uganda. *Ethnomusicology*, 56(2): 206–233.

Oliver, C. 2021. Beyond-human ethics: The animal question in institutional ethical reviews. *Area*, 53: 619–626.

Olufemi, T. 2021. Noise pollution is harming wildlife in Tulum. *Mixmag* [online], 3 September. Available from: https://mixmag.net/read/wildlife-tulum-noise-pollution-mexico-events-news/.

Parikka, J. 2015. *A Geology of Media*. Minneapolis, MN: University of Minnesota Press.

Poliquin, R. 2012. *The Breathless Zoo: Taxidermy and the Cultures of Longing*. University Park, PA: The Pennsylvania State University Press.

Predator University. n.d. Tony's Top Killers [online]. Available from: https://predatoruniversity.store/collections/sound-files/products/tonys-top-killers.

Prior, J. 2017. Sonic environmental aesthetics and landscape research. *Landscape Research*, 42(1): 6–17.

Ritts, M. 2017. Environmentalists abide: Listening to whale music – 1965–1985. *Environment and Planning D: Society and Space*, 35(6): 1096–1114.

Ritts, M. and Bakker, K. 2021. Conservation acoustics: Animal sounds, audible natures, cheap nature. *Geoforum*, 124: 144–155.

Robinson, D. 2020. *Hungry Listening: Resonant Theory for Indigenous Sound Studies*. Minneapolis, MN: The University of Minnesota Press.

Searle, A. and Turnbull, J. 2020. Resurgent natures? More-than-human perspectives on COVID-19. *Dialogues in Human Geography*, 10(2): 291–295.

Searle, A., Turnbull, J., and Adams, W.M. 2023. The digital peregrine: A technonatural history of a cosmopolitan raptor. *Transactions of the Institute of British Geographers*, 48(1): 195–212.

Shirley, M.D.F., Armitage, V.L., Barden, T.L., Gough, M., Lurz, P.W.W., Oatway, D.E., South, A.B., and Rushton, S.P. 2001. Assessing the impact of a music festival on the emergence behaviour of a breeding colony of Daubenton's bats (*Myotis daubentonii*). *Journal of Zoology*, 254(3): 367–373.

Siddik, M.A.B., Shehabi, A., and Marston, L. 2021. The environmental footprint of data centers in the United States. *Environmental Research Letters*, 16(6): 064017.

Tipp, C. 2012. The birth of wildlife sound recording. *Sonic Field* [online], 28 September. Available from: https://sonicfield.org/200/.

Turnbull, J., Searle, A., and Adams, W.M. 2020. Quarantine encounters with digital animals: More-than-human geographies of lockdown life. *Journal of Environmental Media*, 1(1): 6.1–6.10.

United States Fish and Wildlife Service (USFWS). 2021. Endangered and threatened wildlife and plants; removal of 23 extinct species from the lists of Endangered and Threatened Wildlife and Plants. *Federal Register*, 86(187) [online], 30 September. Available from: www.federalregister.gov/documents/2021/09/30/2021-21219/endangered-and-threatened-wildlife-and-plants-removal-of-23-extinct-species-from-the-lists-of.

Walton, S. 2021. *Everybody Needs Beauty: In Search of the Nature Cure*. London: Bloomsbury Circus.

Wright, M.P. 2022. *Listening After Nature: Field Recording, Ecology, Critical Practice*. London: Bloomsbury.

# 3

# Trap-cam of care: conservation and the digital ecology of online lobster entrapment

*Jon Henrik Ziegler Remme*

## Introduction

At 14 metres deep, a lobster is crawling over the sea floor in a calm Norwegian bay, slowly and carefully feeling its way towards a big wooden trap that lies on the seabed. It is probably the pungent scent of the rotten mackerel bait within the trap that has caught its attention. Moving around the trap for a while, the lobster eventually finds its way in, moves towards the bait and starts eating. It does not seem to notice that what appears to be an open roof is actually a transparent acrylic sheet that allows an attached web-camera to film every move it makes. What the lobster probably does not know is that it is now the star of an online stream called 'the lobster trap live' that is watched by hundreds and even thousands of lobster fishers every day during the annual autumn lobster fishing season.[1] In a nearby café, the 'lobster show' is streamed live to a television screen for guests, while local schools and kindergartens stream the lobsters to children while they eat their lunches.

For Norwegian lobster fishers, the lives and trappings of lobsters in the depth of the seas used to be, and to a significant extent still are, shrouded in mystery. How lobsters behave in and around traps has been invisible since trapping began and, for the most part, subject to the fishers' speculative imagination. Indeed, this is part of the attraction for many lobster fishers and what makes this as an occupation and recreational activity fun.[2] However, since 2012, lobster fishers and other enthusiasts have been able to log on to a website and watch a livestream of what is going on in and around a trap 'minute by minute', 24/7, in the first couple of weeks of the lobster fishing season. On a daily basis, the research institute that operates the trap-camera pulls the trap, investigates its contents, restocks its bait bag, and puts it back in the sea, all while streaming it live on their website. Viewers participate, too, by emailing the institute creative and even playful suggestions as to what kind of bait to put in the trap.

The digitally mediated visibility of lobster-trap interactions no doubt provides lobster fishers with valuable information. They get a chance to see how lobsters behave, how they get into the traps, and, surprisingly to many, how they actually are able to crawl out again. This new visibility of lobsters' trap behaviour could very well be a source of knowledge concerning how best to place their traps, what bait is most attractive to lobsters, and when it is best to pull their traps. As such, the trap-cam could be used for making lobster fishing more efficient and putting the already strained lobster stock under increasing stress. However, a closer look at the camera's role in efforts to take care of the strained Norwegian lobster stock through promoting ethical and sustainable fishing reveals that the lobster trap-cam must be understood as much more than a new digital way of enhancing harvest-related knowledge about lobsters. Indeed, as this chapter argues, the trap-cam can also be understood as a virtual affective trap that momentarily captures and reconfigures human–lobster relations by enabling a form of digital intimacy.

The trap-cam is operated by the Norwegian publicly owned Institute of Marine Research. The institute is one of the biggest marine research institutes in Europe, with several research stations in different parts of Norway. Focusing on research, monitoring, and stock assessment, the institute is a leading supplier of scientific knowledge related to marine ecosystems and sustainable management of the country's marine resources. With regard to the lobster, the institute has been a key player in promoting relations of care for the lobster stock. The primary purpose of the lobster trap-cam is not, however, the production of scientific knowledge and neither is it part of any monitoring or stock assessment work. In fact, the trap-cam came about more or less coincidentally when one of the scientists found a web-camera at the research station and thought it might be fun to put it in a lobster trap.[3] Initially it was streamed only on the institute's intranet, but with the popularity it soon gained internally, the institute figured it might be a great way to reach out to the public with information about lobsters, about sustainable lobster fishing, and about the institute's research more generally. From being an experiment conducted for fun, the trap-cam attracted, as soon as live images of lobster were made available to the public, an explosion of interest. For the last three years, what eventually became known and marketed as *'hummerteina live'* – 'the lobster trap live' – the streaming of live images from the lobster trap on the institute's website and Facebook pages have been the institute's most visited sites, with viewers registered in fifty-seven different countries, including Nepal and Trinidad and Tobago. The wide interest in the trap-cam has become an important communication platform for the institute,[4] and apart from providing knowledge about lobster behaviour for the viewers of the stream, researchers from the institute mobilise the trap-cam's popularity to make regular appearances in newspapers and national TV shows where they can reach further out with their attempts at promoting care for and sustainable fishing of the national lobster stock.

Building on fieldwork with lobster fishers, marine scientists, and government fishing agencies on and off in the period 2017–2022, this chapter looks at the contradictory relational effects generated by the trap-cam. Situating the camera in relation to the research institute's effort at cultivating care for, and sustainable fishing of, the Norwegian lobster stock, the chapter demonstrates how the underwater trap-cam allows for a form of digital intimacy with lobsters in a way that other human–lobster encounters rarely enable.[5] The trap-cam thus contributes to fostering a form of conservation based on nurturing near and intimate more-than-human relations through close observation, curiosity, and playfulness.[6] As such, the trap-cam opens a digital contact zone where both humans and lobsters can become what Donna Haraway terms 'response-able' to each other.[7]

However, different from many other camera traps that tend to capture animals in the wild, the fact that the lobster trap-cam actually films the entrapment of lobsters complicates the assumed relation between response-ability and care. As I demonstrate in this chapter, the response-ability produced by the digital mediation of underwater ecologies does not necessarily and unequivocally translate into conservational affectivity and intimate care relations. It may also coincide with and be conducive to generating relations of instrumentalisation and extraction.[8] Aligning with work on digital human–animal relations that sees digitisation as a material, affective, and pluralistic process with no inherent relational effects,[9] the chapter argues that the trap-cam can be understood as a digital entanglement of humans, lobsters, and traps that is shot through with paradoxes of instrumentalisation/care and distance/intimacy. The relational outcomes of digitised human–animal relations are therefore uncertain and contextually variegated.

### Care, instrumentality, and digital encounters in the Anthropocene

The 'lobster trap live' livestream is part of a wider trend of increasing digitisation of human–animal relations. The availability and affordability of webcameras, GoPros, trail cameras, nest cameras, and a range of other digital devices have enabled unprecedented real-time glimpses into the worlds of other animals.[10] While allowing for new forms of proximity with non-human others, the relational outcome of such encounters with 'digital animals' is,[11] however, uncertain. Digitisation may be seen to generate human–animal relations in ways that detach them from real face-to-face encounters,[12] and which thus actually provide, despite the apparent proximity, a disembodied form of encounter. As Ratté puts it, the remote modes of envisioning nature that camera traps provide may actually represent an expansion of human reach into nature while at the same time actually obscuring the human figure and life more generally.[13] While useful for thinking critically about the role of digitisation in the instrumentalisation and objectification of animals, these approaches have tended to see the distance and disembodied nature of such encounters as inimical to fostering relations of care and conservation that many of the digital animals are often in desperate need of.

Others, however, have pointed out that digital encounters with animals are actually far from inadequate simulations of real human–nature relations.[14] Jessica McLean argues that digitised human–nature relations, while often denigrated and seen as inferior to relations in the 'real' world, could actually be understood as 'more-than-real' as they contribute to producing and shaping socio-natural worlds through the affective environmental relations they engender – relations that may foster care and other forms of digital intimacy.[15] Ike Kamphof also suggests that webcams have the potential for digitally enabling species companionship and for providing online affective and ethical spaces where digital intimacy appears as an incentive to care.[16] Similarly, Adam Fish argues that drones used for monitoring fur seals and getting samples from blue whale exhalations can be understood as a tool for intimate, interspecies sensing[17] as they afford 'data intimacy' between pilots and their research subjects.[18] In their study of digital encounters with animals through livestreamed encounters with sanctuary farm animals, dogs in the Chornobyl Exclusion Zone, and bird nestcams during COVID-19 quarantines, Jonathon Turnbull, Adam Searle, and William M. Adams point out that such digital face-to-face encounters opened up a space for dialogue,[19] encouraging compassion and care for animals as well as providing a welcoming invitation to viewers into an alternative atmosphere much appreciated during a difficult time.[20]

In many of these contributions, it is the proximity provided by camera traps that is held as key to fostering interspecies intimacy and care. This is where digital mediations may contribute to untying the evident near-sightedness of embodied ethics. Camera traps may allow for what Beth Greenhough and Emma Roe call 'somatic sensibilities' to develop despite existing distances between animals and human watchers.[21] As such, camera traps may open up a space for interspecies response-ability by providing the possibility for visually mediated care at a distance.

However, while these approaches may alert us to the ways in which camera traps enable encounters with non-human life in ways that foster interspecies response-ability, other studies of human–animal relations show us that it is far from certain that neither response-ability nor proximity translate unequivocally into relations of care. Neither is the apparent distinction between instrumentalisation and care, and the association between proximity and intimacy, so straightforward. As Eva Haifa Giraud and Greg Hollin demonstrate in their study of the breeding of beagles for experimental science,[22] care and affectively charged encounters between human caretakers and dogs were vital not for combatting instrumentalisation but for their crucial role in instrumentalising the dogs as experimental animals. Charlotte Chambers further reminds us that the proximity between birds and birdwatchers provided by digital visual encounters through CCTV may in fact be deceptive since it actually operates upon a hyper-separation between seer and seen that serves to normalise a vision of humanity as inherently separate from wildlife.[23] CCTV-assisted birdwatching thus generates contradictory relational outcomes. It brings nature and humans into proximity but does not necessarily entail intimacy. Elizabeth Johnson's research on laboratory lobsters also shows that extending the temporal scope of human–animal encounters beyond the present allows for a variety of multispecies relations – care, instrumental, or others – to emerge in the encounter itself, requiring a situational attentiveness to the variegated constellations of relations that are operative within them.[24] It is perhaps the potentialities of such constellations that make digital encounters with animals so powerful, enabling a congealment of affective forms of care with instrumentalised forms of relations, be it hunting or other forms of often capital-driven extraction.[25]

The digitisation of human–animal relations thus involves a range of paradoxes as it includes relations of both abstraction and intimacy, care and extractive instrumentalisation, proximity and distance. While earlier approaches to digitisation tended towards two different directions, either emphasising its disconnecting effects or its enabling of new forms of human–nature reconciliation, the complexities and paradoxical relational outcomes of camera traps and other forms of digital mediation invite a more nuanced and situational approach. This chapter draws on approaches that emphasise exactly that: the uncertain relational outcome of digitised human–animal encounters. Jonathon Turnbull and colleagues refer to such encounters as digital entanglements, which hold the potential for connecting and disconnecting.[26] Here, digitisation is understood as a material, affective, and pluralistic process with no inherent relational effects.

From this perspective, the lobster trap-cam is perhaps particularly apt for pointing out the ambiguous character of the digitisation of human–animal encounters. For while the lobster trap-camera in many ways allows for a new form of proximity between humans and lobsters, a proximity that does play a part in the research institute's attempt at cultivating relations of care for the lobster stock, the fact that this is not only a camera trap but a *trap camera* indicates that the relational effects at play here go beyond relations of intimacy and care. Although not a unique form of digital mediation of human–animal encounters, the lobster trap-cam is a rare case of a web-camera that actually provides live, visual images of the entrapment of animals while at the same time linking this entrapment to an effort to conserve and care for lobsters, all while serving as a crucial part of the institute's effort at soliciting attention and funding for its research. In the following, I describe how the 'lobster trap live' provides insights into these relational ambiguities as it enables encounters with individual specimens and relations of play while at the same time enrolling these relations in an instrumentalised form of commodification thought to be necessary for the conservation effort to succeed.

## The context of Norwegian lobster fishing and conservation

To understand the effects of the lobster trap-cam on human–lobster relations, we must first take a look at the history of human–lobster relations, including fishing and conservation in Norwegian waters.

Early in the morning on 1 October every year, thousands of people along the southern and western coast of Norway set out in their small boats to release their lobster traps. The opening of the annual three-month lobster season is much anticipated. Many of the fishers plan this for months. They start fishing bait during the summer, use the following months to soak the bait fish in salt, and when October approaches, they meticulously check their lobster traps, ropes, and buoys, making sure that everything is ready for when the season opens. The vast majority of those who fish for lobsters in Norway are recreational fishers, who do it for, as one of my informants put it, 'the magic, that fabulous feeling when you pull the trap, and you spot that mysterious creature emerging from the depth below'. Some professional fishers engage in lobster fishing, but they too admit that they are in the lobster game as much for the excitement as for the money. In fact, lobster catches are so small that the costs do not justify the minor profits produced. Lobster fishing is thus carried out largely as a recreational activity, where the anticipation, the longing for the season to start, the suspense and magical feeling of getting out on the water in the chilly winter mornings, and the fabulous emotions when the trap, after many empty attempts, finally comes up with a lobster inside. One informant even described this feeling as 'orgasmic'. That the 'cardinals of the seas', as lobsters are called, are also closely associated with luxury, adds an important dimension to the experience of lobster fishing.

Furthermore, the lobster stock in Norway is under heavy strain. Never actually recovering from the nineteenth century's heavy overfishing, the

Norwegian lobster stock is still under pressure from fishing by the 30,000 or so registered lobster fishers. Every year, information campaigns by fishing governments and the Institute of Marine Research make publicly known the threatened condition of the Norwegian lobster stock, inadvertently contributing to a sense of urgency and competitiveness among fishers.

Norwegian lobster fishing is also heavily regulated. There are strict limitations as to when lobstering can take place: between 1 October at 8am and New Year. Recently, moreover, several marine protected areas have been established where lobstering is prohibited. The fishing equipment itself is also strictly regulated with rules defining what kinds of traps are permissible, the size of escape vents, and requirements for the name-tagging of buoys and traps. These regulations are also heavily enforced. Every year in the weeks leading up to the lobster season, the Directorate of Fisheries, the Directorate of the Environment, the police, and the coastguard team up and sweep through parts of the coast, hunting for illegal lobster fishing where they confiscate traps not in accordance with regulations while fining their owners.

Strict, detailed regulations and heavy policing are not the only ways that fishery governments attempt to take care of the lobster stock, however. The coast is long, and as the police and coastguards admitted when I followed them on one of these campaigns, it is virtually impossible to control everyone and everywhere. They rely on fishers controlling themselves, of them becoming part of the effort of caring for the lobster stock. The multispecies biopolitics at work in the Norwegian lobster case is thus aiming towards controlling, conserving, and possibly enhancing the country's lobster stock,[27] but is also as much about cultivating a certain self-government by lobster fishers, thus developing new and sustainable ways for humans to live with lobsters.

So, when the Institute of Marine Research started up their trap-cam project, it soon became a central part of their effort to cultivate a sense of care for, and sustainable harvest of, lobsters by engaging fishers in new ways of relating to lobsters. Could it be that through making visible the oceanic world of the lobster, they could cultivate an attitude and practice of lobster care among fishers? The next section examines how the trap-cam provided opportunities for such relations to emerge between humans and lobsters, looking first at the personalisation of lobsters and second at how the trap-cam project became an arena for playful interactions that enacted lobsters and humans as response-able to each other.

## Personalising lobsters

In his affective approach to visual conservation technology, Jamie Lorimer points out that visual encounters with animals may contribute to forging new forms of environmental subjectivity among viewers.[28] He identifies one tendency in the affective politics this creates: sympathy is often engendered through what he calls 'anthropoidentities',[29] that is, the provision of animals with human-like emotions, relations, and life stories. This affords a form of intimacy between human viewers and non-human animals, and often this is further aided by the animal's 'nonhuman charisma'.[30]

One might say that cultivating an attitude of care towards an animal such as a lobster is not a particularly easy task. If only they had large, comforting eyes and soft fur. But they don't, and as Johnson observes,[31] they are often represented as aggressive, cruel, and cannibalistic creatures, which may reinforce the violent logics of bio- and necro-power that cast some lives as sentient while others are rendered killable.[32] For the staff at the research institute, lobsters' non-human charisma was therefore not something they could easily mobilise for drawing attention and promoting relations of care. However, the way the trap-cam project was set up provided the institute with an opportunity to enact lobsters as individual and even personalised individual specimens that viewers could get to know better.

The spatial location of the trap-cam was an important factor for enabling this. The lobster trap was set in the bay right outside the quay of the institute's research station. This made the wiring of the camera easier, but more importantly, the bay provided ample access to lobsters that researchers already had established some kinds of individual relations with. The bay outside the research station is a marine protected area and has been so for many years. It serves as a central underwater laboratory for the institute, and except for research related purposes, no lobster fishing is allowed. The absence of take-outs from the bay's lobster population means that the bay is well stocked, with lobsters being both plentiful and bigger than what most lobster fishers would get in their traps. Moreover, many of the bay's lobsters have been registered, tagged, and given an ID number in the institute's archives.

Several of the lobsters that were caught in the trap-cam were so called 're-visitors' (*gjengangere*), and when the research staff pulled the trap, they could therefore identify them for the viewers by reading their ID tags and telling viewers about the history of the lobster, when it was caught last, how much it had grown, and so on. For Lene, one of the staff, the recognition that these revisits allowed was part of the trap-cam's virtual encounter value:[33]

> The other day I saw this lobster that was tagged for the first time in 2007 and then it was 20cm, and then it was caught in 2017 and it was 39cm. It's so cool to see lobsters that we catch again and again and again, and you can see how they grow.

In some cases, the behaviour of the lobsters afforded increased individualisation and personalisation. When Sebastian, another researcher at the centre, pulled the trap one morning, he noticed that the acrylic roof sheet had been broken, leaving the trap fully open for lobsters to escape. To Sebastian's surprise, one lobster still sat in the trap: 'Despite the trap being fully open, one lobster just sat there. It was an acquaintance from yesterday. It was the lobster tagged LR1135 that just sat there patiently and waited for me'. Another lobster made its appearance several times and amazed both staff and viewers with its ability to move in and out of the trap in an unusual way. On the camera website viewers could watch the trapped lobster crawling up the trap's back wall before flipping its tail out of the entrance and escaping backwards. Lene eventually named the lobster Houdini, after the escape artist.

For the research institute, these digital encounters with individualised lobsters were central to their promotion of care and conservation for the lobsters. What was streamed through the trap-cam and storytelling that Lene and others did on the YouTube channel thus contributed to the provision of lobsters with anthropoidentities by giving them particular personalities and histories. What is particularly interesting here is how the care relations that this individualising storytelling aimed at drew on techno-scientific relations of control and surveillance,[34] comprising a paradoxical congealment of relations of distance/proximity and care/instrumentalisation.[35]

## Intimacy and difference in human–lobster trap-cam play

Another tendency in the affective politics of visual conservation technologies identified by Lorimer is the creation of awe and respect through the presentation of extremes of difference between humans and the portrayed animals.[36] This often takes place by showing their alien ecologies, unfamiliar anatomies, and inhuman behaviours.[37] Contrasting distinctively from the intimacy created by anthropoidentities, such imagery engenders human–non-human difference, which in many wildlife films is mobilised for forging affective responses such as awe and respect. In the lobster trap-cam case, such human–lobster differentiation was entangled with a playful form of interaction. As noted by C. Anne Claus[38] and others,[39] playful observations of non-human lives may be conducive to creating affective nearness where 'reductionist predator-prey roles give way to reciprocal relationships in which the capacity of nonhumans to think and feel is recognised'.[40] In the lobster trap-cam case, the playful relations between viewers and lobsters that the research centre facilitated worked simultaneously with human–lobster differentiations and a curiosity. It was a play that was stimulated by unlearning commonly held assumptions about lobster behaviour.

In the first year that the research centre launched the trap-cam, it was a rather passive thing for the viewers. They could simply watch what was going on in and around the trap. However, staff at the research centre soon began receiving an enormous number of emails and text messages from viewers, and one thing that the audience asked was if they could experiment with different kinds of bait.

Lobsters are known for being omnivorous, but bait that smells strongly is held to be particularly attractive to lobsters. Most recreational fishers use mackerel, a fish that is easily accessible during summer months. The mackerel is soaked in salt and will eventually, after several weeks, produce an incredibly pungent smell that fishers believe the lobster are particularly fond of. But lobsters are also known to eat pretty much everything that smells bad (to humans), and on Facebook lobster fishing groups, discussions abound each season about all kinds of creative suggestions as to what stinky stuff to use as lobster bait.

With the trap-cam becoming increasingly popular, a lot of this creativity spilled over from Facebook and into the trap-cam website. Viewers emailed the research centre, asking them to try all kinds of bait: bananas, rotten chicken legs, out-of-date sausages, and dog food. The staff responded, put these food items into the trap, and allowed the viewers to watch what happened. Viewers could follow this live, or they could watch short YouTube clips posted on the website the next day where the results were described.

While this experimentation was perceived by many viewers as a way to learn more about what attracted lobsters so that they could apply this in their own traps, the experiments also had a significant playful dimension that enacted human–lobster relations quite differently. On the one hand, the bait experiments were an olfactory-enacted differentiation between lobsters and humans. Lobsters would eat all kinds of things human viewers would find inedible. On the other hand, this form of distance between humans and lobsters combined with a form of curiosity and nearness nurtured by relations of reciprocity, perceptual attunement, and response-ability. The bait experimentation became as much about unlearning lobsters in the sense of 'myth-busting' many of the assumptions that fishers have about lobster behaviour as it was about communicating more efficient entrapment techniques. As Lene explained it,

> You know, people have very strong opinions about what's working and what's not in lobster fishing. Here, we have a protected area with an extreme density of lobsters, and if a certain bait doesn't work here, it's completely unnecessary for people to use it elsewhere … When we're doing more scientific work to monitor the stocks, we consistently use frozen mackerel, just fresh frozen mackerel which fish well. But people believe very strongly in really smelly things … and we actually did get a lot of lobsters on sausages, and I did a

proper leftover party once where I threw in some rotten chops and hot dogs, I got a lot of lobsters, so you never know. But it's fun, seeing what we can get lobsters to eat.

In that sense, the trap-cam bait experiments are ways in which the research centre cultivated curiosity about lobsters' food preferences by meeting lobsters as strangers and experimenting with them in ways that disclosed perplexity.

In one case, this playful engagement with lobsters became quite literal as viewers one day suddenly could see a red toy car attached inside the trap. One of the research staff had the car in the office and had thought it might be a good way to experiment with lobsters' ability to differentiate colours. While many lobster fishers believe that lobster traps covered in black nylon rope are the most efficient, some fishers claim that it is actually orange-coloured pots that fish best. The research staff did not take sides in this ongoing debate, but the red toy car appearing in one of the episodes became a way to invite lobsters to respond. As in many of the playful interactions, the staff at the research centre were uncertain about the relational outcome of these interactions, but they encouraged them and saw them as a way in which they could draw attention and make the trap-cam project more fun. 'It is more like a fun way of testing out things, for making it more exciting and to make new things happen. If we run like nineteen days with the same kind of bait, same things over and over again, many people would lose interest', one of the staff explained. The bait experimentation made it fun and exciting, for both the staff and viewers. The sense of intrigue and excitement created by these experiments became another way to create relations of both intimacy and difference between viewers and lobsters.

## Watching wood

The lobster trap-cam is a rare case in digitally mediated wildlife conservation in that its main focus is the entrapment of an animal. However, to understand the full scope of the trap-cam's role as an affective virtual conservational tool, we need to look closer at what exactly the trap-cam films. As paradoxical as it may seem, the trap itself, which is in one way an equipment of predation, actually played a major role in cultivating relations of care between humans and lobsters.

Up until 2019, the trap-camera was attached to the type of trap that most Norwegian lobster fishers use nowadays: a metal trap covered with nylon rope. In 2020, the institute decided to attach the trap-cam to a different kind of trap – one similar to the lobster traps that dominated lobster fishing up until the 1990s.

Traditionally, lobster fishing in Norway was done with wooden traps. They were often homemade, and if someone did not know how to make one themselves, they needed to know someone who did. In the 1990s, however, new metal and nylon types of lobster traps entered the market. They were considerably easier to obtain since one could just buy them at the local fishing gear store, and they were also much more durable. Soon, cheap hardware stores saw the potential and began importing cheap lightweight lobster traps from China. These became very popular, and many people started fishing who had not fished before, thus putting further strain on the already near-threatened lobster stock.

The new traps also posed a considerable risk to the lobster stock beyond the increased fishing effort they led to. The material composition of the traps themselves represented an additional threat to the lobster stock. Many of these cheap traps are so lightweight that they are very easily moved by ocean currents and wind, which can drag them into deeper waters. There they sink, drawing the rope and buoys with them, and thus become lost to fishers. The traps continue to fish, however, entrapping lobster and other marine life, without ever being pulled, and thereby become what is known as ghost traps. This occasionally also happens with the traditional wooden traps, but the material that these are made of eventually disintegrates and thus stops entrapping.

Ghost traps have become a big problem. About 20,000 traps are lost every season, and today ghost trapping has become one of the most central concerns with the increased popularity of lobster fishing in Norway. Several measures have been introduced to prevent ghost fishing, including the requirement for part of the trap to consist of a cotton thread that disintegrates in seawater over a couple of months. The institute has been actively engaged in combating ghost trapping and has been instrumental in attempts to revitalise the use of wooden traps. In 2019, the research institute initiated a wooden trap project, where they compared the efficiency of metal-nylon traps to wooden traps. As part of this attempt to get fishers to see that wooden traps might be just as good, the research centre decided to use a wooden trap for the 2020 trap-cam season.

In 2020, then, the stream was renamed 'the wooden trap live', emphasising the trap's material quality. The institute collaborated with a local wood workshop and made a wooden trap that was bigger than usual and which made it possible for the bay's unusually large lobsters to easily enter. The trap and the attached trap-cam thus allowed for a digital encounter with exceptionally large lobsters being caught not in modern, seemingly more efficient traps, but in traditional wooden lobster traps.

As mentioned, the trap-cam project's 2020 version became closely linked with the institute's facilitation of the sale of subsidised wooden traps.

Equipped with reused ropes and buoys from salvaged ghost traps, the wooded traps were popular among local lobster fishers and soon sold out. Although the institute itself did not benefit commercially from this facilitation, the staff were not strangers to the potential of commodifying the trap-cam's images. For as one of them pointed out, the attention the trap-cam created – the invitations to TV shows and newspaper articles – was crucial in drawing attention to the institute's scientific work. For a research institute whose main source of income is external funding, the 'lobster trap-live' was a way of making funding agencies aware of the situation of the lobster stock and the urgent need for further conservation-related research. Furthermore, the trap-cam attention was seen by the staff as a way in which the institute's scientific results could be enhanced:

> You know, I work on a lot of other projects besides the trap-cam, and then we have to get people to respond to our surveys. We often have to call people up who have not responded to the surveys we send out, and then the link to the lobster-trap live – a positive association, which has made many people more positively inclined. You give people something they can use, and then they become more interested in helping out.

The digital intimacy that the trap-cam on the wooden trap provided thus also had a more pragmatic use for the institute. It provided a particular virtual encounter value that could be mobilised for drawing attention, eliciting funding through both scientific and affective means.[41] In an almost inverted version of what Giraud and Hollin have shown in relation to dog breeding,[42] instrumentalisation and commodification was central for fostering care and affective encounters with lobsters. No funding, no camera, no publicity, no wooden traps.

## Conclusion

Wildlife cameras and other digital image technologies have become commonplace tools for conservation projects around the world. The effects they have on relations between humans and wildlife are not easily predicted. Rather than having inherent relational effects, camera traps seem to have an inherent ambiguity that may turn effects in different directions at the same time.[43]

While camera traps and other digital mediations of wildlife may contribute to further extension of humans' presence into the wild and enable further extraction and instrumentalisation of animals, they may also draw both human and non-human animals together in encounters that may foster relations of companionship and care. The biopolitics of camera traps is therefore something that cannot be elicited from the technology itself but must rather be understood in relation to the heterogeneous assemblages in which they are entangled. In the lobster trap-cam case, the biopolitics consequently affect both lobsters and humans, including both scientists and fishers.

As such, the trap-cam provokes a rethinking of what the entanglement that the camera engenders actually entails and how it relates to care and the promotion of fishing practices informed by conservation ethics. For while the trap-cam can be understood as a digital entanglement of humans, lobsters, traps, baits, chicken legs, sausages, seawater, conservation ethics, fishing practices, research funding schemes, and so on, entanglement and the proximity or intimacy associated with it is not in itself, as Giraud points out, a guarantee for ethical practice. Rather, the uncertain relational outcomes of the trap-cam as a digital entanglement reminds us to pay attention to the 'frictions, foreclosures, and exclusions that play a constitutive role in the composition of lived reality'.[44]

Does it matter whether the trap-cam provides access not only to the lobster's world but to a world that is an *underwater* world? In her attempt to think media through seawater, Melody Jue alerts us to how milieu specificity matters for how we conceptualise mediation.[45] Aligning with Helmreich's 'theory underwater', thinking with the underwater milieu specificity could here entail not merely theorising underwater things such as the trap-cam, but also 'subjecting theory to unfamiliar conditions … seeing how it deforms as it merges with what it seeks to describe'.[46] Thinking through the underwater trap-cam invites a conceptual displacement, an unlearning of what proximity, distance, care, instrumentality, and response-ability are. This invitation, to a milieu that is materially, affectively, and conceptually fluid all at the same time, is also an invitation to explore and play around with the conceptual bait that the trap-cam might actually be.

## Notes

1 See https://hummerteina.hi.no.
2 This chapter is based on fieldwork among Norwegian lobster fishers, marine researchers, and government fishing agencies on and off in the period 2017–2021. An initial draft was presented at the Digital Ecologies workshop (digitally) in March 2021 at the University of Cambridge. Thanks to Jonathon Turnbull, Adam Searle, and Henry Anderson-Elliot for organising.
3 For a similar case concerning webcams filming peregrine nests, see Searle et al., 'The digital peregrine.'
4 Clements et al., 'Can YouTube save the planet?'; Verma et al., 'Microscope and spectacle.'

5  Kamphof, 'Linking animal and human places'; von Essen et al., 'Wildlife in the digital Anthropocene.'
6  Claus, *Drawing the Sea Near*; Lorimer, *Wildlife in the Anthropocene*.
7  Haraway, *When Species Meet*.
8  Giraud and Hollin, 'Care, laboratory beagles and affective utopia'; Johnson, 'Of lobsters, laboratories, and war'; van Dooren, *Flight Ways*.
9  Turnbull et al., 'Digital ecologies'; von Essen et al., 'Wildlife in the digital Anthropocene.'
10 Turnbull et al., 'Digital ecologies'; Turnbull et al., 'Quarantine encounters with digital animals.'
11 Adams, 'Digital animals.'
12 Virilio, 'The visual crash.'
13 Ratté, '(Un)seen seas.'
14 Jørgensen, 'The armchair traveler's guide.'
15 McLean, *Changing Digital Geographies*.
16 Kamphof, 'Linking animal and human places'; Kamphof, 'Webcams to save nature.'
17 Fish, 'Saildrones and snotbots in the blue Anthropocene.'
18 Calvillo and Garnett, 'Data intimacies.'
19 Turnbull et al., 'Quarantine encounters with digital animals.'
20 Lorimer et al., 'Animals' atmospheres.'
21 Greenhough and Roe, 'Ethics, space, and somatic sensibilities.'
22 Giraud and Hollin, 'Care, laboratory beagles and affective utopia.'
23 Chambers, ' "Well its remote, I suppose, innit?" '
24 Johnson, 'Of lobsters, laboratories, and war.'
25 Büscher, 'Nature 2.0'; Verma et al., 'Microscope and spectacle.'
26 Turnbull et al., 'Digital ecologies.'
27 Pandian, 'Pastoral power in the postcolony'; Porter, 'Bird flu biopower.'
28 Lorimer, *Wildlife in the Anthropocene*.
29 Ibid., p. 137.
30 Ibid., p. 39.
31 Johnson, 'Of lobsters, laboratories, and war.'
32 Wolf, *Before the Law*.
33 Barua, 'Lively commodities and encounter value.'
34 van Dooren, *Flight Ways*; Fish, 'Saildrones and snotbots in the blue Anthropocene.'
35 von Essen et al., 'Wildlife in the digital Anthropocene.'
36 Lorimer, *Wildlife in the Anthropocene*.
37 Ibid., p. 132.
38 Claus, *Drawing the Sea Near*.
39 E.g. Raffles, *Insectopedia*.
40 Claus, *Drawing the Sea Near*, p. 13.
41 Verma et al., 'Microscope and spectacle.'
42 Giraud and Hollin, 'Care, laboratory beagles and affective utopia.'
43 von Essen et al., 'Wildlife in the digital Anthropocene'; Turnbull et al., 'Digital ecologies.'

44 Giraud, *What Comes After Entanglement?*, p. 3.
45 Jue, *Wild Blue Media*.
46 Helmreich, *Sounding the Limits of Life*, p. 186.

## Bibliography

Adams, B. 2020. Digital animals. *The Philosopher*, 108(1). www.thephilosopher1923.org/post/digital-animals.

Barua, M. 2016. Lively commodities and encounter value. *Environment and Planning D: Society and Space*, 34(4): 725–744.

Büscher, B. 2016. Nature 2.0: Exploring and theorizing the links between new media and nature conservation. *New Media & Society*, 18(5): 726–743.

Calvillo, N. and Garnett, E. 2019. Data intimacies: Building infrastructures for intensified embodied encounters with air pollution. *Sociological Review*, 67(2): 340–356.

Chambers, C. 2007. "Well its remote, I suppose, innit?" The relational politics of bird-watching through the CCTV lens. *Scottish Geographical Journal*, 123(2): 122–134.

Claus, C.A. 2020. *Drawing the Sea Near: Satoumi Coral Reef Conservation in Okinawa*. Minneapolis, MN: University of Minnesota Press.

Clements, R., Bickford, D., and Lohman, D.J. 2007. Can YouTube Save the Planet? *Scientist*, 21(9): 26.

Fish, A. 2022. Saildrones and snotbots in the blue Anthropocene: Sensing technologies, multispecies intimacies, and scientific storying. *Environment and Planning D: Society & Space*, 40(5): 862–880.

Giraud, E.H. 2019. *What Comes after Entanglement? Activism, Anthropocentrism, and an Ethics of Exclusion*. Durham, NC: Duke University Press.

Giraud, E.H. and Hollin, G. 2016. Care, laboratory beagles and affective utopia. *Theory, Culture & Society*, 33(4): 27–49.

Greenhough, B. and Roe, E. 2011. Ethics, space, and somatic sensibilities: Comparing relationships between scientific researchers and their human and animal experimental subjects. *Environment and Planning D: Society & Space*, 29(1): 47–66.

Haraway, D. 2008. *When Species Meet*. Minnesota, MN: University of Minnesota Press.

Helmreich, S. 2015. *Sounding the Limits of Life: Essays in the Anthropology of Biology and Beyond*. Princeton, NJ: Princeton University Press.

Johnson, E. 2015. Of lobsters, laboratories, and war: Animal studies and the temporality of more-than-human encounters. *Environment and Planning D: Society & Space*, 33(2): 296–313.

Jue, M. 2020. *Wild Blue Media: Thinking through Seawater*. Durham, NC: Duke University Press.

Jørgensen, F.A. 2014. The armchair traveler's guide to digital environmental humanities. *Environmental Humanities*, 4(1): 95–112.

Kamphof, I. 2011. Webcams to save nature: Online space as affective and ethical space. *Foundations of Science*, 16(2): 259–274.

Kamphof, I. 2013. Linking animal and human places: The potential of webcams for species companionship. *Animal Studies Journal*, 2(1): 82–102.

Lorimer, J. 2015. *Wildlife in the Anthropocene: Conservation after Nature.* Minneapolis, MN: University of Minnesota Press.

Lorimer, J., Hodgetts, T., and Barua, M. 2019. Animals' atmospheres. *Progress in Human Geography*, 43(1): 26–45.

McLean, J. 2020. *Changing Digital Geographies.* London: Palgrave Macmillan.

Pandian, A. 2008. Pastoral power in the postcolony: On the biopolitics of the criminal animal in South India. *Cultural Anthropology*, 23(1): 85–117.

Porter, N. 2013. Bird flu biopower: Strategies for multispecies coexistence in Viet Nam. *American Ethnologist*, 40(1): 132–148.

Raffles, H. 2010. *Insectopedia.* New York: Pantheon.

Ratté, S. 2019. (Un)seen seas: Technological mediation, oceanic imaginaries, and future depths. *Environment and Society*, 10(1): 141–157.

Searle, A., Turnbull, J., and Adams, W.M. 2023. The digital peregrine: A technonatural history of a cosmopolitan raptor. *Transactions of the Institute of British Geographers*, 48(1): 195–212.

Turnbull, J., Searle, A., and Adams, W.M. 2020. Quarantine encounters with digital animals: More-than-human geographies of lockdown life. *Journal of Environmental Media*, 1(Supplement): 6.1–6.10.

Turnbull, J., Searle, A., Hartman Davies, O., Dodsworth, J., Chasseray-Peraldi, P., von Essen, E., and Anderson-Elliott, H. 2023. Digital ecologies: Materialities, encounters, governance. *Progress in Environmental Geography*, 2(1–2): 3–32.

van Dooren, T. 2014. *Flight Ways: Life and Loss at the Edge of Extinction.* New York: Columbia University Press.

Verma, A., van der Wal, R., and Fischer, A. 2015. Microscope and spectacle: On the complexities of using new visual technologies to communicate about wildlife conservation. *Ambio*, 44(Supplement 4): 648–660.

Virilio, P. 2002. The visual crash. In T. Levin, U. Frohne, and P. Weibel (Eds.) *Ctrl [Space]: Rhetorics of Surveillance from Bentham to Big Brother* (pp. 108–113). Karlsruhe: ZKM.

von Essen, E., Turnbull, J., Searle, A., Jørgensen, F.A., Hofmeester, T., and van der Wal, R. 2023. Wildlife in the digital Anthropocene: Examining human-animal relations through surveillance technologies. *Environment and Planning E: Nature and Space*, 6(1): 679–699.

Wolf, C. 2013. *Before the Law: Humans and Other Animals in a Biopolitical Frame.* Chicago, IL: University of Chicago Press.

# 4

## *Our Chicken Life*: byproductive labour in the digital flock

*Catherine Oliver*

### Introduction

In places across the world, if you fall quiet and listen – often not even very hard – you might hear the call of a cockerel at dawn or the bak-bak-baaak song of a hen laying. Despite there being around 26 billion chickens alive on the planet at any one time, this noise is probably not as familiar as it once was. That's where *Our Chicken Life* comes in. With just a few clicks, a fifteen-camera, twenty-four-hour livestream of a flock of seventy chickens in Utah on Twitch allows viewers to hang out with chickens and participate in their care. For a small fee, subscribers can feed 'M&Ms' (mealworms and millet) to chickens, mealworms flying down a chute next to one of the fifteen cameras with a quick command. These cameras are controlled by subscribers, who can focus on different events and individuals around the barnyard.

It's spring in Utah, and the hens have been setting their eggs for weeks. Chicks are finally beginning to hatch. Utah is seven hours behind England. My working day typically runs from 8am to 4pm, meaning that for the first seven hours or so, the chickens at *Our Chicken Life* are asleep. At around 3pm, when my calls have finished, I log into the stream and watch the hens wake up, potter around, and mingle with the rabbits and ducks. Farmer Spence faithfully puts out their food and refreshes their water. A few weeks later, the camera pans to Ada hatching her last chick. In March, broody hen Ada began the incubation of four eggs, placed under her by Spence, the farmer and owner of *Our Chicken Life*. Peeps emerge from under Ada. Her body lifts and falls as she guides the chick out, clucking along with their peeps. Their sibling, born a day earlier, now fluffy and bright-eyed, pokes out to watch the commotion. Ada looks down as a black chick emerges from underneath her, wet and shiny.

*Our Chicken Life* was set up in 2018 by Farmer Spence. Spence has kept a flock of chickens since 2015 and thought that other people might enjoy watching the chickens and interacting with them. With 71,000 followers on Twitch in 2021 and a growing YouTube platform, Spence was not wrong. During the pandemic, the livestream grew at a remarkable pace, with these encounters being part of what Turnbull, Searle, and Adams understood as novel and affective human–animal relations produced by lockdown.[1] It persists in popularity with 91,000 followers on Twitch, and a doubling in YouTube followers at the time of writing. On average, Twitch streamers tune in for forty minutes, indicating an engaged following rather than fleeting encounters.

*Our Chicken Life* allows subscribers to interact via the Twitch chat, primarily through 'feeding' chickens. Subscribers can feed the chickens once per day by posting word commands like 'food' and 'feed', 'noms', 'dindins', 'munchies', or 'chow'. When a subscriber enters one of these commands, 'M&Ms' drop from a chute next to a camera, and the chickens rush towards it. Subscribers can also use commands to switch camera views 24/7, including 'inhouse', 'coop', 'nest', and 'shade', each of which correlates to a space. The feeder is filled once a day and once empty, a message is posted in the chat. This regulates consumption as part of a healthy balanced diet. *Our Chicken Life* presents a novel form of recurrent encounter that produces a digital community of 'carers', supporting the chickens' costs while also controlling their daily lives.

*Our Chicken Life* is a unique case study for digital ecologies where non-human labour, care, and control intermingle with the exploitation of centuries of galline knowledge to find new frontiers of value extraction. In this chapter, I explore the communing of care and control through digital encounters, contending that this galline digital ecology relies on the *byproductive labour* of chickens. Ultimately, I argue that this is a new way of eking capital from non-human bodies, theorising these encounters within ideas of non-human labour, consumption, and commodity in the Anthropocene, with an emblematic Anthropocene species.[2] This builds on digital ecologies' explorations of encounters overlapping with other chapters in this book like Remme's 'relational ambiguities' with individual lobsters who are simultaneously enrolled in commodification; and Adams et al.'s assertion that digital encounters can 'expand the number and diversity of people who can observe wild animals from [a] relatively narrow circle', albeit with chickens not being the 'wild' animals of concern to them.[3]

In this chapter, I look at the livestream in relation to digital ecologies literature and more broadly within more-than-human encounters. Then, I focus on the behaviours and relationships of the chickens; human interactions with the platform and the flock; and *byproductive* labour in the digital flock. I build on Whitney's concept of byproductive labour as both concept and tool, applying it to the role of the digital flock in metabolising waste affects and affective byproducts.[4] I ask how this novel form of encounter builds on and expands previous knowledge about chickens. To quote Haraway:[5] follow the chicken and find the world; following the digital flock, I look at new worlds being created that bring together chickens, technology, and human observers in a unique 'digital ecology'.

## The digital flock

Alexander and Kerr claimed early in the pandemic that two kinds of entertainment nature livestreams had emerged: 24/7 cameras in cages and daily programmed events like feedings.[6] The first resembles 'a nature film in which humans are nowhere to be seen', while the second 'emphasizes the interdependence of humans and animals'.[7] *Our Chicken Life* collapses these categories: there is a constant livestream and Farmer Spence is sometimes on camera, but the real draw is the ability for watchers to 'feed' the chickens themselves. Koch and Miles contend that digital technology changes the possibilities and challenges of encounters with strangers, making them 'a matter of choice as much as chance', and it is certainly under these circumstances that the digital flock has coalesced.[8] The chicken, emblem of the Anthropocene and symbol of capitalist food production, is not, usually, encountered by chance *or* choice in the non-digital realm.

It isn't simply the novelty of the platform that makes *Our Chicken Life* a compelling case study: it is that this form of encounter is with *chickens* – one of the most maligned species on earth, and quite literally the stratigraphic writing of the Anthropocene.[9] Chickens, while the most populous bird on earth, are perhaps the least 'natural' of animals; in 1975, Smith and Daniels argued that 'feathered bipeds bearing a superficial resemblance to the chicken, will continue to exist under the auspices of our technological society, but, and one must insist on this, *they will not be chickens and their eggs will not be eggs*'.[10] In the 50 years since, chickens have continued to morph into creatures that are now forced to grow to twice the size of their 1930s counterparts in half the time.[11]

The chicken is no longer a 'natural' bird and, perhaps, hasn't been since the massification of their labour with the development of egg incubation over 2,000 years ago.[12] By the end of World War 2, the 'tweaking' of chickens reached new heights with the *Chicken of Tomorrow* contest that saw the birth of the industrial hybrid chicken found across the world today. The contest, co-hosted by the US Department for Agriculture and A&P stores, wanted to create a chicken that could feed a growing population: a hybrid bird good for both egg-laying and meat. The contest created new biological conditions for chickens, ushering in a new era of labour and enclosure. This contest set in motion events that would lead to the global chicken population having a mass greater than all other birds on earth combined, and to chickens being the most numerous terrestrial bird on the planet. The chicken is not just a symbol of the *Capitalocene*,[13] but 'vividly symbolize[s] the transformation of the biosphere to fit evolving human consumption patterns'.[14]

The chicken – as both an industrial labourer and commodity – does not fit easily with ideas of 'nature' often explored in digital ecologies and more-than-human studies. Büscher contends that 'online trends influence the politics and political economy of conservation, namely, how they stimulate *and* complicate the commodification of biodiversity, ecosystems and landscapes, and how they help to reimagine ideas, ideals and experiences of ('pristine') nature'.[15] In the political economy of neoliberal capitalism, new ways are always being realised to eke out value and labour from 'nature'. However, the chicken is not a 'natural animal', but rather an Anthropocene animal, produced by and for humans. Where there are arguments for and against virtual commodification of 'nature', how and why does this matter for the chicken? In the digital flock, traditional galline labour – producing meat or eggs – takes a back seat to new kinds of labour that rely on chickens performing 'natural' behaviours; on being willing to interact with the cameras; and on *byproductive* labour – maintaining positive affective atmospheres and metabolising 'waste' affects.

## Notes on methods

It was a chance conversation that initially led me to *Our Chicken Life*. A colleague mentioned the livestream, telling me how their friend had become obsessed with this quirky flock of chickens in Utah. Immediately after that call, I headed over to Twitch. I was hooked. Every day, I would open the stream, soft clucks accompanying my lonely pandemic life. Contextualising my relationship with *Our Chicken Life* is my longer connection with my own small flock. In 2017, my mum and I had rehomed six ex-commercial hens. But, as ex-commercial hens, they didn't live very long. In 2020, when I was a hundred miles away and locked down, the last two hens died. I didn't get to say goodbye, but I deeply felt their absence. *Our Chicken Life* helped me to cope with their loss, offering a new kind of digital network through which I could connect with birds like the ones I loved.

As I watched and listened to the birds, I started to notice that I was being moved by these chickens, building a relationship with them through recurrent encounters. This assemblage of birds, algorithms, screens, camera, and humans made the digital a place of emotionality and connection. While I didn't subscribe to the channel, and therefore didn't comment or interact directly with the flock, I did get to participate in the atmospheres of excitement as birds rushed to scoff mealworms released when someone typed 'nomnoms'. When I was in the Twitch stream, I began to write what I was experiencing. These observations form the basis of this chapter. However, because I could not be watching a livestream 24/7, I have also been watching *Our Chicken Life*'s weekly compilation videos that provide a showreel of the highlights of activity.

## Galline behaviours and relationships

Since 1948, the chicken has transformed. The 50 billion chickens slaughtered annually for meat, and the billions more laying eggs, are for the most part kept in industrial farms. There, 'they just have to *be*, in an existential void, until we kill them'.[16] In Britain, the space given to each chicken in this system is 20×20cm for smaller bantams, and 30×30cm for larger birds. This is equivalent, approximately, to a sheet of standard printer paper. In one square metre, there can be between eleven and twenty-five birds. The reason that I include this detail is that this is how *most* chickens are living; in many cases welfare standards are lower. In these enclosures, chickens are denied the ability to perform their natural behaviours. There is no room to dust bathe, forage, or socialise and the close quarters can lead to conflict as the hens do try to find some distance from one another.[17] Chicken's alienation from their natural behaviours is not just through enclosure; chickens also have their annual laying cycles and moulting strictly controlled. Controlling and limiting these natural behaviours has been essential to the explosion of chicken farming.

At *Our Chicken Life*, the flock live in relative freedom, roaming a large space and living in more 'natural' set-ups than in commercial farms, with cockerels and hens living together, along with other ducks and sheep. I was fascinated with how the very behaviours industrial farming has sought to eradicate were being *encouraged* in part because this is what subscribers are here to see. In the opening encounter of this chapter, as I watched, a subscriber pans the camera to zoom in on Ada hatching her last chick. Embryos develop in eggs once the hen begins sitting on them, meaning that a clutch laid over a period of a week or longer will all develop and hatch together. During the incubation, hens turn eggs to ensure the embryo doesn't get stuck to the shell membrane, that the gases move around, and a steady temperature is maintained. A day or so before they are ready to hatch, a chick begins to peep in the shell, establishing 'a barely audible "communications network"' between chicks and mother.[18] The chick then saws its way out with its egg tooth; the hen does not break the egg but remains sat on her clutch as each chick breaks slowly from their shell.

Ada guides her chick out, clucking along with their peeps. She looks down as a black chick emerges from underneath her, wet and shiny. In the weeks that follow, we watch Ada raise her chicks surrounded by the rest of the flock, to applause and excitement from subscribers. This set-up, of young joining a flock, is unusual for most of the billions of chickens on the planet today. These 'natural' individual and social galline behaviours is exactly what subscribers are paying for.

Subscribers go on a journey with the flock and become invested in their care and wellbeing. This is evident from the hatching season, as we follow along from laying to setting to hatching, cheering them on through the chat, throwing treats through the camera as sustenance. One subscriber posts: '*It is nice to see Ada finally getting at least a little bit of sleep*' and another replies: '*I bet it's difficult when little ones keep wiggling under her*'. This sanitised online space transforms often physically and emotionally gruelling chicken care into something as easy as paying a small monthly fee and clicking a few buttons.[19] But this online platform is not just about the chickens, it's also about building identities and community around them, and encouraging particular kinds of encounter between human and chicken that subvert the usual relation, mediated through capital and commodification. In a world where chickens are usually hidden away, it's revealing that these natural behaviours entice an audience who reward pecking, crowing, dustbathing, preening, and seeing chickens live in a flock.

## Interacting with the digital flock

In *The Emancipated Spectator*, Rancière argues that the theatre is 'the place where an action is taken to its conclusion by bodies in motion in front of living bodies to be mobilized. The latter might have relinquished their power. But this power is revived, reactivated in the performance of the former'.[20] Might it be possible to also conceptualise the digital flock and their spectators in this kind of relationship? In doing so, the chickens shift from pixels and images to creative producers. The galline body becomes a *productive* one, which creates affective (and economic) value through its relationship with the camera and the audience beyond. This section therefore looks at the role of 'care' in these digital encounters with this flock, ultimately questioning what, exactly, this encounter is *doing* in Our Chicken Life – for both chickens and humans.

Guéry and Deleule look to the 'productive body' to think about identity.[21] They insist that 'animal bodies are referred to their nature as living beings, not as producers' and that 'being productive is not the property of whoever transforms, or informs, a previously furnished material ... In truth, being productive is not the property of anyone or anything, whereas products are the *property* of whoever appropriates them'.[22] Instead of insisting upon being *producers*, they look to *productivity* to understand bodies that have already *become*. It is thus important in thinking about the productive bodies of the digital flock in *specificity*. It is because they are chickens – these chickens – that this relationship is produced with the audience.

For its founder, the intention of *Our Chicken Life* doesn't offer a unidirectional gaze of the digital chicken on the human screen, but rather a curated intersubjective encounter with chickens; as he explains:

> The main feature of *Our Chicken Life* is cheering Bits to send M&Ms (mealworms and millet) to the chickens, getting them running to the camera. I've worked hard to shift control of the stream from me to the viewers. There are over fifteen cameras which can be displayed in one of four windows on the stream page and can be changed by using chat commands.[23]

This shift towards collectivity in the livestream is important, relying on a series of human and non-human interactions, digital and visceral, to commune the care of chickens. Subscribers become a digital community of 'carers', supporting the chickens' costs through their monthly fee while also controlling parts of their daily lives. For Giraud and Hollin, 'care is precisely what enables the instrumentalization of life, in being used to gain knowledge about entities that can be exploited for the purpose of control'.[24] Care has dominated recent debates in more-than-human geographies, animal studies, and multispecies ethnography: what does it *mean* to care, what are care's *contours*, can we care and still *kill*?

Caring beyond the human is often argued to go together with violence; van Dooren has gone so far as to think about regimes of violent care, arguing that 'caring is not achieved through abstract well-wishing, but is an embodied and often fraught, complex, and compromised practice'.[25] This raises questions not only over the appropriateness of definitions of care in scientific research on animals,[26] but also in ethnographic[27] and non-invasive research,[28] recognising animals not just as participants but co-producers of knowledge. As Ginn has argued of the 'relational diagnostic' of more-than-human ontology, it 'ignore[s] the non-relational, what may not be vital, and what may precede or be obscured by existing relations ... a focus on connectivity, vitality and belonging obscures as much as it reveals ... [it] has a constitutive violence – it is also an exclusion'.[29]

Thinking about exclusion, Giraud explores how caring can be dismissed when it is caring in the wrong way; when certain 'groups' caring stance is (for instance) perceived as angry or so focused on caring abstractly about a particular cause that it is insufficiently caring toward other interlocutors'.[30] In the digital flock, it at first appears that the stakes are low: who, after all, could object to the livestreaming of animals who are, in a sense, *cared for*? The chat moves on to discuss whether it is too cold for the chickens to be running across to the 'M&Ms' chute. Then, subscribers collectively discuss their release strategy for the day: '*I'd like to wait until it's a bit warmer, make sure everyone has the chance to eat, not just the brave few*'. These discussions are commonplace in the chat: the chicken care is a negotiation, wanting to make sure as many subscribers get to see the chickens rush for mealworms, but also that they get to see as many chickens as possible.

Chickens and humans have a history stretching back 8,000 years, but since the beginning of the twentieth century, as egg and meat production scaled up, knowledge about chickens has exploded,[31] while becoming known to far fewer people. In addition to their biology, intimate knowledge of chicken behaviour was essential to scaling up meat and egg production. The selective breeding of chickens for food dates to at least the sixteenth century but it was the nineteenth century that saw meat production take over the globe.[32] With the rise of chicken eating came a burgeoning of knowledge about chickens, albeit through a lens of exploitation. As chicken consumption scaled up, selection for specific traits has led to significant reductions in effective population size and overall genetic diversity of chickens. As chicken and egg production scaled up, their behaviour and environments became more strictly controlled. To do this, a significant and intimate knowledge of genetic, nutritional, and ethological traits was needed.[33] One lineage, of the less violent kind, has led here, to a farm in Utah, where chickens are conscripted to perform for the camera as a far-flung human audience watches on.

When a spectator 'noms' into the chat and mealworms topple down the chute, this can be conceptualised as communing the care of the chickens – participating through an intricate series of cameras, algorithms, and mechanics in their maintenance, as described on their website: 'many cams are utilized to give our twitch viewers as many viewing options as possible'. When a command is typed into the chat, as detailed in the introduction to this chapter, a signal is sent to a chute to open and release some treat foods into the coop. A camera above the chute can then be controlled by subscribers. In the chat, the audience comment on the chickens: how they look, their behaviours, cooing when treats are released as chickens run towards the camera. The rewards are released to attract chickens towards the camera, to coerce them into encounters, but for the human audience, control or experimentation doesn't consciously seem to come into it. The sense is one of commensality or beneficence: simply participating in communal care. As Sutton has critiqued there is an inherent violence in taming and tempering animals, where 'unequal relations manifest in the "creation" of pets – purposive breeding, coercive training and physical restriction and adornment'.[34] The presence of cameras and interaction open this space while simultaneously shallowing it, centring encounters to produce anthropocentric value.

However, the digital flock is also a new frontier of labour, extracting from chickens the metabolisation of affects through *byproductive* labour, exacerbated by a turn to 'nature' as curative during a pandemic that saw our abilities to engage with the other-than-human world constricted.

## Byproductive labour

*Our Chicken Life* has seen a huge surge in both viewers and paid subscribers during and since the pandemic. While Farmer Spence does not track data on why people are watching or subscribing, the growing popularity of the livestream is related to the temporalities and isolation of lockdowns,[35] and a trend in keeping chickens.[36] Walton engages critically – but seriously – with the connection between (mental and physical) health and nature, including digital nature, by asking if some of the places we seek nature in the future might be entirely virtual.[37] There are, Walton argues, 'ways of experiencing nature from a distance that are just as valid, and maybe more powerful too'.[38] In February 2022, this 'entirely virtual' future was brought to the fore with the WWF releasing 'NFAs' – *non-fungible animals* – to 'raise awareness and funds for the conservation of ten endangered species'.[39] With virtual chickens, this conservation angle is absent but a connection with a *simpler* way of life remains. Through the screen, caring for chickens becomes a digital encounter of and with animal care, where the stakes are passed off onto someone else. If you don't log in for a day to feed treats, there aren't repercussions; the relationship is an optional, non-essential one.

The virtual flock livestream isn't simply a representation of the other-than-human world; there is a real connection between the spectators and the chickens. People are invested in the chickens and come back each day to check in with them. There is a kind of reciprocal relationship, albeit one that is mediated through cameras and in which one species is watched without being able to look back. In the surge of subscribers and viewers during the pandemic, *Our Chicken Life* offered something unique in the digital encounter: the ability to interact. The livestream became somewhere that people could go to put their worries aside and become absorbed in this galline ecology – and in that absorption, pass their excessive affects onto the chickens through the screen by directing their anxieties onto the digital flock. The inability for the chickens to look back – the removal of *their* power to interact – is essential to this encounter.

On the livestream, the chickens perform a *byproductive* labour of affect disposal and affect accumulation. Whitney's 'byproductive labour'[40] builds on ideas of emotional[41] and affective labour,[42] arguing that this is 'not only the work of producing affects for others to consume or the reproductive work that rejuvenates and sustains labor power and social life, but also the work of *metabolizing waste affects and affective byproducts*'.[43] A framework of byproductive labour is aligned with the literal galline labour producing eggs, but one that can also aid in conceptualising these unique Nature 2.0 ecologies that have *nothing* to do with conservation or wildlife. As the emblematic Anthropocene animal worker, the chicken is the antithesis of the usual animal subjects of online environmental spaces.[44]

'Byproductive labour' not only produces affects for others to consume and does the reproductive work of maintaining positive affective atmospheres, but also metabolises 'waste' affects and affective byproducts. The chicken as a byproductive labourer metabolises waste or excess affects and becomes a receptacle for the disposal of affects and emotions,[45] consuming affective waste as the chickens take affects out of circulation. Outside of Whitney's coining of the term, 'byproductive labour' has yet to emerge as a common concept with notable exceptions in feminist and cultural studies. For example, Meegaswatta defines byproductive labour as 'a capitalist patriarchal practice that underpins the creation and perpetuation of female subordination'.[46] Meanwhile, Táíwò uses the byproductive labour of metabolisation to theorise emotional compression and the priority of non-emotionality in patriarchal masculinity.[47] Veldstra pushes back against byproductive labour as 'the shadow side' of productive labour, arguing byproduction is production under neoliberal capitalism.[48] Nonetheless, outside of Whitney's original theorisation, the promise of byproductive labour as a theoretical contribution has largely been unexplored. In the digital flock, byproductive labour finds a new mode of more-than-human elaboration.

The byproductive labour of these chickens intensified as *Our Chicken Life*'s popularity soared during the pandemic, opening and complicating questions of labour, circulation, and commodification through a byproductive lens. In the digital flock, a communing of control and care and conscription of labour exist, uneasily, side by side. The digital flock's conscription in byproductive labour might also be understood as an exploitation of human knowledge about chickens to shape their environments to accommodate human pleasure. The negotiation of care and control through paying to 'treat' the chickens while offering constant insight into their lives demands questions are raised over whether the chickens' observability is a condition of their thriving. Without the camera, (how) would these chickens exist?

Logging in to watch the chickens peck, bathe, and sleep, my anxiety is absorbed through the screen; when a subscriber releases pellets for the chickens, their squawks and excitement break my ruminations of hopelessness. As the chickens scoff their treats, with them goes my own affective waste that otherwise overwhelms the locked-down isolation of my bedroom.

The digital flock are enlisted into byproductive affect-metabolising labour, alongside the traditional re/productive labour of laying and hatching, beginning before they are born. How might we see this as an under-studied consideration in other-than-human labour? How does this novel form of encounter allow us to differently understand chicken–human relationships, and how might it allow us to critique the eking out of capital and conscription of galline labour in ever more intimate ways?

If affective labour is always *byproductive*, this conceptual frame can bring a political economy of affects *to the side* of the distinction between productive and reproductive labour. For chickens in the digital flock, this byproductive labour is not (only) found in the production of egg byproducts, but in their absorption and metabolising of human affective surplus and waste, thus producing 'depleted embodied subjectivities: ones whose affects are diminished in their force as affections, constructed as non-intentional, non-agentic, or nonauthoritative, and who thereby are constructed as affect disposals, sites of affect accumulation'.[49] As well as eroding the distinctions between public and private, affective labour undermines the distinction between work and play, labour, and leisure. Affective labour's byproductive work is twofold: it is (1) affect producing, which is byproductive in its *failure* as productive and reproductive labour, resulting from managing the behaviour of the labourer; and it is also (2) affect metabolising, where the byproductive labourer – here, the chicken – must absorb the waste of excess affects, akin to Ahmed's 'sticky surplus'.[50] The virtual chicken thus becomes a receptacle for affect disposal: consume, metabolise, produce, repeat as the chickens take affects out of circulation through an intricate network of cameras and codes.

If capital's products are *already* byproducts, accumulating nature and binding them to remove them from organic circulation produces indigestible and unwanted waste that needs to be 'dumped'.[51] The digital flock, as well as undertaking productive labour through their eggs and reproductive labour through hatching, are also enlisted into byproductive affect-metabolising and affect-dumping labour. This conscription begins before these chickens are even born, with the hatching process on full display and the communed care of feeding, observing, and overseeing the birth of new chickens imposing the metabolising of affects from their conception.

## Conclusion

The work of the chickens has intensified as *Our Chicken Life*'s popularity soared during the pandemic, opening and complicating questions of labour, circulation, and commodification through this unique byproductive lens.

This unique digital ecology expands new frontiers in digitally mediated human–animal interaction while simultaneously using knowledge of galline behaviours to produce engaging forms of encounter. A digital ecologies approach to theorising more-than-human byproductive labour shows how exploitative relations are not eradicated in the digital world, but rather expand existing modes of relation. In the digital flock, there is a communing of care, but also of control and conscription of labour. The digital flock's conscription in *byproductive* labour might also be understood as an exploitation of human knowledge about chickens to shape their environments to accommodate human pleasure. The negotiation of care and control through paying to 'treat' the chickens while offering constant insight into their lives raises troubling examples of conditional more-than-human digital ecologies. *Our Chicken Life* is a novel case study that aligns with and pushes existing research in the field, while identifying future areas of interest for the field that go further than simply understanding virtual livestreams as a gimmick to also view them as a new frontier of value extraction.

Considerations of virtual nature and digital ecologies have thus far, for the majority, focused on conservation, awareness, and extinction that rose in conjunction with the charismatic turn in conservation since the 1970s.[52] In this context, a small flock of chickens – the most populous bird on the planet – might not seem the most interesting or important case for digital ecologies. But it is precisely *because* the chicken has had such an intimate, exploitative relationship with humans that this case provides such stark insights into how virtual encounters might be new frontiers for value extraction. The chicken, once again, is a keystone species for digital ecologies, much as it has been for the Anthropocene, albeit one that is largely ignored in favour of the spectacular and the charismatic.

Opening my browser as I finish writing this chapter, I can see that the ground in Utah is frozen and it's minus 11 degrees Celsius. The chickens are mostly nestled into their nesting boxes but one bird after another braves the cold to snatch a few pellets of food. The cockerel is crowing to signal dawn and a subscriber posts 'blast' in the chat, seeing food rushing out of the chute by one camera. A few chickens dart out, their red combs bobbing past another camera on their way to the treats. A chicken pecks the frozen ground directly in front of the central pinned camera, her eye level with mine. If humans have a duty to socialise with domesticated animals,[53] this relationship isn't untroubling, often carrying nefarious or dominating tendencies.[54] *Our Chicken Life* might be a less violent space than we might otherwise interact with chickens due to the novel kinds of encounter that digital ecologies can cultivate. It is a new kind of intentional community, but is it one that risks both reproducing and extending pressures on galline life? This digital ecology allows for new forms of access to extract value from non-human animals, creating new ethical and political questions that build on long legacies of troubling human–animal relations in critical animal studies. Following the chicken – once again – leads us to understanding new and changing worlds.

## Notes

1. Turnbull et al., 'Quarantine encounters with digital animals.'
2. Bennett et al., 'The broiler chicken as a signal of a human reconfigured biosphere'; Patel and Moore, *A History of the World in Seven Cheap Things*.
3. Wadiwel, 'Chicken harvesting machine.'
4. Whitney, 'Byproductive labor.'
5. Haraway, *When Species Meet*, p. 278.
6. Alexander and Kerr, 'Animals strike curious poses.'
7. Ibid., p. 3.
8. Koch and Miles, 'Inviting the stranger in,' p. 1380.
9. Bennett et al., 'The broiler chicken as a signal of a human reconfigured biosphere.'
10. Smith and Daniels, *The Chicken Book*, p. 299; italics in original text.
11. Boyd, 'Making meat.'
12. Traverso, 'The Egyptian egg ovens considered more wondrous than the pyramids.'
13. Patel and Moore, *A History of the World in Seven Cheap Things*.
14. Bennett et al., 'The broiler chicken as a signal of a human reconfigured biosphere,' p. 9.
15. Büscher, 'Nature 2.0,' p. 728.
16. Davis, *Prisoned Chickens, Poisoned Eggs*, p. 9; italics in original text.
17. Baxter, 'The welfare problems of laying hens in battery cages.'
18. Smith and Daniel, *Chicken Book*, p. 316.
19. Parker and Morrow, 'Urban homesteading and intensive mothering.'
20. Rancière, *The Emancipated Spectator*, p. 3.
21. Guéry and Deleule, *The Productive Body*.
22. Ibid., p. 58.
23. https://blog.streamelements.com/streamovator-ourchickenlife-98ec3f51c90a.
24. Giraud and Hollin, 'Care, laboratory beagles and affective utopia,' p. 92.
25. van Dooren, *Flight Ways*, p. 92.
26. Greenhough and Roe, 'Ethics, space, and somatic sensibilities.'
27. Oliver, *Veganism, Archives and Animals*.
28. van Patter and Blattner, 'Advancing ethical principles for non-invasive, respectful research with nonhuman animal participants.'
29. Ginn, 'Sticky lives,' p. 533.
30. Giraud, *What Comes After Entanglement?*, p. 105.
31. Boyd, 'Making meat.'
32. Otter, *Diet for a Large Planet*.

33 See Blanchette, *Porkopolis*.
34 Sutton, 'Researching towards a critically posthumanist future,' p. 3.
35 Turnbull et al., 'Quarantine urban ecologies.'
36 Oliver, 'Re-homing hens during Covid-19.'
37 Walton, *Everybody Needs Beauty*.
38 Ibid., p. 262.
39 The Worldwide Fund for Nature, www.wwf-nfa.com. Last accessed June 2021.
40 Whitney, 'Byproductive labor.'
41 Hochschild, 'Emotion work, feeling rules, and social structure.'
42 Hardt, 'Affective labor.'
43 Whitney, 'Byproductive labor,' p. 637; italics in original text.
44 cf. Büscher et al., 'Introduction.'
45 Ahmed, 'Affective economies.'
46 Meegaswatta, 'The balancing act,' p. 160.
47 Táíwò, 'Stoicism (as emotional compression) is emotional labor.'
48 Veldstra, 'Bad feeling at work,' p. 12.
49 Whitney, *Byproductive Labor*, p. 639.
50 Ahmed, 'Affective economies.'
51 Brennan, *Exhausting Modernity*.
52 See, for example, Adams, 'Geographies of conservation II'; Arts et al., 'Digital technology and the conservation of nature'; Oliver, 'Animals in the age of acceleration'; Turnbull et al., 'Digital ecologies.'
53 Scotton, 'Duties to socialise with domesticated animals.'
54 Oliver, *Veganism, Archives and Animals*.

## Bibliography

Adams, W.M. 2019. Geographies of conservation II: Technology, surveillance and conservation by algorithm. *Progress in Human Geography*, 43(2): 337–350.

Ahmed, S. 2004. Affective economies. *Social Text*, 79(22:2): 117–139.

Alexander, N. and Kerr, B.H. 2020. Animals strike curious poses. *Real Life Magazine* [online], 7 May. https://reallifemag.com/animals-strike-curious-poses/.

Arts, K., van der Wal, R., and Adams, W.M. 2015. Digital technology and the conservation of nature. *Ambio*, 44(4): 661–673.

Baxter, M.R. 1994. The welfare problems of laying hens in battery cages. *The Veterinary Record*, 134(24): 614–619.

Bennett, A.E., Thomas, R., Williams, M., Zalasiewicz, J., Edgeworth, M., Miller, H., Coles, B., Foster, A., Burton, E.J., and Marume, U. 2018. The broiler chicken as a signal of a human reconfigured biosphere. *Royal Society Open Science*, 5(12). https://doi.org/10.1098/rsos.180325.

Blanchette, A. 2020. *Porkopolis*. Durham, NC: Duke University Press.

Boyd, W. 2001. Making meat: Science, technology, and American poultry production. *Technology and Culture*, 42(4): 631–664.

Brennan, T. 2000. *Exhausting Modernity: Grounds for a New Economy*. Oxford: Routledge.

Büscher, B. 2016. Nature 2.0: Exploring and theorizing the links between new media and nature conservation. *New Media & Society*, 18(5): 726–743.
Büscher, B., Koot, S., and Nelson, I. 2017. Introduction. Nature 2.0: New media, online activism and the cyberpolitics of environmental conservation. *Geoforum*, 9: 111–113.
Davis, K. 2009. *Prisoned Chickens, Poisoned Eggs*. Summertown, TN: Book Publishing Company.
Ginn, F. 2014. Sticky lives: slugs, detachment and more-than-human ethics in the garden. *Transactions of the Institute of British Geographers*, 39(4): 532–544.
Giraud, E.H. 2019. *What Comes After Entanglement?* Durham, NC: Duke University Press.
Giraud, E.H. and Hollin, G. 2013. Care, laboratory beagles and affective utopia. *Theory, Culture & Society*, 33(4): 27–49.
Greenhough, B. and Roe, E. 2011. Ethics, space, and somatic sensibilities. *Environment and Planning D: Society and Space*, 29(1): 47–66.
Guéry, F. and Deleule, D. 2014. *The Productive Body*. Alresford: Zero Books
Haraway, D.J. 2013. *When Species Meet*. Minneapolis, MN: University of Minnesota Press.
Hardt, M. 1999. Affective labor. *boundary 2*, 26(2): 89–100.
Hochschild, A.R. 1979. Emotion work, feeling rules, and social structure. *American Journal of Sociology*, 85(3): 551–575.
Koch, R. and Miles, S. 2021. Inviting the stranger in: Intimacy, digital technology and new geographies of encounter. *Progress in Human Geography*, 45(6): 1379–1401.
Meegaswatta, T.N.K. 2021. The balancing act: Employed women navigating the Covid-19 lockdown in Sri Lanka. *South Asian Survey*, 28(1): 157–171.
Oliver, C. 2020. Re-homing hens during Covid-19: A rethinking of urban space? *Sociology Lens* [online], 10 August. www.sociologylens.net/topics/collective-behaviour-and-social-movements/re-homing-hens-during-covid-19-a-rethinking-of-urban-space/32056.
Oliver, C. 2021. Beyond-human ethics: The animal question in institutional ethical reviews. *Area*, 53(4): 619–626.
Oliver, C. 2021. *Veganism, Archives and Animals*. Oxford: Routledge.
Oliver, C. Forthcoming. Animals in the age of acceleration. In S. Mosley and G. Bankoff (Eds.) *Cultural History of the Environment*. Vol. 6. London: Bloomsbury.
Otter, C. 2020. *Diet for a Large Planet*. Chicago, IL: University of Chicago Press.
Parker, B. and Morrow, O. 2017. Urban homesteading and intensive mothering. *Gender, Place & Culture*, 24(2): 247–259.
Patel, R. and Moore, J. 2017. *A History of the World in Seven Cheap Things*. Oakland, CA: University of California Press.
Rancière, J. 2008. *The Emancipated Spectator*. London: Verso.
Scotton, G. 2017. Duties to socialise with domesticated animals: Farmed animal sanctuaries as frontiers of friendship. *Animal Studies Journal*, 6(2): 86–108.
Smith, P. and Daniels, C. 1975. *The Chicken Book*. Athens, GA: The University of Georgia Press.
Sutton, Z. 2020. Researching towards a critically posthumanist future. *International Journal of Sociology and Social Policy*, 41(3–4): 376–390.
Táíwò, O.O. 2020. Stoicism (as emotional compression) is emotional Labor. *feminist Philosophy Quarterly*, 6(2): 1–25.

Traverso, V. 2019. The Egyptian egg ovens considered more wondrous than the pyramids. *Atlas Obscura* [online], 29 March. www.atlasobscura.com/articles/egypt-egg-ovens.

Turnbull, J., Searle, A., and Adams, W.M. 2020a. Quarantine encounters with digital animals: More-than-human geographies of lockdown life. *Journal of Environmental Media*, 1(1): 6.1–6.10.

Turnbull, J., Searle, A., and Adams, W.M. 2020b. Quarantine urban ecologies. *Cultural Anthropology* [online], 19 May. https://culanth.org/fieldsights/quarantine-urban-ecologies.

Turnbull, J., Searle, A., Hartman Davies, O., Dodsworth, J., Chasseray-Peraldi, P., Von Essen, E., and Anderson-Elliott, H. 2023. Digital ecologies: Materialities, encounters, governance. *Progress In Environmental Geography*, 2(1–2): 3–32.

van Dooren, T. 2014. *Flight Ways: Life and Loss at the Edge of Extinction*. New York: Columbia University Press.

van Patter, L. and Blattner, C. 2020 Advancing ethical principles for non-invasive, respectful research with nonhuman animal participants. *Society & Animals*, 28(2): 171–190.

Veldstra, C. 2018. Bad feeling at work: Emotional labour, precarity, and the affective economy. *Cultural Studies*, 34(1): 1–24.

Wadiwel, D. 2018. Chicken harvesting machine: Animal labor, resistance, and the time of production. *South Atlantic Quarterly*, 117(3): 527–549.

Walton, S. 2021. *Everybody Needs Beauty: In Search of the Nature Cure*. London: Bloomsbury.

Whitney, S. 2018. Byproductive labor: A feminist theory of affective labor beyond the productive–reproductive distinction. *Philosophy & Social Criticism*, 44(6): 637–660.

# Part II

Digital governance

# 5

# On-bird surveillance: albatrosses, sensors, and the lively governance of marine ecologies

*Oscar Hartman Davies and Jamie Lorimer*

## Introduction

*A wandering albatross soars above the waters in a Southern Ocean gale. The turbulent sea below the bird seethes, but its movements are relaxed. Turning in successive downwind and upwind arcs, the albatross travels at great speed, scouring the ocean surface for a meal. Perhaps the bird sees it first, or its smell wafts into its tube-like nostrils: a fishing boat, emerging in sprays of white-water from a trough between waves. The albatross flies downwind to meet it. An antenna protrudes from its soft back feathers and, as it nears, it picks up the radar signal from the boat's navigational system. Unbeknownst, perhaps, to the boat's crew, they have now become the targets of a surveillance and control mechanism operating through the albatross.*

Novel sensing practices enabled by digital technologies are constructing marine space anew – as dynamic, turbulent, and more fragile than previously imagined. Scholarly accounts of digitised oceans have focused particularly on their monitoring by satellites and robotic sensors, as well as on the role of oceanographic models.[1] Through these technologies, monitoring and surveillance become practices performed by a 'composite figure of distributed human and nonhuman agency'.[2] However, the conceptualisation of the non-human in these accounts remains distinctly technological. Little attention has been paid to the roles that cyborg non-human animals, equipped with various sensing devices, increasingly play in these monitoring assemblages.

Critical scholarship on animal tracking primarily focuses on the surveillance *of* animals.[3] Increasingly, though, oceanic surveillance is also performed *with* animals, as part of a 'wired wilderness'.[4] A range of techniques have become available to derive environmental information directly from animal bodies, and animal-borne digital devices for tracking and 'biologging' – the collection of animal behavioural and environmental data – are now an integral feature of wildlife research.[5] Across conservation, pollution monitoring, and epidemiological contexts, this has facilitated enrolling animals as 'sentinels' or 'biosensors' for monitoring environments.[6]

Marine ecologists suggest these modes of sensing offer new opportunities for ocean research and governance,[7] while others have explored the use of animal-borne devices like 'CritterCams' for entertainment and educational purposes.[8]

This chapter develops a novel, more-than-human framework for understanding digital ocean governance, drawing on interviews with marine ecologists and conservationists and document analysis of published research, popular articles, and technical reports. Through our case study of 'on-bird' fisheries surveillance with albatrosses, we bring together digital and more-than-human geographies, political ecology, and science and technology studies to offer an account that is attentive to the lively agencies of technologies, animals, and oceanic volumes, as well as to the power structures governing these assemblages. We apply this account to critically assess an emerging model of ocean governance and its political and ecological implications, focusing on three key themes. We first outline a new wet ontology[9] of the ocean – the 'movescape'[10] – and its attendant modes of governance. Second, we consider the risks presented by these governance approaches to the animals they enrol. Lastly, we interrogate how these approaches naturalise surveillance as a solution to marine ecological issues. In conclusion, we reflect on the potential for digital ecologies research to address these new data-driven and animal-borne approaches to marine science and governance, and to offer cross-disciplinary, holistic understandings of these novel forms of governance as they emerge.

## Governing the dynamic depleted ocean

The anthropogenic influences of fisheries, plastic waste, deep-sea mining, and climate change are transforming the oceans into more unruly, depleted spaces, renewing calls for improving ocean governance to protect marine ecosystems. Large-scale industrial fishing is among the most destructive of these influences, impacting marine life through the overexploitation of target species and the killing of non-target species (bycatch).[11] Overexploitation is now characteristic of many parts of the oceans globally, driven by massive growth in global fish consumption and the technologically facilitated exploitation of coastal areas and the areas beyond national jurisdiction (known as 'the high seas'). Fishing effort has increased fivefold since the 1950s in the high seas, and illegal, unreported, and unregulated fishing is widespread.[12]

Alongside other regulatory and market-based mechanisms, fisheries regulators foreground monitoring, control, and surveillance activities as vital to addressing issues of overexploitation, bycatch, and illegality on the high seas.[13] These activities are increasingly digitised, particularly through on-board electronic monitoring and satellite monitoring.[14] Electronic monitoring systems, shown in Figure 5.1, turn vessels into sites of on-board surveillance.

In addition, commercial vessels are increasingly required to use vessel-based Automatic Identification Systems (AIS) which transmit location, identity, course, and speed data via satellite. Organisations like Global Fishing Watch are using these data for fisheries compliance monitoring.[15] Together, these technologies promise to collect timely, accurate, and cost-efficient fisheries data, as well as reducing issues such as the intimidation of human fisheries observers.

This transition towards digital MCS reflects a broader shift towards digital sensing as the dominant mode of monitoring marine ecologies.[16] This is transforming the oceans into what Jennifer Gabrys terms 'highly instrumented sensor spaces'.[17] These digital ocean ecologies enable new modes of governing that are increasingly real time and responsive to the dynamism of marine ecologies and human resource users.[18]

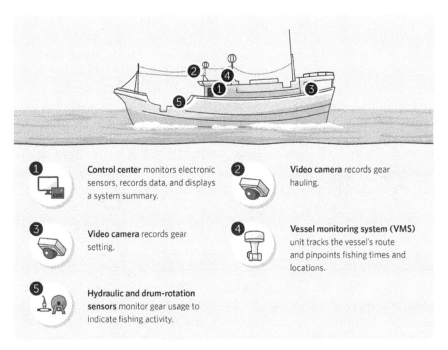

Figure 5.1 The digitisation of fisheries monitoring. (Source: The Pew Charitable Trusts 2019. All rights reserved and permission to use the figure must be obtained from the copyright holder.)

The governance techniques discussed in this chapter exemplify a broader set of emerging environmental governance regimes that operate through intensified surveillance and policing.[19] Conservation surveillance, defined as the 'close watch kept over someone or something for conservation purposes',[20] is an increasingly normalised feature of conservation practice. Geographers have framed these practices in terms of the securitisation and militarisation of conservation.[21] Alongside the human policing of conservation areas, digital technologies like camera traps, drones, and satellites increasingly underpin these regimes.[22] In ocean governance, these technologies open new avenues for securing oceanic space through 'technological objects and the algorithms that operate them'.[23]

Such accounts offer important theorisations of novel forms of governance operating through monitoring technologies, algorithms, and data infrastructures alongside human actors.[24] However, the 'more-than-human sensorium' of ecological monitoring and surveillance increasingly also involves the lively capacities of animals.[25] As Elizabeth Johnson describes, while non-human beings have always been a part of human technological apparatuses for knowing the world, such approaches have developed rapidly in recent years as ways to grasp the severity and multiplicity of ecological changes occurring in the Anthropocene.[26] Through these approaches, 'nonhuman life is revalorized for what it can communicate to humans about the vulnerability of life in the material world'.[27] Animals, and the telemetry and biologging devices attached to them, have not previously been considered conservation surveillance technologies – as able to monitor and communicate human threats to conservation priorities – because they have generally not been implicated in collecting data about 'peoples' spatial and temporal activities'.[28] However, in the following section, we offer an example which demonstrates how this is changing, before reflecting on the implications of enrolling animals in conservation surveillance and digital ocean governance.

## Ocean Sentinel

Between 2015 and 2019, a team of seabird ecologists led by the Centre d'Etudes Biologiques de Chizé worked with New Zealand-based company Sextant Technology to develop new biologgers to detect the fine-scale interactions between albatrosses and fishing vessels. The loggers, called XGPS, XArgos, and Centurion, could sense the radar emissions from vessel navigational systems and transmit this information alongside the birds' locations through the Argos satellite system. They were attached to the back feathers of over 200 Wandering and Amsterdam

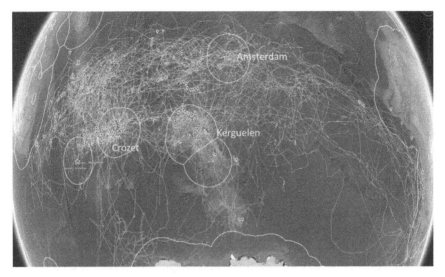

Figure 5.2 Tracking and vessel location data collected by CEBC. Lines show the movement of individual birds from different colonies, location tags show radar detections, and the thicker grey lines delineate jurisdictional boundaries. (Source: Weimerskirch et al. (2020). All rights reserved and permission to use the figure must be obtained from the copyright holder.)

albatrosses breeding across the French Indian Ocean territories of Crozet, Kerguelen, and Amsterdam.[29] Subsequently, these albatrosses journeyed with the loggers over vast areas of ocean from South Africa to Australia and Antarctica, encountering multiple fishing boats on their travels (Figure 5.2).

The loggers were initially developed to investigate albatross bycatch, one of the greatest threats facing the birds globally when they become entangled in fishing equipment and drown while searching for food.[30] However, studying the first data sets collected by the birds, the researchers observed something intriguing: radar detections recorded within the Exclusive Economic Zones around Crozet, Kerguelen, and Amsterdam islands did not correspond to the location data on licensed fishing vessels provided to them by French authorities. This suggested that the birds were encountering illegally operating vessels, the locations of which could be identified by the devices. This finding led the researchers in a new direction. They applied for a European Research Council grant in which they claimed they could combine the characteristics of the birds – large, wide-ranging, attracted to vessels – with the sensing capacities of the devices to develop an 'Ocean Sentinel'.[31] The Ocean Sentinel project proposed 'to use animals as platforms ... for large-scale surveillance',[32] which we term 'on-bird surveillance'.

The purposes of this on-bird surveillance are to identify (illegal) fishing activity and provide this information to enforcement agencies via a system visualised by the researchers in Figure 5.3. To achieve this, the researchers worked with the Terres Australes et Antarctiques Françaises (TAAF) and the Southern Indian Ocean Regional Operational Surveillance and Rescue Center (CROSS) based on Réunion Island. TAAF is responsible for the administration of the French Southern and Antarctic Lands, while CROSS coordinates search and rescue and fisheries control missions to the waters surrounding these territories.[33] As a researcher on the project explained, '[CROSS] cross-compare all their methods of surveillance, of which albatrosses are one, to the declared data'.[34] If a discrepancy emerged between declared and observed vessels, CROSS would send a patrol vessel to investigate. This approach, the researchers working on Ocean Sentinel suggest, could be widely applied across the oceans as part of the digital fisheries monitoring, surveillance, and control toolkit.[35]

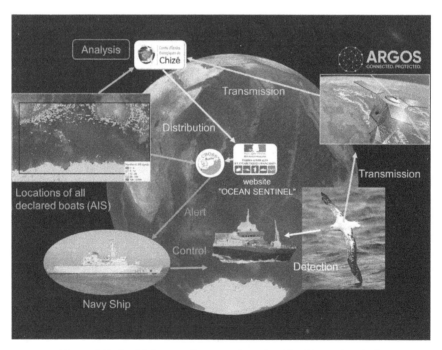

Figure 5.3 On-bird surveillance, as imagined by Ocean Sentinel.
(Source: Weimerskirch et al. (2020). All rights reserved and permission to use the figure must be obtained from the copyright holder.)

## Governing through the 'movescape'

The Ocean Sentinel project expresses a particular ontology of the ocean shared by a range of new governance practices grouped under the term 'dynamic ocean management'.[36] These approaches express a dissatisfaction with spatiotemporally fixed approaches to management, like static marine protected areas, which have often been imported into marine settings from terrestrial conservation. Their proponents suggest the dynamism and fluidity of the oceans require governance approaches that are equally dynamic and responsive to changes in the systems they manage in real time.[37] Marine ecologies, in these approaches, are conceived of as a *movescape*, comprised of dynamic, mobile processes and human and non-human actors whose relations and interactions are monitored and managed in real time.[38] By means of distributed sensor networks, oceanographic models, and communication systems, we suggest that the movescape describes a new, data-driven wet ontology that is becoming institutionalised through dynamic ocean management.[39] Part of a wider 'volumetric' and 'blue' turn in the environmental humanities and social sciences, the notion of wet ontologies recognises that 'a terrestrial ontology of bounded zones and emplaced points of power and knowledge' cannot fully capture (or manage) the material and dynamic qualities of ocean ecologies.[40]

In addition to Ocean Sentinel, the movescape appears in fully operational initiatives like the Hawaiian TurtleWatch bycatch programme, Australian tuna fisheries management, and the prevention of ship collisions with Northern Right Wales in Eastern Canada.[41] In these initiatives, oceanographic and animal movement data are used to manage the activities of marine resource users, for example through dynamic protected areas that move with their target species. Regulation thus works according to a wet ontology, in contrast to conventional management approaches which impose a set of 'landed logics' of territory-making and control upon the ocean.[42] These approaches build upon past research which has enlisted large marine animals as 'oceanographers' or 'platforms' for collecting oceanographic data.[43] Here, though, the data these animals collect additionally enable specific ways of governing. We suggest these forms of digital ecological governance invoke novel forms of environmental biopower and cyborg anatamo-politics.

Dynamic ocean management aims to manage in real time the relations between marine ecologies and humans through attuning and responding to ecologies themselves. Bruce Braun has described the ways in which contemporary modes of power in environmental governance increasingly operate through a 'decidedly fluid and flexible landscape', in which modernist command and control gives way, if only partially, to the modulation of processes and flows.[44] This is increasingly achieved through what David

Chandler terms a 'sensing' mode of governance: big data- and technology-driven approaches to tracing and managing the emergent effects of relations between more-than-human actors.[45] Dynamic ocean management represents one manifestation of this environmental mode of biopower, which Jamie Lorimer suggests is aimed at 'managing the circulation of bodies and things in order to secure desired systemic properties'.[46]

In the case of Ocean Sentinel, these desired systemic properties relate to biodiversity *and* the territorial integrity of French-controlled waters (shown in Figure 5.2). Due to its affiliation with French government agencies, Ocean Sentinel is particularly concerned with policing incursions of illegal fishers into French waters, distinguishing these from the licensed vessels operating in these areas according to catch allowances and protocols to reduce by-catch.[47] The circulation of licensed fishing activity is affirmed, while that of illegal fishers is made visible, by means of the albatross, and controlled. The albatross becomes a form of infrastructure – which Maan Barua defines as 'architectures of circulation, as substrates generating the environments of everyday life and as technologies of regulation and government'[48] – through which environmental biopower operates. Wakefield and Braun suggest these non-human infrastructures frame nature as an appealing solution to climate and ecological crises, as 'there to assist us, provided that we understand what it is capable of doing'.[49]

As a 'natural' solution, albatrosses appear capable of illuminating and policing in real time a set of activities thriving on the invisibility afforded to them by the high seas. The widespread illegality forming the backdrop to Ocean Sentinel's on-bird surveillance practices has inspired media coverage of the project to embrace the figure of 'the albatross cop'. *The Guardian*, for example, wrote: 'Albatross cops may soon be taking to the skies … to scan remote parts of the Pacific Ocean for illegal fishing boats'.[50] *The New York Times* said of these illegal vessels: 'They're stealthy at sea, but they can't hide from the albatross'.[51] The albatross cop signals a key difference between Ocean Sentinel and other examples of dynamic ocean management. Where most other approaches combine data from animal-borne devices with data on human activities from other sources, Ocean Sentinel directly enrols albatrosses in conservation surveillance. This on-bird surveillance exemplifies a 'cyborg anatamo-politics' which is 'reorienting animal bodies into technologies for dealing with shocks and disturbances',[52] clearly expressed by the project leader's description of the birds as 'like drones, only intelligent'.[53]

## Lively surveillance

Despite this comparison to drones, it is the specific sentient and lively qualities of albatrosses that qualify them as 'new beasts of burden' for performing surveillance work.[54] As an Ocean Sentinel project member explained: 'we worked on Wandering and Amsterdam albatrosses because there were conservation issues and because they were large … and they are attracted by vessels so in fact it was a good combination. And they are foraging very far, 2000–3000 km from the colony, and the juveniles disperse across the whole Indian Ocean, so they are very good sentinels'.[55] Albatrosses enable governing through the oceans in ways that digital technologies alone do not (yet), requiring research that is attentive to these hybrid biological-digital affordances. Their vast mobilities and rapid responses to changing oceanographic and atmospheric conditions, as well as to the presence of fishing vessels which they opportunistically seek out when foraging, facilitate lively surveillance.[56]

Indeed, Ocean Sentinel is not alone in viewing particular animal characteristics as attractive for surveillance purposes. Albeit not always informing fisheries enforcement, their method of using birds to monitor fisheries has been taken up in several other contexts.[57] In southern Africa, sentinel animals have been enrolled in early warning systems that use 'an internet-of-things architecture with wearable sensors, wireless data transmission and machine learning algorithms' to sense animal behavioural signatures that indicate the presence and location of poachers in protected areas.[58]

These projects can empower animals to 'collect the data needed for their own conservation', according to Samantha Patrick, a researcher on the Ocean Sentinel project.[59] This is a significant reframing of animals not as passive victims of human exploitation, but as active agents in their own protection and in the surveillance of humans, raising questions concerning the governance techniques described here. In particular, as digital ecological governance increasingly harnesses the agencies of living, sentient beings, what are the consequences for the individual animals themselves?

## On-bird risks

The relations of power at play in fisheries governance place albatrosses in positions of heightened vulnerability rather than authority, rendering the albatross cop an inappropriate and perhaps dangerous framing for these birds. The implications of instrumenting individual animals for research have concerned conservationists since their early use.[60] Seabird researchers have focused on the potentially negative effects of devices on birds in terms of weight, irritation, aerodynamism, and foraging effectiveness.[61] However, by enrolling their wearers in conservation surveillance, these devices now expose animals to potential harms beyond their direct physical effects. In other contexts, researchers have noted the vandalism, destruction, or theft of conservation surveillance technologies by people who object to observation by them.[62] Equally, Steven Cooke and colleagues have noted how people outside of research communities may be able to access animal tracking data to 'locate, disturb, capture, harm, or kill tagged animals'.[63] In examples such as Ocean Sentinel where animals become bodily implicated in surveillance, resistance to surveillance may result not only in the destruction of technologies but also violence towards animals. On-bird surveillance, in other words, inaugurates new on-bird risks.

In several interviews, conservationists commenting on Ocean Sentinel suggested that albatrosses risked being shot by fishers associating them with surveillance and recriminations. This might not be the case only for individual birds wearing loggers, which are hard to identify in turbulent seas, but might become a more general association leading to less discriminate killing. Such negative symbolic associations between particular species and conservation surveillance have also been noted elsewhere. In Malta, where bird conservation is increasingly militarised, hunters have deliberately shot protected species in defiance of conservationists.[64] Given the recency of Ocean Sentinel, and assurances by project members that killings have not occurred,[65] these concerns are currently speculative. However, they complicate the narrative of animals as technologically enabled agents of their own conservation, raising important biopolitical questions concerning the 'entanglement of harm and care' in conservation practice whereby individual animals' lives are often subjugated by biopolitical techniques intervening upon the collective.[66]

Framing encounters between birds and vessels as sources of potentiality and data for governance points to the ways in which birds are not only *instrumented* but also *become instrumental* and, conceivably, expendable. As an Ocean Sentinel researcher points out, 'there will be lines where you put your interests against the animals' interests when putting devices on them'.[67] Across contexts, enthusiasm for the deployment of new technologies to enhance ecological knowledge production and governance outpaces unified approaches to governing their very use.[68] Here too, we note a lack of, and a pressing need for, context-specific ethical and regulatory frameworks that consider the risks to animals enrolled in conservation surveillance.

## The naturalisation of surveillance

Emerging regimes of digital ocean governance also raise a wider set of concerns that relate to how surveillance becomes naturalised as a solution to marine ecological crises. Certainly, there is little doubt that the opacity of the high seas is concerning from regulatory and ecological perspectives.

However, digital technologies do more than simply increase knowledge and transparency. They are also mobilised to support the political and economic interest of specific actors.[69] Indeed, what is made visible by these surveillance technologies are the extractive outposts of complex, global commodities empires (fishers and vessels), while the regimes of value driving destructive practices remain relatively obscured.[70]

In contrast to the participatory decision-making often espoused by fisheries organisations, digital fisheries governance may enable forms of 'green security', shown elsewhere to displace global biodiversity crises onto local sites and often marginalised communities, framed as appropriate sites for intervention.[71] This is not an inevitable outcome though. The use of satellite surveillance to highlight and reduce human rights abuses aboard fishing vessels offers one example of a more progressive vision for digital fisheries governance.[72] However, we are usefully reminded by James Ash and colleagues that 'smart', data-driven governance is often 'rooted in a neoliberal ethos of market-led and technocratic solutions ... that reinforce existing power geometries and social and spatial inequalities'.[73] Given the predominance of socio-economic over environmental interests in fisheries governance, there is clearly more at stake than socio-ecological wellbeing in the uptake of data-driven approaches.[74]

## Conclusion

Many ecologists are actively reaching and embracing a 'transformational point' at which they move from simply studying animals towards assembling a big data ecology that views animals as 'naturally evolved sensors of environments ... [that] help us monitor the planet in completely new ways'.[75] This renders it increasingly feasible to enrol animals in extended more-than-human networks of surveillance. We have suggested that this creates opportunities for new forms of governance attuned to the liveliness of ocean ecologies and to human activities therein – to the ocean as a movescape – but it also inaugurates new risks to individual animals.

We find it important to make two interrelated points of import to scholars in the growing field of digital ecologies. First, we are keen to avoid inscribing projects like Ocean Sentinel as the result of an inevitable trajectory in digital ecological governance towards conservation surveillance or indeed to contribute to the naturalisation of surveillance as an appropriate governance technique. Digital ecologies research recognises the range of potential impacts and affects stemming from the digitisation of knowledge production and governance – from positive and emancipatory, to ambivalent and exploitative. We align with scholars who question the immediate application of a surveillance or biopolitical lens to contemporary developments in ecology. Kristoffer Whitney, for instance, suggests that surveillance obscures the insights and affective intimacy telemetry offers into animals' lifeworlds, while Adam Nicolson's creative non-fiction account of seabirds' lives draws substantially on biologging studies, pointing to alternative modes of relation that might result from the new understandings offered by these technologies.[76]

Yet, remaining attentive to the realities of our case, we also caution against accounts that imply wildlife tracking *could* not be used for conservation surveillance, and suggest that guidelines accounting for the new risks this poses are necessary. By attending ethnographically to the interrelations between animals, ecologies, and technological infrastructures, and drawing on a range of disciplinary approaches, digital ecologies research can offer vital analyses of these emergent hybrid forms of surveillance, situate them in relation to a wider field of digitally mediated relations, and offer practical interventions.

## Notes

1 Gabrys, *Program Earth*; Lehman, 'From ships to robots'.
2 Amoore and Raley, 'Securing with algorithms', p. 7.
3 Benson, *Wired Wilderness*; Bergman, 'Inventing a beast with no body'.
4 Benson, *Wired Wilderness*.
5 Wilmers et al., 'The golden age of bio-logging'.
6 Gabrys, 'Sensing lichens'; Keck, *Avian Reservoirs*.
7 Maxwell et al., 'Dynamic ocean management'.
8 Blue, 'Public attunement with more-than-human others'; Haraway, *When Species Meet*.
9 Steinberg and Peters, 'Wet ontologies'.
10 Bakker, 'Smart oceans'.
11 O'Hara et al., 'At-risk marine biodiversity'.
12 Cullis-Suzuki and Pauly, 'Failing the high seas'; Oral, 'Reflections on the past, present, and future'.
13 Bergh and Davies, 'Fishery monitoring, control and surveillance'; Loefflad et al., *Strategic Plan for Electronic Monitoring*.
14 Toonen and Bush, 'The digital frontiers of fisheries governance'.
15 Drakopulos et al., 'Making global oceans governance in/visible'; Kroodsma et al., 'Tracking the global footprint of fisheries'.
16 Lehman, 'From ships to robots'.
17 Gabrys, *Program Earth*, p. 140.
18 Maxwell et al., 'Dynamic ocean management'.
19 Sandbrook et al., 'Principles for the socially responsible use of conservation monitoring technology'; Simlai, 'Conservation surveillance as a means for state repression?'

20 Sandbrook et al., 'Human bycatch', p. 494.
21 Duffy, 'Waging a war to save biodiversity'; Kelly and Ybarra, 'Green security in protected areas'.
22 Adams, 'Geographies of conservation II'.
23 Johnson, 'The hydra and the leviathan', p. 185.
24 Amoore and Raley, 'Securing with algorithms'.
25 Johnson 'At the limits of species being', p. 283.
26 Ibid.
27 Ibid., p. 283.
28 Sandbrook et al., 'Principles', p. 2.
29 Weimerskirch et al., 'Ocean sentinel albatrosses'; Weimerskirch et al., 'Use of radar detectors'.
30 See Dias et al., 'Threats to seabirds'.
31 European Research Council grant ID 780058, https://cordis.europa.eu/project/id/780058.
32 Weimerskirch et al., 'Ocean sentinel albatrosses', p. 3007.
33 More information about CROSS can be accessed at: www.dm.sud-ocean-indien.developpement-durable.gouv.fr/cross-r24.html.
34 Davide, Interview, 26 August 2020. All names are anonymised throughout.
35 Weimerskirch et al., 'Ocean sentinel albatrosses'.
36 Hobday and Hartog, 'Derived ocean features for dynamic ocean management'; Maxwell et al., 'Dynamic ocean management'.
37 Maxwell et al., 'Dynamic ocean management'.
38 Bakker, 'Smart oceans'; Lowerre-Barbieri et al., 'The ocean's movescape'.
39 See Bear, 'Assembling ocean life'.
40 Steinberg and Peters, 'Wet ontologies', p. 253; see also Braverman and Johnson, *Blue Legalities*; Jue, *Wild Blue Media*.
41 Maxwell et al., 'Mobile protected areas for biodiversity on the high seas'.
42 Peters, 'The territories of governance'.
43 Fedak, 'Marine animals as platforms'; Forssman, 'Staging the animal oceanographer'.
44 Braun, 'A new urban dispositif?' p. 58; see also Barker, 'Biosecurity'; Hinchliffe and Bingham, 'Securing life'.
45 Chandler, *Ontopolitics in the Anthropocene*; see also Latour and Lenton, 'Gaia 2.0'.
46 Lorimer, 'The probiotic planet', p. 82.
47 Weimerskirch et al., 'Ocean sentinel albatrosses'.
48 Barua, 'Infrastructure and non-human life', p. 1469.
49 Wakefield and Braun, 'Oystertecture', p. 201.
50 Roy, "Intelligent drones"', n.p.
51 Kornei, 'They're stealthy at sea', n.p.
52 Barua, 'Infrastructure and non-human life', p. 1481.
53 Weimerskirch, in Roy, ' "Intelligent drones" ', n.p.
54 Barua, 'Infrastructure and non-human life', p. 1479.
55 Michel, Interview, 1 March 2021.

56 See Collet et al., 'Albatrosses redirect flight'.
57 British Antarctic Survey, 'New funding uses seabirds as sentinels'; Gremillet, 'Identifying seabird interactions'; Nishizawa et al., 'Seabird-fishery interactions'.
58 de Knegt et al., 'Timely poacher detection', p. 1.
59 Patrick, 'How we recruited albatrosses', n.p.
60 See Boitani and Fuller, 'Research techniques in animal ecology'.
61 See Phillips et al., 'Effects of satellite transmitters'; Wilson et al., 'Recording devices on free-ranging marine animals'.
62 Mathur, *Crooked Cats*; Simlai, 'Conservation surveillance as a means for state repression?'
63 Cooke et al., 'Troubling issues at the frontier of animal tracking', p. 1205.
64 Campbell and Veríssimo, 'Black stork down'.
65 Arthur, Interview, 10 September 2020.
66 Srinivasan, 'Caring for the collective', p. 501.
67 Davide, Interview, 26 August 2020.
68 di Minin et al., 'How to address data privacy concerns'; Sandbrook et al., 'Principles'.
69 Gabrys, 'Practising, materialising, and contesting environmental data'; Nost and Goldstein, 'A political ecology of data'.
70 See Telesca, *Red Gold*.
71 Kelly and Ybarra, 'Green security in protected areas'.
72 McDonald et al., 'Satellites can reveal global extent of forced labour'.
73 Ash et al., 'Digital turn, digital geographies?' p. 31.
74 See Telesca, *Red Gold*.
75 Kays et al., 'Terrestrial animal tracking', p. 1222.
76 Nicolson, *The Seabird's Cry*; Whitney, 'Domesticating nature?'

# Bibliography

Adams, W.M. 2019. Geographies of conservation II: Technology, surveillance and conservation by algorithm. *Progress in Human Geography*, 43(2): 337–350.

Amoore, L. and Raley, R. 2017. Securing with algorithms: Knowledge, decision, sovereignty. *Security Dialogue* 48(1): 3–10.

Ash, J., Kitchin, R., and Leszczynski, A. 2018. Digital turn, digital geographies? *Progress in Human Geography* 42(1): 25–43.

Bakker, K. 2022. Smart oceans: Artificial intelligence and marine protected areas governance. *Earth System Governance*, 13.

Barker, K. 2015. Biosecurity: Securing circulations from the microbe to the macrocosm. *The Geographical Journal*, 181(4): 357–365.

Barua, M. 2021. Infrastructure and non-human life: A wider ontology. *Progress in Human Geography*, 45(6): 1467–1489.

Bear, C. 2017. Assembling ocean life: More-than-human entanglements in the blue economy. *Dialogues in Human Geography*, 7(1): 27–31.

Benson, E. 2010. *Wired Wilderness: Technologies of Tracking and the Making of Modern Wildlife*. Baltimore, MD: Johns Hopkins University Press.

Bergh, P.E. and Davies, S. 2002. Fishery monitoring, control and surveillance. In K. Cochrane (Ed.) *A Fishery Manager's Guidebook: Management Measures and Their Application* (pp. 373–403). Rome: FAO.

Bergman, C. 2005. Inventing a beast with no body: Radio-telemetry, the marginalization of animals, and the simulation of ecology. *Worldviews: Environment, Culture, Religion*, 9(2): 255–270.

Blue, G. 2016. Public attunement with more-than-human others: Witnessing the life and death of Bear 71. *GeoHumanities*, 2(1): 42–57. https://doi.org/10.1080/2373566X.2016.1166976.

Boitani, L. and Fuller, T.K. 2000. *Research Techniques in Animal Ecology: Controversies and Consequences*. 2nd ed. Issues, Cases, and Methods in Biodiversity Conservation. New York: Columbia University Press.

Braun, B.P. 2014. A new urban dispositif? Governing life in an age of climate change. *Society and Space*, 32: 49–64.

Braverman, I. and Johnson, E.R. 2020. *Blue Legalities: The Life and Laws of the Sea*. Durham, NC: Duke University Press.

British Antarctic Survey. 2019. New funding uses seabirds as sentinels of South Atlantic [online], 21 January. www.bas.ac.uk/media-post/new-funding-uses-seabirds-as-sentinels-of-south-atlantic-ocean/.

Campbell, B. and Veríssimo, D. 2015. Black stork down: Military discourses in bird conservation in Malta. *Human Ecology*, 43(1): 79–92.

Chandler, D. 2018. *Ontopolitics in the Anthropocene: An Introduction to Mapping, Sensing and Hacking*. London: Routledge.

Collet, J., Patrick, S.C., and Weimerskirch, H. 2015. Albatrosses redirect flight towards vessels at the limit of their visual range. *Marine Ecology Progress Series*, 526: 199–205.

Cooke, S.J., Nguyen, V.M., Kessel, S.T., Hussey, N.E., Young, N., and Ford, A.T. 2017. Troubling issues at the frontier of animal tracking for conservation and management. *Conservation Biology*, 31(5): 1205–1207.

Cullis-Suzuki, S. and Pauly, D. 2010. Failing the high seas: A global evaluation of regional fisheries management organizations. *Marine Policy*, 34(5): 1036–1042.

De Knegt, H.J., Eikelboom, J.A.J., van Langevelde, F., Spruyt, W.F., and Prins, H.T. 2021. Timely poacher detection and localization using sentinel animal movement. *Scientific Reports*, 11(1): 4596–4596. https://doi.org/10.1038/s41598-021-83800-1.

Di Minin, E., Fink, C., Hausmann, A., Kremer, J., and Kulkarni, R. 2021. How to address data privacy concerns when using social media data in conservation science. *Conservation Biology*, 35(2): 437–446.

Dias, M.P., Martin, R., Pearmain, E.J., Burfield, I.J., Small, C., Phillips, R.A., Yates, O., Lascelles, B., Borboroglu, P.G., and Croxall, J.P. 2019. Threats to seabirds: A global assessment. *Biological Conservation*, 237: 525–537.

Drakopulos, L., Silver, J.J., Nost, E., Gray, N., and Hawkins, R. 2023. Making global oceans governance in/visible with Smart Earth: The case of Global Fishing Watch. *Environment and Planning E: Nature and Space*, 6(2): 1098–1113.

Duffy, R. 2014. Waging a war to save biodiversity: The rise of militarized conservation. *International Affairs*, 90(4): 819–834.

Fedak, M.A. 2004. Marine animals as platforms for oceanographic sampling: A 'win/win' situation for biology and operational oceanography. *Memoirs of the National Institute of Polar Research*, 58: 133–147.

Forssman, N. 2017. *Staging the Animal Oceanographer: An Ethnography of Seals and Their Scientists*. PhD thesis, UC San Diego. Available from: https://escholarship.org/uc/item/7498c4ww#author.

Gabrys, J. 2016a. Practicing, materialising and contesting environmental data. *Big Data & Society*, 3(2).

Gabrys, J. 2016b. *Program Earth: Environmental Sensing Technology and the Making of a Computational Planet*. Minneapolis, MN: University of Minnesota Press.

Gabrys, J. 2018. Sensing lichens. *Third Text*, 32(2–3): 350–367.

Gremillet, D. 2021. Identifying seabird interactions with fisheries from GPS tracks: Automatic classification validated using bird-borne video recordings. *World Seabird Conference*, online, 6 October 2021.

Haraway, D.J. 2008. *When Species Meet*. Minneapolis, MN: University of Minnesota Press.

Hinchliffe, S. and Bingham, N. 2008. Securing life: The emerging practices of biosecurity. *Environment and Planning A*, 40(7): 1534–1551.

Hobday, A. and Hartog, J. 2014. Derived ocean features for dynamic ocean management. *Oceanography*, 27(4): 134–145.

Johnson, E.R. 2017. At the limits of species being: Sensing the Anthropocene. *South Atlantic Quarterly*, 116(2): 275–292.

Johnson, E.R. 2020. The hydra and the leviathan: Unmanned maritime vehicles and the militarized seaspace. In I. Braverman and E.R. Johnson (Eds.) *Blue Legalities: The Life and Laws of the Sea* (pp. 183–200). Durham, NC: Duke University Press.

Jue, M. 2020. *Wild Blue Media: Thinking through Seawater*. Durham, NC: Duke University Press.

Kays, R., Crofoot, M.C., Jetz, W., and Wikelski, M. 2015. Terrestrial animal tracking as an eye on life and planet. *Science*, 348(6240).

Keck, F. 2020. *Avian Reservoirs: Virus Hunters & Birdwatchers in Chinese Sentinels Posts*. Durham, NC: Duke University Press.

Kelly, A.B. and Ybarra, M. 2016. Introduction to themed issue: 'Green Security in Protected Areas'. *Geoforum*, 69: 171–175.

Kornei, K. 2020. They're stealthy at sea, but they can't hide from the albatross. *The New York Times* [online], 27 January. Available from: www.nytimes.com/2020/01/27/science/albatross-ocean-radar.html.

Kroodsma, D.A., Mayorga, J., Hochberg, T., Miller, N.A., Boerder, K., Ferretti, F., Wilson, A., Bergman, B., White, T.D., Block, B.A., Woods, P., Sullivan, B., Costello, C., and Worm, B. 2018. Tracking the global footprint of fisheries. *Science*, 359(6378): 904–908.

Lehman, J. 2018. From ships to robots: The social relations of sensing the world ocean. *Social Studies of Science*, 48(1): 57–79.

Lenton, T.M. and Latour, B. 2018. Gaia 2.0: Could humans add some level of self-awareness to Earth's self-regulation? *Science Magazine*, 361(6407): 1066–1068.

Loefflad, M.R., Wallace, F., Mondragon, J., Watson, J., and Harrington, G.A. 2014. *Strategic Plan for Electronic Monitoring and Electronic Reporting in the North Pacific*. Silverspring, MD: National Oceanic and Atmospheric Administration.

Lorimer, J. 2020. *The Probiotic Planet: Using Life to Manage Life*. Minneapolis, MN: University of Minnesota Press.

Lowerre-Barbieri, S.K., Kays, R., Thorson, J.T., and Wikelski, M. 2019. The ocean's movescape: Fisheries management in the bio-logging decade (2018–2028). *ICES Journal of Marine Science*, 76(2): 477–488.

Mathur, N. 2021. *Crooked Cats: Beastly Encounters in the Anthropocene*. Chicago, IL: University of Chicago Press.

Maxwell, S.M., Gjerde, K.M., Conners, M.G., and Crowder, L.B. 2020. Mobile protected areas for biodiversity on the high seas. *Science*, 367(6475): 252–254.

Maxwell, S.M., Hazen, E.L., Lewison, R.L., Dunn, D.C., Bailey, H., Bograd, S.J., Briscoe, D.K., Fossette, S., Hobday, A.J., Bennett, M., and Benson, S. 2015. Dynamic ocean management: Defining and conceptualizing real-time management of the ocean. *Marine Policy*, 58: 2–50.

McDonald, G.G., Costello, C., Bone, J., Cabral, R.B., Farabee, V., Hochberg, T., Kroodsma, D., Mangin, T., Meng, K.C., and Zahn, O. 2021. Satellites can reveal global extent of forced labor in the world's fishing fleet. *Proceedings of the National Academy of Sciences*, 118(3): e2016238117.

Nicolson, A. 2017. *The Seabird's Cry: The Lives and Loves of Puffins, Gannets and Other Ocean Voyagers*. Sydney, Australia: HarperCollins.

Nishizawa, B., Sugawara, T., Thiebot, J.B., Young, L.C., Vanderwerf, E.A., Sato, F., Minami, H., Yoda, K., and Watanuki, Y. 2021. Seabird-fishery interactions revealed by bird-borne GPS and camera loggers. *World Seabird Conference*, Online, 6 October 2021.

Nost, E. and Goldstein, J.E. 2022. A political ecology of data. *Environment and Planning E: Nature and Space*, 5(1): 3–17.

O'Hara, C.C., Frazier, M., and Halpern, B.S. 2021. At-risk marine biodiversity faces extensive, expanding, and intensifying human impacts. *Science*, 372(6537): 84–87.

Oral, N. 2020. Reflections on the past, present, and future of IUU fishing under international law. *International Community Law Review*, 22: 368–376.

Patrick, S. 2020. How we recruited albatrosses to patrol the high seas for illegal fishers. *The Conversation* [online], 29 January. Available from: https://theconversation.com/how-we-recruited-albatrosses-to-patrol-the-high-seas-for-illegal-fishers-130621.

Peters, K. 2020. The territories of governance: Unpacking the ontologies and geophilosophies of fixed to flexible ocean management, and beyond. *Philosophical Transactions of the Royal Society of London. Series B. Biological Sciences*, 375(1814): 20190458.

Petit, P. 2020. Everywhere surveillance: Global surveillance regimes as techno-securitization. *Science as Culture*, 29(1): 30–56.

Phillips, R.A., Xavier, J.C., and Croxall, J.P. 2003. Effects of satellite transmitters on albatrosses and petrels. *The Auk*, 120(4): 1082–1090.

Roy, E. 2020. 'Intelligent drones': Albatross fitted with radar detectors to spot illegal fishing. *The Guardian New Zealand* [online], 31 January. Available from: www.theguardian.com/world/2020/jan/31/intelligent-drones-albatross-fitted-with-radar-detectors-to-spot-illegal-fishing.

Sandbrook, C., Clark, D., Toivonen, T., Simlai, T., O'Donnell, S., Cobbe, J., and Adams, W.M. 2021. Principles for the socially responsible use of conservation monitoring technology and data. *Conservation Science and Practice*, 3(5): 374.

Sandbrook, C., Luque-Lora, R., and Adams, W.M. 2018. Human bycatch: Conservation surveillance and the social implications of camera traps. *Conservation and Society*, 16(4): 493–504.

Simlai, T. 2021. Conservation surveillance as a means for state repression? Psychological terror and the spectacles of fear through the use of drones in India. *Drone Ecologies Workshop*, Bristol, 6 July 2021.

Srinivasan, K. 2014. Caring for the collective: Biopower and agential subjectification in wildlife conservation. *Environment and Planning D: Society and Space*, 32(3): 501–517.

Steinberg, P. and Peters, K. 2015. Wet ontologies, fluid spaces: Giving depth to volume through oceanic thinking. *Environment and Planning D: Society and Space*, 33(2): 247–264.

Toonen, H.M. and Bush, S.R. 2018. The digital frontiers of fisheries governance: Fish attraction devices, drones and satellites. *Journal of Environmental Policy and Planning*, 22(1): 125–137.

Wakefield, S. and Braun, B. 2019. Oystertecture: Infrastructure, profanation and the sacred figure of the human. In K. Hetherington (Ed.) *Infrastructure, Environment, and Life in the Anthropocene* (pp. 193–215). Durham, NC: Duke University Press.

Weimerskirch, H., Filippi, D.P., Collet, J., Waugh, S.M., and Patrick, S.C. 2018. Use of radar detectors to track attendance of albatrosses at fishing vessels. *Conservation Biology*, 32(1): 240–245.

Weimerskirch, H., Collet, J., Corbeau, A., Pajot, A., Hoarau, F., Marteau, C., Filippi, D., and Patrick, S.C. 2020. Ocean sentinel albatrosses locate illegal vessels and provide the first estimate of the extent of nondeclared fishing. *Proceedings of the National Academy of Sciences*, 117(6): 3006–3014.

Whitney, K. 2014. Domesticating nature? Surveillance and conservation of migratory shorebirds in the 'Atlantic Flyway'. *Studies in History and Philosophy of Science Part C: Studies in History and Philosophy of Biological and Biomedical Sciences*, 45(1): 78–87.

Wilmers, C.C, Nickel, B., Bryce, C.M., Smith, J.A., Wheat, R.E., and Yovovich, V. 2015. The golden age of bio-logging: How animal-borne sensors are advancing the frontiers of ecology. *Ecology*, 96(7): 1741–1753.

Wilson, R.P., Grant, W.S., and Duffy, D.C. 1986. Recording devices on free-ranging marine animals: Does measurement affect foraging performance? *Ecology*, 67(4): 1091–1093.

# 6

# #AmazonFires and the online composition of ecological politics

*Jonathan W.Y. Gray, Liliana Bounegru, and Gabriele Colombo*

### Digital objects and ecological politics

How are digital objects – such as hashtags and likes – involved in ecological politics? In the wake of the 2019 Amazon rainforest fires, journalists, media outlets, NGOs, and others commented on the role of hashtags, images, links, and other kinds of online devices in mobilising and shaping public concern. For example, Asad Rehman, director of anti-poverty charity War on Want, wrote in *The Independent*:

> As the fires in the Amazon rage into their third week, with smoke blanketing the city of Sao Paolo and even visible from space, the world's attention has been belatedly sparked with the hashtag #AmazonFires trending globally.[1]

Such claims of virality were accorded prominence alongside announcements of the number of fires reported and the number of hectares burnt. For instance, the non-profit news source *Common Dreams* reported: '#PrayForAmazonia goes viral as Twitter users call attention to the "international emergency" of fires devastating Brazil's rainforest'. They presented the hashtag as a device deployed by 'social media users [attempting] to draw the world's attention to the Amazon rainforest' and to '[slam] the media for paying too little attention'.[2]

Others found digital objects were playing more troubling and unruly roles. Zoë Schlanger, environment reporter for *Quartz*, shared screenshots of search engine results for queries related to the fires, writing:

> Right now, if you search for news about the massive fires burning in the Amazon rainforest, you might mostly find stories about the Amazon Fire line of tablets and streaming devices.[3]

The media outlet *Mother Jones* published a piece titled 'Stop sharing those viral photos of the Amazon burning' with the byline 'the Amazon is on fire, but the photos you're seeing on social media don't show it' (see Figure 6.1).[4] Other outlets explored the circulation of images which were considered misleading and provided tips on 'how to spot inaccurate photos

Figure 6.1 Tweet from *Mother Jones* on 'fake' viral photos. (Source: https://twitter.com/MotherJones/status/1166085507861876736. All rights reserved and permission to use the figure must be obtained from the copyright holder.)

on social media'.[5] Some questioned the effectiveness of celebrity-driven online crowdfunding initiatives, as a 'noncommittal solution Americans can partake in from thousands of miles away'.[6]

Prompted by questions and concerns around the digital mediation and mediatisation of public engagement with the 2019 Amazon rainforest fires, this chapter considers the role of digital objects, platforms, and 'methods of the medium' in ecological politics.[7] We draw on a series of empirical vignettes from a series of collective inquiries[8] undertaken with the European Forest Institute, the Public Data Lab, DensityDesign Lab, and graduate students at King's College London.[9] Following research on the social lives of methods, we consider digital devices as 'patterned arrangements' which imply, perform, and attempt to (re-)produce (not always successfully) particular versions of the social.[10] Such devices may be traced, scraped, and 'repurposed' for social and cultural research.[11] For example, from the perspective of a web page author, hyperlinks may be used to reference, acknowledge, or point to other pages, and be understood in relation to a broader background of textual referencing practices.[12] Hyperlinks can also be repurposed to disclose the material organisation of 'issue networks': groups of 'heterogeneous entities' such as 'actors, documents, slogans, imagery' configured around a 'common problematic'.[13]

Repurposing digital devices in this spirit may allow for the examination of how things are organised online, not only considering digital objects (such as hashtags, links, or likes) as a sample or proxy whose value is derived from 'standing in' for broader societal relations, but also considering the role that such objects have in shaping social issues themselves.[14] One may, for example, study how digital devices are involved in 'configured, professional and publicized political culture' when organisations actively participate in public displays of connection by linking to each other online.[15] Digital devices may also serve to study the 'formatting of issues',[16] and the 'politics of association',[17] attending to how actors online form alliances and collectively advance their programmes.

Online data, devices, and methods may be repurposed to study not only 'how well one is doing online' (as often done by marketing professionals) but also who is dominant and who is marginalised, their concerns, positioning, and alignment,[18] or even to study the displacements of politics and politics of displacements, such as when actors or institutions reframe issues to downplay their significance or to emphasise alternative priorities.[19] Digital methods may be approached not only to study dominant voices but also to attend to marginal and excluded positions, with attention to the relations between, as Susan Leigh Star puts it, 'lived experience, technologies ... and silences'[20] in order to care for neglected, undervalued, and marginalised experiences.[21]

How such digital methods are put to work in the context of research and beyond the academic realm should be approached with both caution and care. What does it mean that researchers, public institutions, campaign groups, journalists, and others are using the web, social media platforms, and online devices not only for communication and engagement, but also for understanding and reporting on issues they work on? From the point of view of social research, digital methods have been considered 'not our own', bringing 'alien' assumptions into research.[22] How does one untangle what repurposed digital materials bring to the study of social life, particularly in the context of fields which encourage an empirical sensibility towards how societal categories, groupings, and entities are produced and stabilised?[23]

This is not just a case of asking whether digital methods can be enlisted to do the work of other methods (e.g. can tweets replace surveys?) or whether they may eclipse other research approaches (e.g. are application programming interfaces (APIs) displacing ethnographies?). One may also ask how online devices are involved in rearticulating relations between social life and social analysis and to what ends,[24] as well as how they might play a role in more inventive forms of social inquiry.[25]

In the case of the #AmazonFires project, digital objects served to explore different perspectives on forest–society relations, as well as the role of online platforms and devices in organising these relations. Through a series of workshops and activities with the European Forest Institute (an international organisation concerned with forest issues), online materials were used not only to produce research findings but also to support collective inquiry around the actors, issues, and dynamics of online engagement with the 2019 Amazon forest fires.[26] This was undertaken together with journalists, civil society groups, policymakers, and others. In the sections below we examine how digital objects were involved in formatting, performing, and disclosing different kinds of ecological politics, before concluding with a look at how this may contribute to research on environmental events and empirical, conceptual, and theoretical engagements with digital ecologies.

## What is happening? The algorithmic mediation of environmental events

We began our inquiry *in media res*, in the midst of significant international media coverage of the Amazon forest fires in August 2019. As a starting point we took hashtags which had been mainly associated with the event in predominantly English-language media coverage and used 'hashtag snowballing' – querying and gathering tweets using this initial set of hashtags to discover other ones associated with the fires. We also asked the European Forest Institute and their network of 'issue experts' for further suggestions. This gave us the following set of hashtags: #ActForTheAmazon, #AmazonFires, #AmazonRainforest, #PrayforAmazonia, #SaveTheAmazon, and #SOSAmazonia. We could also have taken a broader set of keywords, but we were particularly interested in what we could learn about the role that these prominent and widely used hashtags played in broader societal engagement. Indeed, such hashtags are considered to play a significant role in assembling and connecting different online posts into trending events.

Robin Wagner-Pacifici writes about how 'events *take* shape' through 'concrete material and formal hosts', such as 'executive orders, letters, trials, handshakes, newspaper articles, photographs, and paintings'.[27] With this spirit, one may take hashtags as a kind of digital object involved in the gathering, making, and shaping of environmental events. Forest fires were implicated with the emergence of hashtagging as a social media practice. While there are longer textual and media histories of hashtags as what one might consider connective keywords,[28] the first widely recognised use of the hashtag on Twitter was said to be #sandiegofire, in relation to the 2007 forest fires in San Diego. This led to comments from Twitter's founder that the platform 'does well' at 'natural disasters' as 'massively shared experiences'.[29]

Using the official Twitter API, we began collecting tweets containing any of the hashtags listed above associated with the 2019 Amazon forest fires using the Digital Methods Initiative Twitter Capture and Analysis Toolset, an open source project which aims to support 'methodological diversity and epistemological plurality' in working with social media data.[30] The collection starts with an initial 'spike' of tweets followed by a rapid tailing off over the coming days (Figure 6.2).

This spike coincides with media and user reports that the Amazon fires were 'trending'. Twitter's Trending Topics algorithm is said to prioritise novelty in the form of spikes or surges over overall volume of interest.[31] The algorithmic mediation of environmental events can be read against a background of longer histories of 'orderly expectations' punctuated by improbable catastrophes in cultural representations of environments.[32] For environmental phenomena to emerge as trending events on Twitter they must be exceptional, prompting a response which is an order of magnitude apart from what is usual.

Within our Amazon fires collection one can see Twitter users engaging with the platform's trending algorithm in various ways, including: (1) as a publicity tactic (e.g. 'let's get this trending'); (2) as event, hook, or social fact ('this is trending'); and (3) as failure, distraction, or displacement ('as the fires burn, look at what is trending'). In the case of Amazon fires, Twitter users respond to, imagine, lament, anticipate, critique, contest, and attempt to intervene with the platform's trending algorithm to obtain public attention – to register the fires as an internationally significant event. As various posts asked: Why are Spiderman, Trump, Sharknado, Miley Cyrus, or Jamie Oliver trending rather than the destruction of the world's largest remaining rainforest? What does this say about Twitter? What does this say about us? What can we do about it? Tweet collections may be considered as authorised records of lively, interactive algorithmic cultures arising from

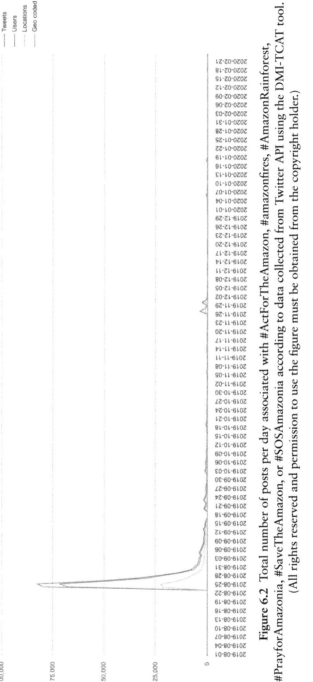

**Figure 6.2** Total number of posts per day associated with #ActForTheAmazon, #amazonfires, #AmazonRainforest, #PrayforAmazonia, #SaveTheAmazon, or #SOSAmazonia according to data collected from Twitter API using the DMI-TCAT tool. (All rights reserved and permission to use the figure must be obtained from the copyright holder.)

an interplay between platform features and user practices,[33] rather than, say, a collection of opinions as one might expect from a survey. Algorithms take part in the making of environmental events not only through computational ordering, but also their reactive effects among users alive to the politics and consequences of this ordering[34] – including what constitutes a significant public event. The hashtags may be seen as part of an attempt to get the fires trending, as well as inviting particular forms of action: to #*Act*ForTheAmazon, to #*Pray*forAmazonia, to #*Save*TheAmazon.

## What is engaging? Querying objects of engagement in environmental events

How might we characterise the 2019 Amazon fires according to this spike in Twitter activity? What kind of event is it? How are Twitter users engaging with it? Digital media scholars have suggested Twitter may be taken as a 'storytelling machine' to facilitate 'remote event analysis', for example by examining the most retweeted tweets in any given day to 'tell the story of an event as it unfolds'.[35] This can be construed as a way of taking metrics and device data into account when making sense of online material, as indicated in the phrase 'quanti-qualitative'.[36] Focusing on a ten-day period from 24 August to 2 September 2019 gave us a collection of 311,483 tweets. We looked at a selection of the top ten most retweeted tweets per day with the European Forest Institute together with Brazilian journalists and scientists and observed a wide variety of narratives, frames, and concerns, including, among others, Amazon fires as: distressing and moving event to pray for (signalled by the use of specific emojis '😢😢😢😢'); as call to action; as displacement of Indigenous communities; as celebrity cause; as space of misinformation; as cattle ranching and meat issue; as deforestation and investment issue; as foreign aid issue; as an environmental event receiving more attention than other comparable events; as scientific issue; and as political issue mobilising for or against Bolsonaro.

In the top ten most retweeted tweets per day, the Amazon rainforests are construed, variously, as 'homes' to people, plants, and animals; the 'lungs of the earth'; Indigenous lands; part of 'our planet'; agricultural sites; and Brazilian territory. Whereas encouragements to pray are most prominent among the most retweeted tweets of the first few days, over the following days, other kinds of calls to action become more visible as users were invited to sign petitions, to share messages, to elevate and give voice to affected communities, to go vegan, to debunk misleading content, to donate funds, to use the Ecosia browser extension to plant trees in Brazil, and to boycott and defund companies who are implicated in deforestation.

There are also voices and perspectives that remain marginal. For example, a graduate student group querying the Twitter data set for the names of all Indigenous communities and territories listed by the Brazilian ministry found that only two – Pataxó and Xingu – appeared in more than a handful of tweets. Among the most retweeted tweets, these two groups featured through the communications activities of climate groups outside of Brazil such as the Sunrise Movement and Fridays For Future Europe, showing how marginalised and local communities obtain visibility only through the voice of European and US-based organisations.

In addition to exploring posts according to 'built-in' platform metrics such as likes and retweet counts, the sharing of links may be taken as another way to characterise online activity associated with the fires. By unshortening,[37] cleaning, aggregating, counting, and reading the contents of the most shared links per day, one can observe a similar plurality of concerns, framings, entities, and invitations to action (Figure 6.3), as different kinds of links indicate different approaches to engaging with the fires.

As well as two peaks of sharing news media links on 24 and 27 August, one could observe petitions among the top shared URLs and social media sites (Twitter, YouTube, and Instagram), as well as NGOs who were active around the fires. The pages associated with these links proposed different framings of the forests and the fires. For example, the most shared link on the first day was an article from Argentinian media outlet *Sitio Andino* framing the forest as habitat and fires as an environmental disaster. The second was a 2006 article from *El Pais* framing the forest as livelihood and fires as a socio-economic crisis. The third was from NASA and showed heat maps and satellite imagery, portraying forests as planetary zones and the fires as planetary events. A Greenpeace petition which remained among the top shared URLs across the ten-day period contrasted 'greedy' and 'land-grabbing' agribusiness interests backed by Bolsonaro's government on the one hand with Indigenous communities, biodiversity, and climate change on the other hand. By days nine and ten there was a rise of promotional content for Etsy merchandise, including bot-like regularly recurring posts.

The most highly engaged-with posts and URLs suggest that this collection is dominated by responses and reactions to the fires, as well as responses to these responses (e.g. accusations that other posts are misleading, reporting on geopolitical exchanges which frame the fires differently). If examining the most engaged-with content can be construed as a form of remote event analysis,[38] then perhaps the event being followed is not only fires spreading in the forests but also different responses to the fires spreading around the world: an algorithmically mediated, reactive archive of the cultural production of an international environmental event.

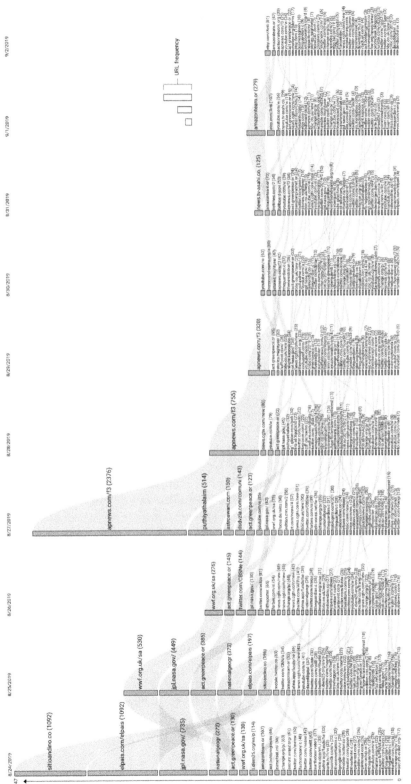

**Figure 6.3** Top 40 most shared links per day, 24 August to 2 September 2019. (All rights reserved and permission to use the figure must be obtained from the copyright holder.)

## What is hashtagging? Hashtags as indicators of environmental issue composition

One may take the web and online platforms as a 'collision space' for different kinds of concerns around the Amazon fires.[39] The Twitter collection of the fires may be considered to exhibit a degree of 'liveliness' to the extent that quite different framings and variation in terms can be detected.[40] How might we unfold the archive to untangle and situate these different kinds of concerns? How might we look beyond what is most engaged with overall in the collection?[41] Researchers in the field of science and technology studies (STS) have employed 'co-word' analysis as a 'relational indicator' in scientific text collections to explore connections among academic publications.[42] Here, 'co-hashtag' analysis has been used as a way into the dynamics and composition of issues.[43]

What is a hashtag? Hashtags form part of media interfaces and platform logics enabling interconnections between posts, users, and other digital objects. They may be used to indicate topics and events, emotions and actions, subjects and subtexts, aspirations, and asides. They may take on 'different emergent qualities' depending on how they are used.[44] We used hashtags appearing at least ten times in the collection as the basis for making a co-hashtag network: that is, a network which shows how hashtags co-occur together in posts (Figure 6.4).[45]

We co-organised a series of collective interpretation moments with the European Forest Institute, including with Brazilian journalists, researchers, and policy experts. These led to the identification of various clusters of hashtags, providing an indication of the composition of the issue on Twitter (Table 6.1). The combination of different issue hashtags can be an indication of 'issue hybridisation'[46] – for example, by connecting trending Amazon fires hashtags to #vegan hashtags. This may be taken as a deliberate tactic ('our issues are related', 'hey vegans, look at what's happening in the Amazon') or as a way to situate the fires within a tangle of concerns that exceeds conventional or professional issue articulation ('this is more than an environmental problem', 'what you eat has consequences'). The variety of concerns in the co-hashtag network may also indicate how these trending hashtags serve as 'cross-cutting networking mechanisms', producing 'unpremeditated combinations across a variety of feeds and networks'.[47] Interpreting and annotating co-hashtag networks with our collaborators served as a way to explore issue composition as well as to situate and explore relations between different concerns.

In examining this network, the prominent role of political personalities was observed, notably a series of heated exchanges between Bolsonaro

#AmazonFires and ecological politics 133

Figure 6.4 Co-hashtag network showing hashtags associated with posts containing prominent Amazon fires related hashtags on Twitter. (All rights reserved and permission to use the figure must be obtained from the copyright holder.)

and Macron and associated pro- and anti-hashtags (e.g. #vivabolsonaro, #MacronLiar). As well as 'issue celebrities'[48] such as American actor #LeonardoDiCaprio announcing a donation of $5 million, one can also see more bottom-up fan culture interventions such as the 'army' of the Korean boy band BTS mobilising in support of Indigenous and conservation organisations ('#ARMYHelpThePlanet'). Various hashtags indicate other ways in which the Amazon fires are connected to supply chains (#soybeans), consumption patterns (#govegan), trade agreements (#stopmercosur), and agricultural practices (#glyphosate). Hashtags may serve to invite, surface, and display relations between heterogeneous situations, issues, entities, and communities involved in the making of environmental events – including contestation around their meaning, significance, and stakes.

Table 6.1 Selection of hashtags identified with EFI to explore issue composition.

| Amazon fires as... | Hashtags |
|---|---|
| Climate activism issue | #climateaction, #climatecrisis, #climateemergency, #extinctionrebellion, #malizia, #unitebehindthescience, #greennewdeal |
| Scientific issue | #sciencematters, #sentinel2, #unitedbehindthescience, #nasa |
| Environmental issue | #nature, #biodiversity, #deforestation, #environmentalprotectionneeded, #endangeredspeciesprotection, #defunddeforestation |
| Meat consumption issue | #beef, #vegan, #govegan, #meatfreelaborday |
| Regional issue | #brazil, #bolivia, #sosbolivia, #buenosaires |
| Brazilian political issue | #bolsonaro, #bolsonaroensueur, #brazil, #illegitimatepresident, #forabolsonaro, #iccforbolsonaro, #vivabolsonaro |
| United States political issue | #trump, #yanggang, #fauxcahontas, #elizabethwarren2020 |
| International political issue | #G7, #g7fr, #g7summit, #g7summit2019, #g7biarritz, #cop24, #mercosur, #Macron, #macronlies, #desculpabrigitte |
| Faith issue | #popefrancis |
| Celebrity issue | #armyhelptheplanet, #army, #방탄소년단, #boywithluv, #bts, #leonardodicaprio, #armypurpleearth, #yoshiki, #kamalhassan |
| Indigenous communities, rights, and land issue | #indigenous, #indigenouspeople, #IndigenousPeoples, #IndigenousRights, #landgrabbing, #landrightsnow, #defendindigenousrights |
| Economic issue | #blackstone, #financing, #billionaires |
| Agricultural issue | #agribusiness, #soybeans, #farmers, #palmoil, #biofuel |
| Fact-checking and misinformation issue | #fakenews |

## What is imaging? From visual misinformation to social lives of environmental images

If pedologists sampling soil in the Amazon forest support a 'long chain of transformations' enabling the circulation of references from field to report,[49] what forms of public knowledge and action are invited when online platforms, devices, and digital objects are involved in the making of environmental events? What role do images play?

Some of the most highly engaged with posts involve contested images and visual representations. For example, fact-checking account HoaxEye wrote 'Not a single photo of #AmazonFires', above images which are portrayed by another viral tweet as 'sad images of Amazon fires'. The fact-checking account also provided source details for the inaccurate images ('Spain, 2006', 'Argentina, 2018', 'Costa Rica, 2016', 'Mexico, 2019'), showing how images from other fires are misleadingly used to tweet about the Amazon fires. The same account highlighted Bolsonaro's contention that Macron is sharing 'fake photos' ('fotos falsas') in order to 'instumentalise an internal issue of Brazil'. In another widely shared post, US conservative commentator Dinesh D'Souza posted: 'Many of the photos of #AmazonFires are bogus. They are taken from years ago – sometimes as far back as 2000. Another case of #FakeNews to advance the climate change hoax'.[50] US magazine *Mother Jones* posted: 'The single most viral photo of the #AmazonFires is fake and you should really stop sharing it since it makes you look silly', and the *Times of India* reported 'These three most-viral images of #AmazonFires are "fake"'.

Our collaborators at the European Forest Institute were keen to know more about these claims about misleading images. When looking into the circulation of some of the most engaged with images in the Twitter collection (both within the collection and across the web and other platforms), we found that many of them were indeed from places and times other than the Amazon forests in 2019. One of the most engaged with posts contained a photo taken in 2016 showing a jaguar which had been rescued by the Brazilian army being held in the arms of a soldier wading through water. Many images of distressed, injured, and dead animals circulating in posts associated with the fires were from other events. Pictures of burning forests – including those shared by Macron, Leonardo DiCaprio, and the footballer Cristiano Ronaldo – were from other fires, as much as a decade and a half earlier. One of the most retweeted tweets contains an image of forest fires in Thailand. A highly shared video of an Indigenous Pataxó woman was from an arson attack outside the Amazon forest.

What is it that makes an image misleading? How might one distinguish between images being shared as direct representations of events and images which are doing other kinds of meaning work? When are images to be taken as evidence of an event, and when might they serve as 'generic visuals'?[51] Previous studies have explored the role of images in environmental and climate communications – from 'issue animals'[52] to 'issue landscapes'.[53] Such images may serve to indicate *types* of animals, landscapes, and environmental events, for the purposes of issue work which often aims to enrol events as part of broader and ongoing issues (e.g. an oil spill as a form of pollution, as one of a series of spills as a result of corporate malfeasance). On the website of an NGO, an image of a forest fire may be to some degree substitutable. Similarly, images in news media coverage may often be selected from stock photography collections, with the image serving as content within a template or layout. Social media posts with images are said to have higher engagement rates than those without.

Looking beyond a focus on the representational (in-)fidelities or faithfulness of images, we traced their circulation and social lives within and beyond our Twitter collection in order to obtain a richer picture of 'instances of image usage'[54] and 'sites of audiencing'.[55] As Hito Steyerl comments, digital images are not just about 'the real thing' but also their 'own real conditions of existence' including their transformation, recontextualisation, appropriation, exploitation, and dispersion.[56] When accounting for the technicity of 'networked images',[57] one may also learn about the features and vernaculars of online spaces and platforms in which they circulate.[58] This shifted the focus of our collaborative interpretation activities with the European Forest Institute from 'misleading images' to 'media recycling' and tracing and telling stories about the social lives of images without necessarily assuming they are used in a way which is misleading.[59] We explored various approaches for analysing and redisplaying social media images in terms of their content, ordering, circulation, and audiencing.[60] For example, taking a forest fire image that the Agence France-Presse (AFP) characterised as misleading as a starting point, we looked at variations, visually similar images, and images which contained this image throughout the collection (Figure 6.5), as well as tracing the texts and contexts in which these images were shared.

In tracing these variations and image variants one can find different visual formats, indicating some of the ways in which they are put to work in different situations. There are several near copies with minor modifications such as cropping or stretching (group A in Figure 6.5). There are also screenshots of the image posted indicating the context of the online space in which it was posted such as Instagram posts and tweets (group B in Figure 6.5), often including additional textual elements. These posts include practices of 'screenshot debunking', where images of news articles and

#AmazonFires and ecological politics 137

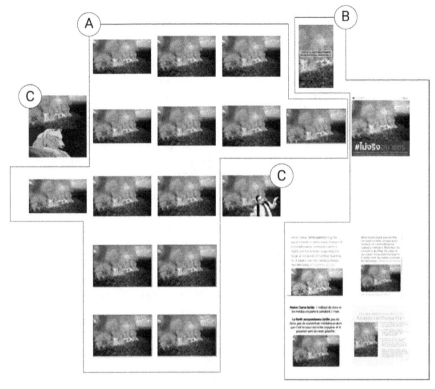

**Figure 6.5** Tracing variations and different visual articulations of pre-2003 burning forest image shared by Macron and others in association with 2019 Amazon fires. (All rights reserved and permission to use the figure must be obtained from the copyright holder.)

tweets flagging the image as potentially misleading have been used together with hashtags like #FakeNews and #misinformation. These kinds of images are also overlaid with fact checking or 'credibility labels' on platforms where they are shared. In looking into these labelling practices, we found that not all versions of an image are treated equally: one widely circulating version of the image on Facebook has a warning from fact-checking organisations, whereas the same image posted by Macron contains no such warning. One can also see memefied versions, with other visual elements overlaid or juxtaposed, repurposing the original image for satirical takes on the event (group C in Figure 6.5), often with an affected dimension, which may be read in a similar vein to 'reaction gifs' (e.g. animated images used to express emotions in online conversations).

## Digital objects, methods, ecologies

What can digital objects tell us about ecological politics? The empirical vignettes in the sections above examine how digital objects may serve as a way to explore: (1) the algorithmic meditation of environment events and how the 2019 Amazon fires were organised, staged, and narrated as trending events; (2) which kinds of concerns, framings, entities, and invitations to action are 'doing well' online by following and querying objects of engagement such as posts and links; (3) how relations between different concerns and groups are invited and displayed by means of the interpretation of co-hashtag networks; and (4) the roles that images played in online activity around the fires, looking beyond misleading photographs to the social lives of networked images and what they disclose.

What kinds of understandings of environmental politics can digital methods enable? Another recent study suggests that following prominent hashtags shows how the 2019 Amazon fires were construed as a planetary problem – for example, with framing such as 'lungs of the earth' – framing Bolsonaro as responsible and animals and Indigenous Peoples as victims.[61] Delving further into the Twitter archive provides further insights into how digital objects were involved in the making, contestation, and negotiation of meanings, representations, and relations around the fires. As well as surfacing different kinds of actors, concerns, and invited action (witnessing, boycotting, donating, debunking, amplifying, sharing, signing), the Twitter archive was used to elicit different conceptions of what the Amazon fires were as an environmental event.[62] Through collaborative interpretation exercises with our civil society and journalist collaborators, digital objects in the archive served as a prompt to rethink the making of environmental events online and what it means to talk about ecological governance, stakeholders, science communication, and misinformation in this context. Amidst the many lively responses and counter-responses in the archive, the absence of live reporting involving affected communities, human and not, present at the scene of the fires is even more conspicuous.

### Notes

1. Rehman, 'Bolsonaro is basically burning the Amazon'.
2. Johnson, '#PrayForAmazonia Goes Viral'.
3. Schlanger, 'Why you won't see much news'.
4. Weinberg, 'Stop sharing those viral photos'.
5. Agence France-Presse, 'Amazon forest fire'.
6. Nguyen, 'People have donated millions'.

7 Rogers, *Digital Methods*.
8 Gray et al., 'Engaged research-led teaching'.
9 We are most grateful to all of the researchers, students, and collaborators who joined us. For other materials from these inquiries, see: https://publicdatalab.org/projects/out-of-the-flames/.
10 Law and Ruppet, 'The social life of methods'.
11 Marres and Weltevrede, 'Scraping the social?'; Rogers, *Digital Methods*.
12 Brügger, 'Connecting textual segments'.
13 Marres, 'Why map issues?'; Marres and Rogers, 'Recipe for tracing'; Rogers and Marres, 'Landscaping climate change'.
14 Mulvin, *Proxies*.
15 Rogers, *Digital Methods*, p. 54.
16 Marres, 'Net-work is format work'; Marres and Rogers, 'Subsuming the ground'.
17 Rogers, *Digital Methods*, p. 5.
18 Rogers, 'Otherwise engaged', p. 450.
19 Marres, 'No issue, no public'.
20 Star, 'Five questions', p. 227.
21 Puig de la Bellacasa, 'Matters of care'.
22 Marres and Gerlitz, 'Interface methods'; Marres and Weltevrede, 'Scraping the social?'
23 Boullier, 'Médialab stories'; Venturini et al., 'An unexpected journey'.
24 Marres, *Digital Sociology*.
25 Lury and Wakeford, *Inventive Methods*; Marres et al., *Inventing the Social*.
26 Gray et al., 'Engaged research-led teaching'.
27 Wagner-Pacifici, *What Is an Event?* pp. 10–11; italics in original text.
28 E.g. Bernard, *Theory of the Hashtag*.
29 Rogers, 'Debanalizing Twitter', p. 360.
30 Borra and Rieder, 'Programmed method'.
31 Gillespie, 'Can an algorithm be wrong?'
32 Ghosh, *The Great Derangement*.
33 Seaver, 'Algorithms as culture'.
34 Espeland and Sauder, 'Rankings and reactivity'.
35 Rogers, *Doing Digital Methods*.
36 Ibid. Cf. Moats and Borra, 'Quali-quantitative methods beyond networks'; Venturini and Latour, 'The social fabric'.
37 Shortened links (e.g. using services such as bit.ly) were unshortened so different posts pointing to the same link could be counted together, enabling exploration of those which were most shared.
38 Rogers, *Doing Digital Methods*.
39 Rogers, *Information Politics on the Web*.
40 Marres and Weltevrede, 'Scraping the social?'
41 Rogers, 'Otherwise engaged'.
42 Courtial and Law, 'A co-word study of artificial intelligence'.
43 Marres and Gerlitz, 'Interface methods'.

44 Rambukkana, *Hashtag Publics*, p. 2.
45 Created using Gephi and the Force Atlas 2 algorithm. See Jacomy et al., 'ForceAtlas2'. Hashtags which co-appear in posts more frequently are closer together in the network.
46 Rogers, *Doing Digital Methods*.
47 Segerberg and Bennett, 'Social media and the organization of collective action', p. 203.
48 GovCom.org, 'Issue celebrities'.
49 Latour, *Pandora's Hope*.
50 See https://twitter.com/DineshDSouza/status/1165631438647103488.
51 Aiello et al., ' "Generic visuals" '.
52 Digital Methods Initiative, 'Issue Animals'.
53 Digital Methods Initiative, 'Issue Landscapes'; Rogers, 'Digital methods'.
54 Rogers, 'Visual media analysis for Instagram and other online platforms'.
55 Rose, *Visual Methodologies*.
56 Steyerl, 'In defense of the poor image'.
57 Niederer, *Networked Images*; Niederer and Colombo, 'Visual methodologies for networked images'.
58 Pearce et al., 'Visual cross-platform analysis'.
59 See http://amazonfires.publicdatalab.org/third-issue.
60 Colombo et al., 'Visual models for social media image analysis'.
61 Skill et al., 'Assembling Amazon fires'.
62 The data for this study was collected in 2019, three years before Elon Musk's purchase of Twitter and associated debates among researchers, civil society groups, activists, and institutions concerning the ownership, economics, governance, and future of the platform. Amidst reports of rising hate speech, the disappearance of historical posts, changing user practices, and loss of API access, the fate of platform data and its role in media research remains to be seen.

## Bibliography

Agence France-Presse. 2019. Amazon forest fire: Pictures shared on social media with hashtag '#PrayforAmazonas' are several decades old or from other countries, reports AFP. *Firstpost* [online], 22 August. Available from: www.firstpost.com/world/amazon-forest-fire-pictures-shared-on-social-media-with-hashtag-prayforamazonas-are-several-decades-old-or-from-other-countries-reports-afp-7204951.html.

Aiello, G., Kennedy, H., Anderson, C.W., and Mørk Røstvik, C. 2022. 'Generic visuals' of Covid-19 in the news: Invoking banal belonging through symbolic reiteration. *International Journal of Cultural Studies*, 24(3–4): 309–330.

Bernard, A. 2019. *Theory of the Hashtag* (trans. V.A. Pakis and D. Ross). Medford, MA: Polity.

Borra, E. and Rieder, B. 2014. Programmed method: Developing a toolset for capturing and analyzing tweets. *Aslib Journal of Information Management*, 66: 262–278.

Boullier, D. 2018. Médialab stories: How to align actor network theory and digital methods. *Big Data & Society*, 5: 2053951718816722.

Brügger, N. 2017. Connecting textual segments: A brief history of the web hyperlink. In N. Brügger (Ed.) *Web 25: Histories from the First 25 Years of the World Wide Web* (pp. 3–28). New York: Peter Lang.

Colombo, G., Bounegru, L., and Gray, J. 2023. Visual models for social media image analysis: Groupings, engagement, trends, and rankings. *International Journal of Communication*. https://ijoc.org/index.php/ijoc/article/view/18971.

Courtial, J.-P. and Law, J. 1989. A co-word study of artificial intelligence. *Social Studies of Science*, 19: 301–311.

Digital Methods Initiative. 2007. Issue Animals [online]. Available from: https://wiki.digitalmethods.net/Dmi/IssueImageAnalysis.

Digital Methods Initiative. 2013. Issue Landscapes [online]. Available from: www.digitalmethods.net/Dmi/MappingClimateConflictVulnerabilityAndVictims.

Espeland, W.N. and Sauder, M. 2007. Rankings and reactivity: How public measures recreate social worlds. *American Journal of Sociology*, 113: 1–40. https://doi.org/10.1086/517897.

Gabrys, J. 2018. Becoming planetary. *e-Flux* [online]. Available from: www.e-flux.com/architecture/accumulation/217051/becoming-planetary/.

Ghosh, A. 2016. *The Great Derangement: Climate Change and the Unthinkable*. Chicago, IL: University of Chicago Press.

Gillespie, T. 2012. Can an algorithm be wrong? *Limn* [online]. Available from: https://limn.it/articles/can-an-algorithm-be-wrong/.

GovCom.org. 2007. *Issue Celebrities* [online]. Available from: https://movies.digitalmethods.net/issuecelebrities.html.

Gray, J., Bounegru, L., Rogers, R., Venturini, T., Ricci, D., Meunier, A., Mauri, M., Niederer, S., Sanchez-Querubin, N., Tuters, M., Kimbell, L., and Munk, A. 2022. Engaged research-led teaching: Composing collective inquiry with digital methods and data. *Digital Culture and Education*, 14. www.digitalcultureandeducation.com/volume-143-papers/gray-etal-2022.

Jacomy, M., Venturini, T., Heymann, S., and Bastian, M. 2014. ForceAtlas2, a continuous graph layout algorithm for handy network visualization designed for the Gephi software. *PLoS ONE*, 9: e98679.

Johnson, J. 2019. #PrayForAmazonia goes viral as Twitter users call attention to 'international emergency' of fires devastating Brazil's rainforest. *The Independent* [online], 20 August. Available from: www.commondreams.org/news/2019/08/20/prayforamazonia-goes-viral-twitter-users-call-attention-international-emergency.

Latour, B. 1999. *Pandora's Hope: An Essay on the Reality of Science Studies*. Cambridge, MA: Harvard University Press.

Latour, B. and Weibel, P. (Eds.) 2020. *Critical Zones: The Science and Politics of Landing on Earth*. Cambridge, MA: MIT Press.

Law, J. and Ruppert, E. 2013. The social life of methods: Devices. *Journal of Cultural Economy*, 6: 229–240.

Lury, C. 2020. *Problem Spaces: How and Why Methodology Matters*. Cambridge, UK: Polity.

Lury, C. and Wakeford, N. (Eds.) 2012. *Inventive Methods. The Happening of the Social*. New York: Routledge.

Marres, N. 2005. *No Issue, No Public: Democratic Deficits After the Displacement of Politics*. Amsterdam: University of Amsterdam.

Marres, N. 2006. Net-work is format work: Issue networks and the sites of civil society politics. In J. Dean, J. Anderson, and G. Lovink (Eds.) *Reformatting Politics: Information Technology and Global Civil Society* (pp. 3–18). New York: Routledge.

Marres, N. 2012. *Material Participation: Technology, the Environment and Everyday Publics*. London: Palgrave Macmillan.

Marres, N. 2015. Why map issues? On controversy analysis as a digital method. *Science, Technology, and Human Values*, 40: 655–686.

Marres, N. 2017. *Digital Sociology: The Reinvention of Social Research*. London: Polity Press.

Marres, N. 2020. For a situational analytics: An interpretative methodology for the study of situations in computational settings. *Big Data & Society*, 7: 2053951720949571.

Marres, N. and de Rijcke, S. 2020. From indicators to indicating interdisciplinarity: A participatory mapping methodology for research communities in-the-making. *Quantitative Science Studies*, 1: 1041–1055.

Marres, N. and Gerlitz, C. 2015. Interface methods: Renegotiating relations between digital social research, STS and sociology. *The Sociological Review*, 64: 21–46.

Marres, N., Guggenheim, M., and Wilkie, A. (Eds.) 2018. *Inventing the Social*. Manchester: Mattering Press.

Marres, N. and Rogers, R. 2005. Recipe for tracing the fate of issues and their publics on the web. In B. Latour and P. Weibel (Eds.) *Making Things Public: Atmospheres of Democracy* (pp. 922–935). Cambridge, MA: MIT Press.

Marres, N. and Rogers, R. 2008. Subsuming the ground: How local realities of the Fergana Valley, the Narmada Dams and the BTC pipeline are put to use on the web. *Economy and Society*, 37: 251–281.

Marres, N. and Weltevrede, E. 2013. Scraping the social? Issues in live social research. *Journal of Cultural Economy*, 6: 313–335.

Moats, D. and Borra, E. 2018. Quali-quantitative methods beyond networks: Studying information diffusion on Twitter with the modulation sequencer. *Big Data & Society*, 5: 2053951718772137.

Mol, A. 1999. Ontological politics: A word and some questions. *The Sociological Review*, 47(S1): 74–89. https://doi.org/10.1111/j.1467-954X.1999.tb03483.x.

Mol, A. 2003. *The Body Multiple: Ontology in Medical Practice*. Durham, NC: Duke University Press Books.

Mulvin, D. 2021. *Proxies: The Cultural Work of Standing In*. Cambridge, MA: MIT Press.

Nguyen, T. 2019. People have donated millions to fight the Amazon fires. Will the money help? *Vox* [online], 27 August. Available from: www.vox.com/the-goods/2019/8/27/20835154/amazon-fires-charity.

Niederer, S. 2018. *Networked Images: Visual Methodologies for the Digital Age*. Amsterdam: Hogeschool van Amsterdam.

Niederer, S. and Colombo, G. 2019. Visual methodologies for networked images: Designing visualizations for collaborative research, cross-platform analysis, and public participation. *Diseña*, 14: 40–67.

Pearce, W., Özkula, S.M., Greene, A.K., Teeling, L., Bansard, J.S., Omena, J.J., and Rabello, E.T. 2018. Visual cross-platform analysis: Digital methods to research social media images. *Information, Communication and Society*, 23(2): 161–180.

Puig de la Bellacasa, M.P. 2011. Matters of care in technoscience: Assembling neglected things. *Social Studies of Science*, 41: 85–106.

Rambukkana, N. (Ed.) 2015. *Hashtag Publics: The Power and Politics of Discursive Networks*. New York: Peter Lang.

Rehman, A. 2019. Bolsonaro is basically burning the Amazon – but Macron is complicit too. *The Independent* [online], 24 August. Available from: www.independent.co.uk/voices/amazon-rainforest-fire-bolsonaro-macron-facism-neoliberalism-agribusiness-a9076631.html.

Rogers, R. 2004. *Information Politics on the Web*. Cambridge, MA: MIT Press.

Rogers, R. 2013a. *Digital Methods*. Cambridge, MA: MIT Press.

Rogers, R. 2013b. Debanalizing Twitter: The transformation of an object of study. *Proceedings of the 5th Annual ACM Web Science Conference* (pp. 356–365). New York: Association for Computing Machinery.

Rogers, R. 2018. Otherwise engaged: Social media from vanity metrics to critical analytics. *International Journal of Communication*, 12, 450–472.

Rogers, R. 2019. *Doing Digital Methods*. London: Sage.

Rogers, R. 2021. Visual media analysis for Instagram and other online platforms. *Big Data & Society*, 8, 1–23. https://doi.org/10.1177/20539517211022370.

Rogers, R. and Marres, N. 2000. Landscaping climate change: A mapping technique for understanding science and technology debates on the World Wide Web. *Public Understanding of Science*, 9, 141–163.

Rose, G. 2016. *Visual Methodologies: An Introduction to Researching with Visual Materials*. London: Sage.

Ruppert, E., Law, J., and Savage, M. 2013. Reassembling social science methods: The challenge of digital devices. *Theory, Culture and Society*, 30(4): 22–46. https://doi.org/10.1177/0263276413484941.

Schlanger, Z. 2019. Why you won't see much news about the devastating Amazon rainforest fires on Google News. *Quartz* [online], 21 August. Available from: https://qz.com/1692755/amazon-fire-tablet-upstages-amazon-rainforest-fires-on-google.

Seaver, N. 2017. Algorithms as culture: Some tactics for the ethnography of algorithmic systems. *Big Data & Society*, 4: 2053951717738104.

Segerberg, A. and Bennett, W.L. 2011. Social media and the organization of collective action: Using Twitter to explore the ecologies of two climate change protests. *The Communication Review*, 14: 197–215.

Skill, K., Passero, S., and Francisco, M. 2021. Assembling Amazon fires through English hashtags: Materializing environmental activism within Twitter networks. *Computer Supported Cooperative Work*, 30: 715–732. https://doi.org/10.1007/s10606-021-09403-6.

Star, S.L. 2007. Five questions. In J.K.B. Olsen and E. Selinger (Eds.) *Philosophy of Technology* (pp. 223–232). US/UK: Automatic Press.

Steyerl, H. 2009. In defense of the poor image [online]. Available from: www.e-flux.com/journal/10/61362/in-defense-of-the-poor-image/.

Tsing, A.L. 2011. *Friction: An Ethnography of Global Connection*. Princeton, NJ: Princeton University Press.

Tsing, A.L. 2015. *The Mushroom at the End of the World: On the Possibility of Life in Capitalist Ruins*. Princeton, NJ: Princeton University Press.

Venturini, T. and Latour, B. 2010. The social fabric: Digital traces and quali-quantitative methods. *Proceedings of Futur En Seine 2009* (pp. 87–101). Paris: Editions Futur en Seine.

Venturini, T., Bounegru, L., Gray, J., and Rogers, R. 2018. A reality check(list) for digital methods. *New Media and Society*, 20, 4195–4217.

Venturini, T., Jacomy, M., Meunier, A., and Latour, B. 2017. An unexpected journey: A few lessons from sciences Po médialab's experience. *Big Data & Society*, 4, 2053951717720949.

Wagner-Pacifici, R. 2017. *What Is an Event?* Chicago, IL: University of Chicago Press.

Weinberg, A. 2019. Stop sharing those viral photos of the Amazon burning. *Mother Jones* [online], 21 August. Available from: www.motherjones.com/environment/2019/08/viral-photos-amazon-fire-fake-macron/.

# 7

# Children and young people's digital climate action in Australia: co-belonging with place, ecology, and Country

*Jess McLean and Lara Newman*

## Introduction

Children and young people continue to engage with and co-create digital spaces to achieve their personal and collective goals, in extraordinary as well as everyday contexts, from protesting against environmental injustices to building social networks. At the same time, climate action in Australia is facilitated by entanglements of the digital with non-digital spaces, enabled by lands and waters that form Aboriginal and Torres Strait Islander Country. One growing and important example of both digital world making and climate action is School Strike 4 Climate Australia (SS4C), which involves children and young people working across digital and non-digital spaces to advocate for safer futures. Based on a close analysis of the digital environmental activism produced by a SS4C 15 October 2021 event, this chapter considers the entanglement of digital and non-digital actors, and what this says about co-belonging with ecologies, Country, and place.

The digital affords the capacity to bring together diffuse SS4C events that have been, and are, held across large spaces, while also supporting the social networks that enable the movement. Digital geographies of the movement are produced by the reporting of place-based protests and descriptions that visually and textually record who engages, where they are situated, and why they are participating. Digital renderings of the strikes and rallies enable a sense of solidarity across vast distances and somewhat countervails Australia's relatively low population density. Further, digital spaces articulate relations between multiple scales of climate action, linking local, state, and national iterations with a global social movement of children and young people striking for climate action.

While Australian federal governments have been slow to take effective climate action, children and young people's grassroots movements that tap into global climate action campaigns are still growing. The SS4C in Australia is inspired by Greta Thunberg's leadership and associated international campaigns to build climate action momentum. Power and resistance are a strong part of these expressions of discontent and they foreshadow an alternative future in which children and young people's desire for sustainable worlds is digitally and non-digitally writ large.

A digital ecologies approach is used in this chapter to analyse the SS4C movement, a climate activist group driven by children and young people creatively making digital and non-digital spaces to address Australian and global environmental crises. The digital content that SS4C creates works to coordinate, record, and amplify the in-person strikes and rallies, and is curated with a view to building solidarity and working towards justice in a framework of co-belonging. Importantly, SS4C centres Indigenous knowledges and argues for climate justice in compelling ways: from starting events with acknowledgements and welcomes to Country to including calls for Indigenous sovereignty within campaign actions, SS4C aims to undermine settler colonial power.

The question that this chapter sets out to answer is: what does the SS4C demonstrate about children and young people working towards reparative digital worlds to counter Australian and global climate crises? By analysing digital data in the lead up to and just after a SS4C event in late 2021, a picture of the aims and qualities of the movement emerges that contributes to our understanding of diverse digital geographies. This chapter offers an analysis of one small part of an international social movement that works with entangled digital and non-digital spaces to foster effective environmental activism.[1]

By examining the role of place and Country in the digital spaces created by SS4C, evidence of how co-belonging is generated within an exciting movement emerges, showing how young people are doing substantial work in seeking better climate governance and reparative futures. We build on recent research on SS4C here to show how co-belonging partly shapes the movement and suggest future research pathways that may extend this digital geographic scholarship.[2] Our positionality contributes to our analysis in this chapter; Jess McLean is parent to a boy who attended the first SS4C event in Sydney in 2018 and is white Australian. Lara Newman is a teacher and academic of diverse heritage who has attended several SS4C events.

### Perspectives on repair, connecting to place, and the digital

Inspired in part by the work of J.K. Gibson-Graham,[3] this chapter offers an analysis of repair in action that is emerging from this social movement. One question that guided Gibson-Graham's work was whether humans could reimagine economies as co-belonging with, and constituted by, ecologies, Country, and place. As we show in this chapter, the SS4C includes calls for action that are grounded in place, centre Country, and seek more sustainable environmental futures. We use a digital ecologies lens to illuminate the ways in which this particular environmental movement emphasises place and Country, as children and young people imagine different environmental futures.

We understand Country as describing a particular area belonging to Aboriginal and Torres Strait Islander peoples, and to which they belong, and that it includes animate and inanimate entities. Aboriginal and Torres Strait Islander peoples' connections to Country may include cultural practices, knowledge, songs, stories, art, non-human life, atmosphere, and waterways.[4] Country is a living thing for which Aboriginal and Torres Strait Islander people care, and which cares for them. The authors of this chapter learn from Aboriginal and Torres Strait Islander peoples about what Country means and how it relates to climate justice.[5] In this context, digital environmental activism that centres Country is one way to articulate connections to place and ecology within Australia.

## Digital ecologies, co-belonging, and repair

As an approach, digital ecologies has its conceptual roots within media studies scholarship, along with multiple related metaphors including 'communication ecology' and 'media ecology', to theorise connections between media and social movements and to capture the complexity in relationships between both spheres. For example, Treré and Mattoni argue that a 'media ecological lens' enables us to understand the communicative complexity within social movements and the media that they employ.[6] The media ecological lens encompasses a diversity of metaphors and these are variably used to explain different theoretical positions and approaches. In research on digital food activism, Giraud uses a communication ecologies lens to analyse interventions targeting multinational food chains,[7] including the tensions between the political goals of such social movements and the use of corporatised digital media. Earlier, Taffel offered a constructive analysis of digital media ecology as forged by entangled scalar relations, emphasising materialist concerns within media studies.[8] Digital media is a focus for Pickerill,[9] who notes how Movement Intellectuals leading environmental activism can 'advocate new ways of viewing and utilising technology – to those within the movement and the general public – ways that might contradict with commercial desires for the technology'. It is within this broad context of digital environmental activism scholarship that this case study sits.

The term 'digital ecology' emerges from two strands of research according to Lyle et al.:[10] one tending to use digital ecologies as an overarching term for digital–human interactions and the other grounded in digital design within pedagogical literature. For the purposes of this chapter, we take digital ecologies to refer to an approach that considers how digital technologies can potentially deepen the ties between humans and more-than-human lifeworlds in generative ways.[11] More-than-human geographic scholarship of the digital is emphasising how digital devices are co-producing environments. For example, Prebble et al. show how smart urban forests are governed in Australia at the local government scale with a policy and document analysis of current digital governance initiatives;[12] this research found that digital interventions of urban forests reinforce and reproduce Western values of nature. Decentring humans is a distant possibility in many smart urban forest practices but Gabrys invites us to do just that and think about how forests walk.[13] Non-human agency is foregrounded in this recent digital and more-than-human geographic research. Indeed, multiple forms of agency have been studied in social movement studies for some time, expanding the focus on individual human and collective agency to other agents of change. For example, Feigenbaum considers non-human actors as key components of the Occupy Movement, ranging from 'the signboard-ready flat surfaces of a canvas marquee to the atmospheric quality of tear gas'.[14] Nature is tangentially included in Feigenbaum's analysis in the form of grass playing a role in the tent assemblage. By extending this earlier de-centring of the human with analysis of Country as a powerful actor in digitally mediated social movements, we hope to continue this conversation on agency.

Digital ecologies captures the interplay and interconnections between 'natural' spaces and data. Morey succinctly argues that 'Nature is digital' in their chapter entitled *Digital Ecologies* for an edited collection on ecology and new media.[15] The compartmentalisation and atomisation of nature in much of modernist thinking is the target of Morey's claim that 'the modern' has warped and reduced nature. Connecting nature with digital technologies via framing these as digital ecologies can open up and challenge this reductionism according to Morey, and we found this perspective productive in our analysis of SS4C.

More recently, Nost and Goldstein introduce a special issue on the political ecology of data with a prescient claim that it is only by understanding digital technologies – including platforms, devices, and the institutions that make up digital ecosystems – that we can understand where we are at in terms of global environmental governance.[16] A Special Issue for *Digital Geography and Society* on 'Digital Natures' also examines how digital technologies and practices reshape how nature is conceptualised and invites political critiques of these transformations.[17] Digital geography scholars are examining human, nature, and digital technological relations and offering conceptual and empirical tools in ways that help us understand our digital worlds.[18] We suggest that the connections and disconnections between digital geographies and digital ecologies literatures are yet to be fully conceptualised: the two research approaches share significant common ground and future theoretical work could examine this terrain.

Building on J.K. Gibson-Graham's thinking on repair in the Anthropocene, this chapter analyses a social movement that is seeking transformation and offers an examination of the social media that is entangled with in-person strikes that remake co-belonging. Gibson-Graham focus on the regional scale in their thinking on a feminist project of belonging for the Anthropocene. They exhort us to reimagine economies as co-belonging with, and constituted by, ecologies, Country, and place, rather than continuing damaging extractive modes of production and consumption. This chapter takes up their challenge and adopts a multi-scaled perspective to show how place is important in grounding the SS4C in the digital, while also connecting to global social movements and confronting this global environmental issue. Gibson-Graham consider co-belonging in the Anthropocene with a regional emphasis, and we build on this framing to think about repair via children and young people's digital activism. Repair may be facilitated by climate action – especially in Australia where so much remains to be done on this front – and plays a key role in realigning human and non-human relations for alternative futures.

## Research on SS4C and children and young people's digital environmental activism

Research on digital platforms and how young people are experiencing, and resisting, climate change has shown that the digital is a primary avenue for 'affectively and politically staging this problem'.[19] Rousell and Cutter-Mackenzie-Knowles started a research project in northern New South Wales prior to the emergence of SS4C, studying how a climate change education app might facilitate young people's agency with respect to climate action. They situate their findings in relation to SS4C and describe it as a globally theatrical political movement, drawing on Deleuzian concepts of affect and differentiation.

Recent research specifically on SS4C includes consideration of citizenship deployment as part of the movement, the role of emotion and affect in SS4C, and how adults are responding to children and young people's protests, but it does not examine the digital geographies of the movement. Before March 2020, when physical distancing and prohibitions of large mass gatherings were made in response to the COVID-19 pandemic, five large School Strike 4 Climate events were held around Australia, supported by digital actions.[20] Analysing how students are engaging in activism, Collin and Matthews describe the SS4C Australian movement in detail from that time, and argue that it is an example of students renegotiating citizenship.[21] Their chapter examines the event on 20 September 2019 that was facilitated by SS4C and draws on surveys with protestors at the time as well as soon after the event. The surveys were complemented by mainstream media analysis and participant observation. Like earlier SS4C events in Australia, the 2019 SS4C event started with a Welcome to Country, this time by Aunty Rhonda Dixon-Grovenor, Gadigal Traditional Owner, and her daughter, Nadeena Dixon.[22] Beginning the SS4C with this protocol is important as it centres Indigenous knowledges in climate justice efforts.

Social and climate justice are an ongoing focus for SS4C leaders and participants. In a survey of SS4C participants, Collin and Matthews found that participants 'were mainly motivated to attend the protest "to put pressure on politicians to make things change," "raise public awareness," and "express solidarity"'.[23] By emphasising citizenship in their analysis of the 2019 SS4C, Collin and Matthews counter the denigration of this emergent social movement by politicians in Australia who were against the political action and outline the ethical framing of SS4C participants by documenting the event. Our chapter builds on Collin and Matthews' offering by examining the SS4C held in late 2021 and the digital activism that enabled, and was intertwined with, the in-person gatherings to produce compelling social movements.

Pedagogical research has included analysis of the dynamics of the SS4C and what it means for education in Australia.[24] Alexander et al. examine how adults framed the protest in mainstream media and categorised these as protectionist narratives or anticipatory narratives.[25] Anticipatory narratives involve asserting that children should be in school and that strikes are inappropriate activities for them to pursue, while protectionist narratives tend to claim that children should be shielded from the political adult world so they are not harmed by the harsh realities therein. Whether anticipatory or protectionist, the fact that SS4C persists demonstrates the commitment to alternative futures that young people in Australia (and elsewhere) seek. Indeed, Verlie and Flynn describe school strikers as themselves becoming climate change educators, in a prefigurative sense, by organising and enacting the climate strikes.[26] In contributing to this burgeoning research on children and young people's activism, this chapter offers a digital ecologies perspective on co-belonging within SS4C.

## Methodology

Digital methods were used to collect data about SS4C social media activities during a strike event. Drawing on Rogers,[27] we examined quantitative and qualitative aspects of the posts that involved organising and then amplifying the event. Data collection focused on the lead-up to, and aftermath of, an Australian School Strike for Climate action held on 15 October 2021. Empirical data were collected from social media accounts in the week leading up to and immediately after this event. The content analysis of this material included noting:

- the type of post (inviting attendance/reporting participation/political critique/outcome of strike action);
- the geographical location of the post;
- the scope of strike action (including an estimate of the number of participants);
- a record of the sort of engagement with the post (number of likes/comments/shares);
- and a sample standout comment/response.

This data collection focused on the national Twitter account for School Strike for Climate in Australia and the Instagram Sydney-based and national accounts for New South Wales (NSW) data (as the official NSW page was only set up after the 15 October strike). The Sydney account tended to focus on the NSW-wide digital strike. National accounts for both Twitter and Instagram contain content from most Australian states and territories; there wasn't much identified as being from the Australian Capital Territory or Victoria, although we understand that some of the photos were from those strikes. A lot of the smaller SS4C social media accounts have been inactive since May 2021 or earlier, probably due to COVID-19 related lockdowns, so there wasn't much content regarding the 15 October strikes on those accounts.

Following this data collection process, data analysis involved coding for significant themes and processes that shape digital action, using a summative and direct content analysis approach.[28] In terms of summative content analysis, we examined word frequency of key words related to digital climate action including young people, protest, hope, future, change, Australia, fossil free, Morrison (for then Australian Prime Minister Scott Morrison). Direct content analysis drew on themes raised from previous research in young people's digital climate action.[29] The data were analysed according to the following dimensions: the scope and scale of the climate action; the demands put forward by the participants; and the themes that shaped the actions. The co-belonging – between protestors, Country, and the digital – that emerges from this analysis is partial rather than a complete representation of the event.

## Tracking children and young people making place and acknowledging Country on SS4C social media

### SS4C Australia and Sydney Instagram accounts

From the SS4C's national Instagram account, there was significant diversity in engagement between types of posts. Political critique of former Prime Minister Scott Morrison received the largest engagement. Inviting attendance to in-person events received moderate engagement. For example, this post on the SS4C Instagram account had nearly 3,000 likes: 'Scott Morrison's voting record is clear. He just could not care less about our futures 😔 It is so important that we make our voices clear and say enough is enough! Join us on October 15 for the National #ClimateStrike! RSVP to your local in-person or online action at: ss4c.info/oct15 #TheYouthAreRising #ClimateStrike #ClimateCrisis #ScottMorrison #WhatACOPOut'.

There were fewer posts on Instagram than on Twitter; however, the national Instagram account posts generally received far more comments and likes than the Twitter account's posts, and more than the NSW/Sydney Instagram account. Posts of memes tended to attract a substantial number of likes. Instagram was strategically used for organising and promotion in the lead-up to 15 October, and to encourage engagement and action on the day – approximately 40% of posts were from 10 to 14 October, 40% were on the day of strike (15 October), 20% were after the strike (16–20 October). Similar styles and branding were used across posts – yellow and purple featured as text colours, tints over images, and in backgrounds of posts on Twitter and Instagram. Posts prior to 15 October focused on engaging politicians, participating on social media, and preparing resources for the strike. The national account posted content on strikes all over the continent.

The Sydney Instagram account tended to focus on NSW-wide action rather than remaining Sydney specific (the official NSW Instagram page was set up after the 15 October), extending the geographical presence of SS4C beyond the largest city in the state. Likes tended to be higher for posts inviting attendance at the digital NSW action. Most posts were sharing content from the national Instagram or Twitter accounts. Overall, the majority of posts (45%) were invites, followed by reporting participation (31%), outcome of strike action (17%), and political critique (8%). The digital is therefore crucial in facilitating participation and engagement for SS4C.

In terms of content relating to Indigenous knowledges in these Instagram accounts, the Queensland rally was particularly interesting. Posts from that SS4C event acknowledged that young people and other Queenslanders are resisting climate inaction and First Nations people have led this resistance of poor governance and settler colonial power for hundreds of years. Extending the articulation of resistance to environmental devastation beyond the immediate climate crisis shows the depth of SS4C understanding with respect to the agents responsible for the Anthropocene.

### SS4C Australian Twitter account

Content of Twitter stories on the SS4C Australian account varied in the lead up to, during, and after the 15 October strike. There were fewer tweets in the lead up to 15 October than posts on Instagram. Use of Twitter seemed to focus on political critique and reporting engagement on 15 October, while Instagram focused more on planning and engagement prior to the event. It is worth noting here that SS4C's different strategies create a decentralised but still cohesive 'collective actor', resonant with media studies scholarship that establishes how collectives have been created in different activist settings such as the Occupy Movement (for example Kavada).[30]

On 15 October, the SS4C national Twitter account was populated by many tweets from the movement and retweets of articles from major news outlets, as well as from supporters such as unions, parent groups, Greens and Labor politicians, business people, and other climate action groups in Australia and one from India. This may indicate an extensive network of adults allied with the student movement and seems to be reflective of a deliberate attempt to make that support visible to politicians and media.

There were more reposts of others' content relating to SS4C on Twitter than on Instagram, especially on the day of the strike. The hashtags #ClimateStrike and #theyoutharerising, as well as the topic 'Morrison' were trending on 15 October. A small percentage (21%) of tweets were invites, which predominantly appeared prior to 15 October, or early on in the Twitter feed. Tweets reporting outcomes of strike action made up only 5% of tweets and featured during or after 15 October. Political critique (36%) and reporting attendance (39%) made up the majority of tweets. Some tweets contained content from multiple categories (for example, political critique and reporting attendance). Political critique focused heavily on Scott Morrison, with occasional references to liberal member Sussan Ley (then Minister of the Environment at the federal level), the National Party (a conservative political party), and the Queensland Labor party (a political party that aims to support equality).

Reports of attendance were celebratory tweets, with some political critique and references to voting politicians out or 'voting climate' at the May 2022 federal government election. Most comments on Twitter associated with SS4C and the strike event were in support of it and the students; however, there were more unsupportive or critical comments on Twitter than on Instagram. Some tweets were also featured on Instagram indicating the strategic and sophisticated quality of social media and community engagement by SS4C. There were far fewer images and videos on Twitter than on Instagram, reflecting the affordances of both platforms.

Examining particular strikes and how they are shared on these social media feeds provides insights into how Country, place, and ecologies are fundamental components of the overarching SS4C movement. For instance, SS4C named the Meanjin/Brisbane Strike (in Queensland) as such in a deliberate move to highlight Aboriginal sovereignty. 'Meanjin' is the Jagera and Turrbal peoples' traditional name for the Brisbane area,[31] and while the Aboriginal custodians of the land and many others frequently use this name, it is not often used as the first name for the city. Inverting its order – naming the strike as in Meanjin/Brisbane rather than Brisbane/Meanjin – is a conscious strategy to undermine colonial naming practices. Approximately 3,000 people participated in the Meanjin/Brisbane Strike and a long video was shared on the SS4C feed of a young person giving a speech and leading chants, accompanied by an adult Auslan (sign language of Australia) interpreter. One chant that started the event was 'Always was, always will be, Aboriginal land', capturing how integral recognition of Indigenous sovereignty is for SS4C.

After this video post, SS4C share another video of a student striker giving a speech on the need for creating space for inclusion of 'diverse' and 'BIPOC' people (Black, Indigenous, and people of colour), and calling for a focus on their voices in climate activism. This speaker discussed how climate justice requires racial justice, respect for intersectionality, and that we need to have conversations about giving land back to Aboriginal and Torres Strait Islander peoples, working to achieve environmental justice and ending climate apartheid. One comment in response to this video was 'Climate Justice is Racial Justice, what a powerful speech!!! 👏🏾👏🏾👏🏾👏🏾👏🏾👏🏾'

Other strike events around Australia aimed to centre Country in meaningful ways. The SS4C event in Tasmania named the location of the event as Indigenous Country: 'NIPALUNA HOBART OCT 15 STRIKE Live footage from Nipaluna the youth are rising strike 🔥'. Nipaluna is the Indigenous name for the place that settler colonial structures label as Hobart. In Sydney, posts mentioned 'Warrang/Sydney' as the location for striking, again centring Indigenous place names.

## SS4C as grounded in place, ecology, and Country

Children and young people involved in SS4C are using digital platforms to express their political agency and work against apathy on climate change. Connected to the international movement of school strikes, Australia's SS4C is grounded in place and centres Indigenous ways of knowing and protocols in their digital and in-person activities to cultivate a strong sense of co-belonging.

The energy, enthusiasm, and spirit of the SS4C is evident in the event studied here, and in previous strikes, both in the digital amplification and organisation of the event and the strikes on the ground. The colourful gatherings, the powerful speeches, the effective posters, the slogans at strike actions, all reflect a motivated and organised collective who are committed to generating change – and are having fun while doing so. The SS4C movement continues to build momentum, even when pandemic lockdown conditions made digital protests the only feasible option, and in the face of despair about inaction on climate crises.[32]

Joining social movements and engendering solidarity has been shown to promote stronger mental health among participants of protest movements, including social media-driven feminist movements.[33] In the context of climate action, Trott has shown how participation in youth-led climate action in the United States helped children feel more positive about the state of the world,[34] and this reflects the atmospheres captured in digital presences of SS4C. The strikers in this case study come together with anger, hope, enthusiasm, despair, humour, and kindness. We could think here of participants 'bearing worlds', as Verlie proposes in her pedagogical work on climate anxiety,[35] which involves enduring and encountering difficult climate realities now while simultaneously building collectives to make more tolerable futures.

Digital ecologies, as an emerging research area, may benefit from drawing on Gibson-Graham's invitation to think about co-belonging in terms of place and ecologies, helping us to ground lived realities of global environmental dilemmas such as climate change. To return to the question set out at the beginning of this chapter, how are children and young people digitally asserting co-belonging to, and with, their places and ecologies in the context of the SS4C? While they rallied in their towns and cities in discrete groups, a sense of unification was generated by digital connections, and these relations will likely be an important feature of future events. The affordances of social media are an especially crucial component of SS4C in this nation that has low population density and persists as a climate action laggard.[36]

The audience for SS4C goes beyond children and young people as the data gathered from primary social media accounts managed by the movement leaders demonstrate. A key theme was 'voting climate' at the studied event, which is clearly impossible for many participants as they are under the current Australian legal voting age of eighteen. The SS4C's demonstration of active citizenship, despite a lack of capacity to realise this citizenship in a formal vote at an election, is indicative of the strategic qualities of the social movement and corroborates with Collin and Matthews' research.[37] With the benefit of hindsight, it is not too much of a stretch to suggest that SS4C most likely played a role in the Liberal Party's loss of the Australian 2022 federal election, which was made possible by a significant wave of support for climate action independents and a solid climate policy from the victorious Labor Party.

Nuanced political engagement of the sort captured on the Twitter account for SS4C shows the sophistication of the movement. For example, the then Prime Minister Scott Morrison-related tweets and Instagram posts received the most engagement by followers and yet this is not the extent of the political targets chosen by SS4C. For context, Morrison is on the record as actively dissuading the strikers from pursuing their social activism,[38] but this did not sway their activism; rather, it may have potentially galvanised their commitment to the cause. Further, instead of just focusing on one political target – the seemingly pro-fossil fuel then PM – the protestors extended their critique to the federal Environment Minister Sussan Ley, the conservative National Party, and the Queensland Labor Party. Sussan Ley followed the party line on climate action, adopting a minimalist approach on carbon emission reductions and continuing to support fossil fuel extraction. The National Party's policies on climate change have been at odds with the realities of the experiences of their supporter base: despite being a rural political party, where the effects of climate change are directly felt in terms of lived experiences with extreme weather events and challenging economic realities, the Nationals have pushed a conservative political agenda and, along with the Liberal Party, opted to take minimal action on climate change.[39]

Effective environmental activism is a part of co-belonging for the SS4C and includes careful political interventions. For example, the SS4C's targeting of the Queensland Labor Party was an attempt to leverage political power they do not directly have as children and young people. The Queensland Labor Party, while nominally a politically progressive party that is in power, has also been reticent to proactively halt logging or block the expansion of coal mining. For the SS4C to encompass multiple targets in this one multi-located event mirrors the depth of the campaign and the sophistication of their claims. Also, the integration and association of the SS4C with other protest movements is evident in their multiple points of intervention. It is also worth noting that the SS4C calls for a just transition for workers, disrupting the historical narrative of environment versus jobs and economy that politicians seem so fond of in Australia and other similar wealthy nations.

Place is important in grounding the SS4C around Australia, reflecting how social transgressions such as protests play out in a range of settings,[40] and that these specificities affect social movements. As we have shown in the digital data of the 15 October event, reporting on where the gatherings were situated played a part in building community and showing how co-belonging can be articulated in such a diverse nation, with numerous gatherings on different Countries. The digital affords the capacity to bring together diffuse events across large spaces and strengthen the social networks that enable the movement, capturing some of the particular qualities of places nationwide. Digital geographies of the movement are made clear in the reporting of place-based protests and descriptions that visually and textually record who engages, where they are situated, and why they are participating. On the role of place in SS4C, the strategy of locating the protest event in multiple sites across the continent at the same time, while invoking adult support across these different states and territories, may have put more pressure on politicians and political parties than if it was just one gathering, in one place. A distributed and digitally amplified protest movement produces a potentially more significant impact than a concentrated, singularly located event.

Centring Country in rethinking how and why humans and non-humans co-belong in the Anthropocene offers another way of approaching the digital. In the SS4C, Indigenous knowledges and protocols are central to the way the events are run, both in person and digitally. As Collin and Matthews describe, a Welcome to Country launched the 2019 large Sydney SS4C event, and climate justice concerns are central to the framing of the movement.[41] The October 2021 event shared this focus with protest signs including calls for Indigenous justice in Perth, and the Brisbane/Meanjin event included a speech by a leader that began with a chant of 'Always was/always will be/ Aboriginal Land'. The Brisbane/Meanjin introductory speech connected this climate fight with the resistance led by First Nations people against settler colonialism since invasion. Multiple posters calling for climate justice and supporting First Nations' people were carried by protestors.

Indigenous scholars have been questioning modernist notions of global environmental collapse for some time, drawing on Indigenous ontologies and epistemologies to counter universalist arguments. For instance, Indigenous science counters the 'new' assignation of living (and dying) in the Anthropocene with sound arguments about how colonial forces have produced environmental, social, and cultural crises for centuries. Kyle Whyte, a Potawatomi scholar-activist, argues that human-induced climate change is an extension and deepening of environmental crises imposed on Indigenous peoples around the world by colonial forces. Rather than accepting the science of environmental dilemmas on multiple fronts as agents producing the Anthropocene, Whyte argues that global environmental crises are another wave of extractive colonial practices.[42] The problematic flattening of responsibility that accompanies Anthropocenic thinking – where all humans are defined as contributing to global environmental crises – deepens colonial thinking rather than overturns past injustices. Whyte suggests that Indigenous climate science is one way to remedy these universalist and marginalising tendencies and construct alternative futures. Another view is offered by Indigenous scholar Zoe Todd,[43] who argues for Indigenising the Anthropocene rather than allowing gentrification and white dominance of this intellectual idea that has captured scientific and social scientific imaginations.

With these critiques in mind, we can read how children and young people in Australia who participate in SS4C are aware of histories and presences of colonialism and the ongoing injustices that Aboriginal and Torres Strait Islander people experience on many fronts. The centring of Aboriginal and Torres Strait Islander people and issues in the running of SS4C events and the digital facilitation, recording, and reflections of those events all provide evidence of this knowledge. Further, the connections between SS4C and organisations such as Seed, Australia's first Indigenous youth-led climate network, are also visible in participation at strike events. It is clear that climate justice arguments are core to the SS4C, including how Country must be recognised and that sovereignty of Australia is contested.

## Digital worlds and future building within SS4C

The SS4C is an example of how children and young people are actively co-creating reparative digital worlds to confront and hopefully renegotiate Australian and global environmental crises. The digital content that facilitates, coordinates, records, and amplifies the in-person strikes and rallies is curated with a view to building solidarity and working towards justice. SS4C centres Indigenous knowledges and argues for climate justice in compelling ways that are building momentum, despite restrictive sociopolitical contexts and relatively limited opportunities to assert their political agency (in formal terms).

The multiple political strategies that undergird SS4C's digital work shows how complex this movement is: rather than simply rehashing critiques and attacks on political leaders, different political targets appear in the materials circulating at the events and in the digital spaces associated with the strikes. As a case study of children and young people carving out space for their personal and collective goals, this SS4C event in late 2021 illustrates how striking digitally and in person can be a generative and hopeful act.

Future digital ecologies research could continue the emerging research on how children and young people are creating interventions in environmental governance. Digital ecologies scholarship might also centre conceptualisations of Country that facilitate involvement of, and respect for, Indigenous peoples and their knowledges. The agency of Country has been foregrounded in Indigenous scholarship of the digital, including within Carlson and Frazer's book *Indigenous Digital Life*.[44] Activism and identity are important aspects of how and why Indigenous people use digital technologies,[45] and grounding both with connections to Country may provide avenues for digital ecologies approaches to continue doing decolonial work.

Digital ecologies as an approach can enable a focus on reparative relations, a repeated theme in this growing literature, and in depictions of creative (digital) social movements that are aiming to transform political, social, environmental, and economic relations. The relationship between the emergent literatures in digital ecologies and digital geographies will also provide productive conversations in these research areas.[46] Digital ecologies approaches that emphasise human and more-than-human relations might continue to provide productive linkages between digital geographic and media scholarship in future work.

In closing, one of the most remarkable qualities of SS4C is how it has managed to generate and express co-belonging, despite heavy critique from national political leaders and in the face of incredibly frustrating social, political, and environmental realities. The atmosphere at SS4C events, and in their associated digital worlds, is supportive, righteous, and joyous, even when climate change policy in Australia has been underwhelming, and despite incredibly high stakes, as reflected in the damaging realities of continuing to live with climate change.

## Notes

1 Pickerill, 'Cyberprotest'.
2 Collin and Matthews, 'School Strike 4 Climate'; Verlie and Flynn, 'School strike for climate'.
3 Gibson-Graham, 'A feminist project of belonging for the Anthropocene'.
4 Australian Institute for Aboriginal and Torres Strait Islander Studies, 'Welcome to Country'.
5 Birch, 'Recovering a narrative of place'.
6 Treré and Mattoni, 'Media ecologies and protest movements'.
7 Giraud, 'Displacement, "failure" and friction'.
8 Taffel, 'Scalar entanglement in digital media ecologies'.

9. Pickerill, 'Cyberprotest', p. 32.
10. Lyle et al., 'What's in an ecology?'
11. Duroux (with the Digital Ecologies Team), 'The slowness of digital ecologies in practice'; Searle et al., 'The digital peregrine'.
12. Prebble et al., 'Smart urban forests'.
13. Gabrys, 'The forest that walks'.
14. Feigenbaum, 'Resistant matters', p. 16.
15. Morey, 'Digital ecologies'.
16. Nost and Goldstein, 'A political ecology of data'.
17. Bori, 'CFP: Digital natures'.
18. Kinsley, 'The matter of "virtual" geographies'; McLean, *Changing Digital Geographies*.
19. Rousell et al., 'Digital media, political affect, and a youth to come', p. 5.
20. Ibid.
21. Collin and Matthews, 'School Strike 4 Climate'.
22. Ibid.
23. Ibid., p. 134.
24. Verlie and Flynn, 'School strike for climate'.
25. Alexander et al., 'More learning, less activism'.
26. Verlie and Flynn, 'School strike for climate'.
27. Rogers, 'Digital methods for cross-platform analysis'.
28. Hsieh and Shannon, 'Three approaches to qualitative content analysis'.
29. Collin and Matthews, 'School Strike 4 Climate'; Nairn, 'Learning from young people engaged in climate activism'.
30. Kavada, 'Creating the collective'.
31. Bhattacharya and Barry, 'On orientations and adjustments'.
32. Nairn, 'Learning from young people engaged in climate activism'.
33. Foster, 'Tweeting about sexism'.
34. Trott, 'Climate change education for transformation'.
35. Verlie, 'Bearing worlds: Learning to live-with climate change'.
36. McLean, 'Connections between energy and ecological democracy'.
37. Collin and Matthews, 'School Strike 4 Climate'.
38. Mayes and Hartup, 'News coverage of the School Strike for Climate movement in Australia'.
39. Crowley, 'Up and down with climate politics'.
40. Cresswell, *In Place/Out of Place*.
41. Collin and Matthews, 'School Strike 4 Climate'.
42. Whyte, 'Indigenous climate change studies'.
43. Todd, 'Indigenizing the Anthropocene'.
44. Carlson and Frazer, *Indigenous Digital Life*.
45. Ibid.
46. Ash et al., *Digital Geographies*; Kinsley et al., 'Editorial'; McLean, *Changing Digital Geographies*.

## Bibliography

Alexander, N., Petray, T., and McDowall, A. 2021. More learning, less activism: Narratives of childhood in Australian media representations of the School Strike for Climate. *Australian Journal of Environmental Education*, 38(1): 96–111.

Ash, J., Kitchin, R., and Leszczynski, A. (Eds.) 2018. *Digital Geographies*. London: Sage.

Australian Institute of Aboriginal and Torres Strait Islander Studies. 2022. Welcome to Country. AIATSIS [online]. Available from: https://aiatsis.gov.au/explore/welcome-country.

Bhattacharya, D. and Barry, K. 2021. On orientations and adjustments: An exploration of walking, wandering and wayfinding in Brisbane–Meanjin, Australia. *Australian Geographer*, 52(3): 257–272.

Birch, T. 2018. Recovering a narrative of place: Stories in the time of climate change. *The Conversation* [online], 26 April. Available from: https://theconversation.com/friday-essay-recovering-a-narrative-of-place-stories-in-the-time-of-climate-change-95067.

Bori, P. 2020. CfP: Digital Natures: Reworking Epistemologies, Ontologies and Politics Special Issue for the journal Digital Geography and Society. *POLLEN website* [online], 1 December. Available from: https://politicalecologynetwork.org/2020/12/01/cfp-digital-natures-reworking-epistemologies-ontologies-and-politics-special-issue-for-the-journal-digital-geography-and-society/#more-4611.

Carlson, B. and Frazer, R. 2021. *Indigenous Digital Life: The Practice and Politics of Being Indigenous on Social Media*. London: Palgrave Macmillan.

Collin, P. and Matthews, I. 2021. School Strike 4 Climate: Australian students renegotiating citizenship. In M. Bessant, A. Mesinas, and S. Pickard (Eds.) *When Students Protest: Secondary and High Schools* (pp. 125–143). Lanham, MD: Rowman and Littlefield.

Cresswell, T. 1992. *In Place/Out of Place: Geography, Ideology, and Transgression* (Vol. 2). Minneapolis, MN: University of Minnesota Press.

Crowley, K. 2017. Up and down with climate politics 2013–2016: The repeal of carbon pricing in Australia. *Wiley Interdisciplinary Reviews: Climate Change*, 8(3): e458.

Duroux, N. (with the Digital Ecologies Team). 2022. The slowness of digital ecologies in practice. *Digital Ecologies Blog* [online], 18 September. Available from: www.digicologies.com/2022/09/18/noemi-duroux/.

Feigenbaum, A. 2014. Resistant matters: Tents, tear gas and the "other media" of Occupy. *Communication and Critical/Cultural Studies*, 11(1): 15–24.

Foster, M.D. 2015. Tweeting about sexism: The well-being benefits of a social media collective action. *British Journal of Social Psychology*, 54(4): 629–647.

Gabrys, J. 2021. The forest that walks: Digital fieldwork and distributions of Site. *Qualitative Inquiry*, 28(2): 228–235.

Gibson-Graham, J.K. 2011. A feminist project of belonging for the Anthropocene. *Gender, Place and Culture*, 18(1): 1–21.

Giraud, E.H. 2018. Displacement, "failure" and friction: Tactical interventions in the communication ecologies of anti-capitalist food activism. In T. Schneider, K. Eli, C. Dolan, and S. Ulijaszek (Eds.) *Digital Food Activism* (pp. 130–150). London: Routledge.

Hsieh, H.F. and Shannon, S.E. 2005. Three approaches to qualitative content analysis. *Qualitative Health Research*, 15(9): 1277–1288.

Kavada, A. 2015. Creating the collective: Social media, the Occupy movement and its constitution as a collective actor. *Information, Communication and Society*, 18(8): 872–886.

Kinsley, S. 2014. The matter of 'virtual' geographies. *Progress in Human Geography*, 38(3): 364–384.

Kinsley, S., McLean, J., and Maalsen, S. 2020. Editorial. *Digital Geography and Society*, 1.

Lyle, P., Korsgaard, H., and Bødker, S. 2020. What's in an ecology? A review of artifact, communicative, device and information ecologies. *Proceedings of the 11th Nordic Conference on Human-Computer Interaction: Shaping Experiences, Shaping Society* (pp. 1–14) [online], 26 October. Available from: https://dl.acm.org/doi/pdf/10.1145/3419249.3420185?casa_token=apuINlorfqEAAAAA:gul1vxqxeyulcbFGyCQVYWxk5nrGgDTzdKv5fONFhrPopD0fvV9Xkow_Zgmfwd7JeHpFaF_d5jtxFQ.

Mayes, E. and Hartup, M.E. 2021. News coverage of the School Strike for Climate movement in Australia: The politics of representing young strikers' emotions. *Journal of Youth Studies*, 25(7): 994–1016.

McLean, J. 2020. *Changing Digital Geographies: Technologies, Environments and People*. London: Palgrave Macmillan.

McLean, J. 2022. Connections between energy and ecological democracy: Considering the Climate Council as a case of climate action in Australia. *Energy Research and Social Science*, 85: 1–10.

Morey, S. 2011. Digital ecologies. In S. Dobrin (Ed.) *Ecology, Writing Theory, and New Media* (pp 114–129). London: Routledge.

Nairn, K. 2019. Learning from young people engaged in climate activism: The potential of collectivizing despair and hope. *YOUNG*, 27(5): 435–450.

Nost, E. and Goldstein, J. 2022. A political ecology of data. *Environment and Planning E: Nature and Space*, 5(1): 3–17.

Pickerill, J. 2003. *Cyberprotest: Environmental Activism Online*. Manchester: Manchester University Press.

Prebble, S., McLean, J., and Houston, D. 2021. Smart urban forests: An overview of more-than-human and more-than-real urban forest management in Australian cities. *Digital Geography and Society*, 2.

Rogers, R. 2018. Digital methods for cross-platform analysis. In J. Burgess, A. Marwick, and T. Poell (Eds.) *The SAGE Handbook of Social Media* (pp. 91–110). London: Sage.

Rousell D., Wijesinghe, T., Cutter-Mackenzie-Knowles, A., and Osborn, M. 2021. Digital media, political affect, and a youth to come: Rethinking climate change education through Deleuzian dramatization. *Educational Review*, 75(1): 33–53.

Searle, A., Turnbull, J., and Adams, W.M. 2022. The digital peregrine: A technonatural history of a cosmopolitan raptor. *Transactions of the Institute of British Geographers*, 48(1): 195–212.

Taffel, S. 2013. Scalar entanglement in digital media ecologies. *NECSUS: European Journal of Media Studies*, 2(1): 233–254.

Todd, Z. 2015. Indigenizing the Anthropocene. In H. Davis and E. Turpin (Eds.) *Art in the Anthropocene: Encounters Among Aesthetics, Politics, Environments and Epistemologies* (pp. 241–254). London: Open Humanities Press.

Treré, E. and Mattoni, A. 2016. Media ecologies and protest movements: Main perspectives and key lessons. *Information, Communication and Society*, 19(3): 290–306.

Trott, C.D. 2021. Climate change education for transformation: Exploring the affective and attitudinal dimensions of children's learning and action. *Environmental Education Research*, 28(7): 1023–1042.

Verlie, B. 2019. Bearing worlds: Learning to live-with climate change. *Environmental Education Research*, 25(5): 751–766.

Verlie, B. and Flynn, A. 2022. School strike for climate: A reckoning for education. *Australian Journal of Environmental Education*, 38(1): 1–12.

Whyte, K. 2017. Indigenous climate change studies: Indigenizing futures, decolonizing the Anthropocene. *English Language Notes*, 55(1–2): 153–162.

# 8

# 'Saving the knowledge helps to save the seed': generating a collaborative seed data project in London

*Sophia Doyle and Katharine Dow*

## Introduction

London Freedom Seed Bank (LFSB) is a small network dedicated to saving, storing, and sharing plant seeds across London and raising awareness of the political importance of seed saving. It holds a small library of open-pollinated seeds that are grown and harvested by its members and shared at seed swap events or, more recently due to the COVID-19 pandemic, via post. At present the LFSB connects 144 crop varieties, 128 growers, and 99 growing spaces across the wider London area and is coordinated by a small, voluntary steering group who manage, record, and share the seed stock with the wider grower network. For this, the steering group keeps detailed records of the seeds in its care, the people who grow them, and the spaces that they are grown in. In 2020, steering group members Richard Galpin and Anna Clow designed a digital database using the free version of the software Airtable to hold information about the LFSB's seed stock and to trace how the seeds move through the network through time. Since its inception, this database, called the LFSBase, has grown into a larger and more ambitious project aiming to also record and share the growers' knowledge and stories alongside the seeds themselves. As Richard explained in a post on the LFSB's blog introducing the database project: 'What has become clearer is that the physical seeds are only a part of the resource that we aim to nurture and share at LFSB – there is also an abundance of social relations, grower knowledge, non-human genetic seed knowledge, and political aspiration'.[1]

For this chapter, we are drawing on our dual roles as researchers and activist members of LFSB. Our close involvement with the organisation has allowed us to observe and participate in the inner workings of the seed network and, through it, insight into the design process of the LFSBase. Witnessing the excitement with which the LFSB growers and the public engaged with the seeds through the mediating environment of the database, we felt a critical potential in how the LFSBase facilitated both material and digital encounters between the plants and the people who grow them, and how it highlighted the interaction between species and environments that are necessary for things to grow. The data presented in this chapter are informed by both authors' previous research on the LFSB, but will focus particularly on our analysis of the LFSBase, drawing on interviews and informal conversations we have had within the steering group and with the creators of the Base.

With this chapter we set out to explore how data technologies such as the LFSBase are implicated in the production of knowledges about the living worlds they record. Rejecting the dominant framing of data technologies as epistemically neutral, ahistorical, and merely representational, we follow Eric Nost and Jenny Elaine Goldstein in their articulation of the ways in which data and data infrastructures are material, governed, practised, and fundamentally a 'product of social, political, cultural and economic circumstance'.[2] With this understanding, data and data technologies are always already engendered in the particular world-making projects that they arise from; we recognise how data are constantly 'at the heart of questions of mattering, and consequently at the heart of the political'.[3] We want to 'look beyond data as a "representational resource", to consider the various forms of epistemic, social and political work that it does and which is done to produce it'.[4] As recent work and the contributions in this volume extrapolate, processes of datafication of everyday life extend beyond the realm of the human to include the so-called 'natural' with increasing intensity. This opens up new ways of reading data itself as a 'political ecology', prompting consideration of the ethical implications that this datafication has for how we relate and act in our ecologies and interspecies relations. With this chapter we aim to show how the design and specific practices of capture of information on the more-than-human world is embroiled in epistemological projects, and how digital technologies can both reproduce and subvert the epistemes in which they were created to facilitate other ways of knowing and being in relation to our ecologies.

In the first two sections we examine how practices of recording, ordering, and storing data on the living world are part of a genealogy of imperial knowledge production as part of the establishment of racial capitalism. This has given rise to a seed regime based on ideas of genetic purity and linearity, which is increasingly mediated and governed through data technologies such as national and international databases which commodify the plant life they record as a legible inventory for a global market. Activists resisting this epistemological framing of seeds as intellectual property/commodity avail themselves of database technologies while also subverting the modern corporate seed regime by saving their own seed, often based in an understanding of seed saving and food growing as collaborative, interspecies practice. We then go on to examine how the LFSBase captures the relationships between the seeds in the care of the network, the growers who grow them, and the places they are grown in. We examine how these lively entangled relationships are translated into the digital environment of the database and what kinds of knowledges are facilitated through the design of the database. Understanding how the 'digitisation of nonhuman life across spaces, species, and scales has profound implications for how we see our place in the world and how we act in it',[5] we ask: what kinds of knowledges and relationalities are fostered in the digital space of the database, and what kinds of ethics emerge from these connections? We feel that such a reading of the LFSBase holds generative potential for a political ecology of data which approaches everyday practices of data management as sites of inquiry and knowledge-making where hegemonic epistemes are (re)produced, but also where relations and meanings are made that exist in tension with and leak beyond the strictures of colonial logics.

## Technologies of collection

Databases first emerged in the mid-twentieth century from innovations in the office-equipment industry as tools to manage the ever-increasing speed and scale of industrial operations in a globalised market, and soon became the primary technology for organising and storing information.[6] Yet practices of collecting and ordering data on the living world date back much further. With the expansion of European empires, the disciples of the budding disciplines of natural science were sent to research, record, and map the flora and fauna of the colonies in search for 'green gold', scouting and extracting specimens that could prove profitable for empire. This led to an explosion of data flooding into imperial centres, which required new practices of recording, storing, and ordering information, a practice which continues to provide the majority of genetic resources for scientific research in the West to this day.[7] This led early botanists such as Carl Linnaeus to experiment with 'different ways of presenting and arranging large amounts of data on plants and animals' in indexes, tables, and manuscripts in their struggle with the resulting 'information overload'. They eventually produced taxonomies and nomenclature which became the basis for modern scientific classification today, producing natural history as a 'prototype of what one could call "data-driven" research'.[8]

These 'technologies of collection' were purposefully engendered in the much larger epistemic project of naturalising the extractive operations of capital in the colonies. As plants were violently extracted from their lively local relations they were reframed within the systematised logics of a universal botanical language and rendered 'legible' as inventory on a global market.[9] Local names, relations, and uses of the plants were substituted with the 'pure' and supposedly superior classifications of empirical science, erasing all previous modes of being and relating 'not premised upon the value, profitability and usefulness of plants that underpins the vampiric logic of capitalism towards nature'.[10] Importantly, these same processes of classification not only ordered the 'plant kingdom' into families, genera, and species, but they also classified humans through racial taxonomies,[11] in order to legitimate colonisation, enslavement, and genocide. The plants extracted from the colonies were cast as discoveries of European explorers and botanists and the inventions of the plant breeders who sought to 'improve' them as cash crops for agronomic use.[12] Situating the development of these early 'technologies of collection' within the political economy of colonialism facilitates a critical understanding of how data management practices today continue to operate through extractive logics which have material and racialised consequences.

## Making modern seeds

This modern dream of 'improvement' fundamentally underpinned the development of scientific plant breeding as a cornerstone of industrial agriculture. With innovations in genetics at the turn of the twentieth century, a broader ontological shift has been observed in the life sciences, in which life began to be increasingly understood through doctrines of linear evolution and genetic purity. Lively organisms came to be understood as 'having an intrinsic genetic identity, sealed off from the vagaries of the environment', which articulated itself in the scientific search for 'purified forms of life', an approach which Christophe Bonneuil and Frederic Thomas have termed 'pure line ontology'.[13] This 'genetic modernism' reduced seeds to the status of genetic resources and marked a prioritisation of 'pure', 'improved', and 'elite' cultivars that were (re)produced through state-sponsored breeding programmes as governments realised the profitability and biopolitical potential of plant breeding, while farmer-bred and saved seeds were cast as 'impure' and unreliable.

This hierarchical ontology was further institutionalised with the development of hybridisation, a breeding practice in which two 'pure lines' are crossed to produce hybrid seed, the first generation (F1) of which usually produces a higher yielding and morphologically uniform crop, making F1 hybrids favourable to the demands of industrialised agriculture. However, because F1 hybrids do not produce 'true to type' in subsequent generations, they cannot be saved by the farmer for future use. This ruptured traditional farming economies in which farmers would save and exchange seeds from their own crops locally. Instead, farmers were encouraged to buy the more productive hybrid seed from commercial producers each year. Increasing state legislation on 'variety protection' further cemented this hegemonic framing of seeds as the intellectual property and 'inventions' of breeders.[14] The professionalisation of plant breeding and seed production disrupted traditional farming economies as 'a new seed regime and a new knowledge production regime' emerged, in which scientific breeders replaced farmers' role in crop evolutionary processes.[15]

The second half of the twentieth century saw the rise of national and international regulatory frameworks which sought to govern farmers' ability to reproduce their own seeds by making it practically illegal for farmers to save their own seeds, as commercial crop varieties must be registered on national lists of protected varieties. These registers, mediated largely through databases such as UPOV's Plant Variety Database or the EU Database of Registered Plant Varieties, have become the primary governance technology on seeds and instruments of globalised industrial agriculture dominated by large agri-chemical giants, three of which control 60% of the global seed trade today.[16] Grounded in the same colonial logics that classified plant life in botanical indexes in the eighteenth century, modern seed registers and their databases determined strict breeding criteria for 'modern' varieties, reproducing a view 'that seeds are the result of individual ingenuity, rather than the collective and intergenerational knowledge that co-evolves with plant genes, soils, and climates'.[17]

The streamlining and genetic homogenisation of varieties under industrial agriculture has led to a drastic drop in crop biodiversity and a rise in state-sponsored gene banking endeavours by international research institutions. Through such 'gene fetishism',[18] seeds are extracted from their in situ worlds and the multispecies webs of relations in which they usually circulate, along with the different practices, knowledges, and ways of relating that those entail.[19] They are subsequently placed into controlled conditions, based on the assumption that this will allow for more precise understandings of their constitution, behaviour, and genetics, which is vital to industrialised breeding. Managed through database technologies, these gene banks have also begun to include the sequenced genomes of the seeds they hold. This has become a major source of concern and resistance from Indigenous and peasant communities and food sovereignty activists, as it gives rise to biopiracy and continues to reduce the animacy and lively relations of the seeds to sequenced code.[20] Parallel to these large-scale ex situ collections of plant genetic material, farmers, growers, and food sovereignty activists have begun politically organising to resist the corporate and state-controlled seed regime by establishing seed libraries and networks for saving and sharing open-pollinated seeds. Some of these initiatives make use of technologies such as databases and digital inventory systems for managing their seed collections and networks.[21] We now turn to the London Freedom Seed Bank as one such project to interrogate how digital data technologies can facilitate alternative ways of knowing and being in the world to the extractive 'pure line ontology' of the modern seed industry.

### Knowledge, relationality, and variability in the LFSBase

Before the LFSBase, the LFSB used a simple Excel spreadsheet to take an inventory of the seeds coming in and out of the bank. For Richard Galpin, the Airtable software presented an opportunity not only to record as much information as possible about saved seeds in London, but also to try to understand and visualise the dynamic relationships between seeds, their growers, and growing spaces. In an online interview along with Anna Clow and both authors in February 2021, Richard explained that, with an Excel spreadsheet, 'there's no real way of easily seeing how that relates to what happened last year and whether that grower features anywhere else and whether that variety features anywhere else'. The LFSBase offers a means to represent these relationships – and, as we will argue in the following, resists some of the hegemonies of ordering and storing data and seeds that are characteristic of more modernist scientific and commercial approaches. Richard had become familiar with Airtable through his work as coordinator of the Walworth Community Food Hub in London, a mutual aid response to increased food insecurity during the COVID-19 pandemic, and felt it could be useful to update the LFSB's record-keeping practices. Anna, a computing technician who had come across Airtable through working with the London Renters' Union, joined the steering group of LFSB in late summer 2020 and worked with Richard (online) to get the LFSBase up and running by November that year.

By outlining how information is recorded in the LFSBase and drawing on Richard and Anna's reflections on the design and constraints of the technology, we interrogate how the LFSBase is able to hold a multiplicity of knowledges and relations that radically depart from the hegemonic narrative of breeding outlined above. We then go on to examine how variability and adaptability are treated in the database.

### *Four views: Growers, Growing Spaces, Varieties, and Seed Batches*

For Anna and Richard, the principles of accessibility, aesthetics, and ease of use determined their design of the LFSBase. Unlike a standard two-dimensional spreadsheet, Airtable is based around different 'views', which allow users to visualise data from several spreadsheets or 'tables', depending on the specific information and relationships they want to comprehend. The option of 'gallery view' presents the data in tiles, making the software both aesthetically appealing and user-friendly. In our interview, Richard, who is a practising artist, explained: 'it was [the] gallery [view] aspect that I initially thought, this would be great for seeds, because it just felt like that will be something that would allow us to enjoy the database more and have more of a visual relationship with it'.

The LFSBase records information in four main tables: Seed Batches, Varieties, Growers, and Growing Spaces (see Figure 8.1). Records from these

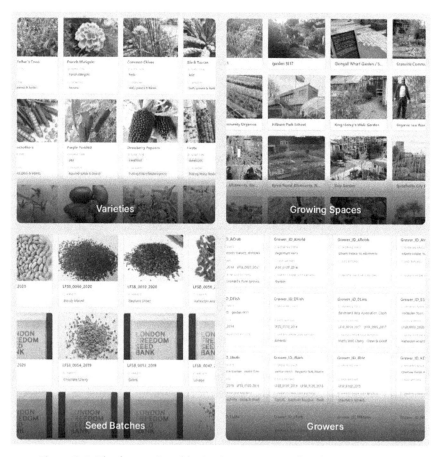

**Figure 8.1** The four main tables in the LFSBase. (All rights reserved and permission to use the figure must be obtained from the copyright holder.)

# Why did we need a database?

**Figure 8.2** Figure created by Anna Clow to illustrate the linked record fields in the LFSBase. (All rights reserved and permission to use the figure must be obtained from the copyright holder.)

tables are linked, which allows them to be read in relation to one another (see Figure 8.2). As Richard explained in a blog post on the LFSB website in which he introduced the LFSBase: 'The relationship between these four elements is key. We may have multiple growers in the same growing space, or multiple seed batches from the same grower. A popular variety that starts with one grower, becomes grown by multiple growers. A standard Excel sheet just couldn't capture this complexity.'

*Stories*

In addition to capturing technical data about the seeds in the network, the database was created with the aim of facilitating the sharing of practical and experiential knowledge from the growers themselves. Richard continued: 'The history and the grower's knowledge are important too. The stories that attach to particular varieties, and the recommendation of how best to grow them, all help to advance the seed's progression from one grower to the next. Saving the knowledge helps to save the seed, and vice-versa.'[22]

When Richard said 'saving the knowledge helps to save the seed', he was using an expansive definition of knowledge, which goes beyond the 'pure' knowledge of a seed's genetic profile or its place in a taxonomic hierarchy to express a sense that seeds circulate between places and people and that growers' embodied and relational knowledge is a crucial factor in saving seeds.

Valuing this lay knowledge pushes against the assumptions that commercial breeders have the monopoly on expertise about seeds, *and* that successful seed saving and breeding should be done in purified ex situ conditions.

Working with Airtable, like any form of data technology, has created dilemmas for Anna and Richard because it involves navigating the assumptions and limitations built into the design of the software alongside their goal of recording diverse information from a range of sources. Richard, at one point in our interview, stated that the Airtable, through its design, forces the user to make decisions, as 'classifying anything forces you to put it in separate boxes … it forces you to think about, if this, then not that'. For example, when entering a new Variety record, the variety still holds a certain primacy, as new seed batches get linked to broader variety records. However, as we argue below, this also expresses an expansive understanding of what a variety is – Anna and Richard want LFSBase to reflect, and facilitate, the interspecies relations and knowledges at the heart of in situ seed saving, so they are sensitive to the ways in which technologies and their design constraints can work against this. This is another dimension to Richard's aspiration to share knowledge about the seeds: sharing is a relational act that decentres the individual in favour of the collective.

These challenges are illustrated by the case of the Bloody Marvel variety of lettuce. In the LFSBase, the Bloody Marvel is described under Variety as 'An experimental new lettuce variety bred by the grower in Walworth, London for resilience to London's challenging growing conditions. Originally inspired by research into the Bloody Cos variety, also known as Spotted Aleppo originating in Syria in the 18th Century. Blood red splotches on an upright open butterhead-cos'. The unidentified grower in the quote is in fact Richard Galpin, who, as the breeder of this new variety, is a repository of knowledge about it. However, the intimate relationship between Richard and Bloody Marvel is obscured in the Airtable (see Figure 8.3). Anna observed, 'It [Airtable] does flatten everything, if you [Richard] were to stop growing Bloody Marvel for four years and somebody was to continue, then … from a purely data way, it would almost look like someone else had more of something to do with it'.

In the days of the Excel spreadsheet, seeds, and information about them, were generally collected on an ad hoc basis, at seed swaps and other events, and Richard described how LFSB co-director Charlotte Dove, who is also a professional gardener, held much of the LFSB's collective knowledge in her own memory. Richard and Anna are aware of the fact that LFSBase is just one element of the ways in which people interact with seeds and each other, that databases can be alienating and spending time in front of a computer inputting data is not necessarily what growers enjoy about seed saving. Richard observed that, to tell stories about the seeds in care of the network,

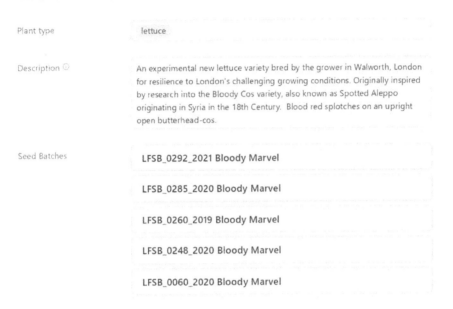

**Figure 8.3** Linked Seed Batches records in the LFSBase Variety record for Bloody Marvel lettuce.

'it needs both narrative and, probably, interaction. These stories need an audience, right?' So, while he is very aware that, as he put it, Airtable is 'not going to write the stories for us, but it'll give us a box to put them in', he is also pragmatic about the fact that this is not its primary purpose, as is reflected in its design. Yet, when we probed him a little more on this issue, he did observe that, since the LFSBase had been established, most seed orders were for those varieties that have 'more background story in the description'. He suggested that this is linked to the fact that people do not rely on the LFSB for their entire seedstock, so are specifically 'looking for something unusual or special that they wouldn't get somewhere else', so here the description or story of the seed, contained within its particular 'box' in LFSBase, becomes a determining factor in which variety they decide to grow.

The LFSB's network values 'stories' about seeds as knowledge, but as Richard and Anna reflected, this is limited by the fact that Airtable is not designed to capture stories. Airtable is based around having 'boxes' to put things in, as Richard described it, and with this go certain assumptions about the absolute nature of categories. By contrast, the design of the LFSBase aims to facilitate, rather than just capture, relationality. The database is envisioned as a mediator of multispecies relationships, driven by the key ethic of sharing upon which the LFSB is built. This decentring of individual authorship and ownership again contrasts with the ontology of modern seeds as deployed by industrial agriculture.

### Diversity

As 'the biggest and most complex field' in the database, as Richard described it in our interview, Seed Batches is the category upon which most of the operations of the database are built. Every new donation of seeds to the seed bank is registered as a new Seed Batch with a unique batch code, which allows the record to be traced through the database and through time. This record is linked to the Variety that it falls under, but captures more specific information about the particular batch at hand, such as how much light or water the crops received, whether the growers selected the healthiest, most vigorous plants for saving, and whether the plants were isolated to prevent cross-pollination – a necessary step for most crop families to ensure the varieties saved reproduce stably over the generations. In addition, growers can comment on the growing process and add memories or reflections in the 'batch notes'. Seed Batches are in turn linked to the records of the grower who grew and donated the seeds and the growing space where they were grown. As such the Seed Batch records emerge from the convergence of the seeds, the growing space, and the care of the grower not only physically, but epistemically within the LFSBase.

Varieties are made up of multiple Seed Batches, which in turn each represent a unique assemblage of relationships from which they have emerged. With each new Seed Batch, the Variety record expands to encompass new information about that variety. As Richard said in our interview, 'What we said about that variety two years ago is probably pretty similar to what they would say about it two years later. But any new information they create becomes part of the record of that variety for us. We subsume that information into the totality of information we have about that variety'. In this, the LFSBase fundamentally departs from the fixist paradigm of the modern seed industry by which varieties have to be 'distinct, uniform, and stable' to be considered agriculturally 'useful' crops. Rather, in the LFSBase, Varieties act as a container for the multiplicity of Seed Batches, the knowledge related to them, and their relationships to people and places.

In his blog post, Richard explains this distinction as it figures in the LFSBase:

Varieties are traditionally seen as static. Different seed batches of the same variety should be genetically identical. But the idea of local adaptability confounds this. Batches are not identical if they continue to adapt. But they do remain attached to a common name and an idea about the particular 'identifiable traits' that a particular variety should aspire to. This is done by 'roguing out' off-type characteristics or undesirable traits – or by only selecting plants for seed saving that exhibit the best of those identifiable characteristics. But the extent of this 'variety maintenance' varies from grower to grower, and year to year, so we know there must be variation across different seed batches of the same variety.[23]

The example of amaranth illustrates this dynamic use of varieties further. In contrast to the relatively controlled knowledge about Bloody Marvel, amaranth has a fluid relationship with the LFSBase's data 'boxes'. Amaranth, a crop that is grown around the world and known for its incredible resilience, is grown by many Londoners, though it is generally less familiar to white growers. As they were compiling the LFSBase, Richard and Anna realised that amaranth had several different identities in the LFSB's records, having also been recorded as different varieties with names including 'latte', 'callaloo', 'amaranthus', and 'tricolor'.

While some seeds in the LFSBase are accompanied by much grower knowledge, the proliferation of amaranths and uncertainty about whether they were different varieties instead demonstrates a lack of knowledge about this particular plant among the (majority white) steering group and growers' network, for whom it is a largely unfamiliar crop. Richard noted, 'Varieties aren't really used in the same way, it seems, within callaloo so much, culturally'. So, while the LFSBase is attempting to take a diverse approach to data curation that is inclusive of non-expert knowledge, when there is a lack of knowledge about a plant, what scant information there is can spill out of its boxes and potentially become confusing or misleading. Richard, in consultation with others in the steering group, decided to split up the seeds saved from the original seeds by their main features, resulting in five Variety entries. This has led the LFSB to conduct a series of 'amaranth trials' with a number of growers who agreed to grow out some of the seed to try and establish the different characteristics within the varieties. The information gleaned from this experiment will then be fed back into the Airtable in order to improve the knowledge about amaranth in the database.

Seeds in the bank are expected to have some genetic variability, partly out of pragmatism about the 'uncontrolled' conditions of home and allotment growing and partly out of a sense that open-pollinated seeds should be allowed to interact with their environments. As well as decentring individual growers and expert scientific knowledge, the LFSBase draws attention to the complex and interwoven relationalities involved in saving and sharing seeds, and unsettles the pure line ontology that epistemically produces seeds as distinct and innate genetic packages. This is further illustrated by the Mamadoli Pumpkin variety of tomato held by the seed bank:

> Donated by Olcay Colak whose family have grown these good sized beefsteak tomatoes in Turkey for many years. The family didn't have a name for them, so we called them 'Mamadoli' after Olcay's father's name in Kurdish - and 'Pumpkin' for their pumpkin-like shape.

The brief description of the seed variety is clearly not one that is bounded by the rigours of genetic purity, or indeed a strict interpretation of variety, but instead reflects a multispecies entanglement between people, place, and plants. While more formalised seed banks might reject this seed because of its uncertain identity, in the LFSB, it is accepted and given a name which reflects its diasporic heritage, memorialising the connection to the original donor's family and country of origin. Here, the fact that the variety 'didn't have a name' is recorded *as part of the knowledge* held about this seed.

When, in contrast to standard commercial practice, seeds are open-pollinated, they are inherently dynamic and adaptive. Each generation receives genetic information from their parents, making them able to adapt to changing environments and thus ecologically resilient.[24] This genetic diversity, and the ability to reproduce true-to-type in subsequent generations, is what distinguishes open-pollinated seeds from F1 hybrids. Because the seeds of the LFSB are grown in situ, they are able to adapt to local growing conditions with each generation, preserving the agro-biodiversity unique to London ecologies. This genetic diversity of OP seeds is reflected in the database through linked record fields in which the Varieties are linked to the records of the Seed Batches that make up that variety stock.

In this practice, the growers, and their corresponding 'Grower' records in the database are not given primacy over the other elements in the database, reworking the modern narrative of agriculture as a manipulation of 'nature' by the human 'grower' protagonist/subject, giving way instead to an understanding of cultivation through its constituent interspecies processes.

In our interview, this tension was framed by Richard as a question of scale, or 'granularity' as he put it. Because open-pollinated seeds are able to adapt to their environments with each generation, if a particular variety is grown out over multiple generations by the same grower and in the same space, it would adapt to that particular ecology. This raised the question of to what degree the 'London-adapted varieties' in the care of the LFSB would be specified. Richard posed the question: 'We often talk about London-adapted varieties, but by the same logic, do you take garden-adapted varieties? So you say well, okay, this seed batch was growing in this garden in these conditions, therefore do we want to mix it with the other version? ... do we consider it the same or do we now consider it different?' This illustrates the fundamental tension between genetic purity and diversity that many seed savers face. It also draws attention to the fragility of the epistemic construct of varieties. With these questions of scalability, the LFSB also negotiates the market logics of specification and homogenisation presented by F1 hybrids, which are bred to reflect the epistemic construct of botanical varieties or cultivars, understood as distinct, uniform, and stable. Any uncharacteristic traits for that particular variety are 'rogued out' and, as such, a pure-line ideology of varieties is produced. However, this roguing out is also an important practice of ensuring that the particular traits a variety has been bred for over generations continue to be passed on, which is why seed saving requires both roguing out and for most species isolating varieties from each other to prevent cross-pollination and thus a 'contamination' of the seed stock. At the same time, maintaining genetic diversity within a variety is important, as lack of diversity can lead to 'inbreeding depression', that is, a generational decline in health and vigour of a variety. After all, it is the genetic diversity *within* varieties that makes open-pollinated seeds more resilient and adaptive. This fundamental tension between genetic purity and genetic diversity is often raised in seed-saving circles, and approaches, opinions, and rigidity vary.

While this tension may be debated at length in grower and seed-saving circles, many also find that, more often than not, seeds behave differently from a grower's expectations. Richard articulated his approach as one of 'happy accidents', and indeed, the LFSB's stock includes varieties that have come about through unforeseen or unintended crossings and evolutions, such as the lettuce variety 'Pandemic', which has the following description in the LFSBase:

> During [the COVID-19] lockdown every plant seemed like it might be needed to help with rising food insecurity. Arguably a bit of a loser in the genetic lottery this sickly-looking lettuce has good nutty flavour. Issuing from the Bloody Marvel breeding project, so tough and well suited to London's parched and depleted soils. Not self-isolated.

Furthermore, what to save and whether to isolate often comes down to the individual grower and to subjective or experiential factors, such as taste, beauty, practicality, and so on. As such, seed saving in the LFSBase is understood as experiential, subjective, and dynamic and, while the basic aim is to maintain the varieties in its care, the LFSB happily includes new, different, or unusual seeds in its collection, demonstrating an approach to genetic diversity akin to decolonial approaches to human–plant co-evolution.[25]

This focus on representing the multispecies relationships that make up the LFSB network sets the LFSBase apart from imperial and commercial uses of recording technologies. The seeds in the network are represented *through* their constitutive relationships, as the Seed Batches unite the different elements that make it possible for seeds to grow and be shared. From this, an understanding of seed saving and cultivation emerges as a conjunction of 'intra-species skills that are cultivated in a dialogue between plants and humans that also involve ... microorganisms, soil, weather, geological conditions and so on'.[26] The seeds, as all ecological beings, 'do not precede their relations with others, rather they constantly emerge through material relations'.[27]

## Conclusion

The LFSBase tells an interesting story about the tension between how technologies are imagined to function by their creators and how they are put to use by users. As this shows, while databases are classificatory technologies that bend towards order and control, they are also being used in unanticipated and subversive ways to effect more radical ends. In one sense, then, the LFSBase works the system, using a software program to facilitate activities that push against political–economic orthodoxies in favour of building multispecies communities, sharing knowledge and experience freely, resisting corporate control of biotic materials, and questioning the need for stringent controls over genetic purity.

The LFSBase offers insights into the epistemic and material implications of digital technologies on human–plant relations. While technologies of collection have historically been employed for imperial purposes and continue to buttress a seed industry based in the colonial disavowal of the relationality and lively dynamism of cultivation practices, the LFSBase demonstrates how such imperial tools can be used by activists resisting these systems on the ground for generative and liberatory aims, facilitating alternative ways of knowing and being in relation to the more-than-human and our species' place in agricultural practices. Resisting the genetic modernism of the industrial seed regime, the LSFBase facilitates an understanding of seed saving and growing as a relational collaborative interspecies practice between people, places, and plants.

Our reading of the LFSBase intends to add to a discourse on how increasing datafication impacts our relationships to our ecologies. Public discourse rightly identifies the challenges that come with these developments, but the LFSBase demonstrates how digital technologies can play an active role in the creation of alternative meanings and relationships beyond the knowledge systems they were built in. Data software can be a practical and integral tool for facilitating the material exchange of seeds and the gathering of stories and knowledges that might normatively be discounted. A range of activist projects such as the Ida B. Wells Justice Data Lab share such an approach and already make use of data technologies for liberatory ends. The LFSBase offers an example of how grassroots organisations can use data technologies to 'design anew' the worlds that we want to live in by offering infrastructures for imagining alternatives and acting as tools for living them. Repurposing the kinds of imperial tools that have historically been used to institute classificatory hierarchies that have divorced us from the interspecies processes of which we are a part, the LFSBase disrupts the prevailing market logics of racial capitalism such as individualism, ownership, and improvement in the modern seed industry and promotes a relational ethic of seeds, growers, and ecologies as co-constitutive, co-evolutionary. It thereby gestures towards a radical otherwise.

## Notes

1. Galpin, 'What is LSFBase?' n.p.
2. Nost and Goldstein, 'A political ecology of data,' p. 10.
3. Barla, 'Technology/technicity/techné,' n.p.
4. Gray, 'Three aspects of data worlds,' p. 4.
5. Turnbull and Searle, *Towards a Research Agenda for Digital Ecologies*, n.p.
6. Castelle, 'Relational and non-relational models in the entextualization of bureaucracy'; Fuller and Goffey, *Evil Media*.
7. Kloppenburg, *First the Seed*, p. 15; Schiebinger, *Plants and Empire*, p. 7.
8. Müller-Wille and Charmantier, 'Natural history and information overload,' pp. 4–5.
9. Schiebinger, *Plants and Empire*, p. 11.
10. Gray and Sheikh, 'The wretched Earth,' p. 165.
11. Ibid., p. 166.
12. Schiebinger, *Plants and Empire*.
13. Bonneuil and Thomas, 'Purifying landscapes,' p. 535; see also Müller-Wille and Charmantier, 'Natural history and information overload'; Sonjasdotter, 'The order of potatoes.'
14. Demeulenaere, 'A political ontology of seeds.'
15. Bonneuil and Thomas, 'Purifying landscapes,' p. 561.
16. Howard, 'Global seed industry changes since 2013.'
17. Montenegro de Wit, 'Beating the bounds,' p. 44.
18. Haraway, *Modest_Witness@Second_Millenium*, p. 147.
19. Aistara, 'Seeds of kin, kin of seeds'; Graddy, 'Situating in situ'; Nazarea, *Heirloom Seeds and Their Keepers*; van Dooren, 'Inventing seed.'
20. Peschard and Randeria, 'Keeping seeds in our hands,' p. 634.
21. See Native American Food Sovereignty Alliance, 'Seed database and inventory systems.'

22 Galpin, 'Introducing our new collaborative data project.'
23 LSFB website, www.londonfreedomseedbank.org/lfsbase/seed-batches/.
24 See also Dow, 'Bloody marvels.'
25 See also Emergence Magazine's interview with Mohawk seedkeeper and activist Rowen White.
26 Sonjasdotter, 'The order of potatoes,' p. 311.
27 Turnbull and Searle, *Towards a Research Agenda for Digital Ecologies*, n.p.

## Bibliography

Aistara, G.A. 2011. Seeds of kin, kin of seeds: The commodification of organic seeds and social relations in Costa Rica and Latvia. *Ethnography*, 12(4): 490–517.

Barla, J. 2018. 'Technology/technicity/techné'. *New Materialism* [online], 18 March. Available from: https://newmaterialism.eu/almanac/t/technology-technicity-techne.html.

Batsaki, Y., Burke, S., and Tchikine, A. 2016. *The Botany of Empire in the Long Eighteenth Century*. Washington, DC: Dumbarton Oaks Research Library and Collection.

Bonneuil, C. and Thomas, F. 2010. Purifying landscapes: The Vichy regime and the genetic modernization of France. *Historical Studies in the Natural Sciences*, 40(4): 532–568.

Castelle, M. 2013. Relational and non-relational models in the entextualization of bureaucracy. *Computational Culture*, 3 [online]. Available from: http://computationalculture.net/relational-and-non-relational-models-in-the-entextualization-of-bureaucracy/.

Cukier, K. and Mayer-Schoenberger, V. 2013. The rise of big data: How it's changing the way we think about the world. *Foreign Affairs*, 92(3): 28–40.

Demeulenaere, E. 2014. A political ontology of seeds. *Focaal – Journal of Global and Historical Anthropology*, 69: 45–61.

Dow, K. 2021. Bloody marvels: In situ seed saving and intergenerational malleability. *Medical Anthropology Quarterly*, 35(4): 493–510.

Emergence Magazine. 2019. Reseeding the food system: An interview with Rowen White [online], 11 October. Available from: https://emergencemagazine.org/interview/reseeding-the-food-system/.

Fuller, M. and Goffey, A. 2012. *Evil Media*. Cambridge, MA: MIT Press.

Galpin, R. 2020. Introducing our new collaborative data project. *London Freedom Seed Bank* [online], 15 December. Available from: www.londonfreedomseedbank.org/introducing-our-new-collaborative-data-project/.

Graddy, T.G. 2014. Situating in situ: A critical geography of agricultural biodiversity conservation in the Peruvian Andes and beyond. *Antipode*, 46(2): 426–454.

Gray, J. 2018. Three aspects of data worlds. *Krisis*, 1. https://archive.krisis.eu/three-aspects-of-data-worlds/.

Gray, R. and Sheikh, S. 2018. The wretched Earth. *Third Text*, 32(2–3): 163–175.

Haraway, D.J. 1997. *Modest_Witness@Second_Millennium. FemaleMan_Meets_OncoMouse: Feminism and Technoscience*. New York: Routledge.

Howard, P.H. 2018. Global seed industry changes since 2013. *Philip H. Howard* [online], 31 December. Available from: https://philhoward.net/2018/12/31/global-seed-industry-changes-since-2013/.

Kloppenburg, J.R. 2004. *First the Seed: The Political Economy of Plant Biotechnology*. 2nd revised ed. Madison, WI: University of Wisconsin Press.

Montenegro de Wit, M. 2019. Beating the bounds: How does "open source" become a seed commons? *The Journal of Peasant Studies*, 46(1): 44–79.

Müller-Wille, S. and Charmantier, I. 2012. Natural history and information overload: The case of Linnaeus. *Studies in History and Philosophy of Science Part C: Studies in History and Philosophy of Biological and Biomedical Sciences*, 43(1): 4–15.

Native American Food Sovereignty Alliance. 2021. Seed database and inventory systems – with the Indigenous Seedkeepers Network & Seed Savers Exchange. YouTube video [online], 2 April. Available from: www.youtube.com/watch?v=7C78QbmbNfc.

Nazarea, V.D. 2015. *Heirloom Seeds and Their Keepers: Marginality and Memory in the Conservation of Biological Diversity*. Illustrated edition. Tucson, AZ: University of Arizona Press.

Nost, E. and Goldstein, J.E. 2022. A political ecology of data. *Environment and Planning E: Nature and Space*, 5(1): 3–17.

Peschard, K. and Randeria, S. 2020. Keeping seeds in our hands: The rise of seed activism. *The Journal of Peasant Studies*, 47(4): 613–647.

Schiebinger, L.L. 2007. *Plants and Empire: Colonial Bioprospecting in the Atlantic World*. Cambridge, MA: Harvard University Press.

Sheikh, S. 2018. Planting seeds/the fires of war. *Third Text*, 32(2–3): 200–229.

Sonjasdotter, Å. 2018. The order of potatoes: On purity and variation in plant breeding. *Third Text*, 32(2–3): 311–329.

Turnbull, J. and Searle, A. 2021. Towards a research agenda for digital ecologies. *Where Next for Digital Geographies? Pathways and Prospects*. Digital Geographies Research Group Annual Symposium, online (Zoom).

van Dooren, T. 2008. Inventing seed: The nature(s) of intellectual property in plants. *Environment and Planning D: Society and Space*, 26(4): 676–697.

# Part III

Digital assemblages

# 9

# Programming nature as infrastructure in the Smart Forest City

*Jennifer Gabrys*

### Introduction

Smart green infrastructures increasingly feature as key components of smart cities and urban development. Along with digitalised infrastructures of water and lighting, buildings and roads, more organismal and ecological infrastructures of vegetation and soil, air, and water are also undergoing networked monitoring, management, and augmentation. Many smart cities technologies that would ensure automated and optimised flows across communication and transport circuits have been implemented to measure air pollution, detect flooding, monitor soil health, and ensure adequate hydration of urban forests. Smart cities now program green as well as grey infrastructure.

This chapter discusses the possible consequences of wiring up organismal and ecological contributors to cities. Proposed and emerging digital-organismal urban connections give rise to networked infrastructures that are meant to achieve new levels of efficiency, responsiveness, and coordination. Even more than merely adding the digital to the natural, programmed green infrastructures strive toward an updated 'infrastructural ideal' of joined-up systems, where the fusing of technology and nature could be a way to stave off planetary collapse. Yet such projects are as likely to result in fragmented and 'splintering urbanisms' and inequalities,[1] whether from differential investment in networked systems, varying degrees of interoperability, and green space deserts that elude digitalisation. The socio-technical formations of smart green urbanism do not overcome urban inequalities; instead, they have the potential to amplify them. As Susan Leigh Star suggests, the study of infrastructures can surface 'essential aspects of distributional justice and planning power'.[2] What are the specific social-political effects of these programmed green infrastructures and digital ecologies? And how do they potentially exacerbate extractive economies and social inequalities at the same time that they attempt to mitigate environmental impacts?

To address these questions, I first consider how digital–natural urbanisms materialise through plans to incorporate green spaces into the logic of smart cities. The wiring up of green spaces and urban forests is an infrastructural project that operationalises green infrastructures as useful urban processes and services through digitalisation. In this sense, digital–natural infrastructures remake urban ecologies as particular functions and relations meant to contribute to distinct imaginings and materialisations of urban life. In the second section of this chapter, I discuss an architectural proposal for a Smart Forest City in Cancún, Mexico, by Stefano Boeri Architects. The Smart Forest City is a speculative master plan that programs nature as infrastructure through a digital–vegetal approach to sustainable development. In working through different approaches to programming nature as infrastructure, I outline how the smart and sustainable city moves beyond energy efficiency and sustainable transport to incorporate digital-ecological programs that operationalise 'nature' through distinct logics of exchange, coordination, repair, and mitigation.

The programming of vegetal infrastructures aligns in part with natural climate solutions and ecosystem services that would mobilise more-than-human ecologies as key operators in addressing and averting climate crisis while realising green growth.[3] Yet it also indicates how these digitalised natures function less as purified ecologies in the outmoded binary sense of nature as a world apart, and more as environments and systems that quicken to the logic of circuits, chips, and capital. Here, vegetation becomes technological, operating within digital functions that are co-extensive with smart urbanism. But such programs of efficiency and responsiveness are as likely to render obsolete and inassimilable any bodies, practices, or organisms that would not contribute to the productive augmentation of smart green economies and ecologies. To become infrastructural, in other words, nature must fit within the productive logic of the smart green city.

### Networking green infrastructure, infrastructuring digital natures

Transport, utilities, and communications have formed a basic mix of grey infrastructure that informs urban life. Grey infrastructure typically refers to the built and engineered components of urban life. The provision of safe drinking water, readily available electricity, and public roadways are among the infrastructural projects that are meant to undergird the development of 'modern' cities.[4] These infrastructures continue to be updated in the form of smart systems – from smart energy grids to automated transport and surveillance systems – that digitalise urban functions toward greater efficiency. At the same time, infrastructure projects have served as the basis for near-future projects that would 'build back better' by bouncing back from the effects of COVID-19 while forming anticipatory responses to the infrastructural destruction and decay that climate change threatens. Debates about what constitutes infrastructure run through these projects, where airports and roads are held up as most obviously infrastructural, while parks and social services are rendered the 'softer' approach. Infrastructure is thus highly contested and subject to power struggles, even when its many modalities are contributing to the integration of social and spatial life.

So too do digitalisation and digital infrastructures constitute distinct modes of power, governance, and everyday exchange.[5] As many studies of smart cities and smart infrastructures have demonstrated, the digitalisation of urban spaces can reorder social life, variously enable or constrain political engagement, and amplify inequalities by creating new zones of exclusion.[6] The governance of urban environments can become a project delegated to automated systems, detection devices, and control architectures. The digital organisation and management of everyday urban life, in other words, can constitute a type of environmentality, where digital governance is distributed through and within cities.[7] Such environmentality coordinates not just to the movement and conduct of human bodies, however, but also the processes and relations of multiple non-humans.

In the context of climate change and environmentally stressed urban environments, infrastructure is increasingly more than the concrete and the cabled. It is also the green and growing. Green infrastructure is often used in contrast to grey infrastructure as the 'natural' systems that also enable urban functioning. In many smart green city proposals and projects, urban natures are reconstituted to perform particular work that is meant to achieve the infrastructural ideal of sustainable urbanism.[8] Trees become carbon sinks, low-lying vegetation acts as flood defences, shrubs and vines take up air pollution, and mass planting mitigates urban heat island effects. Ecosystem services, natural capital, and natural climate solutions are just a few of the common concepts that describe how nature has become infrastructural as it mitigates and prevents the overheating, flooding, and collapse of cities.[9] These increasingly common practices seek to ensure the liveability of cities in the context of environmental change,[10] yet such developments also raise concerns about what infrastructural collectives and exclusions could materialise. They also point to the reworking of governance through digital-ecological arrangements that operationalise nature through an 'ecological urbanism' that undertakes the work of staving off ecosystem collapse.[11]

In this way, green infrastructures are increasingly digitally monitored and managed to ensure optimal contributions to urban processes. Networked green urbanisms do not simply involve planting and preserving what otherwise would have been paved over. Instead, these digital processes program nature as infrastructure that operates and responds to the demands of ongoing environmental change and climate crisis.[12] Digital technologies undertake remote and in situ sensing to assess carbon storage capacity of trees and soil. Mapping technologies geo-locate trees and vegetation as 'natural assets' that can mitigate environmental stress. Robots plant, climb, and manage trees for improved growth and efficiency. Sensors detect water moisture levels and track chlorophyll levels. Citizen-sensing initiatives track and maintain urban tree planting, and joined-up digital systems contribute to real-estate development projects for creating future smart forest cities.[13]

Such digitalisation of urban ecologies forms what some advocates refer to as an 'Internet of Nature'.[14] As part of the Fourth Industrial Revolution, nature is brought online to perform in 'the next frontier of ecosystem management' that is meant to 'change our relationship with the natural world in the urban age'.[15] The Internet of Nature merges 'existing natural ecosystem dynamics and IoT infrastructure', where plants can become biosensors for more resilient ecosystems, wearable technologies can monitor human health for wellbeing nearby green space, blockchain and crypto-currency can support green initiatives, sensors can monitor urban heat islands, and 'ecosystem intelligence' will reside in the cloud.[16]

Networked urbanism here involves amplifying communications within ecosystems by constructing cities through connections that also are a process of programming, operationalising, and making functional according to distinct logics for urban environmental governance. The smart green city is one of efficiency and automation, coordination and measurement, contingency and response. At the same time, the logics of digital operations – including processes for gathering data, apportioning ownership, realising value, and managing property – permeate digital-vegetal operations. Green infrastructure, including smart urban forests, in turn would function as automated systems mitigating, ventilating, and conditioning the effects of environmental change.

As an updated infrastructural ideal that would address planetary environmental change, the seamless functioning of smart green infrastructure relies on a sort of cyborgian organicism that fuses technologies and ecologies. These are forms of digital governance that unfold across multiple registers and trajectories, where environmental governance is remade, regularised, and optimised through digital systems. Digital governance here refers to the forms of environmental governance that become possible and regularised through digital systems. Smart green infrastructures and smart forest cities become bound up with the emerging practices of digital governance, where the operations and attunements of technologies inform distributions of power and resources. Forests governed through digital technologies play an increasingly central role in retooling the planet to contend with environmental change. Yet such eco-digital technologies and infrastructures implement specific compositions of justice, power, and democratic possibility, as noted earlier in this chapter.

In this sense, the emergence of any infrastructure has consequences for politics, social interactions, inequality, and distribution of resources.[17] Infrastructures present distinct ways of making collectives and of joining up urban environmental life. They can also create specific barriers and exclusions, where infrastructural operations might be available to some but not others. The privatisation of infrastructure can cause fragmentation of services. So too do monopolistic formations of infrastructure have the potential to establish technocratic and inflexible exchanges, which constrain social and political life. Moreover, the resources required to create and sustain infrastructures can cause vast disparities across regions, where digital infrastructures in one location could contribute to extractive and unequal economies and relations in another. Smart green infrastructures must inevitably be considered within this longer trajectory of infrastructural problematics, rather than presented as an easy solution to pressing planetary problems. The next section outlines in more detail one example of how these infrastructural problematics erupt in a Smart Forest City.

### Programming infrastructure in a Smart Forest City

The Smart Forest City in Cancún, Mexico, is a speculative project and master plan that raises such questions about the consequences of smart green infrastructure developments. Stefano Boeri Architects, a group well known for green city and building projects, developed the Smart Forest City plan in 2019. The architecture group developed the Smart Forest City plan in Cancún for the Honduras-based multinational textile manufacture and real estate developer Grupo Karim. In addition to manufacturing personal protective equipment (PPE), Grupo Karim has developed a number of smart cities as part of its broader real estate portfolio that includes commercial, residential, and industrial properties. Smart cities developed by Grupo Karim often take the form of business parks in Central America, where call centres cluster together in San Pedro Sula in Honduras; and outsourcing industries integrate with a university, residences, shopping, and a 'corporate/diplomatic zone' in the capital city Tegucigalpa.[18]

The Smart Forest City in Cancún fits within this range of developments, as a 'unique investment opportunity' within the smart city space.[19] Just south of the Cancún International Airport, and moments from the beach on the Caribbean Sea, the Smart Forest City is designed as a smart green city of networked systems. This 'innovation hub' is meant to be regenerative, giving back to nature what would have otherwise been developed into a shopping mall.[20] Flood-proof waterways, drones, glass and steel office towers, and palm trees garlanding solar panels form a tranquil setting where families with prams, men in speedboats, and leisurely onlookers studying desalination towers populate the scenes of this imagined Smart Forest City. Electric vehicles provide smarter transport options and provide a low-carbon way to navigate this zone of high-tech research and sustainable living. Social life unfolds in scenes of seamless integration with the Smart Forest City, where city-subjects are economically privileged knowledge workers inhabiting a relatively protected enclave.

Here, technology, nature, and society harmoniously commingle in scenes of manicured and digitalised urbanism that might be slotted into the genre of 'the eco-fantasy project' that especially focuses on 'performance and optimization'.[21] The work that nature will perform to keep the Smart Forest City operational and balanced includes absorbing and stocking more than 116,000 tons of carbon dioxide. The site includes '400 hectares of green spaces with 7,500,000 plants of 400 different species', selected by a botanist and landscape architect. This mix of vegetation will ensure that there are 2.3 trees to every inhabitant. The project and press literature stresses that the layout will ensure that 'public parks, private gardens, green roofs, and green façades will all contribute to achieving a perfect balance between nature and building footprint'.[22] Here, natural capital and green growth are meant to work towards a more perfectly organised environment.

However, in many ways extractive logics continue to inform how nature is put to work in support of existing socio-economic systems.[23] The human and non-human labour that would build, maintain, repair, and operate the Smart Forest City is not evident in the scenes of leisurely and automated digital-vegetal urban life. Resources required to construct and operate the Smart Forest City are dematerialised, where lithium, copper, coltan, iron, and water recede from the verdant views. The mining and harvesting of resources, as well as the disposal of obsolete and decaying devices, are activities that take place in locations distant from this more purified location. The digital–vegetal city, however, inevitably requires resources, labour, and waste sites to operate. Green infrastructure here would seem to add to the apparent immateriality of the digital, rather than make evident the materiality of these infrastructures.[24] Indeed, the disparity between digital–vegetal urban havens and sites of extraction could become even more entrenched through the privatisation of smart green infrastructural enclaves situated within areas of broader socio-economic depravation. Caribbean spaces and islands have served as spaces of ongoing respatialisation in the context of offshore economies, tourism, mobility, and digital infrastructures, which can reinforce colonial forms of territoriality.[25]

Similar to many development schemes, the Smart Forest City is designated as a 'forest' less because anything traditionally resembling a forest materialises here, and more because it conveys a seemingly ecological approach to transforming a greenfield site into a business park. The development is proposed to be self-sustaining, producing its own energy and food through adjacent fields and solar panels, desalinating its own water, irrigating its crops, regulating floods, and achieving resilience through carefully orchestrated networked connections watched over by industrious drones. Behind the scenes, digital technologies with a high environmental footprint are meant to ensure the balance and self-sufficiency that this city would achieve.

Yet this organicism of technologies and ecologies is generative of an exclusive enclave that is self-sufficient on its own terms, while still requiring the ongoing extraction of resources from – and fortification against – a wider world. The social milieu that unfolds within this proposed natural-technological harmony includes carefully surveilled spaces where humans operate according to programs as productive and networked as those that would manage vegetation. With these programmed natural infrastructures, there is an absence of weeds and discord. Such balanced systems do not make space for struggle and protest. Order prevails in this master plan, which transforms cities and forests toward urbanisms that resemble a biosphere experiment caught in an idyllic state of homeostasis. Smart green infrastructures seem to soften the edges of the usual extractive and inequitable digital urbanisms, but reproduce many of the same infrastructural problematics of these developments.

## Otherwise infrastructures

Infrastructures not only sustain forms of urban and environmental organisation. They also construct collective worlds.[26] As Lauren Berlant notes, infrastructures are not mere structures. Rather, they inform the movements of collective social life by generating politics and struggle. Social life is not merely an expression of perpetual balance, but includes disagreement, 'brokenness', and crisis.[27] In other words, while infrastructure informs social and urban life, it also generates moments for extending it in other ways, beyond seamless functioning and towards transformative challenges and connections. Infrastructural practices – and their transformation – can spark political potential.

However, such urban unfoldings of process and practice are less evident in plans such as the Smart Forest City and similar smart urban forest initiatives. These projects would program nature as productive and harmonious infrastructure. Climate change in the form of sea-level rise, resource depletion, and overheating are meant to be addressed through adaptive waterways, self-sufficient agriculture and energy, and vegetative air conditioning that together create digital, green, and resilient urbanisms. Such infrastructural imaginings often elide the inequalities, political struggles, environmental crises, and extractive economies that undergird plans such as the Smart Forest City. These smart green infrastructures run the risk of reproducing and amplifying environmental crises and injustices, rather than transforming them.[28]

In this way, and following LaDuke and Cowen, programmed green infrastructure projects force encounters with the 'profoundly practical work of infrastructure'.[29] In their project to 'reimagine the critical infrastructures of everyday life on Turtle Island' by working towards 'collective futures hinge[d] on remaking socio-technical systems'.[30] Such practical work could even break with the destructive qualities of what these authors refer to as 'Wiindigo infrastructure', which requires relentless extraction and inequality to realise its operative ideals. Instead, infrastructure as practice requires developing projects that would work towards 'justice, decolonisation, and planetary survival' as joined-up concerns.[31] These are 'otherwise infrastructures', which recognise the work that infrastructures do to sustain social life. A project of infrastructuring otherwise points to the question of what the work of infrastructure does. Rather than speed and delay, automation and optimisation, La Duke and Cowen draw attention to accumulation and dispossession as markers of the Wiindigo economy and infrastructure, while also considering flourishing and reciprocity as conditions that would allow for infrastructural transformations. Such transformational work – an indication of the 'public works' that are synonymous with infrastructure – can become a way to transition towards less extractive infrastructural projects and to rework the socio-technical formations of everyday life.

## Conclusion

Infrastructures form as material commitments to environmental–social worlds, both in their formation and building, and in their cultivation and continuation. This analysis of the digital–ecological infrastructures of the Smart Forest City points to the consequences of these infrastructural arrangements. Smart green infrastructures co-constitute and join up urban entities in the interests of optimisation and efficiency, which contribute to a version of sustainability that would often leave existing inequalities and extractive practices unchecked. These digital–ecological and socio-technical formations organise the capacities and inhabitations of urban life. Such digital infrastructures further operate as environmentalities, where human and non-human life and relations materialise through automated and digitalised forms of governance.

As this analysis of smart green infrastructure shows, infrastructures are not mere physical objects, in the form of fixed roadways or 'grey' engineering works. Instead, they are the very stuff of social life. Materiality, in this sense, is in process and transformation, made and remade by social practices, as well as by more-than-human relations and environmental change that are now testing the stress points of infrastructure and pushing infrastructure to breaking points. If urbanisms, more-than-humans, democratic political life, and social justice are to converge in more generative ways, then infrastructures – grey, green, and otherwise – need to be engaged with as key sites and processes of social and political transformation. The practical work of infrastructure could then be wrested from the property developer's portfolio and architect's plan to become an ongoing collective project and political struggle for more liveable urban worlds.

## Acknowledgements

This project has received funding from the European Research Council (ERC) under the European Union's Horizon 2020 research and innovation programme (Grant agreement No. 866006, Smart Forests).

An abbreviated version of this chapter was first published as 'Programming Nature as Infrastructure in the Smart Forest City' by Jennifer Gabrys © 2022 The Author(s), taken from *Journal of Urban Technology* 2022, Volume 29, Issue 1 © Informa UK Limited, trading as Taylor & Francis Group 2022, reprinted by permission of Taylor & Francis Ltd, www.tandfonline.com/

## Notes

1. Graham and Marvin, *Splintering Urbanism*.
2. Star, 'The ethnography of infrastructure,' p. 379; also cited in Marvin and Graham, *Splintering Urbanism*, p. 16.
3. Sullivan, 'Banking nature?'.
4. Although see Simone, 'People as infrastructure.'
5. Maguire and Winthereik, 'Digitalizing the state.'
6. Marvin et al., 'Smart urbanism.'
7. Gabrys, 'Programming environments'; cf. Foucault, *The Birth of Biopolitics*.
8. Gabrys, 'Plastic and the work of the biodegradable.'
9. Carse, 'Nature as infrastructure.'
10. Karvonen, 'Pathways of urban nature.'

11 Adams, 'Natura urbans'; Wakefield, 'Making nature into infrastructure.'
12 Gabrys, *Program Earth*; cf. Blok et al., 'Infrastructuring environments'; Jensen and Morita, 'Introduction: Infrastructures as ontological experiments'.
13 Nitoslawski et al., 'Smarter ecosystems'; see also Gabrys, 'Smart forests'; and https://smartforests.net.
14 Galle et al., 'The Internet of Nature.'
15 Ibid., p. 279.
16 Ibid., p. 282.
17 Graham and Marvin, *Splintering Urbanism*.
18 Grupo Karim, 'Smart cities.'
19 Grupo Karim, 'About us.'
20 Stefano Boeri Architetti, 'Smart Forest City Cancun.'
21 Barber and Putalik, 'Forest, tower, city,' n.p.
22 Design Boom, 'Stefano Boeri plans Smart Forest City.'
23 For a related text, see Fletcher et al., 'Natural capital.'
24 Gabrys, *Digital Rubbish*.
25 Sheller, 'Infrastructures of the imagined island.'
26 Foucault, *A Reader*, p. 239; also cited in Graham and Marvin, *Splintering Urbanism*, p. xxxi.
27 Berlant, 'The commons'; see also Larkin, 'The politics and poetics of infrastructure'; McFarlane and Rutherford, 'Political infrastructures.'
28 For a related text, see Masucci et al., 'The smart city conundrum for social justice.'
29 LaDuke and Cowen, 'Beyond Wiindigo infrastructure,' p. 244.
30 Ibid., p. 245.
31 Ibid.

## Bibliography

Adams, R.E. 2014. Natura urbans, natura urbanata: Ecological urbanism, circulation, and the immunization of nature. *Environment and Planning D: Society and Space*, 32(1): 12–29.

Barber, D. and Putalik, E. 2018. Forest, tower, city: Rethinking the green machine aesthetic. *Harvard Design Magazine*, 45: 234–243. www.harvarddesignmagazine.org/issues/45/forest-tower-city-rethinking-the-green-machine-aesthetic.

Berlant, L. 2016. The commons: Infrastructures for troubling times. *Environment and Planning D: Society and Space*, 34(3): 393–419.

Blok, A., Nakazora, M., and Wintherik, B.R. 2016. Infrastructuring environments. *Science as Culture*, 25(1): 1–22.

Carse, A. 2012. Nature as infrastructure: Making and managing the Panama Canal Watershed. *Social Studies of Science*, 42(4): 539–563.

Design Boom. 2019. Stefano Boeri plans Smart Forest City with more than 7 million plants in Cancun, Mexico [online]. Available from: www.designboom.com/architecture/stefano-boeri-smart-forest-city-cancun-mexico-10-30-2019.

Fletcher, R., Dressler, W.H., Anderson, Z.R., and Büscher, B. 2019. Natural capital must be defended: Green growth as neoliberal biopolitics. *The Journal of Peasant Studies*, 46(5): 1068–1095.

Foucault, M. 2008. *The Birth of Biopolitics: Lectures at the Collège de France 1978–1979.* (trans G. Burchell). New York: Palgrave Macmillan.

Foucault, M. 1984. *A Reader* (P. Rabinow, Ed.). New York: Pantheon.

Gabrys, J. n.d. Smart Forests [online]. Available from: www.smartforests.net.

Gabrys, J. 2011. *Digital Rubbish: A Natural History of Electronics.* Ann Arbor, MI: University of Michigan Press.

Gabrys, J. 2013. Plastic and the work of the biodegradable. In J. Gabrys, G. Hawkins, and M. Michael (Eds.) *Accumulation: The Material Politics of Plastic* (pp. 208–227). New York and London: Routledge.

Gabrys, J. 2014. Programming environments: Environmentality and citizen sensing in the Smart City. *Environment and Planning D: Society and Space,* 32(1): 30–48.

Gabrys, J. 2016. *Program Earth: Environmental Sensing Technology and the Making of a Computational Planet.* Minneapolis, MN: University of Minnesota Press.

Gabrys, J. 2020. Smart forests and data practices: From the Internet of Trees to planetary governance. *Big Data & Society,* 7(1): 2053951720904871.

Galle, N.J., Nitoslawski, S.A., and Pilla, F. 2019. The Internet of Nature: How taking nature online can shape urban ecosystems. *The Anthropocene Review,* 6(3): 279–287.

Graham, S. and Marvin, S. 2001. *Splintering Urbanism: Networked Infrastructures, Technological Mobilities and the Urban Condition.* London: Routledge.

Grupo Karim. n.d. About us [online]. Available from: www.grupokarims.com/about_us.htm.

Grupo Karim. n.d. Smart Cities [online]. Available from: www.grupokarims.com/smart_cities.htm.

Jensen, C.B. and Morita, A. 2016. Introduction: Infrastructures as ontological experiments. *Ethnos,* 82(4): 615–626.

Karvonen, A. 2015. Pathways of urban nature: Diversity in the greening of the twenty-first-century city. In H. Jeffrey, B. Spencer, T. Way, and K. Yocom (Eds.) *Now Urbanism: The Future City is Here* (pp. 274–285). London: Routledge.

LaDuke, W. and Cowen, D. 2020. Beyond Wiindigo infrastructure. *The South Atlantic Quarterly,* 119(2): 243–268.

Larkin, B. 2013. The politics and poetics of infrastructure. *Annual Review of Anthropology,* 42: 327–343.

Maguire, J. and Winthereik, B.R. 2019. Digitalizing the state: Data centres and the power of exchange. *Ethnos,* 5: 530–551.

Marvin, S., Luque-Ayala, A., and McFarlane, C. (Eds.) 2016. *Smart Urbanism: Utopian Vision or False Dawn?* London: Routledge.

Masucci, M., Pearsall, H., and Wiig, A. 2020. The smart city conundrum for social justice: Youth perspectives on digital technologies and urban transformations. *Annals of the American Association of Geographers,* 110(2): 476–484.

McFarlane, C. and Rutherford, J. 2008. Political infrastructures: Governing and experiencing the fabric of the city. *International Journal of Urban and Regional Research,* 32(2): 363–374.

Nitoslawski, S.A., Galle, N.J., Van Den Bosch, C.K., and Steenberg, J.W.N. 2019. Smarter ecosystems for smarter cities? A review of trends, technologies, and turning points for smart urban forestry. *Sustainable Cities and Society,* 51: 101770.

Sheller, M. 2009. Infrastructures of the imagined island: Software, mobilities, and the architecture of Caribbean paradise. *Environment and Planning A,* 41(6): 1386–1403.

Simone, A. 2004. People as infrastructure: Intersecting fragments in Johannesburg. *Public Culture*, 16(3): 407–429.

Smart Forests. n.d. [online]. Available from: https://smartforests.net.

Star, S.L. 1999. The ethnography of infrastructure. *American Behavioral Scientist*, 43(3): 377–391. https://doi.org/10.1177/00027649921955532.

Stefano Boeri Architetti. n.d. Smart Forest City Cancun [online]. Available from: www.stefanoboeriarchitetti.net/en/project/smart-forest-city-cancun.

Sullivan, S. 2013. Banking nature? The spectacular financialisation of environmental conservation. *Antipode*, 45(1): 198–217.

Wakefield, S. 2020. Making nature into infrastructure: The construction of oysters as a risk management solution in New York City. *Environment and Planning E: Nature and Space*, 3(3): 761–785.

# 10

# Ecological computationality: cognition, recursivity, and a more-than-human political actor

*Andrew C. Dwyer*

Computation has become a key mediator and contributor to almost all aspects of collective everyday life. It is, in various places and at differing temporalities, at work. Computational processes and their associated *outputs* are engaged in the retrieval of information using the Internet, the geolocation infrastructure that mobile devices are entangled with, and the 'background' databases and algorithms utilised across numerous industries and governments, as much as in the monitoring and cataloguing of animals and plants for conservation and ecological restoration. In this chapter, I pursue an argument – drawing on research from software studies and media studies[1] – that computation should be considered ecological, albeit distinct to its (in) organic counterparts. To do so, I develop the concept of *computationality* as a performative collective of materials consisting of hardware, software, and networks with a capacity for (re)cognition, which topologically intersect with certain people, places, and communities.[2] Rather than computation understood as a tool, interface, surface, or network upon which to appreciate the (digital) ecologies of plants, animals, and other forms of organic and inorganic materials, I argue that computation is a recursive and cognitive *political* actor. By this, I mean that computation is engaged in forms of reasoning that are sustained by iterative, and often non-linear, feedback loops that are formative of a recursivity across, in, and through, multiple ecologies. Computation, from this perspective, then, not only represents ecologies but is actively reworking them too. Machine learning algorithms, at their greatest extent, have become indicative of recursive computation's capacity to optimise and make inferences: whether in the (mis)identification of faces, in assessing the likelihood for a person to commit fraud, or – crucially, in the context of this book – suggesting the best areas for ecological intervention. Hence, exploring the role of computationality in societies is essential for understanding how it is productive of, and is shaped by, ecologies that we collectively live in.

To articulate the complex relationships between computationality, ecology, and computation as entangled political actors in this chapter,

I provide two vignettes from an (auto)ethnography of the analysis and detection of malicious software. My analysis draws on seven months of fieldwork, training to become an analyst at an analysis and detection laboratory, that relied on computationality and ecological methods for practising cybersecurity. Malware, as it is frequently known, has historically been referred to as its derivatives in the computational virus and worm. Today, malware has become a seemingly persistent and ever-present part of contemporary interconnected societies, with recent cases affecting the Irish Healthcare Safety Executive[3] and against the software provider SolarWinds, in a supply-chain compromise of the US government.[4] Since the late 1980s, privatised responses to secure against computational viruses materialised in anti-virus engines. Today, anti-virus technologies have been integrated into *endpoint detection* products that offer a broader range of techniques and strategies for malware detection by a range of household names such as Norton and McAfee. Unlike the 'script kiddies' of the latter part of the twentieth century,[5] malware is now primarily written by states and organised criminal gangs to exploit computational vulnerabilities, with ransomware the most egregious contemporary example.[6] However, in this chapter, I do not focus on the essential analysis ongoing elsewhere on how to attend to such threats, but instead conceptualise how malware is analysed and detected through thinking of endpoint detection – and cybersecurity generally – as engaging with computational ecologically.

By arguing for an ecological appreciation of computation through computationality, I embrace perspectives from across software studies, media studies, and more-than-humanism, as well as the philosophy of computation.[7] In emphasising computationality, I wish to extend, twist, and bend the 'outputs' of computation so that it is rendered a societal and political thing, one which cannot be simply disentangled from its relations or presented as an abstracted mathematical machine, but as embedded in complex, recursive, political, and more-than-human ecologies. In the case of this chapter, I demonstrate, through the exemplar of endpoint detection, how software is categorised as malicious and then becomes detected in ways that embrace the cognitive capacity of computation in various ecologies. The chapter thus proceeds by (1) giving a brief background to how computation is conceptualised as a technology that is incapable of exerting agency and politics; (2) how conceptual developments have repositioned how the human can assist in assessing computation and recursivity in more-than-human and ecological forms; before (3) engaging more deeply with computational (re)cognition as a more-than-human political ecology that distances itself from readings on technological affordances, complexity, and agency; and then (4) concluding with openings of what computation as a political actor means for the study of digital ecologies.

## Computation: from technology to ecology

Within the (computing) sciences, the dominant interpretation of computation has long regarded it as an axiomatic and logical system that is bound to certain mathematical rules, upon which it can be controlled and rendered knowable. This frequently assumes that computation's agency is limited to its authors, with reference to software authors' capacity to generate ever-greater sophisticated forms of reasoning. The central figure of the (human) author is sustained by a 'tech bro' culture where resolutions to our problems are exclusively addressed by a supposed elite of coders to construct new worlds – such as through recent branding and materialisation of the 'metaverse'.[8] McKenzie Wark's critique of such Silicon Valley culture, identifies the importance of coders in the formation of a new iteration of capitalism in 'vectorialism', which splices society and power according to the ability to code and create new societal 'vectors'.[9] In such accounts of the importance of software authors and coders from Wark to Zuckerberg, however, there is a pervasive centring of the human – or coding elites – as being in control of computation. Such a position makes computation devoid of its political agency and often ascribes it to complexity,[10] where agency in some accounts manifests in *bugs, glitches*, and *errors*.[11] Together, these perspectives suggest that computation's agency emerges from either an inherent environmental complexity or from an intending and political human.

Computation as a complex tool, or one that has certain technological affordances or affects, rests on multiple genealogies of *our* relationship to technology,[12] which extend back into the (Western) Enlightenment that sought to categorise and offer a world of rationality and order.[13] Although there is not space to fully explore the often-conflicting historical lineages of technological thought, Yuk Hui has noted how the body became understood as mechanical at the same time as René Descartes made a distinction between humans and non-human animals.[14] Animals – and bodies generally – became considered 'machine-like' as they were 'devoid of mind and consciousness, and hence lacking in sentience'.[15] In this privileging of the human mind through a mind–body dualism, it is not only computation that is devoid of an ability to participate in politics, but also all non-human organic animals and plants. Friedrich Leibniz likewise creates a further division between natural and artificial machines, with the former more complex than the latter.[16] In this reading, animals and organic matter are of a higher ranking than technology. These collectively produce an implicit hierarchy with the dominance of the human mind at the top, followed by their bodies, 'natural' machines, and at the bottom, artificial, technological machines subservient to humans and less sophisticated than other organic matter.

In contrast, cybernetics, led by individuals such as Norbert Wiener,[17] advocated for understanding animals, humans, and machines through abstracting their interactions to information.[18] Although N. Katherine Hayles has been critiqued for her over-simplification of the complex emergence of the study and various orders of cybernetics,[19] early cybernetics' abstraction and equivalence of things, permitted by an emphasis on information and feedback systems, enabled computational and human intelligence to be routinely compared and contrasted. Cybernetic equivalence has let computation – most prolifically in discussions on machine learning algorithms – to be compared to human forms of intelligence.[20] However, with dominant lineages from Western thinking identified above, computation is still rendered a tool below human forms of intelligence. This is not to claim that the abstraction and equivalence of things should be ascribed to all cyberneticists or indeed technological thought but, I argue, this offers one foundation to understand how and why computation can be both perceived as more 'intelligent' than humans as much as it remains regulated as another technology at the lowest rung of the hierarchy of politics and agency. Although such distinctions are often unsettled in popular anxieties of robotic domination and control in post-anthropogenic landscapes, they derive from an anxiety of our relationship to computation as a political actor that *we* cannot place. That is, computers are either seeking to control us or us computers. Together, this leaves computation lacking a more-than-human politics or agency, and when it does, it is shrouded in the hyperbole of domination.

## More-than-humanism, ecology, and recursivity

Since the 1990s, there have been moves, sometimes unrelated to technological thinking, across the social sciences, humanities, and beyond to address the position of the human in contemporary thought and practice. This has sought, often through enmeshed and interlinked genealogies, to understand and recognise the role of non-human agencies and their impact upon our societies and politics, whether that be, for example, through new materialisms,[21] Actor–Network Theories,[22] and in animal studies.[23] In geography, these have often consolidated and been promoted through a focus on 'more-than-humanism'[24] that advocate for an expanded 'we' as much as for experimentation in research praxis.[25] Likewise, the philosophy of computation has attended to computational agency, logics, and the capacities for inductive processes of artificial thought.[26] Collectively, these bodies of thought have productively questioned the central role of the human and continued (feminist) traditions of deconstructing the dualism of the mind and body, both within and outside of geography.

In veins like more-than-humanism within geography, the concept of ecology within media studies and software studies frequently pursues and develops related paths in continental philosophy, noting how software works across and through various different materials and in different socio-cultural interactions.[27] This suggests that technology is generative of affordances on, through, and in response to societal dynamics. Ecological thinking has likewise been adopted in human geography through the feminist thinking of Donna Haraway,[28] in thinking about the 'Anthropocene',[29] and in association with the concept of Gaia.[30] This has been accompanied by questioning the Eurocentrism – and thus the positionality of the human – of such approaches and its impact on other ways of living.[31]

When considering ecological computationality within geography, I combine two streams of thought from software studies, media studies, and the philosophy of computation on the one hand and more-than-humanism on the other. This permits two things: first, it takes seriously the former's empirical and conceptual contributions on computation's technological affordances and logics to shape society in ways similar to core work in geography on the matter,[32] whereas, second, this chapter draws on geography's complementary repositioning of differently positioned peoples and communities, experimental practice, and working alongside the agencies of animals and plants in more-than-human ways.

As software studies and media studies have explicitly examined, the ecologies of computation must attend to the sheer volume of computational materialities exhibiting greater interdependencies, which have enhanced the complexity, negotiation, translation, and intertwining of human subjectivities and technological affordances. This deepening spatial distribution – and environmental complexity – of computation, alongside growing processing capacities, has been accompanied by the decreasing cost of computing hardware. This has enabled sensors, actuators, cameras, and other forms of computation to become commonplace in the monitoring and assessment of a range of ecologies.[33] In the process, computational interdependencies, supported by big data collection, have enabled the possibility of enhanced recursion, especially with machine learning algorithms, enabling affects and effects to be generated at scale.[34] However, this does not only occur at supposed large scales. For example, when one types into a text document on a computer, it is not simply a word appearing on a screen. Instead, there are a whole host of processes, to first read the electronic signal from a keyboard, interpret this, and find and access a place in memory to a stored value, which in turn requires various other processes to retrieve, translate, and display this through a text-processing program on a screen. Often, such interactions *function as expected*; however, there is always a potential for a mistranslation, a misreading within the ecology of processes, which often expresses itself when a program crashes or glitches.[35]

One common embrace of more-than-humanism in human geography engages with various new materialisms that have often built upon and underacknowledged similar veins of thought.[36] New materialisms emphasise the capacity of things to have agency, with philosopher Jane Bennett making a distinction between the 'big agency' of humans and the 'small agency' of worms.[37] Yet, this distinction suggests a primacy of the human as 'big' or hierarchically atop of other things. Whereas, turning to discussions on the agencies of algorithms, with their interconnections, big data relations, and capacities for recursive reasoning,[38] such a hierarchical distinction begins to decompose. Thus, it may be pertinent to consider how there are various gradients of capacity for agency, dependent on the capacity for recursive reasoning, where computation allows for ecologies to be deconstructed and reconstituted by 'deep' machine learning algorithms.[39] To summarise, in contemporary new materialist thinking, computation – and other technologies, as well as organic and inorganic ecologies – can be understood through either environmental complexity (such as slippages, errors, and bugs) or through an expanded view of agency, which gives emphasis to the capacity of inorganic technologies to be generative of affordances and to perform that extend and complicate human-centric notions of the term. Hence, ecologies of computationality consist of the environment complexities of computation as much as the affordances they permit, shaping and contouring societies through the performances computation engages in. This could, for example, involve computational materials such as sensors with certain material qualities, generating big data, and software that affords a capacity to render knowable, in certain ways, an environment. Yet, in developing such productive lines of thought, new materialisms have not explicitly attended to computation's capacity for recursive reasoning and have regulated computation to being another inorganic *agent*.

## Analysing and detecting malware

When conducting an autoethnography of a malware analysis and detection laboratory, I often encountered the affordances of computational materials as much as I glimpsed at ecologies of computational materials as distinctive political actors. The majority of the labour I performed in the laboratory consisted of the production of malware detections using techniques that have existed since the earliest days of anti-virus technologies. Detection 'signatures' I crafted sought to prevent software identified as malicious from executing, using code matching against unique attributes found in the software and code. Contemporary endpoint detection itself now utilises a much wider range of techniques and strategies in addition to detection signatures, including 'behavioural' analyses that monitor computational environments for changes, as well as machine learning algorithms that use big data from a range of sources to create features to identify malicious attributes in analysed software. The detection engines of endpoint detection enterprises are today installed on millions, if not billions, of devices, analysing environments and used to detect malware and suspicious behaviour in an industry worth billions of US dollars each year. Endpoint detection is widely used, and perhaps forms one of the most data-intensive, spatially complex, yet under-studied, areas of cybersecurity. It is, in many forms, an attempt to monitor, transform, and shape a planetary ecology of computation to limit malicious and suspicious activity.

At Sophos, in Oxfordshire, England, where I conducted my (auto)ethnography, multiple different forms of analysis and detection were in concurrent use, intermingling and threaded across one another. When sitting at my desk, I was confronted with a bewildering amount of data, from various databases both internal and external (such as Alphabet-owned Virus Total, a malware repository). This also included learning how to analyse software at the lowest levels of human-readable code (known as 'assembly language') so that code instructions could be intricately read and understood, and sometimes incorporated into detection signatures. Although I do not have space to go into further detail here, what I seek to highlight is how the environments of the laboratory were already ecological – drawing together various tools for analysis, multiple, competing streams of big data generation and analysis, as well as analysts' affective and embodied relations to maliciousness honed through experimentation and time spent conducting analysis of malware 'in-depth'.[40] However, such an ecology, where one is using computation as both the 'tool' of detection as much as the object of analysis, made it exceptionally difficult to ascertain who and what was doing the analysis and thus was practising cybersecurity. For example, when I was sitting at my desk in the laboratory, looking at my screens, I had 'automated' percentages with colours presented to me of the malicious likelihood of the artefact being analysed, as well as tools which could execute software in a simulated environment to assess whether it was malicious or not. Hence, it was not only me or the other analysts partaking in the protection of computers, but also computers in performance in ecologies, engaging in crucial political choices about what is or is not malicious.

## Vignette 1: A false positive, 22 June 2017

I had just returned from lunch at the cafeteria on the ground floor of the headquarters of Sophos, wondering what I was going to do that afternoon. Before I had left for lunch, I had been working with a large group of software samples that had been tagged by other endpoint detection vendors as SupTab – a browser modifier.[41] SupTab was variously tagged as either malicious or, in some cases, as a 'potentially unwanted application'. The different tags applied to the same software are reflective of the social construction of 'maliciousness'. Such tags are reflective of an affective and financial economy, affective through what is considered normal by analysts and financial through the time and labour that laboratories can devote to the production of detections. However, big data analysis and sharing has enabled an ecological practice to identify samples for further detection and to structure and direct the limited labour of the laboratory. In this case, I was allocated a range of software samples that had been identified by other vendors as SupTab and needed to be detected by Sophos. To do so, I had generated a method to identify various 'missed' SupTab detections through an *unusual* set of strings to *uniquely* detect the software (or, at least, I thought).[42] However, it was after lunch, when my detection encountered the curated ecologies of quality assurance processes to ensure that my detection would *execute* as expected and not detect 'benign' or 'clean' software out 'in the wild',[43] that things went wrong.

Due to the increasing reliance on big data across cybersecurity to develop ecological awareness, there are persistent issues with data quality, especially when one relies on data feeds and comparisons to other endpoint detection vendors. This quickly destroyed any post-lunch malaise. When I unlocked my computer, a message was flashing from Elliott, another malware analyst, stating that I had submitted a detection for SupTab that was producing quality assurance errors. This was preventing the release and distribution of a range of detections packaged as part of that afternoon's release to computers that had Sophos' endpoint detection installed on them. I therefore quickly turned my attention to the analysis screens on my computer. What Sophos called the 'false positive rig' contained a data store of what software was deemed 'benign' or 'clean' by other endpoint detection vendors. The rig had identified my detection as 'detecting on software' tagged as non-malicious. The rig was used by quality assurance to ensure detections produced by Sophos did not detect 'clean' software. In the case of my detection, it appeared I had not written a sequence of instructions precise enough to only refer to the unique attributes of SupTab. I had to investigate, and quickly.

As I dug into the case and worked line by line through my detection and examples of the supposedly 'clean' software, I found that the rig had samples that were incorrectly identified by other endpoint detection vendors as non-malicious. The misidentification was down to one endpoint detection vendor incorrectly identifying files as 'clean' and therefore claiming they were not malicious or potentially unwanted, transforming the Sophos infrastructure of quality assurance. Such infrastructures, as much as they are reliant on big data sharing, offer a baseline of comparison to produce detections that are less likely to incorrectly detect software that is not malicious. By focusing on the infrastructural condition of big data sharing, I do not seek to single out Sophos. Rather, all endpoint detection vendors are dependent on similar infrastructures and are indicative of the great interdependencies and complexities of embracing ecological computationality in cybersecurity. By engaging in greater recursivity through big data analysis, cybersecurity is not only shaping conditions on customer computers, but cybersecurity itself is dependent on an ecology of unknown environments and infrastructures, as well as as computational analysis 'tools' that have been constructed based on the affective engagements of analysts at other endpoint detection vendors. Thus, the ecology of Sophos' laboratory had been disrupted by the complexity of the ecologies of big data sharing and computational networks as well as being reliant on 'automated' quality assurance techniques dependent on computationality. Thus, the *false positive* identified by the rig on my detection was one rupture, caesura, on a warm June afternoon that exposed the complex ecologies at work in cybersecurity today.

## Recognition and politics

However, as much as these ecological ruptures could be plausibly attributed to computational complexity, complexity did not appear to wholly explain what was going on in the laboratory. Drawing on the work of N. Katherine Hayles,[44] and associated work on thinking about recursive societies,[45] I found the argument about computation's capacity to (re)cognise as a cognitive actor supported by its recursive capacities fruitful. Such thinking allows for more-than-human political hybrids, which alternatively enable facial features to be matched with databases of 'suspicious' individuals at state borders, often folding entrenched forms of injustice.[46] This approach also extends to identifying plants through mobile applications, such as PictureThis, or ascertaining whether software is malicious or not in cybersecurity. Hayles' work specifically engages with materials according to their capacity to be either cognisers or non-cognisers in contrast to a hierarchy based on human centrism. Cognisers include a broad polity of different things that include organic things including people, animals, plants, and even viruses, but crucially also computation. In contrast, non-cognisers include things that do not read, interpret, or act upon signs[47] – including rocks, ocean waves, and plastics – that could be understood to dynamically interact and afford properties as in much new materialist thought.

Hayles' expansive notion of cognition opens up a plural, and political, 'we' by exploring how cognisers make *choices* and collectively develop meaning and communities. This makes computation distinct to other forms of technology with its capacity to recursively *read* the environments and ecologies it is within, *interpret* these, and then *act* by shifting bits, producing 'outputs', and more. Computation is not simply acting according to the forces exerted upon it, but is about making choices. As I have expressed with the notion of grammars of malware elsewhere,[48] this thinking is productive of complex ecological computationalities, involving people writing software and various computational materials making choices, alongside infrastructures and more. Certain grammars of cognitive capability are embedded in computational materials, enabling malware to make *choices* that lead to particular transformations in computation (as much as other computational materials and people are making choices too!) Focusing on the capacity for cognition also opens up polities for all organic matter to make choices, albeit at different gradients and with different affects. For some plants, the cognitive scope and choices may be exceptionally limited, such as how to orientate towards light or seek nutrients in soils. Debates on such capacities of both plants and animals to cognise, be intelligent, and otherwise have been widely debated within geography and elsewhere.[49] However, I claim that a broadening of choice-making is intimately political without recourse to saying that all forms of cognition are equal, comparable, or commensurable to one another. So, rather than conceptualising computation through the figure of a tool, instead computationality enables a political acknowledgement of the complex processes that occur during the various readings, interpretations, and then choices that emerge in such a process. This also suggests an alternative view of computation beyond the glitch, bug, or error, and rather of an expression of choices that do not align with our humanly, representational, aspirations.

### *Vignette 2: Machine learning algorithms, colours, and percentages*

The importance of the recursive cognitive capacities of computationality were most clearly expressed to me in what was a relatively new addition to Sophos' capabilities to both analyse and detect malware: convolutional neural network machine learning algorithms.[50] Although algorithms have pervaded endpoint detection for many years, machine learning algorithms offer the promise of identifying the 'unknown' malware, as has been promised with 'threats' in other security domains.[51] This is because, most simply, machine learning algorithms leverage the cognitive capacity of computation to recursively iterate digital data in feedback loops. This process (re)constitutes various ecologies, establishing new abstract features to categorise and render the world in new formations. In one use at Sophos, an algorithm processed a software byte distribution presented as an image to identify malicious features.[52] This was achieved through training on the big data of previously identified malware that had been shared as detections (itself an ecology of contemporary cybersecurity).

However, to a malware analyst, recognising human-sensible features from this bit distribution is exceptionally difficult and remains mainly incommensurable to them. I may be able to recognise some patterns, but not in the way that the algorithm did, creating new features of maliciousness that are broadly nonsensical to the analysts I worked with. Thus, such machine learning algorithms produce new formations of what is malicious or not. *They literally perform new forms of security* (and what is 'normal', a profoundly political act). Such algorithms provide a basis for a new form of recognition to take place, where the algorithm can be 'grounded' in the affective and embodied forms of maliciousness practised by malware analysts through the learning data used to train the algorithm. This produced, ultimately through computational recognition, new forms of what may be considered malicious, albeit still infused with norms established by malware analysts both at Sophos and elsewhere. In many ways, this is a more-than-human communal 'we' upon which different political actors work together in often incommensurable forms.

Computational cognitive capacities also permit a speeding up, and expanded reach, of cybersecurity and endpoint detection. Yet, it is also perilously reliant on more-than-human politics with alien forms of recognition embedded within it. When I was at my desk in the laboratory, the outputs of the machine learning algorithm were presented on my screen as the potential likelihood of maliciousness as a percentage, with an associated hue of colour on the interface before me. When conducting the autoethnography, *becoming-analyst*, those colours and percentages obscured the recognition of the machine learning algorithm, infusing my affective relations with malware as computational materials, and thus what maliciousness was. It changed how I viewed the software I was analysing, transforming my perception and relationality to this structured arrangement of code. I was being trained not solely by people, but by an ecology of computation itself. In this sense, malware analysis and detection are a truly more-than-human endeavour.

However, computation was not only transforming my perception in the laboratory, but actively constructing other ecologies by deeming what features were malicious or not. This leads to an increasing standardisation of what is considered 'good' software practice and establishing precedents over what a 'good' cybersecurity ecology may look like. Yet, in many ways, what happens when computation recognises and performs its choices, is it truly recognising 'malware' or something rather more unsettling, simply anomalous software? Anomalous to what? To our society's capitalist response to computational vulnerability? I therefore assert that computation is not simply a tool with a unidirectional form of control and knowability from its authors. Computation actively participates in the political through its choices – which can intersect with our more humanly concerns. This occurs in ways that make its study all the more difficult, yet equally fascinating – whether that be through models of climate change or addressing concerns over disinformation on social media. Yet, political capacities occur across all forms of computationality, not just with machine learning algorithms, such as in the translations required to write in a text document, albeit with a varying gradient of the choices that are available to be made. It is only in machine learning algorithms – and increasingly their integration with robotics – that there has become a need to address computation's explicit political capacities as it becomes imbricated across vast digital ecologies.

## A political digital ecology?

In Félix Guattari's *Three Ecologies*, he argues for ecologies to be understood across environments, social relations, and human subjectivity as three registers of an 'ecosophy'.[53] Guattari was aware, even in 1989, of the potential 'of the technological and data-processing revolutions, as prefigured in the growth of a computer-aided subjectivity, which will lead to the opening up or, if you prefer, the unfolding [*dépliage*], of animal-, vegetal-, Cosmic- and machinic-becomings'.[54] In contemporary thinking of ecologies of, and digitised through, computation, their recursive cognitive ability has radically transformed our societies by rearticulating forms of knowing and politics. Rather than as some backdrop for understanding animal or vegetal matter – to use Guattari's phraseology – computation, in this chapter, has been presented as an active interlocutor and political actor enmeshed in communal more-than-human polities. This has drawn upon insights of ecology from software studies and media studies alongside the work on more-than-humanism and the philosophy of computation to argue that it is a cognising *political actor*, making choices aided by its recursive technological capacity. There is thus an incessant negotiation and translation going on all around us. It is not just an unfolding, but instead a *recursive folding* engaging in contested terrains, with alien relations of computational recognition,[55] with multiple forms of *subjectivity* that do not wholly ascribe to humanly ways of recognising, thinking, and doing.

In my reading of computation, unlike Hayles, choice is a foundation to understanding a performative, recursive, and, crucially, political ecological computationality. This situates computation as distinct to other technologies that do not make choices and creates a more-than-human ecological polity alongside other forms of organic life. This does not neglect that there are important technological affordances – and indeed by all things – but these affordances should not be confused with political actors; ones that actively choose how to read, interpret, and act in the world compared to those which afford certain properties that shape those engaging in choice-making (albeit political actors can afford certain properties too, such as through what is written in malware). Such choices as political negotiations and frictions across terrains in ecologies may be incommensurable to our humanly representations, and even greater capacity for choice-making in more abstracted computational forms in machine learning algorithms increase this. I thus advocate for a more-than-human, expanded 'we', where computation is one of a broader range of political actors at work in (digital) ecologies. Thus, as much as computational representations are not always as complex as in machine learning algorithms, drawing on software studies and media studies' close empirical attention to the fissures, ruptures, and interrelationship with our capitalist societies, it is possible to glimpse at how more-than-human relationships,[56] between computation, people, other technologies, organic life, and more, can enable a more expansive appreciation of our contemporary ecologies.

In this chapter, I have used two vignettes of the Sophos malware analysis and detection laboratory to demonstrate how ecological computational practices are used – computationality – in cybersecurity. In identifying software as malicious, computation affords some properties to collect and store vast amounts of big data; but this is also made 'useful' through the politics of recognition and choice. This means that computation is not just about setting up a tool for analysis – but rather as an analyst, I was experimentally negotiating with a political actor that is defuse, not whole, known, nor localisable as much as it is distributed across customer endpoints and the sites of big data generation and collection. Cybersecurity, as one example, is then a complex hybrid of ecologies with various political actors, complex environments, in more-than-human collectives. Thus, researching digital ecologies, as this book proposes, means to also study the computationality upon which other ecologies may interface, interact, and be articulated afresh through computation's capacity to be an entangled political actor. It is not simply enough to understand how computational media and interfaces may shape our perceptions, or how sensors may be able to understand *other* places in new ways, but also how computationality must be studied to understand the emergence of more-than-human modes of knowing, thinking, and politics.

## Notes

1. Taffel, *Digital Media Ecologies*.
2. I have developed this thinking elsewhere in relation to security studies through topology and scene in Dwyer et al., 'Topologies of security.'
3. PwC, *Conti Cyber Attack on the HSE*.
4. FireEye, 'Highly evasive attacker.'
5. 'Script kiddies' are often referred to as novice, or relatively unskilled, individuals who use common techniques and tools to gain access or attack other computer systems.
6. Ransomware is a category of malware that encrypts – or mathematically 'locks' – files on a computer so that the user cannot access such files without the decryption key to 'unlock' them. This is accompanied by a ransom 'note' that informs the victim that they must pay a fee to gain access to their files.
7. Fazi, *Contingent Computation*; Fuller and Goffey, *Evil Media*; Parikka, *Digital Contagions*.
8. Zuckerberg, 'Founder's letter.'
9. Wark, *Capital Is Dead*.
10. Such a position on complexity can be considered with regard to the 'black box' of machine learning algorithms, where it is simply the complexity of recursive practices that needs to be 'opened' to observe the rationality of an algorithm's outputs.
11. Parikka and Sampson, *The Spam Book*. However, see Leszczynski and Elwood, 'Glitch epistemologies' for a geographical perspective on the openings that glitches offer, albeit in a different context but which could offer glimpses into similar arguments I make regarding ecological computationality.
12. Pedwell, 'Speculative machines and us.'
13. Bowker and Star, *Sorting Things Out*.
14. Hui, *Recursivity and Contingency*.
15. Hatfield, 'René Descartes,' n.p.
16. For more on this, see Raymont, 'Leibniz's distinction between natural and artificial machines.'
17. Wiener, *Cybernetics*.
18. Hayles, *How We Became Posthuman*.
19. Taffel, *Digital Media Ecologies*, p. 33.
20. Pedwell, 'Speculative machines and us.'
21. Devellennes and Dillet, 'Questioning new materialisms.'
22. Law, 'After ANT.'
23. Barua, 'Volatile ecologies.'
24. Dowling et al., 'Qualitative methods II'; Greenhough, 'More-than-human geographies.'

# Ecological computationality 211

25 Whatmore, 'Materialist returns.'
26 Fazi, 'Can a machine think (anything new)?'; Parisi, 'Critical computation.'
27 See Fuller, 'Media ecologies'; Fuller and Goffey, *Evil Media*; Montfort et al., *10 PRINT CHR*; Spencer, 'Creative malfunction.' Ecological thinking has multiple different avenues that this chapter cannot delve into to, but it uses the position from theoretical media studies (particularly software studies) rather than those of social movement media studies (for a genealogy of the latter, see Treré and Mattoni, 'Media ecologies and protest movements').
28 Haraway, *Staying with the Trouble.*
29 Castree, 'The epistemology of particulars.'
30 Latour, *Facing Gaia*; Stengers, *In Catastrophic Times.*
31 Panelli, 'More-than-human social geographies'; Povinelli, *Geontologies*; Yusoff, *A Billion Black Anthropocenes or None.*
32 Kitchin and Dodge, *Code/Space.*
33 Gabrys, *Program Earth.*
34 Beer, 'The problem of researching a recursive society.'
35 This is not to say that computation cannot be very tightly articulated and programmed, especially in high-assurance software. Yet, this is because each step of the translation process is heavily scrutinised. This, typically, however limits software to being highly attuned to a particular task and cannot *reason*, which is more often than not the allure – and *value* – of our contemporary attention towards machine learning algorithms.
36 Rosiek et al., 'The new materialisms and Indigenous theories.'
37 Bennett, *Vibrant Matter.*
38 Beer, 'The problem of researching a recursive society'; Hui, *Recursivity and Contingency.*
39 Amoore, *Cloud Ethics.*
40 Dwyer, *Malware Ecologies.*
41 For more information, see Microsoft Security Intelligence, *Microsoft Security Intelligence Report 22.*
42 These are concatenations of alphanumerical symbols. I do not provide any further detail on what these were, as it is highly likely that these are still used in active detections.
43 'In the wild' is a common term in cybersecurity to refer to spaces – and ecologies – outside of a closed computational network or environment.
44 Hayles, 'Can computers create meanings?'; Hayles, *Unthought.*
45 Beer, 'The problem of researching a recursive society'; Pedwell, 'Speculative machines and us.'
46 Amoore, 'Machine learning political orders.'
47 For more on a discussion on signs and information in computational cognition, see a conversation between N. Katherine Hayles and Tony Sampson – in Hayles and Sampson, 'Unthought meets the assemblage brain,' – nor should this thinking be directly associated with the cognitive sciences.
48 Dwyer, 'Cybersecurity's grammars.'
49 Lawrence, 'Listening to plants.'

50 Although the details of these algorithms are too complex to note here, these types of algorithms analyse images.
51 Amoore, 'The deep border.'
52 The bytes (8 bits) of a software program were transformed into a distribution that could then be visualised, with various colours, depending on whether it was encrypted or not, for instance.
53 Guattari, *The Three Ecologies.*
54 Ibid., p. 25.
55 Fazi, 'Beyond human.'
56 Mackenzie, 'Machine learners.'

# Bibliography

Amoore, L. 2020. *Cloud Ethics: Algorithms and the Attributes of Ourselves and Others.* Durham, NC: Duke University Press.
Amoore, L. 2021. The deep border. *Political Geography*, 110: 102547.
Amoore, L. 2023. Machine learning political orders. *Review of International Studies*, 49(1): 20–36.
Barua, M. 2014. Volatile ecologies: Towards a material politics of human–animal relations. *Environment and Planning A*, 46(6): 1462–1478.
Beer, D. 2022. The problem of researching a recursive society: Algorithms, data coils and the looping of the social. *Big Data & Society*, 9(2): 20539517221104996.
Bennett, J. 2010. *Vibrant Matter: A Political Ecology of Things.* Durham, NC: Duke University Press.
Bowker, G.C. and Star, S.L. 1999. *Sorting Things Out: Classification and Its Consequences.* Cambridge, MA: MIT Press.
Castree, N. 2005. The epistemology of particulars: Human geography, case studies and 'context'. *Geoforum*, 36(5): 541–544.
Devellennes, C. and Dillet, B. 2018. Questioning new materialisms: An introduction. *Theory, Culture & Society*, 35(7–8): 5–20.
Dowling, R., Lloyd, K., and Suchet-Pearson, S. 2016. Qualitative methods II: 'More-than-human' methodologies and/in praxis. *Progress in Human Geography*, 41(6): 823–831.
Dwyer, A.C. 2019. *Malware Ecologies: A Politics of Cybersecurity.* PhD thesis, University of Oxford. Available from: https://ora.ox.ac.uk/objects/uuid:a81dcaae-585b-4d5b-922f-8c972b371ec8/.
Dwyer, A.C. 2023. Cybersecurity's grammars: A more-than-human geopolitics of computation. *Area*, 55(1):10–17.
Dwyer, A.C., Langenohl, A., and Lottholz, P. 2023. Topologies of security: Inquiring in/security across postcolonial and postsocialist scenes. *Critical Studies on Security*, 11(1): 1–13.
Fazi, M.B. 2018. *Contingent Computation: Abstraction, Experience, and Indeterminacy in Computational Aesthetics.* London: Rowman & Littlefield International.
Fazi, M.B. 2019. Can a machine think (anything new)? Automation beyond simulation. *AI & Society*, 34(4): 813–824.

Fazi, M.B. 2021. Beyond human: Deep learning, explainability and representation. *Theory, Culture & Society*, 38(7–8): 55–77.
FireEye, 2020. Highly evasive attacker leverages SolarWinds supply chain to compromise multiple global victims with SUNBURST backdoor. *Threat Research* [online], 13 December. Available from: https://web.archive.org/web/20210312010850/www.fireeye.com/blog/threat-research/2020/12/evasive-attacker-leverages-solarwinds-supply-chain-compromises-with-sunburst-backdoor.html.
Fuller, M. 2005. *Media Ecologies: Materialist Energies in Art and Technoculture*. Leonardo (Series). Cambridge, MA: MIT Press.
Fuller, M. and Goffey, A. 2012. *Evil Media*. Cambridge, MA: MIT Press.
Gabrys, J. 2016. *Program Earth: Environmental Sensing Technology and the Making of a Computational Planet*. Minneapolis, MN: University of Minnesota Press.
Greenhough, B. 2014. More-than-human geographies. In A. Passi, N. Castree, R. Lee, S. Radcliffe, R. Kitchin, V. Lawson, and C. Withers (Eds.) *The SAGE Handbook of Progress in Human Geography* (pp. 94–119). London: Sage.
Guattari, F. 2014. *The Three Ecologies*. Bloomsbury Revelations. London: Bloomsbury.
Haraway, D.J. 2016. *Staying with the Trouble: Making Kin in the Chthulucene*. Experimental Futures. Durham, NC: Duke University Press.
Hatfield, G. 2018. René Descartes. In E.N. Zalta (Ed.) *The Stanford Encyclopedia of Philosophy*, Summer 2018. Metaphysics Research Lab, Stanford University [online]. Available from: https://plato.stanford.edu/archives/sum2018/entries/descartes/.
Hayles, N.K. 1999. *How We Became Posthuman: Virtual Bodies in Cybernetics, Literature, and Informatics*. Chicago, IL: University of Chicago Press.
Hayles, N.K. 2017. *Unthought: The Power of the Cognitive Nonconscious*. Chicago, IL: University of Chicago Press.
Hayles, N.K. 2019. Can computers create meanings? A cyber/bio/semiotic perspective. *Critical Inquiry*, 46(1): 32–55. https://doi.org/10.1086/705303.
Hayles, N.K. and Sampson, T. 2018. Unthought meets the assemblage brain: A dialogue between N. Katherine Hayles and Tony D. Sampson. *Capacious: Journal for Emerging Affect Inquiry*, 1(2): 60–84.
Hui, Y. 2019. *Recursivity and Contingency*. Media Philosophy. London: Rowman & Littlefield International, Ltd.
Kitchin, R. and Dodge, M. 2011. *Code/Space: Software and Everyday Life*. Cambridge, MA: MIT Press.
Latour, B. 2017. *Facing Gaia: Eight Lectures on the New Climatic Regime*. Cambridge, UK: John Wiley & Sons.
Law, J. 1999. After ANT: Complexity, naming and topology. *The Sociological Review*, 47(S1): 1–14.
Lawrence, A.M. 2022. Listening to plants: Conversations between critical plant studies and vegetal geography. *Progress in Human Geography*, 46(2): 629–651.
Leszczynski, A. and Elwood, S. 2022. Glitch epistemologies for computational cities. *Dialogues in Human Geography*, 12(3): 361–378.
Mackenzie, A. 2017. *Machine Learners: Archaeology of a Data Practice*. Cambridge, MA: MIT Press.
Microsoft Security Intelligence. 2017. *Microsoft Security Intelligence Report 22* [online]. Available from: www.microsoft.com/en-us/security/business/security-intelligence-report.

Montfort, N., Baudoin, P., Bell, J., Bogost, I., Douglass, J., Marino, M.C., Mateas, M., Reas, C., Sample, M., and Vawter, N. 2012. *10 PRINT CHR $(205.5+ RND (1)); GOTO 10*. London: MIT Press.

Panelli, R. 2009. More-than-human social geographies: Posthuman and other possibilities. *Progress in Human Geography*, 34(1): 79–87.

Parikka, J. 2016. *Digital Contagions: A Media Archaeology of Computer Viruses*. 2nd ed. New York: Peter Lang.

Parikka, J. and Sampson, T.D. 2009. *The Spam Book: On Viruses, Porn, and Other Anomalies from the Dark Side of Digital Culture*. Cresskill, NJ: Hampton Press.

Parisi, L. 2019. Critical computation: Digital automata and general artificial thinking. *Theory, Culture & Society*, 36(2): 89–121.

Pedwell, C. 2022. Speculative machines and us: More-than-human intuition and the algorithmic condition. *Cultural Studies*, 38(2): 188–218.

Povinelli, E.A. 2016. *Geontologies: A Requiem to Late Liberalism*. Durham, NC: Duke University Press.

PwC. 2021. *Conti Cyber Attack on the HSE*. Dublin: PwC [online]. Available from: https://web.archive.org/web/20220110205442/ www.hse.ie/eng/services/publications/conti-cyber-attack-on-the-hse-full-report.pdf.

Raymont, P. 1998. Leibniz's distinction between natural and artificial machines. *The Paideia Archive: Twentieth World Congress of Philosophy*, 11: 148–152.

Rosiek, J.L., Snyder, J., and Pratt, S.L. 2020. The new materialisms and Indigenous theories of non-human agency: Making the case for respectful anti-colonial engagement. *Qualitative Inquiry*, 26(3–4): 331–346. https://doi.org/10.1177/1077800419830135.

Spencer, M. 2021. Creative malfunction: Finding fault with Rowhammer. *Computational Culture*, 8. http://computationalculture.net/creative-malfunction-finding-fault-with-rowhammer/.

Stengers, I. 2015. *In Catastrophic Times: Resisting the Coming Barbarism* (A. Goffey, Trans.). London: Open Humanities Press.

Taffel, S. 2019. *Digital Media Ecologies: Entanglements of Content, Code and Hardware*. London: Bloomsbury Academic.

Treré, E. and Mattoni, A. 2016. Media ecologies and protest movements: Main perspectives and key lessons. *Information, Communication & Society*, 19(3): 290–306. https://doi.org/10.1080/1369118X.2015.1109699.

Wark, M. 2019. *Capital Is Dead: Is This Something Worse?* London: Verso.

Whatmore, S. 2006. Materialist returns: Practising cultural geography in and for a more-than-human world. *Cultural Geographies*, 13(4): 600–609.

Wiener, N. 1948. *Cybernetics: Or Control and Communication in the Animal and the Machine*. New York: J. Wiley.

Yusoff, K. 2018. *A Billion Black Anthropocenes or None*. Minneapolis, MN: University of Minnesota Press.

Zuckerberg, M. 2021. Founder's Letter, 2021. *Meta* [online], 29 October. Available from: https://web.archive.org/web/20220115154749/https://about.fb.com/news/2021/10/founders-letter/.

# 11

# Mediated natures: towards an integrated framework of analogue and digital ecologies

*Mari Arold*

In recent decades, the proliferation of information technologies has given rise to the so-called 'digital turn' in geography and cognate social science disciplines.[1] The continuously renewing repertoires aim at grasping how digital tools, platforms, and interactions shape our perceptions of phenomena mediated through them. In carefully capturing the specificities of digital mediation, however, these efforts have sometimes under-emphasised: (1) the wider milieu of digital and non-digital elements involved in empirical contexts; and (2) what digital and analogue mediations have in common and could thus be consolidated under a shared framework.

This chapter considers an ongoing policy debate in Estonia as a case study to explore the significance of forest's conceptual disparity for environmental conflict resolution. Through fieldwork snapshots from the 'Forest War', the chapter looks at how different versions of forest are generated and shaped via digital and analogue mediations. Empirical observations reveal how forest is experienced and (re)produced in sacred groves and institutional vlogs, behind a harvester's dashboard and over a mushroom basket. These competing and converging conceptualisations of forest reaffirm the epistemological and ontological multiplicity of nature, space, landscape, and environment – as conceived in Indigenous ecologies and certain strands of political ecology.[2] Such multiplicity gives rise to what Jennifer Gabrys and colleagues have termed 'political forests' – environmental governance entities co-constituted by historical and modern technologies.[3] As the fate of forest – whether as a biogeographical or cultural entity – depends on its perception and communication, a deeper empirical inquiry into how people engage with it is due. A better understanding of how people relate to forest can help us fathom how this conceptual and experiential diversity can hamper conflict resolution.

Online and offline observations of digital and analogue technologies and practices will shed light on the diverse material relations and myriad ways of knowing forest. To interpret these conceptualisations, a rejuvenated framework for digital ecologies scholarship is needed – one that can simultaneously account for digital/analogue, discursive/material, and tangible/

ethereal mediations of phenomena. In media studies, a well-established body of work conceives of media as a 'hybrid system', where so-called analogue media (posters, placards, protests chants, radio shows) are entangled with a range of digital platforms, in ways that collectively shape, constrain, and mediate protest.[4] This chapter's observations of different forest users' day-to-day activities, stakeholders' websites, and forest and forestry events bring some of these insights into conversation with digital ecologies. This affiliation paves the way towards an at least partially shared language on digital and analogue mediations beyond anthropogenic communication systems.[5]

The first part of the chapter sets the contextual and epistemological stage for the case studies, sketching out a more-than-digital ecology approach with a focus on mediations. Mediation is conceptualised as an ontogenetic event forging all phenomena. The empirically driven second and third parts revisit a selection of everyday and organised forest-mediating events amid Estonia's heated forest policy debate. It appropriates the concept of mediation for more-than-human encounters, using notions of *attunements and conductivity*; *mediative loops*; *augmented and compressed realities*; *synchronies and sequences*; and *multimodal complementarity*. The chapter proposes a movement from *digital* towards *mediated* geographies that also accommodate the analogue. It concludes with five theoretical premises for any future research that wishes to pursue a holistic framework of mediations in the context of more-than-human worlds.

## Forest in the forest war: following the shifting notion

Covering approximately 50% of Estonia's land area, forest is an important habitat, economic resource, and recreational space for the country's inhabitants. Forest and wood industries have consistently contributed about 4% of Estonia's GDP,[6] and, in 2021, provided 4.5% of the country's employment.[7] So, despite the lack of correlation between felled timber volume and employment (oft purported in industry lobby),[8] the sector's service for the workforce and the state's budget remains significant. This argument has been behind a series of relaxations in forestry regulations. Since the beginning of the twenty-first century, the law has undergone the highest number of individual property-related liberalisations across the European Union,[9] and the felling volume has more than doubled since 2008.[10] These legal concessions cast doubt on the effort to balance ecological, economic, social, and cultural needs,[11] as prescribed by the national Forest Act. While environmental organisations criticised the law in the 1990s, the numerous deregulations since have brought concern to the masses. Alongside its economic and ecological functions, forest plays a central role in Estonian culture and identity.

Residents enjoy free access to public and private forests – whether for foraging, leisure, or to draw energy from one of the country's sacred groves – *hiied*.[12] As clear-cut sites have proliferated and moved closer to settlements, public discontent has intensified in sync with logging.

In the country, where the closest forest from whichever starting point is no more than a short bicycle ride away and internet access is near ubiquitous, the forest debate continually switches between online and offline environments. Since 2016, the sharpening polarisation between industry advocates and critics has manifested in the foundation of a series of environmentalist citizen movements, protests, petitions, court cases, and incessant media and Facebook debates. The profound incommensurability between stakeholders' concepts of 'forest' hampers the outlook for conflict resolution, begging for better apprehension of how the notions emerge and evolve. Forest is socially co-constructed – regarding its cultural meanings, as well as materiality: every story, image, and experience of forest is conducive to how it is governed and used. Forest concepts differ widely between individuals, who define the 'forestness' of land by its purpose, appearance, dimensions, species composition, or history. But forest is also phenomenologically constructed – its affective expressions in each embodied experience shape its physical and discursive manifestations in the future.[13] The material semiosis of embodied and discursive ingredients comprise versions of forest that can, but do not always, have geographical coordinates or physical presence.[14] These versions of forest are challenging to reconcile intellectually and in governance. For example, forests are multiple, and can be understood in many forms (Table 11.1).

The lack of universal reference points problematises the singular reality of forest and complicates research that would resonate with all stakeholders. How to understand how something emerges, disseminates, and wanes if there is no 'thing' to follow but a mere 'family resemblance' between the uses of the concept?[15] Political ecology's notion of 'pluriverse' captures the ontological multiplicity of nature,[16] but its tendency to focus on macro-level power dynamics risks carving a static image of parallel worlds (usually Indigenous/colonised vs neoliberal/Western/colonising) that do not leave much room for transformations and variations across and within these worlds. To fathom the diverse conceptions, experiences, and manifestations of an elusive phenomenon, we must find a way to *follow the shifting notion*. Applying Leszczynski's articulation of spatiality as 'always-already mediated' to all phenomena,[17] forest becomes a *processual socio-environmental artefact* – a concept continually redefined by material and symbolic mediations. It manifests in images and utterances, policies and myths, maps and statistics, flying squirrels and bilberries. This definition lets us include more evasive forest perceptions alongside those already sharing

**Table 11.1** Forests understood through different conceptual lenses.

| Concept | Definition | Examples |
| --- | --- | --- |
| Landscape | An aesthetic-symbolic abstraction that has an areal element but is not necessarily linked to any specific geo-coordinates | 'National' scenery |
| Resource | A directly or indirectly, quantitatively or qualitatively measurable entity, whose location is often inconsequential ... | Timber |
|  | ... but not always | Health and wellbeing from a peri-urban woodland |
| Place | A defined space inherently tied to its location | Grandmother's 'mushroom forest' |
|  |  | *Hiis* |
| Space | A geographical entity that is related to physical locations but may accommodate some fungibility | Nature reserve (ecosystem) |
|  |  | Green corridor (infrastructure) |
|  |  | Real estate (spatial commodity) |
| Diverse unarticulated versions of forest | Interpreted non-verbally and/or subconsciously, or affectively felt and embodied | Source of identity or wellbeing |

a touchstone. Viewing forest as an ontogenetic process, rather than a static object viewed from different angles, pushes us to let go of 'the thing' and look for new reference points.

The ways to conjure images and tell stories of forest have proliferated through technological developments such as forest and forestry apps, digital media and digital tools, making it ever more urgent to review the epistemologies of nature and environment. Understandings of digital(ised) knowledges to date carry a risk of content reification. Despite the oft-attributed omniscience, digitally born or mediated knowledges are not immune to discursive path dependencies, offline contexts, or the affordances and constraints of the technologies themselves. Prompted by digital developments and concomitant data optimism, an array of epistemological writing disputes the new and revamped old cognitive regimes that order our engagements with nature.[18] Explicitly or implicitly drawing from hybrid and assemblage theories, these studies reject distinctions between representation and reality or between nature and technology. Digital structures and content are parts of more-than-human, socio-technological entanglements[19] – encroached but not solely defined by binary code – which put into question the ontological security of digital (research) objects.[20] The vagrant agencies and classificatory ambiguities in such topologies necessitate new, processual epistemologies that include offline worlds and embodied practices in explorations of (digitally) mediated phenomena. This chapter does not hunt for stable definitions of forest. Instead, it seeks to decrypt forest in its transformational moments – mediative events – not its essence.

## A word on terminology

### The digital

The design, affordances, and reputation of 'the digital' create and legitimise space, socio-spatial relations, and the environment.[21] Unlike in early digital geographies, dualistic perspectives of parallel 'digital/virtual' and 'real' worlds are increasingly rare in recent scholarship.[22] Most agree that the two are effectively a hybrid,[23] or ontologically inseparable.[24] Building on colleagues' critiques, Jessica McLean observes how 'terms like "virtual reality" reinforce the seeming non-realness of digital geographies'.[25] After all – as Tom Boellstorff exemplifies – German learnt over the Internet gets you by in Germany and money lost through online gambling is real money.[26] Conversely, in light of dynamic conceptions of landscape, nature, and space as socially constructed,[27] and becoming,[28] it should be added that terms like 'reality' reinforce the deceptive realness (or ontological security) of *non*-digital geographies: spatiality is always already mediated.[29] This chapter concurs with the recent scholarship, conceiving 'the digital' as more-than-digital: a dimension of contemporary reality that alters but is inseparable from (material and semiotic) analogue phenomena.

### Media and mediations

Digital geographies and anthropologies have enlivened conversations about media, mediations, and human perception. The myriad ways in which objects, spaces, and other phenomena manifest through different software, hardware, and on-the-ground contexts have introduced volatility to mediations, which earlier, pre-digital geography alone is inapt to envisage.[30] The governance of material landscapes or 'spatialities' has always been contingent on how they are perceived.[31] But due to the cardinally changed and changeable tempo, networks, trending and attention economies, contexts, technological affordances, and dispersed authorship in the increasingly digitalised world – perceptions need to be regarded as parts of lively mediation *events*. This chapter expands upon Leszczynski's take on *mediation* as an *ontological claim* whereby everyday spaces are produced at the 'conjunctions of code, content, social relations, technologies, and space/place'.[32] These conjunctions include, but are not limited to, *media* – that is, socio-technological *communication structures*. Viewing mediation as an event helps reveal its components' interplay and changing prevalence, as perception takes shape. Digital developments have heightened and highlighted the dynamism of communicated objects and spatialities.

## *Conductivity*

When I was listening to my fieldwork recordings, I often heard sounds I had not discerned while in the forest with participants. Sometimes a conspicuous birdsong had gone unnoticed, sometimes my own small talk with mushrooms, as I was engaged with my non-auditory senses. A single-minded search for mushrooms, the smell of moss, and uneven ground under my feet had shut my attention to background noises from further afield, whereas the taped birds only had to compete with an intermittent conversation between the participants and me. In an interplay of senses and thoughts, signals from some channels became foregrounded while others stepped aside. I call this variable prominence of channels their *conductivity*. A channel's conductivity is contingent on technology's (or any medium's) affordances, and affective and discursive distractions from other channels. When a roamer opens a plant identification app or Wikipedia in the forest, the prevalence of the information they register changes. Their peripheral vision may narrow upon focusing on the screen; their thoughts might start switching between their native language and English or Latin. At the break of a rainstorm, articulated ideas, perhaps, take a backseat altogether while bodily sensations become more pronounced. The conductivity of mediating channels such as senses, weather elements and other affective phenomena, media and social media, digital and analogue tools, and other humans and non-humans fluctuates constantly, calling for methods that appreciate the complexity of perception's mutable composition and, consequently, the intricacy of (mediated) phenomena.

## Empirical axis: an approximated human perceiver

Like forest, any spatiality – and any (digitally) mediated space, nature, phenomenon, or object – is a processual artefact. How, then, to observe and describe these fleeting notions? While political ecology has rightfully emphasised digital materiality,[33] the meaning of a digital object is larger than the sum of its silicon and syntactic parts and the economic forces driving them. As the computer engineer and philosopher Yuk Hui remarked, deconstructing a digital artefact down from programming languages and binary code to signals generated by voltage values and logic gates 'doesn't tell us much about the world'.[34] Just like deconstructing bodies down to chemical elements and electric currents is limited in what it can tell us about humans and human society. The social life of humans and objects cannot be explained solely in material terms. And understanding the infrastructures' economic drivers helps us apprehend the *received*, but less so the *perceived* phenomena. Perceived objects do not equate with what is communicated. They are composed through an interplay of digital data and infrastructure, history and memory, aesthetic and computational rationalities, neurotransmitters and selves. Bringing the analogue/digital, material/discursive, and living/non-living onto an even ground continues to be rehearsed in more-than-human scholarship, but these structurally liberating non-atomic assemblage philosophies pose a problem: how do we study something in perpetual ontogenesis – incessantly reinvented through material, discursive, algorithmic, and embodied mediations? We want to avoid reifying research objects before the inquiry even begins, but how to do so without surrendering our entire analytical ammunition? To find our feet in this fickle landscape, this chapter employs an artificially stable starting point – the perceiving human. While tacitly acknowledging non-human actants' interventions, as well as humans' multispecies, cyborgian composition,[35] it pragmatically approximates the agency of a human perceiver for studying protean natures. Of course, human perception is but one in a series of manifestations of phenomena, but – considering its impact on the world – it holds prime airtime for a reason.

The approximated human perceiver grounded the fieldwork observations amid the ongoing Forest War in Estonia. The socio-environmental conflict is trapped in a conundrum: how to resolve a forest policy dispute when the variously mediated 'forest' is conceptually and experientially so divided that stakeholders cannot so much as agree on the object of the debate? The remainder of this chapter considers how humans experience forest through everyday and organised events. The empirical observations form the bedrock for a conceptual quest for variously perceived natures in a way that accommodates (more-than-)digital, as well as analogue mediations.[36]

## Mediative events

Strands in new media studies have flagged the need to pay more attention to media's experiential and material aspects[37] and historical contexts.[38]

Participant observation in media and mediations that encompasses online and offline realms can address this need and avoid techno-determinist conclusions divorced from heterogenic offline circumstances. Carefully contextualised, on-the-ground case studies can unveil the configuration of phenomena through mediative events, in a dynamic interplay of channels, messages, and technologies. The following sections exemplify the latent potential of studying everyday mediative events through participant observation, awaiting to be incorporated into new conceptual frameworks.

### Attunements and conductivity

> While I was taking the shot, everything was normal. But when I uploaded the photos onto my computer, I was astounded to discover dancing beings on them – like floating, translucent balls. (Riho, forest dweller)

The dancing beings Riho – a forest dweller nicknamed Forest Troll – observed were not an anomaly, but merely one of many reported sightings of forest fairies in Estonian collective spiritual consciousness. Some years ago, life-changing personal affairs and environmental injustice had impelled Riho to look for new alliances. Local animist tradition and forest's affective properties attuned him to find them in the 'more-than-human' territory. Ever since their first encounter, various ethereal forest beings have offered Riho moral guidance and, he asserts, punished environmental wrongdoers. Intangibly but surely, they mediate a version of forest and environmental ethics that Riho abides by. Of course, Estonian folk belief is not the only forest discourse Riho has been exposed to.[39] He has encountered the paper industry's publications, ecologists' articles, environmentalists' outcries, and artists' expressions. But not all information lands on fertile ground, just like not everyone would have identified the translucent balls as living creatures. Even Riho only spotted them thanks to his camera. It took digital mediation and Riho's disposition to recognise and classify them as such.

Alongside the geographical and cultural context, the camera's technological affordances and Riho's attunement to the ethereal co-determined how the moment by a forest spring was mediated between formats and locations (from the forest to a digital desktop to Riho's eyes and memories). Paraphrasing the influential media theorist Marshall McLuhan's idea that 'the medium is the message' (i.e. mediative technology is more formative than content to a message),[40] we could say that *the recipient is the (co-) mediator is the message*. Riho's perception is not defined solely by forest discourses circulating the society, nor by mediative technology, nor by forest as material, independent externality. It is a configuration of all of the above, plus Riho as a mediating agent in his own right. In reply to a question about

Mediated natures 223

which information channels he uses to keep up to date with developments in the forest, Riho replies, 'You go, look, listen to what the forest has to tell. If you go in the direction where you are guided, you'll find [what you need]'. By 'listening', Riho and several other research participants seemed to mean openness to non-visual, non-articulated signals that do not neatly fit into our familiar scheme of five independent senses. This generative listening is reminiscent of synthesisers turning mushrooms' internal bioelectronic signals into sounds, the videos of which can be found on YouTube.[41] While the ordinarily imperceptible 'mushroom music' is foregrounded by synthesisers, Riho practises silent attentiveness to amplify forests' stories out of inconspicuous vibrations and signals. His attunement is his amplifier. 'You must be quiet and listen to what the forest is telling', he teaches his children.

Riho's evident mediative agency that can alter the strength of signals available to him emphasises the audience's active role in meaning-making and cautions against the technological determinism some media studies have been criticised for.[42] It demonstrates that the salience of a message is not decided merely by mediating channels and technologies but also by the perceiver's disposition and attunements. Message, conductivity, and attunements shape each other.

## Mediative loops

> Twenty plus, three, nine, and the fourth is from nine to thirteen. Thirteen plus, nine. Yes. Yes-yes-yes. Four begins from thirteen. There will be more of the others – yeah, it's thicker. Three-nine is thick, isn't it. Yes-yes. There's more of the thin ones. (Sepo, harvester operator)

Sepo hangs up the phone. Irregular beeps, creaks, and clatter join the harvester's low droning as its jaw-like head chomps through trees, making the cabin shake whenever it encounters a rebellious knobbly trunk. A GPS device had guided Sepo to the workplace a few days ago. With GIS software, the forest had already been turned into management plots, whose straight boundaries cut across the land's wonky topology.

At the start of the day, the harvester's computer interface prompted Sepo to divide the forest into a table of dominant tree species and size classes and ignore whatever did not fit into the pregiven categories (see Figure 11.1). The computer is programmable, but as a rule, out of the fifty-one native tree species in Estonia, six at the most make it to the interface. The software then converts trees into financial returns, guiding the operator's decisions about cutting and sorting the timber as the harvester chunters up and down the plot, leaving a clear path behind.[43] Sepo's forest concept is almost entirely defined by his work. Fourteen-hour days and long commutes at weekends

Figure 11.1 Harvester cabin. (All rights reserved and permission to use the figure must be obtained from the copyright holder.)

leave him short of time and desire to experience forest in any other way in the little time he has off. To a question about which forests he likes, Sepo responds, 'straight [trees and] little variety'. Smoothness and homogeneity of trunks mean efficiency and more money.

Riho and Sepo should neither be seen as types nor anomalies in the widely heterogeneous participant sample I worked with. They appear in this chapter merely for their strikingly different forest experiences – so we can judge whether a conceptual common ground for such diverse cases can be achievable. To do so, let us contemplate some of the co-mediating channels and filters that contribute to Sepo's forest experience, displayed in Table 11.2.

Despite entirely different technologies and the proportion of digital and analogue engagements with forest, the mediative compositions of Riho and Sepo's experiences are comparable. The next step would be to evaluate the dynamics between each mediative event's components that make the encounters so different. As days unfold, media channels and other components of perception alternate in their influence; neither digital nor any other aspect is pre-eminent by default. The parallel channels may enhance or hinder each other's conductivity and the salience of a particular broadcasted (or unicasted) version of forest. Let us, for instance, consider

Table 11.2 Co-mediating channels and filters shaping Sepo's forest experience.

| Mediation channels and filters | Descriptions |
| --- | --- |
| Aspects of the forest environment and inhabitants | The visual-pallaesthetic simulcast of the forest seen through the windshield and felt corporeally: soil and delimbed timber variously shift and shake the harvester's frame – expressing selected characteristics of the forest floor and trees. Occasionally, a large mammal or an environmental activist with a camera may appear within the field of vision, while birds and bird nests – to their misfortune – tend to stay hidden between tree branches. |
| Immediate (machine) environment | The roaring and shaking cabin that insulates aspects of the surrounding landscape – such as sound, smell, and weather elements – from the operator and replaces them with others – like air-conditioning, radio, and beeping hardware. |
| Technology | Extensions of body and environment, including hardware, software, and other material and cognitive tools (levers and buttons, GPS, language, decimal numerals, binary code, etc.).<br>The kinaesthetic human/machine hybrid apprehending the perils of soft patches and protruding stumps.<br>Like Riho's collaboration with his camera, this 'taskscape' is also subject to the harvester's technological affordances.[44] |
| Discourse | The industry's rationalised view of forest as a timber resource, which informs the technology's production and the operator's training and instructions. |
| Disposition | The operator's previous life experiences that shape their discursive and embodied attunements upon the forest encounter. |
| Distant communications | Infrequent phone conversations with the employer or a colleague. |

Sepo's harvester computer as a mediator. The kinaesthetic dialogue between Sepo, the computer, and the dashboard fuses the external discourses with mutually embodied attunements to manage the land and tree cover according to the industry's definition of forest. The encounter is managed through software and hardware, but its rationale can be seen on crunched-up printouts and heard in occasional oral instructions. While code, indeed, increasingly mediates processes – in this case by delimiting, hierarchising, and quantifying forest species and their qualities – its role is sometimes over-emphasised in digital geographies. Not only must we remember that every experience and manifestation is *co*-mediated by numerous channels (not least the recipient's cognitive agency), but also that there is no set precedence between technology and discourse.[45] Instead, they feed back to each other in a continuous *mediative loop*. So, too, the harvester's software draws its forest parameters from the industry's (on-the-ground) priorities, while workers operating the computer may internalise this model in their own forest articulations and reinforce it in their future communications. But these feedback loops are not closed. They are continuously negotiated between perceiving selves and various mediating channels, calling for conceptual avenues that entertain processual mediations.

### *Augmented and compressed realities*

Among anthropologists, and to a lesser extent in digital geographies, studies have emerged that accommodate processual conceptualisations of mediation. Mark Graham and colleagues call digitally co-designed moments 'augmented realities':[46] changeable, subjective realities arising from partly digitised relationships with the world. However, we must not assume that realities are infinitely augmentable – being consumed by an increasing wealth of information, attention is a limited resource.[47] Like coins accumulating in a penny pusher, augmented realities build pressure along their edges, and something has got to give. We are not necessarily seeing collective experiential enrichment, either. While digital and hybrid events appear to create more stimuli and perceptual possibilities, these part-digital experiences generate both perceptual diversity and assimilation. Consider a mushroom identification app. It reveals information not apparent when encountering a specimen in the forest: who are their taxonomic relatives,[48] what do they look like when they are older or younger, and are they poisonous or edible? But scrolling and clicking through this information, mushroom aficionados may overlook other aspects relevant to the specimen: what do they smell like, how do they feel against the skin, who are their symbiotic companions surrounding them, or indeed, what do they sound like? Mobile digital interfaces and app content homogenise encounters with different specimens in diverse offline contexts. Distracting from the on-the-ground context, they part-standardise human–mushroom encounters. Thus, talking about augmentation without regard to compression, simplification, and other possible transformations can only give us a partial picture of the mediated artefact's evolution in (digital) transmission. Visions of infinitely augmentable realities turn a blind eye to what is omitted or blurred in the mediation process. In Riho's encounters, perhaps, the socio-economic dimensions of forest went unnoticed; for Sepo – forest's spiritual manifestations. Conversely, analysing attention deficit without regard to *multi-channel complementarities* fails to acknowledge the strategic ways political actors make digital/analogue and discursive/affective communication channels support each other. The final sections of the chapter will exemplify this point, but let us first consider one more aspect of multi-channel mediations – time.

### Synchronies and sequences

Compatible with a contextual emphasis in mediation analyses are the studies that have drawn inspiration from the language of sound. To counterbalance the long-standing textual and visual favouritism in cultural geographies and to coalesce human perception with technical aspects of interface design, James Ash and colleagues[49] argue that '[j]ust as sound can be simultaneously heard and felt and these sounds and feelings depend on the environment the sound travels through [[50]], so are parts of interfaces experienced on multiple sensory levels depending on what they are placed in relation to'. Paul C. Adams – also inspired by sound waves – suggests viewing communications non-media-centrically as open-ended, collaborative, transformative arcs – consisting of a series of referrals and resonances.[51] In line with non-representational theory,[52] communicating subjects are transformed as resonance ripples through them. 'Arc of communication' as a unifying, more-than-representational metaphor that encompasses discursive, material, and performed interpretations of landscape (or other phenomena) allows us to imagine perceiving subjects simultaneously as information receivers and mediating agents in a communicative chain.

The analogy with sound waves, however, poses a limit: vibrating through space, an arc of communication is conditioned by linear time. But mediation – which is what every communication is – is both sequential and synchronic. As Adams himself notes, 'An arc has the property of directionality but is not merely a one-way, causal or sequential link'.[53] A harvester operator's conception of forest, for instance, is negotiated through various synchronous and asynchronous transmissions. It is shaped by preceding (asynchronous) communications, such as employer instructions, mainstream and social media posts, and peer conversations. But forest is also materialising through the operator's real-time encounters with it – co-created between the harvester, forest inhabitants, and the operator at each moment of their workday. To capture the simultaneity of multiple communications in each mediation, we must also reckon with its synchronous elements.

By addressing the concerns raised in new media studies through participant observation, more-than-human and digital geographies approaches can unleash great cross-fertilising potential for digital ecologies. If the chapter so far has sought these synergies from participants' day-to-day activities, then the following section considers forest manifestations as they are negotiated across multi-channel and multi-actor architectures at politically tinged events.

## Multimodal complementarity

As touched upon above, due to competing channels and attention scarcity, mediation can result in reduced or distracted realities. Yet, the potential complementarity of discursive, affective, and embodied modes of information mediation can be and is harnessed by political actors, stakeholders, and activists.

### *Narrated and performed climate optimism*

Estonian forest industry publicity deploys forest's affective properties alongside narrative strategies to increase support for its activities. As a for-profit state agency, the State Forest Management Centre (SFMC) collaborates closely with the private forest industry. Long-term supply agreements and subcontracted services align the interests of SFMC and the private sector, evident in shared discourses in their public relations. Mirroring Sweden's forestry publicity (e.g. LRF Skogsägarna and Skogsindustrierna's *Swedish Forest* campaign[54]), one recent trend to expand support for the industry has developed around the narrative of intensive forestry as the climate change solution. SFMC's rendition weaves the message into Estonian national and vocational forest-related identities through discursive and embodied outputs and events. In its 'Climate Heroes' vlog (Figure 11.2), various forestry workers convey the industry's carbon-optimist story, invoking authority from their 'forestman' identities handed down from fathers to sons. The message is reinforced with drone shots of seemingly infinite Nordic forests that the forestmen protect from nature's perils, such as pests and rot.

SFMC and the private forestry sector also mobilise the intended audience to absorb its messages affectively. Nature lovers are invited to join the 'climate heroes' ranks by tree planting on SFMC's clear-cut sites. Fresh air,

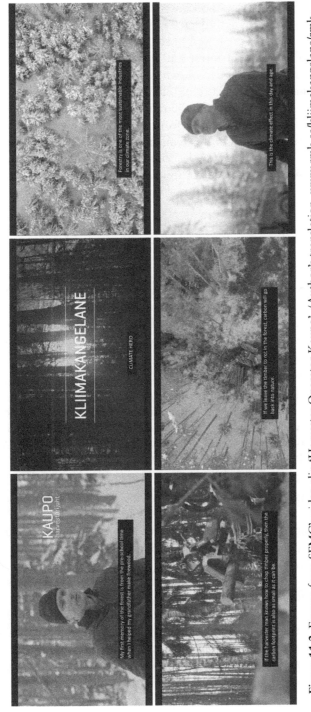

**Figure 11.2** Frames from SFMC's video clip 'Harvester Operator Kaupo'. (Author's translation. www.rmk.ee/kliimakangelane/rmk-kliimakangelased/harvesterijuht, accessed 7 July 2022. All rights reserved and permission to use the figure must be obtained from the copyright holder.)

good company, and exercise-induced endorphins allow the volunteers to feel as if they are bringing nature into being under the guidance of mindful forest stewards. Industry-organised 'forest days' offer nature walks propagating a particular vision of forest and forestry. Families are encouraged to partake in multisensory activities, where they can smell wood dust from arborists' saw-handling competitions, climb trees, make wooden toys, and operate a harvester simulator. Fist-bumping a rabbit mascot and posing with stuffed wolves, visitors are performatively co-producing a gamified, happy forest – reassured by forest owners' badges stating 'Estonian forest is in good hands'. These fun activities supplement the industry's media and social media communications advocating contested forestry practices. The industry's online discourse is performed by its audience on the ground.

## Mobilisation of more-than-earthly assemblages

Organised tours to *hiied* similarly utilise forests and trees' affective properties, alongside oral heritage, to performatively and discursively interlink nature conservation with ethnic and spiritual identity. *Hiied* are sacred groves in Estonia, revered by followers of *maausk* (see note 39), but also visited and respected by many others. Ahto Kaasik – a leading *maausk* practitioner, researcher, and campaigner – describes *hiied* as follows:

> Natural sacred sites ... are permanent landmarks, anchors of Estonianness that keep old place names, place and family heritage, beliefs, customs, knowledge and attitudes. They offer shelter to plants and animals, rocks and bodies of water, nature spirits, and most of all, Maaema[55] ... Hiied adorn the landscape, offer refuge to the body as well as soul, preserve our connection with ancestors and [related] tribal nations. In hiied, love for homeland and will to defend are grown. ... [H]iied keep the roots of us as an indigenous nation.[56]

The tours include runic singalongs, gift-giving to forest beings, skidding down healing rocks, and trading good thoughts and silver for energy from holy springs. The tour guide dons traditional clothing elements and an Estonian flag affixed to his bag, kindling participants' sense of shared national identity.

*Hiied* are simultaneously a pretext and a weapon in the Forest War. On the one hand, their preservation is of existential importance to people who habitually visit these places of worship in search of a connection with ancestors and forest beings, or physical and mental wellbeing. On the other hand, most natural holy sites are not mapped, with only scarce oral or archival heritage marking their location and history. To legitimise the protection expectation of *hiied* and their immediate surroundings, this heritage must endure.[57] Awareness campaigns are increasingly utilising new channels to enliven the groves' cultural relevance, as many are no longer distinguishable from their surroundings or, indeed, even tree covered. *Hiied* are looped through digital infrastructures, popping up on Facebook and thematic photo competitions. Cash prizes and a GIS-navigable map of *hiied* encourage contestants to learn about, visit, and breathe new life into less known or perished sacred sites by connecting their photos to stories and database entries.

By deploying a combination of technological affordances, forest's affective properties, multisensory physical engagement, and forest-related identities, different event series mediate and weaponise versions of forest that align with the organisers' discursive and political aims (see Figure 11.3). Further research within a holistic digital-analogue mediation framework can uncover, in more nuance, how individual, institutional, technological, and spiritual actors forge natures through competing and complementing mediative architectures: that is, more-than-human, more-than-representational, more-than-real, more-than-digital, and more-than-earthly assemblages.

Figure 11.3 Gathering energy and photographs from a holy oak on a sacred groves tour. (All rights reserved and permission to use the figure must be obtained from the copyright holder.)

## Conclusion and future directions for studying mediated natures

This chapter sought to move from digital towards mediated geographies that also accommodate the analogue. It deemed all phenomena as always already mediated, and defined natures (or landscapes, spaces, places) as processual socio-environmental artefacts, which transcend their digital and analogue dimensions. To disentangle mediative assemblages and more accurately predict their outcomes, the chapter proposes five premises for future research: (1) Artefacts evolve through mediative events, where the conceptual product is negotiated between the perceiver's disposition and attunements, on the one hand, and multiple channels of variable conductivity, on the other. A channel's conductivity is co-determined by the affordances of the technology/medium and distractions from competing channels; (2) Technology and discourse feed back into each other in a non-hierarchical loop, continuously transforming realities; (3) Digital realities can be augmented or compressed but are not inherently either; (4) Perception is simultaneously a sequential and synchronic event, requiring a broadened interpretation of causality that transcends linear time; and (5) Mediative events entail multimodal complementarity, which political actors harness. The communicative potential of such additionalities should be recognised alongside the approaches that emphasise attention deficit in the information age.

This indefinite list of premises invites redactions and additions with the caveat that – to fit into a holistic framework – each attribute is applicable to digital and analogue, material, and discursive contexts.

## Notes

1 Ash et al., 'Digital turn, digital geographies?'
2 For a political ecological overview of 'multinaturalism', see Lorimer, 'Multinatural geographies for the Anthropocene.'
3 Gabrys et al., 'Reworking the political in digital forests.'
4 For a foundational text on hybrid media, see Chadwick, *The Hybrid Media System*. For an application of media ecological theory that cuts across the digital and analogue, see OAPEN Foundation and Costanza-Chock, *Out of the Shadows, into the Streets!* For a text that draws these themes together, see Treré, *Hybrid Media Activism*.
5 See 'A word on terminology' section below for this chapter's definitions of 'media' and 'mediations' as two related but not synonymous terms.
6 Estonian University of Life Sciences and Environmental Investment Center, 'Mapping and analysis of financial flows in forestry.'
7 Estonian Qualifications Authority, 'Forestry and timber industry.'
8 Environment Agency, *Yearbook Forest 2020*, p. 133. https://keskkonnaportaal.ee/sites/default/files/Teemad/Mets/Mets2020.pdf.

9 Nichiforel et al., 'Two decades of forest-related legislation changes in European countries.'
10 Vihma and Toikka, 'The limits of collaborative governance.'
11 Estonian Environmental Law Center, 'Forestry regulation.'
12 In Estonian, sing. *hiis*, pl. *hiied* – an ancient nature worship site in a forest or grove, inhabited by ancestors' spirits and ethereal forest beings and charged with life force, *vägi*, which can be harnessed at the site.
13 Ash et al., 'Unit, vibration, tone'; Ingold, *The Perception of the Environment*.
14 Wylie, *Landscape*.
15 Wittgenstein, *Philosophical Investigations*.
16 Escobar, *Designs for the Pluriverse*.
17 Leszcsynski, 'Spatial media/tion.'
18 E.g. Leszczynski, 'Quantitative limits to qualitative engagements'; Nost and Goldstein, 'A political ecology of data.'
19 Berland, *Virtual Menageries*; McLean, *Changing Digital Geographies*; Taffel, *Digital Media Ecologies*; Turnbull et al., 'Digital ecologies.' See also Turnbull et al., 'What Is *Digital Ecologies*?' in this collection.
20 Salmond, 'Digital subjects, cultural objects.'
21 See also Leszczynski, 'Spatialities.'
22 Graham et al., 'Augmented reality in urban places'; Leszczynski, 'Spatialities.'
23 E.g. de Souza e Silva, 'Location-aware mobile technologies'; Zook and Mark Graham, 'Mapping DigiPlace.'
24 Boellstorff, 'For whom the ontology turns.'
25 McLean, *Changing Digital Geographies*, p. 254.
26 Boellstorff, 'For whom the ontology turns.'
27 Cosgrove, *Social Formation and Symbolic Landscape*; Crang and Thrift, *Thinking Space*; Williams, 'The country and the city.'
28 E.g. Crang and Thrift, *Thinking Space*; Massey, *For Space*.
29 Leszczynski, 'Spatial media/tion,' p. 729. See also Dodge and Kitchin, 'Code and the transduction of space.'
30 E.g. Rose, 'Rethinking the geographies of cultural "objects".'
31 Cosgrove, *Social Formation and Symbolic Landscape*; Scott, *Seeing Like a State*.
32 Leszczynski, 'Spatial media/tion,' p. 732.
33 Nost and Goldstein, 'A political ecology of data.'
34 Hui, 'What is a digital object?' p. 387.
35 E.g. Haraway, *Simians, Cyborgs, and Women*; Hird, 'Volatile bodies, volatile Earth'; Tsing, 'More-than-human sociality.'
36 Strictly speaking, 'the analogue' is *more-than*-analogue, as most present-day experiences are at least indirectly impacted by digital technology.
37 Kaun, *Crisis and Critique*; Kaun, 'Time of protest.'
38 Mattoni, 'A situated understanding of digital.'
39 With no dogma or scripture, Estonian native religion (sometimes called *maausk* – 'land belief'; 'country belief') is a loose set of syncretic traditions characterised by nature and ancestor worship, polytheism, and animism.
40 McLuhan, *Understanding Media*, p. 7.
41 E.g. MycoLyco, 'Five minutes of blue oyster mushrooms talking.'

42 Barassi, *Activism on the Web*; Lim, 'Roots, routes, and routers'; Treré, *Hybrid Media Activism*.
43 In Estonia, wood is cut and sorted immediately into piles according to species and product type (e.g. roundwood, pulp, and fuel) and subtype (e.g. size of sawlogs).
44 Ingold, *The Perception of the Environment*.
45 Pink, *Digital Ethnography*.
46 Zook et al., 'Augmented reality in urban places.'
47 Taffel, *Digital Media Ecologies*.
48 Non-gender-specific pronouns are characteristic of formal and informal Estonian language, while animate pronouns for mushrooms (and less often plants) follow the colloquial rather than official language use.
49 Ash et al., 'Unit, vibration, tone,' p. 169.
50 Gallagher, 'Sound as affect.'
51 Adams, 'Geographies of media and communication II.'
52 Thrift, *Non-Representational Theory*.
53 Adams, 'Geographies of media and communication II,' p. 591.
54 See www.svenskaskogen.nu, accessed 7 May 2022 (page no longer live).
55 Estonian for Mother Earth.
56 Kaasik, *Põlised Pühapaigad*, p. 9, author's translation.
57 The legal protection of each *hiis* is decided on a case-by-case basis. However, some owners choose to leave legally unprotected *hiied* untouched, either out of respect or conformism to social acceptability. In such cases – or when suggesting additional sites for legal protection – the fate of a *hiis* hinges on the awareness of the site's significance and, antecedently, the vitality of its heritage.

## Bibliography

Adams, P. 2018. Geographies of media and communication II: Arcs of communication. *Progress in Human Geography*, 42(4): 590–599.

Ash, J., Anderson, B., Gordon, R., and Langley, P. 2018. Unit, vibration, tone: A post-phenomenological method for researching digital interfaces. *cultural geographies*, 25(1): 165–181.

Ash, J., Kitchin, R., and Leszczynski, A. 2018. Digital turn, digital geographies? *Progress in Human Geography*, 42(1): 25–43.

Barassi, V. 2015. *Activism on the Web: Everyday Struggles against Digital Capitalism*. London: Routledge.

Berland, J. 2019. *Virtual Menageries: Animals as Mediators in Network Cultures*. Cambridge, MA: MIT Press.

Boellstorff, T. 2016. For whom the ontology turns: Theorizing the digital real. *Current Anthropology*, 57(4): 387–407.

Chadwick, A. 2017. *The Hybrid Media System: Politics and Power*. 2nd ed. Oxford: Oxford University Press.

Cosgrove, D. 1998. *Social Formation and Symbolic Landscape*. Madison, WI: University of Wisconsin Press.

Crang, M. and Thrift, N. 2000. *Thinking Space*. London: Routledge.

de Souza e Silva, A. 2013. Location-aware mobile technologies: Historical, social and spatial approaches. *Mobile Media & Communication*, 1(1): 116–121.

Dodge, M. and Kitchin, R. 2005. Code and the transduction of space. *Annals of the Association of American Geographers*, 95(1): 162–180.

Environment Agency. 2022. *Yearbook Forest 2020* [online]. Available from: https://keskkonnaportaal.ee/sites/default/files/Teemad/Mets/Mets2020.pdf.

Escobar, A. 2018. *Designs for the Pluriverse: Radical Interdependence, Autonomy, and the Making of Worlds*. Durham, NC: Duke University Press.

Estonian Environmental Law Center. 2013. *Forestry Regulation: Legal Analysis of the Restrictions Provided for in the Forest Act in 1998–2013* [online]. Available from: www.k6k.ee/keskkonnaigus/materjalid/teemavaldkonnad/metsandus.

Estonian Qualifications Authority. 2021. Forestry and timber industry [online]. Available from: https://oska.kutsekoda.ee/en/field/forestry-timber-industry/.

Estonian University of Life Sciences and Environmental Investment Centre. 2020. Mapping and analysis of financial flows in forestry [online]. Available from: https://dspace.emu.ee/items/4a570876-4594-4258-8205-9b2b17295d88.

Gabrys, J., Westerlaken, M., Urzedo, D., Ritts, M., and Simlai, T. 2022. Reworking the political in digital forests: The cosmopolitics of socio-technical worlds. *Progress in Environmental Geography*, 1(1–4): 58–83.

Gallagher, M. 2016. Sound as affect: Difference, power and spatiality. *Emotion, Space and Society*, 20: 42–48.

Graham, M., Zook, M., and Boulton, A. 2013. Augmented reality in urban places: Contested content and the duplicity of code. *Transactions of the Institute of British Geographers*, 38(3): 464–479.

Haraway, D.J. 1991. *Simians, Cyborgs, and Women: The Reinvention of Nature*. New York: Routledge.

Hird, M.J. 2012. Volatile bodies, volatile Earth: Towards an ethic of vulnerability. In G. Martin, D. Mincyte, and U. Münster (Eds.) *Why Do We Value Diversity? Biocultural Diversity in a Global Context* (pp. 67–71). RCC Perspectives, 9. Munich: Rachel Carson Center for Environment and Society.

Hui, Y. 2012. What is a digital object? *Metaphilosophy*, 43(4): 380–395.

Ingold, T. 2000. *The Perception of the Environment: Essays on Livelihood, Dwelling & Skill*. New York: Routledge.

Kaasik, A. 2016. *Põlised Pühapaigad*. Tallinn: Pegasus.

Kaun, A. 2016. *Crisis and Critique: A Brief History of Media Participation in Times of Crisis*. London: Zed Books.

Kaun, A. 2020. Time of protest: An archaeological perspective on media practices. In H.C. Stephansen and E. Treré (Eds.) *Citizen Media and Practice: Currents, Connections, Challenges* (pp. 113–126). New York: Routledge.

Leszczynski, A. 2009. Quantitative limits to qualitative engagements: GIS, its critics, and the philosophical divide. *The Professional Geographer*, 61(3): 350–365.

Leszczynski, A. 2015. Spatial media/tion. *Progress in Human Geography*, 39(6): 729–751.

Leszczynski, A. 2019. Spatialities. In J. Ash, R. Kitchin, and A. Leszczynski (Eds.) *Digital Geographies* (pp. 13–24). London: Sage.

Lim, M. 2018. Roots, routes, and routers: Communications and media of contemporary social movements. *Journalism & Communication Monographs*, 20(2): 92–136.

Lorimer, J. 2012. Multinatural geographies for the Anthropocene. *Progress in Human Geography*, 36(5): 593–612.

Massey, D. 2005. *For Space*. London: Sage.

Mattoni, A. 2017. A situated understanding of digital technologies in social movements: Media ecology and media practice approaches. *Social Movement Studies*, 16(4): 494–505.

McLean, J. 2020. *Changing Digital Geographies: Technologies, Environments and People*. London: Palgrave Macmillan.

McLuhan, M. 1964. *Understanding Media: The Extensions of Man*. New York: McGraw Hill.

MycoLyco. 2020. Five minutes of blue oyster mushrooms talking. YouTube video [online], 28 November. Available from: www.youtube.com/watch?v=J-nIBA0V_No.

Nichiforel, L. 2020. Two decades of forest-related legislation changes in European countries analysed from a property rights perspective. *Forest Policy and Economics*, 115. https://doi.org/10.1016/j.forpol.2020.102146.

Nost, E. and Goldstein, J.E. 2022. A political ecology of data. *Environment and Planning E: Nature and Space*, 5(1): 3–17.

OAPEN Foundation and Costanza-Chock, S. 2014. *Out of the Shadows, into the Streets!* Cambridge, MA: MIT Press.

Pink, S. 2016. *Digital Ethnography: Principles and Practice*. Los Angeles, CA and London: Sage.

Riigimetsa Majandamise Keskus. n.d. [online]. Available from: www.rmk.ee/kliimakangelane/rmk-kliimakangelased/harvesterijuht.

Rose, G. 2016. Rethinking the geographies of cultural 'objects' through digital technologies: Interface, network and friction. *Progress in Human Geography*, 40(3): 334–351.

Salmond, A. 2012. Digital Subjects, Cultural Objects: Special Issue introduction. *Journal of Material Culture*, 17(3): 211–228.

Scott, J.C. 1998. *Seeing Like a State: How Certain Schemes to Improve the Human Condition Have Failed*. New Haven, CT: Yale University Press.

Svenska Skogen. n.d. [online]. Available from: www.svenskaskogen.nu (accessed 7 May 2022; page no longer live).

Taffel, S. 2019. *Digital Media Ecologies: Entanglements of Content, Code and Hardware*. New York: Bloomsbury Publishing.

Thrift, N. 2007. *Non-Representational Theory: Space, Politics, Affect*. New York: Routledge.

Treré, E. 2019. *Hybrid Media Activism: Ecologies, Imaginaries, Algorithms*. London and New York: Routledge.

Tsing, A. 2014. More-than-human sociality: A call for critical description. In K. Hastrup (Ed.) *Anthropology and Nature* (pp. 27–43). New York and Abingdon: Routledge.

Turnbull, J., Searle, A., Hartman Davies, O., Dodsworth, J., Chasseray-Peraldi, P., Von Essen, E., and Anderson-Elliott, H. 2023. Digital ecologies: Materialities, encounters, governance. *Progress In Environmental Geography*, 2(1–2): 3–32.

Vihma, P. and Toikka, A. 2021. The limits of collaborative governance: The role of inter-group learning and trust in the case of the Estonian "forest war". *Environmental Policy and Governance*, 31(5): 403–416.

Wittgenstein, L. 1953. *Philosophical Investigations*. New York: Macmillan.

Wylie, J. 2007. *Landscape*. London: Routledge.

Zook, M. and Graham, M. 2007. Mapping DigiPlace: Geocoded internet data and the representation of place. *Environment and Planning B: Planning & Design*, 34(3): 466–482.

# Part IV

Digital ecological directions

# Afterword: digital ecologies and digital geographies

*Gillian Rose*

I start this afterword in whole-hearted agreement with the argument made by the editors of this fascinating collection, which is that the mediation of human and non-human life by technologies means that there is no direct access to a pristine real world, let alone to a nature unsullied by human intervention. Human life has always depended on and been shaped by tools and technologies; human relations to environments as well as to other humans are always mediated by devices and discourses – digital technologies are just some of the most recent of these. This implies that technologies, including digital technologies, are always productive.[1] They co-produce ecologies and geographies. They are generative rather than reductive or selective in relation to a 'real'. They multiply natures, environments, and ecologies. This is also the case because digital processes of mediation are now extraordinarily diverse, dissimilar, and differentiated. As the chapters in this collection attest, and as Andrew Dwyer's chapter in particular emphasises, there are very many such technologies of many different kinds, deployed by many human and non-human actors, converting the world into digital data in diverse ways with very different consequences. Entirely invented digital animals; animals translated into pictures and sounds and routes; animals charismatic and edible; trees wired up as urban infrastructure: these are hybrid and perhaps even undecidable figures.

I have to confess, though, that I remain particularly interested in one sort of animal that appears in all the chapters gathered here, which is what most contributors call the 'human'. The notion of the 'human' has itself also been reconfigured somewhat by digital technologies of course. Digital data and computational processes are often cited as one of the more recent material innovations that mean that 'the human' cannot be understood as a uniquely self-reflexive actor inhabiting a (particular kind of) corporeal body. Human life is also mediated by digital devices of many kinds. And of course there are many arguments that that sovereign notion of the human was always a Western idea in any case, aligned far too closely with only particular forms of embodiment and reason. Hence a new label for such animals: the posthuman. A more capacious sense of multiple posthuman lives intimately entangled with all sorts of ecologies and technologies, including the digital, thus has some potential for displacing the Eurocentrism of much critical theory. Rather than the familiar roll call of social theorists, for example, a more relational and generative sense of digital geographies might emerge if, in different ways with diverse Indigenous knowledges, we proactively engaged in 'making kin with machines'.[2]

This broad orientation towards multiple forms of the digital mediation of organic life aligns with the gist of many of the chapters here, all of which sidestep simplistic accounts of the digital. Many of the specific examples of digital mediation discussed here are approached ambivalently. In the context of the contemporary biodiversity crisis, much of this ambivalence circles around whether a particular digital process will contribute to the conservation of animal life or to its depredation. Some chapters suggest that the answer is – probably – both. This is particularly the case when not only the digital content which renders an animal visible or audible is considered, but also the materialities of that digitality. What kind of cost-benefit analysis could calculate the balance between a digital game that generates empathy with a charismatic non-human animal, the environmental impact of the mining of the materials needed to make the game's hardware, and the carbon footprint of the energy used to produce that hardware and to play that game? I'm not sure, but that kind of calculation is certainly implicit in some chapters here. Other contributors grasp that sort of balance sheet as an impossibility and instead describe digital mediation as inherently paradoxical, as Jon Henrik Ziegler Remme does with some lobsters. As Mari Arold argues, there is a need to 'simultaneously account for digital/analogue, discursive/material, and tangible/ethereal mediations of phenomena'.[3] To which might be added, human and non-human, technological and natural. This complexity certainly aligns with emerging arguments in digital geography which are particularly attentive to digital technologies as a complex site of potentiality rather than a tool wielded by the powerful to capitalism's gain.[4]

Emphasising the complexity of digital mediation – its ambivalence, or paradoxicality – means that questions about the power dynamics of any particular mediation must also be nuanced. Several of the chapters here flag the political economy of platforms as one of those dynamics, as does Bram Büscher's influential account of Nature 2.0.[5] However, the contributors to this collection do not give a lot of attention to the big social media platforms. Few contributors interrogate their harvesting of user data and their algorithmic mediation of environmental data, or their commodification of non-human life. In relation to the subdiscipline of digital geographies and its current focus on platforms, this is an interesting and provocative swerve. It

## Afterword: digital ecologies and digital geographies 241

suggests that platforms are not the only digital organisations making digitally mediated worlds, and that profit-making is not the only dynamic at play in that making.

Some chapters prefer to explore, for example, the ways in which digital data and datafication are being incorporated into pre-existing archives, tools, and models. Hannah Hunter, Sandra Jasper, and Jonathan Prior discuss a museum archive,[6] for example, and Sophia Doyle and Katherine Dow examine an online seedbank database.[7] Here the focus is more on how digital data harvested from ecological worlds replicate and reproduce, but also modify, existing power dynamics of power/knowledge. The truth claims made with data, whether in terms of science or empathy, are often complicit with governance institutions and processes. But digital technologies also have their own material affordances. Uniquely 'digital objects' such as hashtags and hyperlinks are the focus of Rogers' definition of digital methods,[8] and are used by Jonathan W.Y. Gray, Liliana Bounegru, and Gabriele Colombo here to explore the specific mediation of fires in the Amazon forest by Twitter and its users.[9] While topics through which the fires were framed were fairly diverse, perhaps the most striking finding is the temporality of the concern expressed via the platform, which peaked very rapidly and dissipated equally swiftly. This attention to both digital affordance and posthuman practice and discourse is a valuable methodological orientation implicit in much of this collection.

One digital device that struck me because of its repeated appearance in this collection is the online camcorder-with-a-website.[10] A webcam that just sits and watches and shares its watching with online viewers – I wonder if that is a somewhat novel form of digital visuality which might deserve more attention? It's slightly distanced, a little fascinated, a little wary, boring after a while but never bored, its attentiveness performing in(post)human endurance. A lot has been written about operative images – which don't represent the world but are part of a machine's functioning – and webcams aren't quite that, or at least not the ones discussed here. They don't seem to be defined by a particular purpose, though as Catherine Oliver suggests, they do some things with some viewers.[11] So the always-on webcam seems to me to perhaps be another form of inhuman photography for which this collection offers some context.[12]

Indeed, we might supplement discussions about the generative gaze of the webcam with other extended, posthuman ways of seeing.[13] Drone vision is another example,[14] and Oscar Hartman Davies and Jamie Lorimer in this volume examine other forms of surveillance-at-a-distance.[15] Satellite imagery is yet another. Remotely sensed data are received as radio frequency data which are impossible for human corporeal vision to perceive and converted into images. Yet the framing of these images by the notion of a 'cosmic zoom' from outer space to the innermost workings of cellular life is familiar and fascinating.[16] It can be found everywhere from conservation documentaries to video adverts for smart cities to Hollywood movie special effects and art projects. It creates the ambiguous effect of being 'close up at a distance',[17] a viewing position occupied by no one yet powerfully productive.[18] It is also a view increasingly often created by algorithmic calculations to create what have been called 'synthetic geographies'.[19] There's also another finding by Jonathan W.Y. Gray and colleagues, which is that many images shared on Twitter purporting to show the 2019 Amazon fires were of other fires entirely.[20] Rather than dismissing these as fake, they link them to the importance of stock images in the viewing of social media feeds,[21] in which images signify fleetingly and gesturally. Instead, they offer the kind of generic imagery that floods the adverts, blogs, and websites of digital culture.[22] Like the online webcam, none of these images stand in for what humans might witness directly. They are not photographic in that sense. These forms of technologically augmented vision are distinctively posthuman, neither embodied nor representational, and several chapters here find it particularly distressing that no animal can similarly augment or extend its vision.

That visual cosmic zoom is dependent on a specific spatial organisation of the visual field. It assumes three-dimensional space, as a volume through which bodies – corporeal or virtual – can travel. There are histories to the digital mediation of spatialities, of course. Early geographic information systems focused on urban areas, both because data were available there and some use could be seen for GIS there. However, one of the earliest GIS technologies was a land management tool, and efforts to create three-dimensional GIS models on two-dimensional printouts and, later, display screens were there from the very beginning of GIS too (as were animated GIS graphics). Increasingly extensive sensing technologies have extended this three-dimensional spatiality organised through x, y, and z coordinates through oceans and atmospheres and across land, enrolling animal life in various ways, as the chapter here by Oscar Hartman Davies and Jamie Lorimer points out.[23] More recently, satellites have generated the data for Global Positioning Systems. According to William Rankin, GPS technology organises the physical environment differently from the cartographic assumptions embedded in GIS design, less in terms of territories and sovereignties and more through points and connections.[24] These different spatialising technologies reconfigure animal (and posthuman) distribution and mobility somewhat differently, just as forests are configured differently through different spatialities in Mari Arold's discussion here.[25] Different again is the 'movescape' through which some ocean spaces are mediated by many digital devices, which consists of mobile wet territories. One of the devices mentioned in several chapters are the tags attached to animal bodies that allow them to be tracked; it would be interesting to learn more about the specific spaces enacted by that animal-tracker hybrid as it is enrolled in these different spatial formations.

Emphasising the multiplicity of these spatialities is important. As Jennifer Gabrys argues, drawing on the work of Spivak and Wynter, the planetary is a geography that is made rather than discovered, and while it may constitute vast distances, planetary knowledge is neither comprehensive nor universal. 'The planetary is the difference, distance, and duration with, within, and against which it might be possible to think differently about being human and becoming collective', she suggests.[26] The chapter by Jess McLean and Lara Newman in this collection makes this point as it centres the Indigenous force of Country in its account of digital climate activism in Australia.[27] As many of the chapters here imply, it is vital that digitally mediated gaps, multiple knowledges, and uncertainties remain alert not only to differentiations within processes that are spatially extensive, but also to those gaps where such extension dissipates or fails, where understanding or data give out.

Alongside their various emphases on multiplicity, lurking in most of these chapters is a particular version of the posthuman. Most authors are concerned about posthuman capacities to enact relations of care and compassion – or, rather, how and whether the use of digital technologies might evoke such feelings for the animal by the human. The chapters are concerned about the exploitation of animals, their entrapment, and disappearance. The desired human response to such threats is often described as affective: feeling empathy with a snow leopard or a lobster, being hopeful for change, effecting repair. Humans should feel differently, feel more, when they consider animals, and digital technologies may enable that feeling. Action to protect and nurture will follow, it is hoped (though several authors seem less than convinced that nice feelings convert into nice actions). Catherine Oliver's chapter here complexifies this framing, in its recognition that care can also be a form of violence.[28] These affective or emotional ambiguities perhaps deserve more attention. For example, Oliver's chapter also offers a precise account of one posthuman-animal relationality in its discussion of 'byproductive labour'. Byproductive labour maintains 'positive affective atmospheres, but also metabolises 'waste' affects and affective byproducts',[29] and in her account that labour is undertaken by the farm chickens watched by – yes, you guessed it – webcams. The outcome of byproductive labour in this instance is a somewhat ambiguous viewing human who is feeling less intensely, and it's not entirely clear in Oliver's chapter whether this is a good thing or not.

Of course, posthumans don't just feel. They may also calculate, for example, and play, have spiritual experiences, and do many things without consciously thinking at all. Their feelings can be multiple and contradictory, and relations between feeling and doing are highly convoluted (to which the notion of cogniser as decision-maker may add something). Some feelings are not nice: shame, anger, and fear also motivate actions. Violence and apathy are also actions. So too are remembering and memorialising. I was particularly struck by the chapter by Hannah Hunter, Sandra Jasper, and Jonathan Prior on digital audio recordings, and their suggestion that archiving and listening to recordings of extinct animals is a means of grieving their loss.[30] These complex emotional dynamics are felt but they are also themselves mediated through things like archive recordings. Elsewhere I have argued that the multiplicity and diversity of such exteriorised mediations enable posthuman invention of many kinds.[31] What emerges from memory, imagination, and speculation is one kind of posthuman agency.

So while digital entanglements with non-human life are crucial to explore, I don't think that can mean not thinking about posthuman life. The human genome project has converted posthuman life into digital information too;[32] human life is watched by millions of surveillance cameras and hundreds of satellites; GPS systems track human crowds; facial recognition software continues to attempt to sort human bodies into types; drones track and kill humans as well as animals; posthumans track their mobility, their menstrual cycles, their heart rate, their screen time. While many scholars have questioned the continued relevance of Foucauldian notions of biopower when embodiments of so many kinds are now so thoroughly datafied, there is an intriguing sense here that all and any carbon-based lifeforms are increasingly enacted through similar technologies.

To push this provocation a little further, I was struck by Andrew Dwyer's description of digital eco-logics as processes through which materials 'read, interpret, or act upon signs'.[33] Interpreting signs is one of the key ways that the academic disciplines in the human and social sciences have approached the human, of course. As a form of sentience, however – or cognisance, to use Dwyer's term – it is something shared by animals as well as humans and computers (and those environments in which computers are embedded).[34] There are big-data-based approaches to 'human' agency that constitute humans no more and no less as 'cognisers', for example agent-based modelling approaches to understanding human behaviour. Now that so much of posthuman and animal behaviour is turned into data, algorithms can be used to find patterns in both equally, and to simulate such behaviour in many scenarios. Driverless cars can learn about the behaviour of humans on roads from simulated bodies rather than risking live bodies, for example, and though I haven't come across any examples of chickens being added to the models, that may only be a matter of time.

In short, there are many ways that the chapters in this collection extend the range of digital geographies. They pay careful attention to the

# Afterword: digital ecologies and digital geographies

specifically digital affordances of technologies and to their enactment in a range of different situations. These chapters suggest that various forms of power and agency are at work in these enactments, often in complex and contradictory ways. They suggest that there are new spatial formations emerging in these enactments, from huge extensions of three-dimensional space to the fluid mobilities of wetscapes. Given the importance of screen interfaces to so much digital technology, these chapters also provide a rich account of some of the spatial formations which structure specific kinds of digital images in particular ways: the surveillant zoom, for example, now accompanied by the ongoing flow of what Hito Steyerl calls 'the wretched of the screen':[35] the stock image, the meme, and the gif. Perhaps most intriguing to me, as a scholar who can't quite shrug off her early training in human and cultural geography, they also offer rich and nuanced accounts of the posthuman life that is also part of these many paradoxical digital-ecological entanglements.

## Notes

1. Ruppert et al., 'Reassembling social science methods'; see also Dwyer, 'Ecological computationality' and Oliver, '*Our Chicken Life*' in this collection.
2. Lewis et al., 'Making kin with the machines.'
3. See Arold, 'Mediated natures' in this collection.
4. See the exemplary statement by Elwood, 'Digital geographies, feminist relationality, Black and queer code studies.'
5. Büscher, 'Nature 2.0'; Büscher, *The Truth about Nature*.
6. See Hunter et al., 'Digital sonic ecologies' in this collection.
7. See Doyle and Dow, '"Saving the knowledge helps to save the seed"' in this collection.
8. Rogers, *Digital Methods*; Rogers, *Doing Digital Methods*.
9. See Gray et al., '#AmazonFires' in this collection.
10. Gabrys, *Program Earth*.
11. See Oliver, '*Our Chicken Life*' in this collection.
12. Zylinska, *Nonhuman Photography*.
13. McLuhan, *Understanding Media*.
14. Gregory, 'From a view to a kill.'
15. See Hartman Davies and Lorimer, 'On-bird surveillance' in this collection.
16. Horton, *The Cosmic Zoom*.
17. Kurgan, *Close Up at a Distance*.
18. And see Oliver's discussion of 'byproduction' in this collection: Oliver, '*Our Chicken Life*.'
19. Gil-Fournier and Parikka, 'Ground truth to fake geographies'; and see Wilken and Thomas, 'Vertical geomediation.'
20. See Gray et al., '#AmazonFires' in this collection.

21  See Aiello, 'Perfect strangers in the city.'
22  Frosh, *The Image Factory*.
23  See Hartman Davies and Lorimer, 'On-bird surveillance' in this collection.
24  Rankin, *After the Map*.
25  See Arold, 'Mediated natures' in this collection.
26  Gabrys, 'Becoming planetary,' n.p.
27  See McLean and Newman, 'Children and young people's digital climate action in Australia' in this collection.
28  See Oliver, '*Our Chicken Life*' in this collection; see also Hartman Davies and Lorimer, 'On-bird surveillance' in this collection.
29  See Oliver, '*Our Chicken Life*' in this collection.
30  See Hunter et al., 'Digital sonic ecologies' in this collection.
31  Rose, 'Posthuman agency in the digitally mediated city.'
32  Clough, 'Biotechnology and digital information'; Clough, 'The affective turn.'
33  See Dwyer, 'Ecological computationality' in this collection.
34  See Thrift, 'The "sentient" city and what it may portend.'
35  Steyerl, *The Wretched of the Screen*.

## Bibliography

Aiello, G. 2022. Perfect strangers in the city: Stock photography as ambient imagery. In G. Rose (Ed.) *Seeing the City Digitally: Processing Urban Space and Time* (pp. 233–250). Amsterdam: Amsterdam University Press.

Büscher, B. 2016. Nature 2.0: Exploring and theorizing the links between new media and nature conservation. *New Media & Society*, 18(5): 726–743.

Büscher, B. 2021. *The Truth about Nature: Environmentalism in the Era of Post-Truth Politics and Platform Capitalism*. Oakland, CA: University of California Press.

Clough, P.T. 2007. Biotechnology and digital information. *Theory, Culture and Society*, 24(7–8): 312–314.

Clough, P.T. 2008. The affective turn: Political economy, biomedia and bodies. *Theory, Culture and Society*, 25(1): 1–22.

Elwood, S. 2021. Digital geographies, feminist relationality, Black and queer code studies: Thriving otherwise. *Progress in Human Geography*, 45(2): 209–228.

Frosh, P. 2003. *The Image Factory: Consumer Culture, Photography and the Visual Content Industry*. London: Berg.

Gabrys, J. 2016. *Program Earth: Environmental Sensing Technology and the Making of a Computational Planet*. Minneapolis, MN: University of Minnesota Press.

Gabrys, J. 2018. Becoming planetary. *E-Flux Architecture* [online], October. Available from: www.e-flux.com/architecture/accumulation/217051/becoming-planetary/.

Gil-Fournier, A. and Parikka, J. 2020. Ground truth to fake geographies: Machine vision and learning in visual practices. *AI & Society*, November.

Gregory, D. 2011. From a view to a kill: Drones and late modern war. *Theory, Culture & Society*, 28(7–8): 188–215.

Horton, Z. 2021. *The Cosmic Zoom: Scale, Knowledge, and Mediation*. Chicago, IL: University of Chicago Press.

Kurgan, L. 2013. *Close Up at a Distance: Mapping, Technology, and Politics.* First hardcover edition. Brooklyn, NY: Zone Books.

Lewis, J.E., Arista, N., Pechawis, A., and Kite, S. 2018. Making kin with the machines. *Journal of Design and Science*, 3(3). https://jods.mitpress.mit.edu/pub/lewis-arista-pechawis-kite/release/1.

McLuhan, M. 1964. *Understanding Media: The Extensions of Man.* London: Routledge and Kegan Paul.

Rankin, W. 2016. *After the Map: Cartography, Navigation, and the Transformation of Territory in the Twentieth Century.* Chicago, IL: University of Chicago Press.

Rogers, R. 2013. *Digital Methods.* London: MIT Press.

Rogers, R. 2019. *Doing Digital Methods.* London: Sage.

Rose, G. 2017. Posthuman agency in the digitally mediated city: Exteriorization, individuation, reinvention. *Annals of the American Association of Geographers*, 107(4): 779–793.

Ruppert, E., Law, J., and Savage, M. 2013. Reassembling social science methods: The challenge of digital devices. *Theory, Culture & Society*, 30(4): 22–46.

Steyerl, H. 2012. *The Wretched of the Screen.* Berlin: Sternberg Press.

Thrift, N. 2014. The 'sentient' city and what it may portend. *Big Data & Society*, 1(1): 1–21.

Wilken, R. and Thomas, J. 2022. Vertical geomediation: The automation and platformization of photogrammetry. *New Media & Society*, 24(11): 2531–2547.

Zylinska, J. 2017. *Nonhuman Photography.* Cambridge, MA: MIT Press.

# Afterword: making digital ecologies visible

*Dolly Jørgensen and Finn Arne Jørgensen*

We watch the seabed for hours at a time. The muddy sea bottom is punctuated with rocky outcrops or mountains of dead coral or cold seeps that form a lake in the underwater landscape. Mostly we're watching for the life – the bamboo coral, black coral, sponges, jellies, squat lobsters, rattail fish, octopuses, and more – that the eye catches a glimpse of. We watch them interact with humans and each other as shrimp and squat lobsters guard their coral hosts, squid are attracted to the camera light, and fish scurry away from the churned-up sand.

Yet neither of us have ever gone deep sea diving; we are watching from the comforts of home via the live feed of the *Okeanos Explorer*. The ship was commissioned by the National Oceanic and Atmospheric Administration (NOAA) in 2008 as a deep-sea research vessel with telepresence capabilities that allow scientists on shore to have real-time access to the remotely operated vehicle (ROV) feed and converse with the on-board personnel while also allowing the feed to be broadcast online. This means that when you watch the live feed from *Okeanos Explorer*, you are getting not only the images but also expert commentary on the biology, geology, chemistry, archaeology, and other aspects of the dive. It is an augmented view of underwater ecologies that is only available in the digital realm.

The limitation to the digital is key. As Stacy Alaimo has observed, 'most aquatic zones, species, and topics exist beyond human domains, requiring the mediation of science and technology'.[1] While a *Homo aquaticus* has been proposed in science fiction (and to some extent even worked on by serious scientists),[2] humans are primarily a terrestrial species that can only encounter life underwater at limited depths and for limited times without high-tech interventions.

NOAA's director of the Education Program at the time of its launch, Paula Keener-Chavis, wrote that *Okeanos Explorer* would enhance teaching ocean science to anyone. *Okeanos Explorer* was 'the ship upon which learners of all ages embark together on scientific voyages of exploration to poorly known or unexplored areas of the global ocean'.[3] It would

*Afterword: making digital ecologies visible* 249

mobilise 'sophisticated technological capabilities that have made the ocean more "visible" and more accessible than ever before'.[4] The public interest in seeing this deep unseen is large: each exploration cruise of the *Okeanos Explorer* gets hundreds of thousands of views of the live video on its YouTube channel.[5]

The digital ecologies of *Okeanos Explorer*, which are made visible to thousands of onlookers through digital interfaces, resonate with this essay collection. The editors have highlighted that investigating the materialities, encounters, and governance of digital ecologies helps researchers to understand the uneven geographies of the digital encounter. In reflecting upon the collection, we will argue that, even more fundamentally, these constellations of materialities, encounters, and governance make organisms, humans, and technology visible. Bruno Latour argued that modernity depends on immutable mobiles, which are objects which can not only move to other settings (i.e. they are mobile) but which also can be presented and read in the same way no matter where they move (i.e. they are immutable).[6] Inscriptions of phenomena, whether in the form of mathematical equations, photographs, drawings, or textual descriptions, are immutable mobiles that allow others at a distance from the phenomenon to partake in it. The digital creates immutable mobile inscriptions which can facilitate seeing far away from the object of sight. It is through this digital visibility that more-than-human geographies can be constructed.

## Making organisms visible

As much as the rock formations or even the patterns on the sand of the seabed might be interesting, to be honest, we are mostly fascinated by the organisms encountered by *Okeanos Explorer*. We have watched a crab voraciously eating a brittlestar and an armoured sea robin 'walking' on the rocks on small modified fins.[7] The digital resolution of the ROV camera livestreaming video from hundreds or even thousands of feet underwater is amazing – individual coral polyps, hairs on crab legs, and starfish feet are all crystal clear. These are digital ecologies for making organisms visible.

Environmental humanities scholarship has stressed the need to investigate multispecies relations by being attentive to diverse ways of life.[8] This kind of multispecies approach 'focuses on the multitudes of lively agents that bring one another into being through entangled relations' rather than just focusing on the relationship of humans to other species.[9] It is an act of noticing to take time with a squat lobster in the branches of a *Chrysogorgia* octocoral and appreciate their lives on our shared planet. Likewise, listening to a group of disembodied voices belonging to a group of scientists scattered across the planet chatting to identify a mysterious siphonophore that you are all simultaneously watching on screens is also an act of noticing.

The lobster trap-cam discussed by Jon Henrik Ziegler Remme in this volume is a potential site of noticing. Remme describes a 'digital intimacy' between human and lobster through playfulness facilitated by the online live camera. Although the relations are ambiguous – after all, the point of a commercial lobster trap is to trap a lobster to eat it – the Marine Institute's trap-cam creates a digital space in which lobsters can be known as individuals, as beings with preferences.

The attentiveness to individuals and their beings (past or present) is also stressed by Hannah Hunter, Sandra Jasper, and Jonathan Prior in this volume. Sound recordings make the calls of species, or even single individuals, audible to humans far from the locations and times of those animals' lives. Sound archives emerge 'as a space for ecological memorialisation' as species decline and ecosystems are permanently disrupted. Such is the case with the lonely Kaua'i 'ō'ō calling for a mate who never comes, and the spread of that song through digital media highlighted the loss of the 'o'o. Sound is 'an affective, relational, ephemeral force that vibrates through our entire bodies, literally moving us'. One lesson of the Hunter et al. chapter is that attentiveness can involve many senses – organisms are made visible through more than just the visual. Listening to the audio is part of noticing what it is to be another.

The *Our Chicken Life* platform with its multicamera video feed of a chicken flock also places attention on the chicken's way of being. Catherine Oliver shows how *Our Chicken Life* exposes innate chicken behaviours to subscribers, who gleefully observe how a chick hatches and is guided by the mother hen, and allows them to participate in chicken lives by feeding them mealworms as distance caretakers. However, this care only goes so far since both the physical and digital flocks are entangled in capitalist systems of production. As Oliver notes, 'it is precisely because the chicken has had such an intimate, exploitative relationship with humans that this case provides such stark insights into how virtual encounters might be new frontiers for value extraction'. Even being attentive has its limits.

Humans being attentive and paying attention also comes with risk to the organism. As Hunter, Jasper, and Prior note, digital sound recordings can make animals visible by attracting them to the location of the replayed sound, which may be useful for conservationists trying to count individuals but can also be mobilsed by hunters. Oscar Hartman Davies and Jamie Lorimer comment in their chapter that albatrosses (only some of which are equipped with geolocators) might be intentionally shot by fishermen in order to combat ocean surveillance. Even in the case of wiring forests

*Afterword: making digital ecologies visible* 251

up to smart grids discussed in the chapter by Jennifer Gabrys, the focus on one thing (in this case the trees) might 'render obsolete and inassimilable any bodies, practices, or organisms that would not contribute to the productive augmentation of smart green economies and ecologies'. Visibility is not equally just.

### Making humans and their technologies visible

The *Okeanos Explorer* feed is not only about encounters with pristine natures. We remember a dive in 2017 that was set up to investigate a potential shipwreck archaeological site which had been identified through a survey. When the ROV got there, however, it turned out to be a debris field of washing machines from a shipping container that had been lost at sea.[10] Trash is a relatively common sight on dives. One study of the video feed from ROV expeditions of *Okeanos Explorer* and another ship found that debris was spotted on 17.5% of the dives in the Pacific; nearly half the debris was metal, whereas fishing gear and plastic each made up 20% of the total.[11] These mundane encounters with garbage in the deep sea reveal the extent to which human activity expands into the oceans. Michael Brennan and colleagues argue that telepresence-enabled exploration is providing opportunities for archaeology beyond targeting a specific wreck through an 'archeology of discard' that stresses the accidental nature of most marine debris disposal.[12] Looking at debris also allows coupling of archaeological and biological investigations, seeing the organisms growing on or inhabiting the human artefacts as in relation with those artefacts.[13]

As we have seen watching the *Okeanos* feed, humans and their things are everywhere. The Anthropocene, while not yet an official stratigraphic designation, is certainly our living condition. While environmental humanities scholars have often criticised the Anthropocene label for its homogenisation of all humans as the culprit for radical environmental change rather than pinpointing capitalist or production structures (such as in the names Capitalocene or Plantationocene), they have also acknowledged the need to recognise that the speed and scale of change is creating 'severe discontinuities; what comes after will not be like what came before'.[14] Human influence on the planet's biota is deep and wide.

Emerging digital ecologies can make visible human effects on animal behaviours and on the planet writ large. Davies and Lorimer in this volume show how digital ocean governance is facilitated on the back of albatrosses. Trackers attached to albatrosses – 'on-bird surveillance' as they label it – help to identify illegal fishing activities because albatross movement is associated with ships. Making visible the geography of the birds makes visible the geography of humans and their effects on bird behaviour. The birds do not live their lives apart from humans; they are entangled in larger human production structures.

Humans and their technologies can also be made visible in distant seeing. Wildlife documentaries have often been critiqued for the disembodiment of the camera and camera operators who have captured the film; they are not supposed to appear except in special 'behind-the-scenes' additional tracks.[15] This is not the case with *Okeanos Explorer*. There are typically three live camera feeds – one from the main ROV, one from the companion ROV, and one from the control centre – which means that a view of technology is always available. Even when watching the camera on the main ROV, the broadcast includes audio from the technicians discussing ship movements, sampling techniques, time left in the dive, and so on, and the ROV arms are often visible in the wide bottom shots as well as when samples are being collected. The technological components of the digital ecology are made visible with *Okeanos Explorer*.

Technology is more than a tool or network in which other ecologies live; it is an active member of ecosystems, as Andrew Dwyer makes clear in his chapter on computation and malicious software. Computational choices – whether they interpret a piece of code or an image as one thing or another – leads to other choices (by non-organics and organics) in the system. Malware detection software often makes itself and its identified targets visible to the human user, even if the processes it uses to come to that conclusion are opaque. Hashtagging as social practice similarly creates, rather than just reports on, events. The digital ecosystem of #AmazonFires discussed by Jonathan W.Y. Gray, Liliana Bounegru, and Gabriele Colombo contains fires, organisms, and humans, just as the Amazon in Brazil does. More than flames, the event of #AmazonFires is constructed through posting, sharing, and liking content. The Estonian *hiied* sacred groves of Mari Arold's chapter are constructed as much by GIS maps and Facebook posts as they are by the trees themselves. Just as ecocritics Serenella Iovino and Serpil Oppermann have argued that matter configures both meanings and substances through interactions, so is matter a site of narrativity; technologies have both narrative and material repercussions on digital ecologies.[16]

Humans inhabiting these digital spaces also become visible in distinct ways. As Jess McLean and Lara Newman show in their chapter on the digital environmental activism of School Strike 4 Climate Australia, social media posts can amplify local place-based action and give a voice to those not heard through other means. Distributed digital protest can highlight on-the-ground environmental justice activism. Like the work of gardeners who grow plants and collect seeds for the London Freedom Seed Bank discussed by Sophia Doyle and Katharine Dow, human knowledge and action become inscribed in digital databanks.

### Seeing and not seeing

The digital video from *Okeanos Explorer* is more than an ephemeral experience. It has been used to identify and describe numerous species new to science. Christopher Mah, a starfish specialist with the Smithsonian Institution and whose voice is often heard on the *Okeanos Explorer* broadcast as a telepresent scientist, has used ROV video in addition to physical samples to describe twelve newly discovered sea stars.[17] The video provided occurrence and behavorial observation data, as well as still images of the species in their natural habitat.

Yet caution is warranted about thinking that digital ecologies are always transparent and revealing. Although digital ecologies make visible many organisms, humans, and technologies, we should also not overestimate their effects. As Alaimo notes, 'Extinction and "discovery" may happen simultaneously in the Anthropocene seas, paradoxical places that are greatly altered but little known, harboring both compressed and expansive temporalities'.[18] The absence of knowledge about the deep sea is real, leading environmental humanities scholar Michelle Bastian to propose situating ethnographies of unknown extinctions (like the commensals of whale falls which no longer happen because of decreased whale populations) on 'suspended ground' that embraces the uncertainty.[19] At the same time, it's not coincidence that Bastian ends her article with a reflection about a live video feed of a whale fall from the Exploration Vessel *Nautilus*, a ship similar to the *Okeanos Explorer* run by the independent Ocean Exploration Trust. It is through the digital that deep sea whale falls – and their potential absence – have become seen by scientists and lay watchers alike.

The deep sea is a world to itself, a vast ecology that has been inaccessible to humanity for most of human history. Rendered inhospitable for humans by lack of oxygen, low temperatures, deep darkness, and crushing pressure, it is nevertheless full of life. Over time, various technologies have allowed for new ways of sensing this life. With *Okeanos Explorer* and similar ROV-based telepresence technologies, we as watchers can connect with these remote underwater ecologies. But our presence also changes everything. The deep sea is no longer unseen, and more and more of it is mapped for potential exploitation. In particular, deep-sea mining threatens these recently discovered vistas and ecologies. Digital ecologies in the previously unseen oceans become exploitable in new ways. The big test for digital ecologies like these is whether our acts of noticing and our digital presence will shape future governance to facilitate relations or to break them.

## Notes

1  Alaimo, 'Introduction,' p. 429.
2  Rozwadowski, 'Bringing humanity full circle back into the sea.'
3  Keener, 'Enhancing ocean science literacy in the U.S,' n.p.
4  Keener-Chavis, 'The NOAA ship Okeanos Explorer,' n.p.
5  For example, the 23-day telepresence-enabled expedition to the Gulf of Mexico from November to December 2017 had over 280,000 live views on the YouTube channel in addition to live events at universities and aquariums: White et al., 'Cruise report: EX-17–11 Gulf of Mexico,' p. 54. The live feeds are supplemented by a slew of educational activities, including the digital NOAA Ship *Okeanos Explorer* Education Materials Collection.
6  Latour, 'Visualisation and cognition.'
7  The first incident is available to watch online on the NOAA site: https://oceanexplorer.noaa.gov/video_playlist/ex1806-badday.html.
8  van Dooren et al., 'Multispecies studies.'
9  Ibid., p. 3.
10  White et al., 'Cruise report: EX-17–11 Gulf of Mexico,' p. 35.
11  Amon et al., 'Deep-sea debris in the Central and Western Pacific Ocean.'
12  Brennan et al., 'Telepresence-enabled maritime archaeological exploration in the deep,' p. 115.
13  Ibid., p. 119.
14  Haraway, 'Anthropocene, Capitalocene, Plantationocene, Chthulucene,' p. 160.
15  E.g. Garrard, 'Worlds without us'; Bagust, ' "Screen natures".'
16  Iovino and Oppermann, 'Material ecocritism.'
17  Mah, 'New Genera.'
18  Alaimo, 'Introduction,' p. 430.
19  Bastian, 'Whale falls, suspended ground, and extinctions never known.'

## Bibliography

Alaimo, S. 2019. Introduction: Science studies and the blue humanities. *Configurations*, 27(4): 429–432.
Amon, D.J., Kennedy, B.R.C., Cantwell, K., Suhre, K., Glickson, D., Shank, T.M., and Rotjan, R.D. 2020 Deep-sea debris in the Central and Western Pacific Ocean. *Frontiers in Marine Science*, 7: 369.

Bagust, P. 2008. 'Screen natures': Special effects and edutainment in 'new' hybrid wildlife documentary. *Continuum*, 22(2): 213–226.

Bastian, M. 2020. Whale falls, suspended ground, and extinctions never known. *Environmental Humanities*, 12(2): 454–474.

Brennan, M., Cantelas, F., Elliott, K., Delgado, J.P., Bell, K.L.C., Coleman, D., Fundis, A., Irion, J., Van Tilburg, H.K., and Ballard, R.D. 2018. Telepresence-enabled maritime archaeological exploration in the deep. *Journal of Marine Archaeology*, 13: 97–121.

Garrard, G. 2012. Worlds without us: Some types of disanthropy. *SubStance*, 41(1): 40–60.

Haraway, D. 2015. Anthropocene, Capitalocene, Plantationocene, Chthulucene: Making kin. *Environmental Humanities*, 6(1): 159–165.

Iovino, S. and Oppermann, S. 2012. Material ecocritism: Materiality, agency, and models of narrativity. *Ecozon@*, 3(1): 75–91.

Keener, P. 2011. Enhancing ocean science literacy in the U.S. and abroad through NOAA Ocean Exploration. *OCEANS'11 MTS/IEEE KONA*. Conference, 19–22 September 2011, Quebec City, Canada [online]. Available from: https://ieeexplore.ieee.org/abstract/document/6107313.

Keener-Chavis, P. 2008. The NOAA ship Okeanos Explorer: Continuing to unfold the president's panel on Ocean Exploration recommendations for ocean literacy. *OCEANS 2008*. Conference, 15–18 September 2008, Quebec City, Canada [online]. Available from: https://ieeexplore-ieee-org.sheffield.idm.oclc.org/document/5152101.

Latour, B. 1986. Visualisation and cognition: Drawing things together. *Knowledge and Society: Studies in the Sociology of Culture and Present*, 6: 1–40.

Mah, C.L. 2022. New genera, species and occurrences of deep-sea Asteroidea (Valvatacea, Forcipulatacea, Echinodermata) collected from the North Pacific Ocean by the CAPSTONE Expedition. *Zootaxa*, 5164(1): 461–508.

Rozwadowski, H.M. 2022. 'Bringing humanity full circle back into the sea': *Homo aquaticus*, evolution, and the ocean. *Environmental Humanities*, 14(1): 1–28.

van Dooren, T., Kirksey, E., and Münster, U. 2016. Multispecies studies: Cultivating arts of attentiveness. *Environmental Humanities*, 8(1): 1–23.

White, M.P., Kennedy, B.R.C., Amon, D., Messing, C., and Avila, A.M. 2020. *Cruise Report: EX-17–11 Gulf of Mexico 2017 (ROV and Mapping)*. OER Expedition Rep. 17-11. Washington, DC: Office of Ocean Exploration and Research, NOAA.

# Afterword: finding the media in digital ecologies

*Eva Haifa Giraud*

I've been told, anecdotally, that a classic question asked after papers in geographical conferences is 'where's the geography in this?' As an editor coming to this collection from a slightly different disciplinary context than my co-editors, and who has worked in media studies departments for the best part of a decade, I expected my central question when reading through chapters might be 'where's the media in this?' or – perhaps more pointedly – 'where's the media *studies* in this?' In part my (erroneous) assumption stemmed from defensiveness at the way media studies has often been maligned (by the mass media) or overlooked (in academia), dynamics that have been more visible as digital media have become an object of study for an expanding range of disciplines, but frameworks from media studies have not. I was excited, therefore, to read chapters written within a paradigm of more-than-human geography drawing upon heterogeneous strands of media scholarship – from software to social movement media studies – as well as work from the digital humanities that was informed by insights from more-than-human geographies. This afterword, then, is not an attempt to redress a lack of digital ecologies research that draws upon media studies, but to reflect on some of the connections made across chapters that I found especially productive, in order to deepen these connections and ask how they might be suggestive of future research directions.

This book's account of digital ecologies is developed iteratively, through chapters that coalesce around specific media technologies: apps, camera traps, livestreams, sensors, social media platforms, databases, software, digitised sound recordings, and online images. Yet, even as digital technologies assume a central role throughout the book, the account of mediation offered by the collection exceeds narrow conceptions of 'the digital'. Instead, the processes traced by authors resonate with influential theory that has expanded how media are conceived, such as scholarship that has articulated non-human animals and elements as themselves being media;[1] research examining how the affordances of media emerge relationally and

# Afterword: finding the media in digital ecologies

through practice;[2] and work situating digital media in centuries-old historical and material contexts.[3]

The expansion of ecological thinking to conceptualise digital media has not, however, been without criticism. As Erich Hörl argues in the introduction of *General Ecology*:

> There are thousands of ecologies today: ecologies of sensation, perception, cognition, desire, attention, power, values, information, participation, media, the mind, relations, practices, behavior, belonging, the social, the political ... There seems to be hardly any area that cannot be considered the object of an ecology and thus open to ecological reformulation.[4]

For Hörl, the conceptual expansion of ecology is ambivalent because it comes at the same time as the term's association with 'nature' is contracting. Ecology might retain a connection with so-called natural environments in the life sciences, or perhaps in lay uses of the term. However, in many branches of the humanities and social sciences, the interventions made by more-than-human thought have frayed any neat boundaries between nature and culture that would enable 'ecology' to be reduced to the former. Digital technologies play an important role in these discussions. At the heart of Hörl's arguments, for instance, is concern that the concept of ecology has: 'begun to switch sides within the nature/technics divide, undoing the sutures that bound it to nature'.[5] These arguments have high stakes; if anything can be understood in ecological terms, but what ecology *means* has shifted away from any association with 'nature' and towards 'cybernetic paradigms of regulation and control', then there is no domain that can be defended against technocratic manipulation and intervention.[6] Hörl's contention, drawing on Frédéric Neyrat, is that a means must be found to 'reintroduce the gap into the bad immanence of the global technological system': a gap that Neyrat suggests can be found by reclaiming 'nature' as a discrete realm.[7]

While critiques of ecology's expansion and evolution are important, it is important to remember that the unsettling of nature/culture divisions has often been spearheaded by feminist, postcolonial scholarship. For many thinkers, recasting the world in terms of naturecultures offers a means of contesting anthropocentric modes of praxis that place 'humanity' as removed from (and holding dominion over) anything rendered 'nature'.[8] When categories such as 'nature' and the 'human' have been subject to such enduring histories of violence, is it desirable – or even possible – to reinstall an analytic or ethical separation between a human realm of (digital) media and a 'nature' entirely populated by those deemed non-human?[9] The chapters in *Digital Ecologies* go to the heart of these debates, grappling with, on the one hand, the analytic and ethical value of recognising digitally enabled more-than-human entanglements and, on the other hand, laying bare the violence that can be materialised through socio-technical infrastructures, mediated encounters, and emerging forms of governance.

One of the reasons I found the chapters in this book so generative is the routes they offered into navigating these (sometimes fraught) academic debates, precisely through the way they weave different conceptual traditions together. Below I reflect on two areas where I believe especially fruitful disciplinary relationships are emerging, focusing first on the ethics of digital ecologies before moving on to broader discussion of the theoretical implications of how these ecologies are conceived.

## Mediating ethics

As elaborated upon in the Introduction, this book's editors have understood digital ecologies as an epistemological framework, or 'mode of investigation', which traces mediated entanglements that inform more-than-human worlds. This framework is oriented around a series of questions that are intended to reveal the socio-technical relations, technologies, and infrastructures that mediate life in particular contexts, by asking (among other questions) which material relations constitute digital ecologies, who is rendered encounterable by these relations and to what ends, and what regimes of governance emerge from these ecologies? Individual chapters bring the stakes of these questions into focus. What happens, for instance, when the 'byproductive' labour of chickens is monetised through livestreams (Oliver), fisheries and forests become subject to continuous monitoring with digital sensors (Hartman Davies and Lorimer; Gabrys), or when pangolins, tigers, and elephants are enrolled into gamified practices of self-quantification (Adams, Sandbrook, and Tait)?

As underlined throughout each chapter, and as some of the book's editors have put it elsewhere, one of the book's aspirations is to resist simply tracing novel more-than-human entanglements and to instead ask 'what comes after digital entanglement?'[10] What this means in practice is moving beyond the description of entanglements between non-human animals, environmental actors, and media technologies, to instead centralise questions about the ethics and epistemology of these unfolding (or perhaps enfolding) relationships. The ecological approach advocated throughout this collection, therefore, might use the terminology and frameworks associated with more-than-human thought but combine this approach with an explicitly critical edge.

For example, many of the processes described in this book – from trap-cams that foster attentiveness and affection toward lobsters (Remme) to databases of heritage seeds (Doyle and Dow) – rely on carbon-intensive infrastructures and that wreak ecological damage when extracted from the earth. These tensions are epitomised by Hannah Hunter, Sandra Jasper, and Jonathan Prior, in the context of digital sound archives of endangered species, where the authors point out that:

> every new format, whether it is shellac, vinyl, tape, or digital data, has come with its distinctive histories and geographies of extraction. The process of extraction that makes digital sound technologies involves raw materials, more-than-human labour relations, supply chains, toxic waste, and obsolescent media that are distributed unevenly across the globe.

Shellac, in particular, underlines how materials important in conserving futures for some non-human animals are constituted by the bodies of other creatures.[11] Such observations offer a reminder that, in Thom van Dooren's words, 'care that is practised at the dull edge of extinction is often intimately and inextricably entangled with various forms of violence'.[12] What chapters from this book articulate, however, is the pivotal role of *media* in fostering regimes of violent-care or instrumentalising affective relations.

William M. Adams, Chris Sandbrook, and Emma Tait, for instance, draw novel connections between game studies, sociological work on gamification, and animal geographies to trace ways that human self-quantification practices are entangled with the extraction of data from non-human animals in exercise apps. Catherine Oliver's important intervention, likewise, traces complex relationships between the lives of livestreamed chickens and the affective labour of audiences who intervene in these lives through typing commands that drop treats into their coop. What is especially valuable in theorising these relations in terms of byproductive labour is the reminder to situate encounters in relation to the political economy of digital media. Moving forward, these lines of enquiry open up important potentials for grasping how the surplus (encounter-)value derived from relations with non-human beings might intersect with unfolding discussions about the imbrication of digital infrastructures with informational capitalism.[13]

Jon Henrik Ziegler Remme, in contrast, articulates how the role of mediation in lobster conservation 'inverts' the relationship between care and instrumentalisation. As traced in the chapter, a growing body of scholarship has foregrounded how knowledge generated through caring for non-human animals can be used for future purposes of instrumentalisation and control. Remme, however, describes how an experimental lobster trap-cam – which intervened in and instrumentalised lobster behaviour to attract audiences – was integral in generating resources to replace modern lobster traps (which often become 'ghost traps' that continue to kill sea life if lost at sea) with traditional wooden alternatives. Here, he suggests: 'instrumentalisation and commodification was central for fostering care and affective encounters with lobsters. No funding, no camera, no publicity, no wooden traps'.

More broadly, many of the chapters in the book point to the way that conservation work is increasingly bound up with the surveillance, datafication, and capture of environments, or what a number of scholars term 'logics of environmentality' or 'eco-logics'.[14] These concerns are brought to the fore – and again complicated – in Jennifer Gabrys's account of the rise of smart forests (Chapter 9) and Oscar Hartman Davies and Jamie Lorimer's analysis of how surveillance is not just something that happens to non-human animals, as 'oceanic surveillance is also performed *with* animals, as part of a "wired wilderness"' (Chapter 5). Both chapters post important questions about the metamorphosis of surveillance away from neo-colonial national park models, where boundaries are violently policed through static technologies and patrols, to more dispersed modes of governance that enrol non-human beings into a constantly shifting surveillance apparatus.[15] A critical question, then, is how the ethical implications of this metamorphosis in the relationship between violence, encounter, and mediation will unfold as these technologies become ever more pervasive.

In sum, therefore, many chapters in *Digital Ecologies* reveal the role of media in ecological reformulation and instrumentalisation, elucidating how a focus on media can complicate more-than-human narratives of care as emerging through encounter. Other chapters in the book, however, offer a slightly different focus: revealing promise as well as perils in digitisation, through making generative connections with slightly different strands of media studies research.

## Mediated ecologies versus media ecologies

As touched on in the introduction to this afterword, I have often been worried at the lack of meaningful dialogue between disciplines that take 'the digital' as their object of study. A number of chapters in this book, however, made me excited at seeing potential for further dialogue between fields such as more-than-human geographies, media sociology, and social movement studies, which can offer one another informative empirical insights, theoretical coordinates, and methodologies.

Chapters 6 and 7, for instance, foreground the value of digital methods in understanding how awareness – and mobilisation – can emerge in relation to environmental crisis, making insightful contributions to scholarship on the affective circulation and meaning-making that ground online narratives.[16] These chapters' approaches, however, are different in emphasis: while Jonathan W.Y. Gray, Liliana Bounegru, and Gabriele Colombo

*Afterword: finding the media in digital ecologies* 261

(Chapter 6) chart how concern about forest fires was engaged with – akin to a form of front-stage 'connective action' – Jess McLean and Lara Newman's (Chapter 7) account of climate strikes grounds online activities in the place-based 'back-stage' collective action of youth climate activists.[17] In doing so, both chapters speak in productive ways to social movement media studies, which has emphasised the value of framing activist media use in ecological terms. Emiliano Treré and Anne Kaun, for instance, argue that:

> By embedding digital activism within a history of never ending adaptations, displacements, and abandonments, a media ecology approach allows us to appreciate not only how different technologies co-exist but also how, why, and under what circumstances they co-evolve and subsequently how their role changes.[18]

The conception of media ecologies offered by Treré and Kaun, however, also reveals some points of theoretical (and perhaps disciplinary) divergence, offering a slightly different lens to the epistemological approach to that offered by this book's editors elsewhere.[19] Here it is the relationship *between media* that is being understood in ecological terms, rather than using the framework of 'digital ecologies' to conceptualise the novel ways that digital media are entangled with non-human life. Treré and Kaun's usage of 'media ecology', in contrast, has emerged from a long history of within media studies, albeit one where uses of 'ecology' have shifted over time: from early medium theory in the 1960s, which used ecosystem metaphors to understand the relations between media (wherein the ecological niche of a particular medium might be lost with the ascendency of newer communications technologies), to Deleuzian-inspired scholarship in early 2000s software studies that stresses how the dynamic relations between media and user practices create media-ecological affordances that structure worlds.[20]

Andrew Dwyer's (Chapter 10) work complements this exploration of how conceiving of media itself in ecological terms might add another layer of complexity to digital ecologies research, in his examination of the agency of software. Engaging with, but moving beyond, software studies' focus on glitches and breakdowns as the elements that disrupt human mastery over technological systems, Dwyer reframes the agency of software as 'recursive' wherein socio-technical systems are mediated by code that is responding to previous code.[21] Through vignettes of research in a malware detection lab, Dwyer charts how software's own recursive agency might disrupt socio-technical infrastructures in unexpected ways, prompting questions about how to account for this additional layer of agency when researching digital ecologies. Sophia Doyle and Katharine Dow's (Chapter 8) beautiful exploration of seed databases, likewise, draws productive connections with software studies, pointing to the underlying cultural techniques that regulate ways of engaging with seeds as knowledge is formatted into databases.[22] What is so inspiring and hopeful about this chapter, however, is the ongoing presence of resistance to these cultural techniques, as seed activists resist and subvert technology to contest regimes of intellectual property.

Mari Arold's (Chapter 11) vital rejoinder to 'remember the analogue' offers an important through-line between these bodies of literature, making me excited at the potential for expanded narratives about the processes of mediation that constitute digital ecologies. Just as media scholarship has traced all matter of media that constitute the communication ecologies of protest movements – from posters and placards to messaging apps and front-stage social media platforms – Arold foregrounds the importance of processes of mediation to digital ecologies scholarship that exceed narrow conceptions of 'the digital' itself.[23]

## Conclusion

Through their varied approaches to digital media, the chapters in this book offer valuable pathways for me to reflect on future dialogue between more-than-human geographies and media studies that, I feel, is useful in conceptualising and grasping the ethical implications of digital ecologies. What many chapters reveal is not just that digital ecologies foster both ethical potential and harm in turn, but that potentials are perhaps inextricable from harm. The environmental potentials and pitfalls of digital infrastructures can thus prove difficult to parse.[24] In such contexts, perhaps the only recourse is to offer a reminder that, in line with important interventions made in feminist science studies, no relations or entanglements are ever 'innocent'.[25]

Yet while refrains about the non-innocence of more-than-human entanglements are important, they are less helpful in exploring how to actually navigate choppy ethical waters wherein processes of ecological damage require intervention, redress, and repair.[26] To revisit Susan Leigh Star's valuable reminder: technology can order the world in particular ways that embed relations of power and domination through mundane processes of classification as well as large-scale computational infrastructures. If these socio-technical arrangements are invisible, then so too are these oppressive relations which – in turn – makes it difficult to grasp where more hopeful potentials for intervention and resistance might exist. For me, what was most hopeful about the chapters in this book were the set of potential tools that digital ecologies research might have for the relations emerging as more-than-human worlds become entangled with digital media in ever more complex ways.

*Afterword: finding the media in digital ecologies*

## Notes

1 Parikka, *Insect Media*; Peters, *The Marvelous Clouds*; Jue, *Wild Blue Media*.
2 Couldry, *Media, Society, World*; Stephansen and Treré, *Citizen Media and Practice*; Treré, *Hybrid Media Activism*.
3 Cubitt, *Finite Media*; Ma, *The Stone and the Wireless*; Mattern, *Code and Clay, Data and Dirt*.
4 Hörl, *General Ecology*, p. 1.
5 Ibid., p. 2.
6 Ibid., p. 4.
7 Ibid., p. 24.
8 Touchstones throughout this book that speak to these ethical commitments include Haraway, *When Species Meet*; Whatmore, 'Materialist returns.'
9 For a compelling account of the violence of the category 'human', see Jackson, *Becoming Human*.
10 Turnbull et al., 'Digital ecologies.' Framed in STS terms, this approach could be seen as a shift away from an actor–network theory focus on 'following the actors themselves' by engaging with questions more central to feminist science studies, which might share ANT's recognition of non-human agency and concern with tracing relations and the work of mediators, but also centralises questions of power and domination. The specific phrase 'what comes after entanglement' is something I've used in previous work to argue that rather than celebrating entanglement, the focus should be on asking which relationships and ways of being are rendered impossible through the materialisation of particular entanglements.
11 Particularly influential media studies scholarship on the relationship between media and environmental degradation includes Cubitt, *Finite Media*; Parikka, *A Geology of Media*.
12 van Dooren, *Flight Ways*, p. 116.
13 For valuable media and sociological research on this theme, see Bowsher, *The Informational Logic of Human Rights*; Franklin, *The Digital Dispossessed*.
14 While 'environmentality' is informed by Foucauldian governmentality, ecologics is a term derived from Deleuze. Andrew Dwyer's work offers a valuable sense of how these frameworks have been taken up in digital geographies (see Chapter 10, this collection). For further discussion about logics of environmentality and capture see Hörl, 'General ecology.'
15 Rosaleen Duffy's landmark work charts the key features of securitisation in conservation contexts, with specific focus on the role of media technologies. See Duffy, *Security and Conservation*.
16 For valuable media studies scholarship on digital storytelling, counter-narratives, and affective publics, see Jackson et al., *#HashtagActivism*; Papacharissi, *Affective Publics*.
17 Distinctions between collective and connective action, and frontstage/backstage communication, are widespread within sociological approaches to the study of media ecologies; see Bennett and Segerberg, 'The logic of connective action'; Treré, 'The banality of WhatsApp.'

18 Treré and Kaun, 'Digital media activism,' p. 198.
19 Turnbull et al., 'Digital ecologies.'
20 For more on this history of media ecological thought, see Treré and Mattoni, 'Media ecologies and protest movements.'
21 See, for instance, Fuller and Goffey, *Evil Media*.
22 For an overview of scholarship on how the cultural techniques imposed by particular media (such as databases) intersects with 'cognitive capitalism', see Parikka, 'The cultural techniques of cognitive capitalism.'
23 For especially valuable applications of media ecological frameworks which traverse digital/analogue lines, see Feigenbaum et al., *Protest Camps*; OAPEN Foundation and Constanza-Chock, *Out of the Shadows, into the Streets!*
24 A point underlined helpfully in relation to Bernard Stiegler's late scholarship; see Bishop and Simone, 'Volumes of transindividuation.'
25 This important sentiment is made most famously in the work of Haraway's *When Species Meet* and *Staying with the Trouble*.
26 For an important explication of the complexity of this task, see Liboiron, *Pollution Is Colonialism*.

## Bibliography

Bennett, L. and Segerberg, A. 2012. The logic of connective action. *Information, Communication & Society*, 15(5): 739–768.

Bishop, R. and Simone, A. 2023. Volumes of transindividuation. *Cultural Politics*, 19(3): 297–317.

Bowsher, J. 2022. *The Informational Logic of Human Rights*. Edinburgh: Edinburgh University Press.

Constanza-Chock, S. 2015. *Out of the Shadows, into the Streets! Transmedia Organizing and the Immigrant Rights Movement*. Cambridge, MA: MIT Press.

Couldry, N. 2012. *Media, Society, World: Social Theory and Digital Media Practice*. Cambridge: Polity.

Cubitt, S. 2016. *Finite Media: Environmental Implications of Digital Technologies*. Durham, NC: Duke University Press.

Duffy, R. 2022. *Security and Conservation*. New Haven, CT: Yale University Press.

Feigenbaum, A., Frenzel, F., and McCurdy, P. 2013. *Protest Camps*. London: Zed Books.

Franklin, S. 2021. *The Digital Dispossessed*. Minneapolis, MN: University of Minnesota Press.

Fuller, M. and Goffey, A. 2012. *Evil Media*. Cambridge, MA: MIT Press.

Haraway, D.J. 2008. *When Species Meet*. Minneapolis, MN: University of Minnesota Press.

Haraway, D.J. 2016. *Staying with the Trouble*. Durham, NC: Duke University Press.

Hörl, E. 2017. *General Ecology: The New Ecological Paradigm*. London: Bloomsbury Academic.

Jackson, S., Bailey, M., and Welles, B.F. 2020. *#HashtagActivism: Networks of Race and Gender Justice*. Cambridge, MA: MIT Press.

Jackson, Z.I. 2020. *Becoming Human: Matter and Meaning in an Antiblack World*. New York: New York University Press.

Jue, M. 2020. *Wild Blue Media: Thinking through Seawater*. Durham, NC: Duke University Press.
Liboiron, M. 2021. *Pollution Is Colonialism*. Minneapolis, MN: University of Minnesota Press.
Ma, S. 2021. *The Stone and the Wireless*. Durham, NC: Duke University Press.
Mattern, S. 2017. *Code and Clay, Data and Dirt: Five Thousand Years of Urban Media*. Minneapolis, MN: University of Minnesota Press.
Papacharissi, Z. 2015. *Affective Publics*. Oxford: Oxford University Press.
Parikka, J. 2010. *Insect Media: An Archaeology of Animals and Technology*. Minneapolis, MN: University of Minnesota Press.
Parikka, J. 2014. The cultural techniques of cognitive capitalism. *Cultural Studies Review*, 20(1): 30–52.
Parikka, J. 2015. *A Geology of Media*. Minneapolis, MN: University of Minnesota Press.
Peters, J.D. 2015. *The Marvelous Clouds: Towards a Theory of Elemental Media*. Chicago, IL: University of Chicago Press.
Stephansen, H.C. and Treré, E. (Eds.) 2019. *Citizen Media and Practice: Currents, Connections, Challenges*. London: Routledge.
Treré, E. 2018. *Hybrid Media Activism: Ecologies, Imaginaries, Algorithms*. London: Routledge.
Treré, E. 2020. The banality of WhatsApp: On the everyday politics of backstage activism in Mexico and Spain. *First Monday*, 25(1). https://firstmonday.org/ojs/index.php/fm/article/view/10404.
Treré, E. and Kaun, A. Digital media activism. 2021. In G. Balbi, N. Ribeiro, V. Schafer, and C. Schwarzenegger (Eds.) *Digital Roots* (pp. 193–208). Berlin: De Gruyter.
Treré, E. and Mattoni, A. 2016. Media ecologies and protest movements. *Information, Communication & Society*, 19(3): 290–306.
Turnbull, J., Searle, A., Hartman Davies, O., Dodsworth, J., Chasseray-Peraldi, P., Von Essen, E., and Anderson-Elliott, H. 2022. Digital ecologies: Materialities, encounters, governance. *Progress in Environmental Geography*, 2(1–2): 3–32.
van Dooren, T. 2014. *Flight Ways*. New York: Columbia University Press.
Whatmore, S. 2006. Materialist returns: Practising cultural geography in and for a more-than-human world. *cultural geographies*, 13(4): 600–609.

# Index

Page numbers in italics and bold refer to figures and tables, respectively. Page numbers followed by 'n.' denote Notes.

78s *see* shellac discs

Aboriginal and Torres Strait Islander peoples
   Country of 147, 154, 159
   Indigenous knowledges 150, 153, 155, 157–158
   sovereignty of 154
   SS4C *see* School Strike 4 Climate (SS4C)
Adams, William M. 14, 55, 56, 73, 87, 88, 259
Adams, Paul C. 227
affective labour 41, 95, 97, 259
affordances
   of computation 201, 202, 209
   and conductivity of mediating channels 220
   of media 10, 11, 222, 256
   of social media 154, 155
agency 202, 244
   of computation 199, 200, 261
   of media 18
   non-human 12, 13, 16, 58, 148, 200, 263n.10
   political, of children/young people 155, 158
   posthuman 244
Ahmed, Sara 97
Airtable (software) 164, 169, 170, 172, 173–174, 175
Alaimo, Stacy 248, 253
Alexander, Neta 89, 150
algorithms 244
   machine learning 197, 201, 202, 203, 206–208, 209, 210n.10, 211n.35
   mediation of environmental events 126–127, *128*, 129
amaranth 175
Amazon rainforest fires (2019) 123–124, 138, 241, 252, 261
   algorithmic mediation of 126–127, *128*, 129
   hashtags as indicators of issue composition 132–133, **134**
   images of 135–137, *137*, 242
   querying objects of engagement 129–130, *131*
amplified music, impact on urban ecologies 62
animal behaviour research, role of games in 40
anthropoidentities 77, 78
anti-virus technologies 198
archives/archiving, digital
   material footprints of 58
   of sound 52–57, *54*, 58, 60, 63–64, 244, 250, 259
   Twitter 17, 138
   *see also* Amazon rainforest fires (2019)
arc of communication 227
Arold, Mari 18, 240, 242, 252, 262
artificial intelligence (AI) 52
   *see also* machine learning algorithms
artificial machines 199
Ash, James 7, 115, 227
augmented reality (AR) 14, 38–39, 226
Automatic Identification Systems (AIS) 107

Barad, Karen 23n.63
Barua, Maan 37, 41, 112
Bastian, Michelle 253
Bates, Victoria 57
*BeastBox* game 56, 65n.23
Bennett, Jane 202
Benson, Etienne 32
Berland, Jody 10–11
Berlant, Lauren 18, 191
big data 52, 115, 201, 203, 204, 205, 207, 209, 244
Big Tech 52
bioacoustics 51–52, 53, 61
biologging 108–109, 116
biopolitics 18, 76, 82–83, 114
  see also lobster trap-cams
biopower 8, 244
  environmental 111, 112
  non-human 41
birding/birdwatching
  CCTV-assisted 74
  use of digital playback in 60, 65n.43
birdsongs 53, 59, 64n.8
Bishop, Ryan 3
Bloody Marvel (lettuce variety) 172, *173*
Boellstorff, Tom 219
Bonneuil, Christophe 167
Bounegru, Liliana 17, 241, 252, 260
Bowker, Geoffrey 12, 16
Braun, Bruce 111, 112
Brennan, Michael 251
British Library 53, *54*, 56, 58
Büscher, Bram 90, 240
byproductive labour 41, 88, 90, 95–97, 98, 243, 258, 259

Callon, Michel 23n.63
camera traps 2, 73
  see also lobster trap-cams
care
  and digital encounters with animals 73, 74
  and lobster trap-cams 71, 72, 73–75, 76, 77, 78, 80, 82, 259
  and *Our Chicken Life* 88, 92, 93–94, 98, 250
  and violence 15, 93, 243, 259
Carlson, Bronwyn 159

CCTV 2, 74
Centre d'Etudes Biologiques de Chizé 108
Chambers, Charlotte 74
Chandler, David 111–112
charisma, non-human 41, 56, 77
*Chicken of Tomorrow* contest 89
chickens 89–90, 91, 94
  see also *Our Chicken Life* (Twitch livestream)
choice-making, and computation 206, 208, 209, 252
citizenship, and SS4C 149, 150, 156
Claus, C. Anne 78
climate change 3, 228
  education apps 149
  and green infrastructure 187, 192
  see also School Strike 4 Climate (SS4C)
Clow, Anna 164, 169, 172, 173, 175
co-belonging 145, 146, 147, 149, 151–152, 155, 156, 157, 159
  see also School Strike 4 Climate (SS4C)
cognitive capacities of computation 205–206, 207, 208
co-hashtag analysis 132, *133*
Collin, Philippa 150, 156, 157
Colombo, Gabriele 17, 241, 252, 260
colonialism 15, 61, 157–158, 166, 167, 168
communication ecologies 18, 147, 262
computation 197, 239
  affordances of 201, 202, 209
  agency of 199, 200, 261
  and choice-making 206, 208, 209, 252
  cognitive capacities of 205–206, 207, 208
  ecological computationality within geography 201
  environmental complexity of 199, 201, 202, 205
  and human intelligence 200
  machine learning algorithms 206–208
  malware detection 18, 198, 202–205, 206–208, 209, 252, 261
  materialities 201
  philosophy of 200, 208

as a political actor 197, 200, 202, 208, 209
  and recursivity 197, 201, 202, 205, 206, 208, 261
  as a tool 199, 200, 203
conductivity of mediating channels 220, 222–223, 232
conservation games 35, 45n.77
conservation surveillance 108, 112, 113–114, 116
content analysis 151
Cooke, Steven 114
Cornell Laboratory of Ornithology (CLO) 53, 56
cosmic zoom 241–242
Couldry, Nick 8
COVID-19 pandemic 2, 37, 62, 87–88, 89, 95, 150, 169
Cowen, Deborah 192
credibility labels of digital images 137
crop biodiversity 168
crop registers 168
Cubitt, Sean 9
curators of digital sound archives 60, 63–64
Cutter-Mackenzie-Knowles, A. 149
cybernetics 3, 200
cybersecurity 198, 203, 204, 205, 207–208, 209
  see also malware detection

Damerell, Peter 45n.77
Daniels, Charles 89
data 9, 165, 239, 241
  big 52, 115, 201, 203, 204, 205, 207, 209, 244
  data centres 58
  -driven governance 115
  political ecology of 148, 165, 166
  technologies 165, 166–167, 168, 169, 178–179
databases 16, 20, 166, 168, 178, 241, 261–262
  see also LFSBase
datafication 20, 165, 178, 241, 260
Daubenton's bats 62
Davies, Oscar Hartman 16, 241, 242, 251, 260
de la Bellacasa, Maria Puig 23n.63
Deleule, Didier 92

de Peuter, Greg 34
Descartes, René 199
Despret, Vinciane 36
digital, meaning of 7, 219
digital animals 34, 35–36, 38–40, 55, 72, 239
  *BeastBox* 56
  *Run Wild* 31–32, 38, 39–41, 42
digital Anthropocene 32
digital empathy 14, 36–38, 39, 40
digital entanglement 5, 6, 8, 10, 12, 32, 257–258, 261
digital environmental activism 1, 147, 149–150, 252
  see also School Strike 4 Climate (SS4C)
digital fisheries governance 115
digital games 33–35, 240, 259
  animals in 38–40
  *BeastBox* 56, 65n.23
  *Run Wild* 31–32, 38, 39–41, 42
  tagging and surveillance of animals 41
digital geographies 6, 13, 145, 146, 149, 157, 159, 219, 226, 239–245
digital images 135–137, 137, 241–242, 245
  see also Amazon rainforest fires (2019)
digital intimacy 15, 35, 36, 37, 70–71, 72, 73, 78–80, 82, 250
digitalisation 55, 57–58, 186, 187, 188
digital library 58
digital media 1–2, 3, 4, 13, 14, 63, 147, 257
digital mediation 2, 5, 13, 14, 73, 215, 239, 256
  ambivalence of 240
  and games 34, 35
  and glitches of technonatural present 6
  of human life 239
  materiality of 6
  modes of 7–8
  paradoxicality of 240
  of spatialities 242–243
  as technological present 4, 5
digital methods 125–126, 138, 151, 241, 260

Digital Methods Initiative Twitter Capture and Analysis Toolset (DMI-TCAT) 127, *128*
digital natures 13, 32, 33, 34, 57, 95, 98
digital objects 17, 219, 241
   and ecological politics 123–126, 138
   hashtags 126–127, *128*, 129–133, *131*, *134*, 138, 252
   images 135–137, *137*, 241–242, 245
   meaning of 221
   repurposing digital devices 125
digital solutionism 5
digital sound 15, 50–51, 244, 250
   accessibility of digital recording devices 53
   archives 52–57, *54*, 58, 60, 63–64, 244, 250, 259
   *BeastBox* 56, 65n.23
   ecologically attuned recording techniques 54–55
   and extraction process 58–59, 259
   future directions 63–64
   and human–non-human relationships 54, 55–56, 60
   impact on sonic space of animals 59–61
   listening to recording 55–56
   and material ecologies 57–62
   producing and using recordings in the field 63
   recording technologies 52
   and risk for animals 250
   single-species recordings 53, 54
   therapeutic role of 57
digital tracking 16, 35–36, 38, 40, 41
digital visibility 248–249
   humans and technologies 251–253
   organisms 249–251
   underwater ecologies 248–249, 251, 252, 253–254
digitisation 2, 6, 7–8, 14, 15, 17, 32–33, 55, 166
   and disembodied nature of encounters with animals 72–73
   of extinct species 1
   of fisheries monitoring *107*
   of human–nature relations, paradoxes 73–74
   as productive of multiplicity 7

direct content analysis 151
Dove, Charlotte 172
Dow, Katherine 16, 241, 253, 261
Doyle, Sophia 16, 241, 253, 261
drones 73, 228, 241
D'Souza, Dinesh 135
Duffy, Rosaleen 263n.15
Dwyer, Andrew C. 18, 239, 244, 252, 261, 263n.14
Dyer-Witherford, Nick 34
dynamic ocean management 111–112

early warning detection systems 52, 113
eBird 21n.3
ecological urbanism 187
eco-logics 244, 260, 263n.14
ecomedia 9–10
ecosophy 208
Electronic Numerical Integrator and Computer (ENIAC) 3
elemental media 11
empathy 35, 56
   digital 14, 36–38, 39, 40
   embodied 36, 40
encounter value 15, 41, 77, 82
Endangered Species Act 59, 65n.39
endpoint detection 198, 203, 204, 205
entanglement *see* digital entanglement
environmental biopower 111, 112
environmental governance 2, 8, 108, 111, 148, 159, 188, 215
   *see also* ocean governance
environmental humanities 11, 12, 18, 23n.64, 249, 251
environmental sound archives 52–57, *54*
Estonia, forests in 216–217
   mediating events 221–228
   narrated and performed climate optimism 228, 230
   tours 230–231, *231*
Eurocentrism 201
European Forest Institute (EFI) 126, 129, 132, 134, 135, 136
Extinction Rebellion 1
extinct species 1, 15, 50, 56–57, 59–60, 250

extraction 158, 166–167
  and digital mediation 6
  and digital sound 58–59, 259
  and smart green infrastructures 190, 191, 192

Facebook 71, 79, 137, 252
Feigenbaum, Anna 148
feminist science studies 12, 21n.17, 23n.64, 263n.10
Fish, Adam 73
Fletcher, Robert 5
Flynn, Alicia 150
forest(s) 215
  as an ontogenetic process 218
  conceptual lenses for understanding **218**
  mediating events 221–228
  phenomenological construction of 217
  political 215
  as a processual socioenvironmental artefact 217
  smart urban forests 148
  social construction of 217
  *see also* Amazon rainforest fires (2019); Estonia, forests in; Smart Forest City, Mexico
Frazer, Ryan 159

Gabrys, Jennifer 18, 107, 148, 215, 243, 251, 260
Galpin, Richard 164, 169, 170, 171, 172, 173, 174, 175, 176, 177
games 14, 259
  conservation games 35, 45n.77
  digital 33–35, 38–41, 42, 240
  and digital animal sounds 56
  of multitude 34
  for nature 34
  role in animal behaviour research 40
  serious 34
gamification 14, 34, 38, 39–40, 230
gene banks 168
genetic diversity of seeds 176–177
genetics 167, 168
geographic information systems (GIS) 35, 223, 231, 242, 252
ghost traps 81, 259
Gibson-Graham, J.K. 146, 149, 155

Ginn, Franklin 93
Giraud, Eva Haifa 74, 82, 83, 93, 147
glitches of technonatural present 6
Global Fishing Watch 107
Global Positioning Systems (GPS) 36, 223, 242
Goldstein, Jenny Elaine 148, 165
Graham, Mark 226
Gray, Jonathan W.Y. 17, 241, 242, 252, 260
Greenhough, Beth 73
green security 115
grey infrastructure 186
grey wolf 59, 65n.39
Grupo Karim 189
Guattari, Félix 5, 208
Guéry, François 92
Gulf toadfish 62

Halpenny, Matthew 6
Hampe, Max 58
Haraway, Donna 21n.17, 23n.63, 72, 88, 201
Harding, Sandra 23n.63
hashtags 123, 138, 252
  algorithmic mediation of environmental events 126–127, *128*, 129
  as indicators of environmental issue composition 132–133, **134**
hashtag snowballing 126
Hayles, N. Katherine 3, 200, 205–206
Helmreich, Stefan 11, 83
*hiied* (sacred sites) 230–231, *231*, 233n.12, 234n.57, 252
Hollin, Gregory 74, 82, 93
Hörl, Erich 257
Horst, Heather 7
howlbox 59
Hui, Yuk 199, 221
human, notion of 239
human geography 201, 202
Hunter, Hannah 15, 241, 244, 250, 259
hunting, use of digital sound recordings in 60
hybridisation (plant breeding) 167–168
hydrophones 52, 64n.7
hyperlinks 125

images, digital 135–137, *137*, 241–242, 245
immutable mobiles 249
inbreeding depression 177
Indigenous knowledges 150, 153, 155, 157–158
industrial agriculture 10, 167, 168, 174
industrial fishing 106
inequalities
   and digital governance 115
   and digital infrastructures 12
   and digitalisation of urban spaces 187
   and smart green infrastructures 18, 185, 192
infrastructures
   data 165
   digital 12, 52, 231, 259, 262
   grey 186
   mediation of categories and standards 12
   otherwise 18, 191–192
   Smart Forest City (Mexico) 189–191
   smart green 185, 187–189, 192–193
   and social life 191
   vegetal 186
   Wiindigo 192
Instagram 151, 152–153
Institute of Marine Research, Norway 71, 76
instrumentalisation of animals 73, 74, 75, 82, 259–260
Internet of Elephants 31, 38, 45n.77
Internet of Nature 188
interspecies epiphanies 56
intimacy
   and anthropoidentities 77
   digital 15, 35, 36, 37, 70–71, 72, 73, 78–80, 82, 250
   emotional 55
   and proximity in digital encounters 73, 74
Iovino, Serenella 252
ivory-billed woodpecker 59–60

Jacobi, Jim 50
Jasper, Sandra 15, 241, 244, 250, 259
Javan mynas 61
Johnson, Elizabeth 74, 77, 108
Jue, Melody 11, 83
Just Stop Oil 1

Kaasik, Ahto 230
Kamphof, Ike 73
Kauaʻi ʻōʻō 1, 15, 50, 250
Kaun, Anne 9, 10, 261
Keener-Chavis, Paula 248
Kerr, B.H. 89
Kitchin, Rob 7
Koch, R. 89
Krause, Bernie 54

Labour Party (Australia) 156
LaDuke, Winona 192
Latour, Bruno 23n.63, 249
Leibniz, Friedrich 199
Leszczynski, Agnieszka 4, 6, 7, 217, 220
Ley, Sussan 153, 156
LFSBase 164–165, 166, 169, 178–179
   background stories about seeds 171–174
   and genetic diversity 176–177
   linked record fields in *171*
   and relationality 174, 175–176
   Seed Batches category 174, 176, 178
   tables in 170–171, *170*
   unintended crossings and evolutions 177
   Variety category 172, *173*, 174–175, 176
Liberal Party (Australia) 156
Linnaeus, Carl 166
lobster trap-cams 15, 37, 70–72, 74–75, 250, 259
   bait experimentation 79–80
   biopolitics 83
   and care 71, 72, 73–75, 76, 77, 78, 80, 82, 259
   digital intimacy 37, 72, 78–80, 82, 250
   human–non-human differentiation 78–80
   images, commodification of 82
   and instrumentalisation of animals 73, 74, 75, 82, 259–260
   and milieu specificity 83

personalisation of lobsters 76–78
playful relations between viewers and lobsters 78, 79, 80
spatial location of 77
trap type 80–82
London Freedom Seed Bank (LFSB) 16, 164–165, 169, 253
*see also* LFSBase
Lorimer, Jamie 16, 38, 56, 76–77, 112, 241, 242, 251, 260
Lyle, Peter 148

Macaulay Library 53
machine learning algorithms 197, 201, 202, 203, 206–208, 209, 210n.10, 211n.35
McLean, Jessica 17, 73, 146, 219, 243, 252, 261
McLuhan, Marshall 221
Mah, Christopher 253
malware detection 18, 198, 202–205, 206–208, 209, 252, 261
Mamadoli Pumpkin 176
marine ecologies
marine debris 251
*see also* lobster trap-cams; ocean governance
material ecologies, and digital sound 57–62
mathematical theory of communication 8–9
Matthews, Ingrid 150, 156, 157
Mattoni, Alice 147
media 220, 256
affordances of 10, 11, 256
agency of 18
as complex environment 10
deterministic understanding of 10
elemental 11
as a hybrid system 216
materiality of 9–10
political ecology of 13
relationship between 261
studies 8, 20, 147, 153, 201, 208, 209, 216, 223, 256, 260, 261
and transformation 9–10, 11
*see also* digital visibility; social media
media ecologies 10–11, 17, 18, 147, 261
mediation 1, 3, 216, 219–220, 239
and digital sound archives 55

and ethics 9–10, 11–12
mathematical theory of communication 8–9
as a process that makes a difference 8, 11
*see also* digital mediation
mediative events 232
attunements 222–223, 232
augmented and compressed realities 226–227, 232
co-mediating channels and filters 224, **225**
conductivity of channels 220, 222–223, 232
mediative loops 223–224, 226, 232
multimodal complementarity 228, 230
synchronies and sequences 227–228, 232
Meegaswatta, Thilini N.K. 96
mental health of participants of protest movements 155
Michael, David 66n.61
Miles, Sam 89
Miller, Daniel 7
mind–body dualism 199
minimal animal 32
Mirin, Ben 56
Mishra, Charu 32
misleading images 123, 135–136, 137
MOJO Triple Threat E-Caller 50
more-than-human geographies 12–13, 148, 200, 201, 249, 256
Morey, Sean 148
Morrison, Scott 152, 153, 156
*Mother Jones* 123–124, *124*, 135
movescape 111, 242–243
multimodal complementarity, and mediative events 232
multispecies ethnography 40
multispecies relations 14, 16, 74, 168, 174, 177, 249
*see also* LFSBase
Mundy, Rachel 51
music events, impact on animals 62

National Film and Sound Archive of Australia 1
National Oceanic and Atmospheric Administration (NOAA) 248

National Party (Australia) 153
natural machines 199
nature 2–3, 62, 90, 112, 218
   and culture, division between 257
   and digital animals 35, 38, 39
   digital natures 13, 32, 34, 57, 95, 98
   and digital technologies 148–149
   and ecology 257
   games for 34
   human–nature relations 7, 8, 14, 73, 74
   as infrastructure 186, 187–188, 191–192
   Internet of Nature 188
   and Smart Forest City (Mexico) 18, 186, 189–191
   smart green infrastructures 185
nature deficit disorder 5
nestcams 36–37, 56
Newman, Lara 17, 146, 243, 252, 261
new materialisms 202
Neyrat, Frédéric 257
Nicolson, Adam 116
non-fungible animals (NFAs) 95
non-human agency 12, 13, 16, 58, 148, 200, 263n.10
non-human charisma 41, 56, 77
Norway
   Institute of Marine Research 71, 76
   lobster fishing and conservation 75–76
   *see also* lobster trap-cams
Nost, Eric 148, 165

Occupy Movement 148, 153
ocean governance 106–108, 251–252, 260
   digitisation of fisheries monitoring 107
   dynamic ocean management 111–112
   naturalisation of surveillance 114–115
   *see also* Ocean Sentinel project
Ocean Sentinel project 108–110, *110*, 251–252
   environmental biopower 112
   lively surveillance 112–113
   media coverage of 112
   movescape 111, 242–243
   risks for birds 113–114, 250

*Okeanos Explorer* 248–249, 251, 252, 253
Oliver, Catherine 14, 41, 241, 243, 250
on-bird surveillance 16, 108–114, *110*, 251–252
Operation Turtle Dove 21n.3
Oppermann, Serpil 252
otherwise infrastructures 18, 191–192
*Our Chicken Life* (Twitch livestream) 14–15, 41, 87–91, 97–99, 250, 259
   byproductive labour 95–97, 98, 243, 258, 259
   and care 88, 92, 93–94, 98, 250
   galline behaviours and relationships 91–92
   interactions 94, 95
overexploitation of marine life 106

Pandemic (lettuce variety) 177
Patrick, Samantha 113
Peters, John Durham 11
pet trade, use of digital sound recordings in 60
Pickerill, Jenny 147
planetary 243
plants 188
   breeding 167–168
   classification of 166–167
   cognitive capacity of 206
   *see also* seeds
platform capitalism 15
play 14, 33
   and digital games 34, 40
   and lobster trap-cams 78, 79, 80, 250
   *see also* games
pluriverse 217
*Pokémon Go* 38
Poliquin, Rachel 55
political ecology 198, 209, 217, 220–221
   of data 148, 165, 166
   of digital sound 63
   of media 13
political forests 215
posthuman 240, 241, 242, 243–244, 245

power 12, 62, 65n.23, 146, 240, 262, 263n.10
  biopower 8, 41, 111, 112, 244
  and byproductive labour 95–96
  and digital sound archives 54
  in environmental governance 111
  in fisheries governance 113
  and mediation 240, 241
  and pluriverse 217
  and smart green infrastructures 188, 189
  and theatre 92
  and trap cams 37
Prebble, Sarah 148
Prior, Jonathan 15, 241, 244, 250, 259
productive body 92–93
proximity in digital encounters 37, 72, 73, 74
pure line ontology 167, 169, 176

Quantified Self (QS) movement 36, 39
Queensland Labor Party (Australia) 153, 156

*Race the Wild* 39, 45n.77
Rancière, Jacques 92
Rankin, William 242
ransomware 198, 210n.6
Ratté, Stephanie 73
recursivity, and computation 197, 201, 202, 205, 206, 208, 261
Regional Operational Surveillance and Rescue Center (CROSS) 108
Rehman, Asad 123
Reich, Carl 58
Remme, Jon Henrik Ziegler 15, 37, 240, 250, 259
remote event analysis 129, 130
repair 149, 159, 243
  *see also* School Strike 4 Climate (SS4C)
response-ability 72, 73, 76
Roe, Emma 73
Rogers, R. 151, 241
Rose, Gillian 20
Rousell, David 149
Runtastic (app) 31, 39
*Run Wild* 31–32, 38, 39–41, 42
Russell, Legacy 6

Safari Central game 39
Sandbrook, Chris 14, 259
satellites 105, 107, 115, 241, 242
School Strike 4 Climate (SS4C) 17, 145–146, 252, 261
  and co-belonging 146, 147, 151–152, 155, 156, 157, 159
  and Country 147, 154, 159
  digital geographies of 145, 157
  digital worlds of 158–159
  events 150
  and Indigenous knowledges 150, 153, 155, 157–158
  Instagram posts 152–153
  in mainstream media 150
  and place 154, 155, 157
  and political engagement 152, 153, 156–157, 158
  research methodology for studying 151–152
  research on 149–150
  Twitter posts 153–154, 156
  and voting climate 154, 156
science and technology studies (STS) 11–12, 23n.63, 23n.64, 132, 263n.10
screenshot debunking 136
Searle, Adam 56, 73, 87
seeds 261–262
  genetic diversity of 176–177
  and hybridisation 167–168
  open-pollinated 169, 175, 176, 177
  registers 168
  sharing of growers' knowledge about 171–172, 173
  *see also* LFSBase
self-tracking 36, 38
sensing mode of governance 112
sensing technology 73, 105–106, 107, 241, 242
serious games 34
Shannon, Claude 8
shellac discs 58–59, 259
Simone, AbdouMaliq 3
single-species recordings 53, 54
*Slow Serif* (art installation) 6
smart cities 185, 186, 187
Smart Forest City, Mexico 18, 186, 189–191

smart green infrastructures 185, 187–189, 192–193, 251
    see also Smart Forest City, Mexico
Smith, Page 89
social lives of environmental images 136–137
social media 1, 17, 20, 31, 123–126, 124, 240, 242, 252
    see also Amazon rainforest fires (2019); digital objects; School Strike 4 Climate (SS4C)
software studies 6, 10, 201, 208, 209, 261–262
somatic sensibilities 73
sonic weapons, use of digital sound as 61
sound deterrents 61
soundscapes 52, 53, 55
spatialities 217, 219, 220
    digital mediation of 242–243
    multiplicity of 243
Spivak, Gayatri 243
Star, Susan Leigh 12, 16, 125, 185, 262
State Forest Management Centre (SFMC), Estonia 228, 229, 230
Steensen, Jakob Kudsk 1
Stefano Boeri Architects 189
Steyerl, Hito 136, 244
Stiegler, Bernard 3
Sumida Aquarium, Tokyo 37
summative content analysis 151
surveillance 2, 115–116, 241, 260
    of animals 41, 105
    conservation 108, 112, 113–114, 116
    sonic 63
    see also camera traps; Ocean Sentinel project
Sutton, Zoei 94
synthetic geographies 242

Taffel, Sy 5, 6, 10, 13, 147
tags, digital tracking 35, 38, 40, 41, 242–243
Tait, Emma 14, 45n.77, 259
Táíwò, Olúfẹ́mi O. 96
taxidermy 55
'tech bro' culture 199
techno dystopia 5–6
technological present 4, 5
technonatural histories 2, 3
technonatural present 4, 5, 6

techno utopia 5–6
telepresence technologies 248, 251, 253, 254n.5
Terres Australes et Antarctiques Françaises (TAAF) 110
Thomas, Frederic 167
Thunberg, Greta 145
thylacine 1
Tipp, Cheryl 53, 56, 60, 66n.59
Todd, Zoe 158
Trending Topics algorithm (Twitter) 127
Treré, Emiliano 9, 10, 147, 261
Trott, Carlie D. 155
Trump, Donald 65n.39
Turnbull, Jonathon 56, 73, 74, 87
Twitter 31
    and Amazon rainforest fires (2019) 123–138, 241, 242
    and School Strike 4 Climate (SS4C) 151, 153–154, 156
Twitter API 127
Tyler, Tom 34, 35

ultrasonic bird repellers 61
underwater ecologies 248–249, 251, 252, 253–254
    see also lobster trap-cams; marine ecologies; ocean governance

van Dooren, Thom 23n.64, 93, 259
vectorialism 199
vegetal infrastructures 186
Veldstra, Carolyn 96
Verlie, Blanche 150, 155
virtual reality 1, 219
Vivek, Anandhi 45n.77

Wagner-Pacifici, Robin 127
Wakefield, Stephanie 112
Walton, Samantha 57, 95
Walworth Community Food Hub 169
Wark, McKenzie 199
Watson, Chris 66n.61
Weaver, Warren 8
webcams 2, 9, 73, 241, 243
    see also lobster trap-cams; *Our Chicken Life* (Twitch livestream)
Webster, Mike 56–57
wellness industry, use of digital sounds in 57

wet ontology 111
Whitney, Kristoffer 116
Whitney, Shiloh 88, 95, 96
Whyte, Kyle 157–158
Wickberg, Adam 3
Wiener, Norbert 200
Wiindigo infrastructure 192
*Wildeverse* game 38
Wildlife AR 39
wildlife documentaries 252

Wildlife & Environmental Sounds (WES) archive, British Library 53, *54*
Williams, Raymond 9
Wolfe, Cary 19
wooden lobster traps 81–82
Wynter, Sylvia 243

xeno-canto 53, 64n.8

Printed in the USA
CPSIA information can be obtained
at www.ICGtesting.com
JSHW011715251024
72425JS00003B/35